WHAT PEOPLE ARE SAYING

This is a dynamite book! In an age seemingly beset by selfishness, defensiveness, and personal insecurity, Glenn Van Ekeren provides a smorgasbord of rich insights, thoughtfulness, and civility. This book will enrich you in every way that counts.

– Joe Batten, Author, *Tough-Minded Leadership*, *The Master Motivator* and *The Leadership Principles of Jesus*

Read this book. Take it to heart. Not for what others can do differently, but for what you can do to make a difference in your relationships.

– Bob Pike, CSP, Chairman, CEO, Creative Training Techniques International, Inc.

In a world of high tech, we still need high touch. This book gives the right touches in a practical and useful way. Great personal stories that motivate you to apply the "secrets."

– Steve Siemens, President, Siemens People Builders

Glenn Van Ekeren weaves the lessons he's learned in life into a delightful book packed with stimulating stories, powerful quotes, and practical suggestions for enhancing relationships – not only at home, but anywhere you deal with people.

– Michele Matt Yanna, Author, *Attitude: The Choice Is Yours*

12 SIMPLE SECRETS *of* HAPPINESS

12 SIMPLE SECRETS *of* HAPPINESS

FINDING JOY IN EVERYDAY RELATIONSHIPS

Glenn Van Ekeren

Foreword by Jack Canfield and Kimberly Kirberger

PRENTICE HALL PRESS

Library of Congress Cataloging-in-Publication Data

Van Ekeren, Glenn
12 simple secrets of happiness : finding joy in everyday relationships / Glenn Van Ekeren ; foreword by Jack Canfield and Kimberly Kirberger.
p. cm.
ISBN 0-7352-0139-0
1. Interpersonal relations. 2. Friendship. 3. Happiness. I. Title: Twelve simple secrets of happiness. II. Title.
HM1106.V362000 1999
158.2—dc21 99-051643
CIP

Printed in the United States of America

10 9 8 7 6 5 4 3 2 1

ISBN 0-7352-0139-0

PRENTICE HALL PRESS
Paramus, NJ 07652

On the World Wide Web at http://www.phdirect.com

ACKNOWLEDGMENTS

My heartfelt thank you goes to the following people . . .

To my wife, Marty, for her continual encouragement, friendship, and willingness to stick with me through thick and thin.

To my children, Matt and Katy, for believing in their dad and allowing me to tell stories about them.

To Lois Baartman and Jill Vanden Bosch, my fantastic assistants, who give of themselves without fanfare or recognition. I treasure our relationship.

To Phil Grove, my next door editor, who takes the time to read all of my writing with a sharp eye and always provides helpful insights to improve the message.

To my previous employer, Village Northwest Unlimited, who encouraged me to pursue my dreams.

CONTENTS

FOREWORD

We have enjoyed tremendous success with the *Chicken Soup for the Soul*(R) books by sharing powerful stories of hope, inspiration, and encouragement with people of all ages – stories about people living their dreams, overcoming obstacles, and making a difference.

One of the people whose work we have drawn heavily on is Glenn Van Ekeren. We have used many stories from his previous books as well as his personal life in several of our Chicken Soup books.

That's why we are very excited and deeply honored to highly recommend Glenn's new book to you. We know you are going to love *12 Simple Secrets of Happiness: Finding Joy in Everyday Relationships*. Glenn's unique storytelling ability combined with his commitment to people and his willingness to share his personal insights with his friends – which includes you, the reader – make this an extraordinary book. While you will find it inspiring and easy to read, you will also find that it is profound in its depth and, most important, easy to apply. When you apply these principles, you will see dramatic changes in your life.

As we are sure you are painfully aware, relationships these days can be a challenge. Whether it's a brother and sister relationship (like ours), a marriage, friendship, or a relationship with your co-workers, relationships take commitment, energy and a bit of Chicken Soup to warm the heart. Glenn offers loads of encouragement, solid support and lots of insightful understanding. Each selection goes right to the heart of real-world, timeless relationship principles.

Some pages will make you laugh. Others will get you thinking. Some will make you feel good. Others will encourage you to take action. And every page will fill you with a greater appreciation of yourself and how you can make a difference in the lives of others.

We have every confidence that with this book you are about to begin an enjoyable adventure, a journey that will lead you to more enriching and fulfilling relationships. The principles are all here. Read them! Believe them! Absorb them! But most important...apply them! The biggest secret in this book is this: If you work the principles, they will work for you!

Kimberly Kirberger
Jack Canfield

INTRODUCTION

Relationships are as old as creation. They are the driving force behind most everything we do in life. The older I get, the more convinced I am of the direct correlation between our success with relationships and virtually everything of significance in life. When relationships are successful, life is good, but when they fail, along with them go health, prosperity, happiness and the joy of living.

Wherever we go. Whatever we do. No matter what career we have chosen or activity we are involved in, there is a common denominator...people. We can't live without them and sometimes it's tough to live with them. Relationships can be a source of wonderful fulfillment, satisfaction, and joy in life. They can also be a major pain in the neck. There is a constant pull between what we want our relationships to be and what they are. *12 Simple Secrets of Happiness: Finding Joy in Everyday Relationships* is about those simple, yet often forgotten, accumulations of little things that contribute to building our relationships into what we want them to become.

So many books have been written about relationships; so many seminars given on the topic; and so many poems, songs and letters are inspired by them, that it might seem like the secrets to good relationships are known to everyone. Considering all the advice we've received, it should be easy to sustain harmonious, cooperative, and mutually beneficial relationships. In reality, we haven't reached that point. Maybe we read but don't respond, listen but don't understand, or know what to do but fail to take action. Whatever the case, relationships are either getting better, being nurtured, and growing, or they are slipping and sliding downhill.

The ability or inability to cultivate quality relationships is a choice. If we choose to live for ourselves, relationships will suffer and become dissonant. If we choose to focus our attention and invest our energies in our spouse, children, friends, neighbors, and co-workers we'll reap positive returns. Successful relationships are a natural outgrowth of the principle that the way we treat others affects the way they treat us. The tricky part is to not allow the way another person treats us to determine the way we treat that person.

I remember reading a *Dennis the Menace* cartoon where good old Mr. Wilson is sitting in his chair reading the newspaper. Mrs. Wilson is looking out the window as Dennis the Menace walks past the house. You can almost hear the sigh of relief from Mr. Wilson. He looks up from his paper and says to his wife, "There goes a Maalox moment waiting to happen."

It is virtually impossible to live through the day or week, much less a lifetime, without encountering someone who becomes our "Maalox moment." In the same breath, I must admit there are an equal number of people who radiate sunshine and encouragement wherever they go. They are the bright spots in our lives.

I can only hope that when people see me coming, or walking by, their first thought is not, "There goes the thorn in my life." I sincerely strive each day to be a positive influence in people's lives, to become what I often call a picker-upper person. These people are masters at building and maintaining quality relationships. They understand the dynamics for improving their casual and most intimate interaction. To them, love is a verb, and genuinely caring for others is a way of life. Picker-upper people transform lives and relationships by activating the qualities of a people builder.

This book is all about making a positive difference in people's lives. I probably wrote it for myself as much as anyone else. It contains the relationship principles I teach to audiences, preach to my children, and struggle to activate in my daily encounters. As I wrote, new ideas continually surfaced on ways in which I could improve my effectiveness with people. It is packed with timeless wisdom, proven principles, simple actions, and contemporary insight that will help you create increased enjoyment in your relationships.

You can become a picker-upper person. Choose any topic or any selection in this book and discover a variety of insightful comments, entertaining illustrations, and practical strategies that will help you:

Accept people for who they are.

Identify what people need to feel good about themselves.

Make your relationships bloom.

Get along with difficult people.

Effectively deal with conflict.

Develop a sincere interest in others.

Build on people's positive qualities.

Forgive hurtful actions.

Help others feel encouraged, uplifted and motivated to become all they can be.

Become the type of person people enjoy being around.

I assume that you're reading this book because you want more out of your relationships. If so, great! If you're looking for strategies to get your own way, sorry. If you want people to enjoy being with you, help is here. If you want a scheme to manipulate others, don't bother reading any further. If you're willing to commit yourself to the people in your life, the journey through the 12 secrets of happiness shared with you in this book will be a pleasurable and beneficial one.

Renew your desire, increase your awareness and learn new skills to become a life-long picker-upper person. This down-to-earth and thought-provoking book is filled with insights for finding happiness through more fulfilling relationships. You'll be inspired to rekindle the warmth in your friendships, marriage, family, and work relationships.

12 Simple Secrets *of* Happiness

GENEROSITY

The measure of life is not its duration,

but its donation.

PETER MARSHALL

A GIVING SPIRIT

Remember the biblical story of the widow's mite. Jesus watched the rich come to the temple to give their gifts for the temple treasury. He noticed a widow drop in two very small copper coins. Moved by her unselfish giving, Jesus told those who would hear that the value of her gift far exceeded all others. Most people gave gifts from their wealth. This poverty-stricken woman gave sacrificially.

It has been calculated that if the widow's two mites had been deposited in an account bearing 4-percent interest compounded semiannually, by today it would be valued at $4.8 billion trillion. Making a consistent small investment in people can also reproduce itself to create an outstanding return. A generous spirit exposes itself through an attitude that continually searches for ways to add value to people's lives. When a giving spirit permeates a relationship, the rewards are usually greater than either party expected. As Jesus commended the widow for her sacrificial giving, so, too, should we never underestimate the potential of the small things we do with the right motives.

In May of 1997, the Associated Press released a story about an outstanding high-school track runner and his sacrifice to help a teammate be successful. Troy Weiland ran for Canistota High School in South Dakota. He was an outstanding track star headed for Iowa State University on a track scholarship.

Troy decided his mission at the Danielsen Invitational track meet was to help his teammate Brad Jensen earn his varsity letter instead of scoring a victory for himself. If Jensen could finish sixth or better in the two-mile run, the varsity letter was his. Here's the play-by-play action as reported by the Associated Press.

"Troy kept telling me I was going to place," said Jensen. "Man, I was getting pumped."

For almost half the race, the runner trying to earn a varsity letter had one of the state's best high-school distance runners ever as his escort.

"Troy ran back with Jensen and kept an eye on the guys in the lead," said Canistota track coach Jerry Price. "I'd say he was about half a lap behind the leaders."

Weiland provided continual encouragement as he ran alongside Jensen.

"I said, 'Brad, you have to beat two people to place.' He was like 'OK, man, I can do this,'" Weiland said.

With a final few words of encouragement, Weiland took off for the leaders, now some 200 yards ahead, and not only caught them but soon lapped the field, coming upon Jensen again, who was battling another runner for seventh place, not good enough to place.

"Troy came up to me again and kept saying, 'You can do it,'" Jensen said. "He said if I kept running hard he was going to drop out. I said 'No, don't do that.' I tried to talk him out of it, but then he disappeared."

Weiland stepped off the track just before crossing the finish line. With Weiland out, Jensen now was battling for sixth place—good enough to earn his varsity letter.

Jensen used a late sprint to finish in sixth place. His time of 12:15 was 41 seconds faster than anything he had run before.

What a great story epitomizing a generous and giving spirit in a normally competitive environment. Not only is it difficult to get excited about other people's success but to

The miracle is this—the more we share, the more we have.
LEONARD NIMOY

give up your own success so someone else can be successful is virtually unheard of. Weiland's actions were captured by the press, recognized by teammates, and I guarantee you the fans were talking about his actions for days.

I'm not sure all happy people are generous, but I'm convinced that generous people are happy. Just remember you don't have to "be happy" to be generous, but your generosity will produce happiness—in others and you. John Bunyon believed, "You have not lived today until you have done something for someone who can never repay you." Give what little you can to someone who needs what you have and you'll not only produce happiness but the realization that life doesn't get much better than the internal rewards you'll experience.

A SCENARIO OF TOUCHING KINDNESS

Jerry Jenkins, writing for *Moody Monthly*, recalled a situation he observed while attending the premiere showing of Francis Schaeffer's film *How Should We Then Live?*. Dr. Schaeffer was fielding questions from the audience when a man with cerebral palsy struggled to ask a question. His slow, broken, and difficult-to-understand speech irritated some of the people in the audience. But not Schaeffer.

People can do this for one another, can love one another with understanding.
HAROLD S. KUSHNER

"I'm sorry," Schaeffer responded as the man finished his question. "Would you please repeat your last three words?" The man complied. "Now the last word one more time." The man again painstakingly repeated himself. Schaeffer went on to graciously answer the man's question.

Then, to the dismay of the audience, the young man had a second question. The entire process began again. Dr. Schaeffer continued to work kindly and patiently answering the question to the man's satisfaction.

Keep in mind that the true meaning of an individual is how he treats a person who can do him absolutely no good.
ANN LANDERS

What would have been your reaction? Dr. Schaeffer revealed a kindness that set an example for the entire audience. He treated the man with a disability with the same dignity and respect he gave to others.

People don't care how much you know until you show them how much you care by your small acts of kindness. As you go about your daily activities, be especially giving to those who need your touch of kindness.

A SURPRISING ACT OF COMPASSION

I read a great story about Fiorello H. LaGuardia. As New York City's mayor in 1935, he showed up in court one night in the poorest area of New York City and suggested the judge go home for the evening as he took over the bench.

LaGuardia's first case involved an elderly woman arrested for stealing bread. When asked whether she was innocent or guilty, this soft reply was offered, "I needed the bread, Your Honor, to feed my grandchildren." "I've no option but to punish you," the mayor responded. "Ten dollars or ten days in jail."

Proclaiming the sentence, he simultaneously threw $10 into his hat. He then fined every person in the courtroom 50 cents for living in a city "where a grandmother has to steal food to feed her grandchildren." Imagine the surprise of those in the room who I'm sure thought this was a black-and-white, open-and-shut case. When all had contributed their 50 cents, the woman paid her fine and left the courtroom with an additional $47.50.

How far you go in life depends on your being tender with the young, compassionate with the aged, sympathetic with the striving, and tolerant of the weak and strong, because someday in your life, you will have been all of these.

GEORGE WASHINGTON CARVER

Kindness in words creates confidence; kindness in thinking creates profoundness; kindness in giving creates love.
LAO-TSE

It has been said that kindness is the oil that takes the friction out of life. So often it is easy to be grit, rather than oil, by judging, condemning, or berating those going through trials and tribulations. Yet, an act or word of kindness can cool the friction and help someone keep pressing on. Look around you. To whom will you show generosity like that experienced by the grandmother?

SPEAK OF OTHERS GRACIOUSLY

I don't think there is anything I despise worse than gossip. Gossips cause undue contention and strife. The wise King Solomon said, "The words of a whisperer are like dainty morsels, and they go down into the innermost parts of the body." Both the gossip and the unfortunate victim are injured by these "tiny morsels."

There is so much good in the worst of us, and so much bad in the best of us, that it behooves all of us not to talk about the rest of us.
ROBERT LOUIS STEVENSON

Listen to this conversation. Mary says, "Ellen told me you told her the secret that I asked you not to tell her." Alice responds, "Well, I told her I wouldn't tell you that she told me, so please don't tell her I did." Oh what a tangled web we weave when we betray someone's trust.

There will always be people who believe everything they hear and feel compelled to repeat it. Gossips are simply people with a "sense of rumor." Don't be one of them.

I remember occasions when word got back to me concerning a betrayed confidence. What a devastating feeling. Trust is destroyed and friendships are broken when the poisonous contents of a rumor leak.

Why do people gossip? Could it be that we think we make ourselves look better and gain greater acceptance with peers? Does confidential information make us feel important, more knowledgeable or superior so surely people will listen to us? Have you ever been jealous of somebody's achievements or the attention they receive, and by pointing out their weaknesses you look a little better? If somebody has injured us, how easy it is to put them in a bad light as a way of retaliating and balancing the scales. Gossip can also be used to win others to our side of a conflict. There is a tendency to think that the more people we can get to agree with us, the healthier our self-worth.

No matter what reason we give, there is no reason to gossip!

There is a legend about a person who went to the village priest for advice after repeating some slander about a friend and later finding out it wasn't true. He asked the priest what he could do to make amends for his thoughtless act.

The priest told the man: "If you want to make peace with yourself, you must fill a bag with feathers, and go to every door in the village, dropping a feather on each porch."

The peasant found a bag, filled it with feathers, and made his way throughout the village doing as he was told to do. He then returned to the priest and asked: "What else can I do?"

"There is one more thing," responded the priest, "take your bag and gather up every feather."

The peasant reluctantly began his quest to gather all the feathers he had distributed. Hours later he returned, saying, "I could not find all the feathers, for the wind had blown them away."

The priest responded, "So it is with gossip. Unkind words are easily dropped, but we can never take them back again."

The next time you are tempted to say an unkind, possibly untrue or unflattering word about someone, ask yourself how this information will benefit the receiver, yourself, and especially the person you are talking about. Be really clear on this one irrefutable fact: Once you say it, you can't take it back.

If you have an affinity for spreading rumors or welcoming gossip about other people, ask yourself if this is how you would want to be spoken of. Then strive to speak of others as you would want to be spoken of: only with graciousness and charity. And when you have nothing gracious or charitable to say, learn to say nothing at all.

A gossip is one who talks to you about others, a bore is one who talks to you about himself, and a brilliant conversationalist is one who talks to you about yourself.
LISA KIRK

Hope

People love others not for who they are but for how they make us feel.

IRWIN FEDERMAN

HOW DO YOU MAKE PEOPLE FEEL?

I wish you could meet my daughter. Katy is a vibrant, enthusiastic young lady with a fabulous approach toward life. As a fourth grader, she committed herself to an enviable work ethic, developed a magnetic personality, and earned the respect of her teacher. (Of course, I'm entirely objective about my assessment.)

At the end of Katy's first semester as a fourth grader, a parent–teacher conference was scheduled for Thursday afternoon at 4:30 P.M. She was especially excitable during the week and confirmed the meeting time with her mother and me on several occasions. We assured her both of us planned to attend this special event.

On Wednesday morning Katy approached her teacher before school started. "I sure wish my conference was today!" she exclaimed. "Isn't tomorrow a good day for your parents to come?" her insightful teacher, Mrs. DeJong, queried.

"Oh no, they'll both be here," Katy responded, "I just wish my conference was today."

My son, here is the way to get people to like you. Make every person like himself a little better, and I promise that he or she will like you very much.
LORD CHESTERFIELD

Fascinated by this unusual student attitude, Mrs. DeJong probed further. "Why would you like me to meet with your parents today, Katy?"

Katy flashed one of her heart-warming smiles as she blurted, "I just can't wait for them to come home and tell me how good I am!"

Being a good student, Katy knew the parent–teacher conference was one avenue for her to receive a bit of recognition. She also knew my wife and I made it a habit to discuss the conference with the kids. It doesn't take a rocket scientist to see why Katy was anxious for her conference. This was her opportunity to hear how good she was even though she already knew.

My wife and I have ample reason to support and encourage our children. They are good kids. I'm concerned that I spend far too little time looking for ways to encourage and an excessive amount of time searching for things to correct. It's amazing how conditioned I've become—conditioned to believe a parent's role is to correct, discipline, and direct. I'm all right with that when it's balanced with support, recognition, and encouragement. Oh, to find that perfect balance.

"Three billion people on the face of the earth go to bed hungry every night," said Cavett Robert. "But four billion people go to bed hungry for a simple word of encouragement and recognition."

Encouragers support our dreams, understand our difficulties, recognize our efforts, and celebrate our achievements with us. They keep us from going to bed with an aching stomach, broken heart, or damaged spirit. They seem to know what to say and when to say it. They provide nourishment for the soul. Encouragers build hope.

Become an encourager. Make it possible for people to say: "I like myself better when I'm with you."

LEARN TO GIVE YOURSELF AWAY

Only those who have learned the power of sincere and selfless contribution experience life's deepest joy: true fulfillment.
ANTHONY ROBBINS

There are two seas in the Holy Land. The famous Sea of Galilee takes in fresh water from a nearby brook, uses it to generate a variety of marine vegetation, and then passes it on to the Jordan River. The Jordan does its part by spreading the life throughout the desert, turning it into fertile land.

The Dead Sea, on the other hand, comes by its name for a reason—it's dead. The water in the Dead Sea is so full of salt that no life can exist. The major difference between these two bodies of water is that the Dead Sea takes in the water from the Jordan River and hangs on to it. It has no outlet.

What a perfect example of the differences in people. People who live without giving themselves away become stagnant and find that what they keep stifles their life. Those who freely give of themselves multiply life. Eric Butterworth said, "A committed giver is an incurable happy person, a secure person, a satisfied person, and a prosperous person."

There's a life-enhancing lesson here. If you don't sow anything today, you'll have nothing to reap in the future. A rich life is the direct result of enriching others. "Don't judge each day by the harvest you reap," advised Robert Louis Stevenson, "but by the seeds you plant."

According to a *New York Times* article, Mr. Milton Petrie enjoyed giving his money away. He researched New York papers "for stories of people life had kicked in the face. He then reached for his checkbook."

Petrie, the son of a Russian immigrant pawn-shop owner, built his fortune with a chain of women's clothing stores. When he died at the age of 92, his lifelong commitment to being a generous giver continued. The newspaper headline reporting his death said: MILLIONAIRE'S DEATH DOESN'T STOP HIS GENEROSITY. He reportedly named 451 beneficiaries of his $800 million estate.

"What keeps our interest in life and makes us look forward to tomorrow is giving pleasure to other people," advised Eleanor Roosevelt. "Happiness is not a goal, it is a by-product."

Did you know Elvis Presley never took a tax deduction for any of the millions of dollars he donated to charities? The "king" said he believed it would violate the spirit of giving.

General William Booth had a passion for the poor of London and committed himself to a mission of meeting those needs. By the time of his death, Booth's local mission had spread across the world. His final sermon, delivered from a hospital bed to an international convention of Salvation Army "soldiers," was simply a one-word telegram that read: "Others!"

Booth's one-word sermon encapsulated everything he believed about the purpose of living—giving unselfishly of yourself to benefit others.

Billionaire John D. Rockefeller lived the first part of his life as a miserable man, unable to sleep, feeling unloved, and surrounded by bodyguards. At age 53, he was diagnosed with a rare disease. He lost all of his hair, and his body became shrunken. Medical experts gave him a year to live.

Rockefeller started thinking beyond his current life and sought meaning to his existence. He gave away his money to churches and the poor, and he established the Rockefeller Foundation. His life turned around, his health improved, and contrary to the doctor's prediction, he lived to be 98.

John D. Rockefeller's life exemplified the transformation that's possible when the joy of giving is discovered. You might be tempted to think that if you had Rockefeller's wealth, giving to others would be easy. Although it's easy to find examples of people with wealth who gave it away, what we're talking about here is much more than writing a check to your favorite charity. That's only a minute portion of the message.

"Every person passing through life will unknowingly leave something and take something away," reflected Robert Fulghum. "Most of this 'something' cannot be seen or heard or numbered. It does not show up in a census. But nothing counts without it."

Dwight Moody made this "something" Fulghum alluded to a way of life. Moody said, "I wish to do all the good I can, for all the people I can, in as many ways as I can, for as long as I can."

You can keep the waters of life flowing and add tremendous value to others by giving yourself to others. Put others first in your thinking. Find ways to enrich their lives. Give unselfishly. It is a natural law of life that the more of

Lock your house, go across the railroad tracks, find someone in need, and do something for him.

DR. KARL MENNINGER

yourself you pass on to others with no expectation of receiving in return, the more your life will be blessed.

If you want to experience ongoing success, learn to give yourself away and give hope to others. "Success is not rare—it is common," believed Henry Ford, Sr. "It is a matter of adjusting one's efforts to obstacles and one's abilities to a service needed by others. There is no other possible success. But most people think of it in terms of getting; success, however, begins in terms of giving."

YOU CAN MAKE A DIFFERENCE

Let's suppose for a moment you just received a card in the mail from your best friend. The message it contained went like this:

> First, I want to apologize. I've intended to send you this card for several months but never got around to it.
>
> You are a special person! I appreciate your acceptance of me just the way I am, and your friendship is the most valuable thing I have. I marvel at your positive attitude toward work, family, and life in general. It shows in everything you do. Thank you for being an exemplary role model. Most of all, I appreciate you for being you.
>
> Have a great day!

How would you feel? Would you sense a tinge of embarrassment along with a broad internal smile? How might

The purpose of life is not to win. The purpose of life is to grow and to share. When you come to look back on all that you have done in life, you will get more satisfaction from the pleasure you have brought into other people's lives than you will from the time that you outdid and defeated them.

RABBI HAROLD KUSHNER

this note affect your day, your interactions at work, or your feelings about yourself? Most important, how many times have you sent or received such an encouraging message?

Contrast that uplifting scenario with the reality of how many people feel about their relationships. The following story from John Powell, S.J.'s *Will the Real Me Please Stand Up?* sadly but realistically depicts the dire need for us to become sensitive to the needs of those around us.

"Early on Sunday morning, August 5, 1962, Marilyn Monroe was found dead. The coroner would later call it 'suicide.' When Marilyn's maid discovered her lifeless body on that Sunday morning, she noticed that the phone by her bedside was dangling off the hook. Marilyn had obviously made a last attempt to communicate with someone. When her last attempt failed, she gave up and died alone.

"Claire Booth Luce wrote a poignant article for *Life* magazine entitled, 'What Really Killed Marilyn?: The Love Goddess who never found any love.' Luce suggests that the dangling phone was an apt symbol of Marilyn's life. She tried for a long time to say that she was a person, but few ever took her seriously. Only after her death on a Saturday night, when all beautiful women are assumed to be out on the arm of a handsome escort, did many of the facts of her life surface.

"Marilyn Monroe was seriously disliked by most of her Hollywood contemporaries. She was dubbed a 'prima donna.' Very often, she would arrive hours late for a filming. As she casually strolled into the studio, no one suspected that she had been at her home nervously vomiting. She was terrified, afraid of cameras. No doubt her emotional reactions were the result of a sad and troubled childhood. Her father, an itinerant banker, had deserted the family. Her mother was repeatedly committed to mental institutions. Marilyn was raped at age eight by a boarder in her foster home. She was given a nickel not to tell.

"Now at age 35, her mirror kept telling her that the only thing others ever noticed about or praised in her was fading. She must have felt like an artist who is losing his vision or a musician whose hands are becoming arthritic. Marilyn had endured a painful childhood, had moved through several marriages, and had made many movies, but few ever took her seriously . . . until she was dead."

We need each other, yet we live in an age where actions of kindness and encouragement are far too rare. There is a tendency to be nit-picking and fault-finding and often positive, uplifting messages are buried in the desire to make people what we want them to be rather than appreciating them for who they are. We must learn to appreciate and find joy in our relationships, rather than constantly seek to reform those with whom we interact. We must learn to spread hope when others only express despair.

The chance to make a difference in someone's life can present itself at home, at work, with friends or strangers.

Look for an opportunity to lift someone's spirits, to make someone feel appreciated. Opportunities for offering hope to others present themselves everyday, we just have to pay attention and tune in.

As Albert Einstein stated, "Man is here for the sake of other men—above all for those upon whose smile and well-being our own happiness depends, and also for the countless unknown souls, with whose fate we are connected by a bond of sympathy."

KINDNESS

Our worst fault is our preoccupation with the faults of others.

KAHLIL GIBRAN

BEWARE OF BECOMING A FAULT-FINDER

Charlie Brown suffered from the "can't-do-anything-right" syndrome. Lucy is always there to remind him of the error of his ways.

On one occasion Lucy puts her hands on her hips and says, "You, Charlie Brown, are a foul ball in the line drive of life! You're in the shadow of your own goal posts! You are a miscue! You are three putts on the eighteenth green! You are a seven–ten split in the tenth frame! You are a dropped rod and reel in the lake of life! You are a missed free throw, a shanked nine iron, and a called third strike! Do you understand? Have I made myself clear?"

As unfair as Kahlil Gibran's comment might seem, that "Our worst fault is our preoccupation with the faults of others," the tendency to be a Lucy is tempting. How easy it is to point out to people what they aren't, haven't been, or never will become. Whether you are raising a family, running a company, or building a relationship, be sensitive to these words of wisdom from Will Rogers: "There is nothing as easy as denouncing. It don't take much to see that something is wrong, but it does take some eyesight to see what will put it right again."

In most cases, criticism is a futile and destructive process. It forces people to be defensive and usually causes them to make attempts at justifying their actions. Insensitivity will bruise pride, reduce people's sense of importance, and promote resentment within our relationships.

Have you thought lately about someone you would like to change, control, or improve? Fine. Begin with yourself. It has been said that most of us find it difficult to accept the imperfections in others that we possess ourselves. It's uncomfortable to watch people displaying the same negative qualities we ourselves have been unable to overcome. Confucius once said: "Don't complain about the snow on your neighbor's roof when your own doorstep is unclean." Attempting first to improve ourselves will provide us with a greater degree of tolerance concerning the weaknesses or undesirable traits of others.

The late John Wanamaker once reflected, "I learned 30 years ago that it is foolish to scold. I have enough trouble overcoming my own limitations without fretting over the fact that God has not seen fit to distribute evenly the gift of intelligence." Using Wanamaker's advice, concentrate on "me" first, with my heavy load of shortcomings, faults, and areas needing improvement. This enhances my ability to accept the limitations of others.

If you're thinking, "I wish my spouse, boss, friend would read this," then the message hasn't soaked in. Avoiding a fault-finding lifestyle is first and foremost your responsibility. An upbeat, encouraging, nourishing relationship begins with you.

Most fault-finding begins with something like this: "Perhaps I shouldn't say this, but . . ." Another common way to slip into critical remarks is by prefacing our comments with, "I don't mean to criticize, but . . ." And then we go on to do what? Criticize. Once we've shared our inspired observations, we justify them by saying: "I was only trying to help."

There is a huge gap between destructive criticism and constructive feedback that grows out of a sincere desire to enrich someone's life. You can make a positive difference in someone's life by avoiding a fault-finding approach and endorsing a spirit of affirmation and help. Consider these approaches:

1. Uphold People's Self Esteem. "I give up." "What's the use?" "I never do anything right." These are common feelings of people who feel defeated and deflated by personal attacks.

The apostle Paul wrote to the church in Rome: "Why then do you criticize your brother's actions, why do you try to make him look small?" Looking small hurts. People can tell us all day long how wonderful we are and how great it is to be our friend. Then one person criticizes us and we are devastated. The human recorder plays that tape over and over, forgetting the positives and bemoaning the one critical comment.

Be kind. Be gentle. Never forget that a person's spirit is easily crushed. Let people know how much you care for them before ever offering corrective advice. After giving negative feedback, offer additional affirmation of your respect, love, and concern for the person.

2. Focus on Abilities Rather than on Vulnerabilities. I've never met a person who has the ability to do anything worthwhile using his or her weaknesses. Tell people what you like about their performance before you suggest improvement. Find something, no matter how small or insignificant it might seem, that you can compliment them for. It's much easier to swallow criticism that is preceded by a sincere affirmation of what we do well.

3. Check Your Motives. Criticism is often an attempt to raise our own self-concept by comparing our faults to the weaknesses we observe in others. If I can point out some glitch in your life, then mine doesn't look so bad. When I am especially sensitive to an area in my life that needs adjustment, it is wise for me to be careful about what I am looking for in others. Lord Chesterfield said, "People hate those who make them feel their own inferiority." Ouch! Are you really trying to help or are you motivated by an effort to boost your own ego? An unknown author adds, "It is often our own imperfection which makes us reprove the imperfection of others; a sharp-sighted self-love of our own which cannot pardon the self-love of others."

Alice Duer Miller advised: "If it's painful for you to criticize your friends—you're safe in doing it. But if you take the slightest pleasure in it—that's the time to hold your tongue."

A critic is someone who never actually goes to the battle yet who afterwards comes out shooting the wounded.
TYNE DALY

4. *Keep Your Attitude in Check.* Fault-finding communicates the attitude: "I want you to feel as miserable as I do." We don't actually say that to others. Think about it. When do you criticize others the most? When life is flowing along like a dream? Probably not. How about when you are experiencing a trying day? Being sensitive to your emotions will help you refrain from communicating an attitude that because you're a crab, someone is about to get dumped on. Be careful not to blame others for the way you feel.

5. *Offer Assistance.* "What can I do to help?" That is a powerful question. Abraham Lincoln believed that, "He has a right to criticize who has a heart to help."

Fault-finding poisons people's spirits. It chips away at self-worth. Withdrawal seeks security. Defensiveness surfaces. Trust is broken. Love wilts. Growth, cooperation, love, sensitivity, encouragement, and understanding cannot exist in a relationship plagued with criticism. If you persist in pointing out limitations, destruction is imminent.

Offer caring suggestions. Discuss unmet expectations honestly and objectively. Provide educated advice. Encourage people to be the best they can be. Accept people for who they are—mistakes and all.

ENLARGE YOUR CIRCLE OF INFLUENCE

How thick is your Rolodex? How many people have you determined important enough to list in the telephone and address section of your day planner? When is the last time you added someone to your list of valued resources?

How many times have you entered the room of a meeting, seminar, social gathering, or community event and quickly scanned the audience to find someone you know? How many interesting people did you overlook by cozying up to and attaching yourself to familiar people?

Not only is it advisable to align yourself with activities and a lifestyle that breeds a broader vision of life, but it is equally important to align yourself with an ever expanding circle of influence. Surround yourself with exceptional people who have discovered the world in a way different from you.

Most of us become so comfortable with our acquaintances. We play golf with the same foursome, associate with the

You can make more friends in two months by becoming really interested in other people than you can in two years by trying to get other people interested in you.

DALE CARNEGIE

I am going to be meeting people today who talk too much—people who are selfish, egotistical, ungrateful. But I wouldn't be surprised or disturbed, for I can't imagine a world without such people.
MARCUS AURELIUS

same people at work, have lunch with our select network, attend social events with a small inner circle, and enjoy philosophical conversation with those we have repeated the same conversation with over and over.

Capitalize on and create every window of opportunity possible to get acquainted with at least one new person every week. Step out of your comfort zone and introduce yourself to someone.

When you fill up with gas next time, strike up a conversation with the gas station attendant. Ask your next server at the restaurant about the most interesting situation he or she dealt with that day. When ordering over the phone from mail-order catalogs, question the order takers about the things they enjoy most about their job. Make contact with a half dozen people in your community and ask them to tell you about their profession.

The opportunities are endless. But, you must begin seeing every person you encounter as an opportunity to learn, grow, and expand your intelligence.

Blast through the barriers of shyness, fear, self-consciousness, or even apathy to show others how interested you are in their lives and experiences. You'll be amazed how accommodating people are when you express a sincere interest in them. It takes a variety of people to challenge us, encourage us, promote us, and most of all, help us achieve a broader dimension of ourselves.

DON'T OVERLOOK LITTLE ACTS OF KINDNESS

At the hour of death, when we come face to face with God, we are going to be judged on love—not how much we have done, but how much love we put into our actions.
MOTHER TERESA

Calvin Coolidge was invited to a dinner hosted by Dwight Morrow, the father of Anne Morrow Lindbergh. After Coolidge had excused himself for the evening, Morrow expressed his belief that Coolidge would make a good president. The others disagreed and a discussion ensued concerning Coolidge's qualifications. Those not believing in his presidential potential felt he was too quiet and lacked charisma and personality. He just wasn't likable enough, they said.

Anne, then age six, spoke up. "I like him," she said. Displaying a finger with a bandage around it, she continued, "He was the only one at the party who asked about my sore finger, and that's why he would make a good president," said little Anne.

Anne had a good point. Maybe asking a little girl about her sore finger isn't necessarily a bona fide qualification for the presidency, but a spirit of kindness is a surefire way to impress others. Kindness, the sincere expression of love, makes the people around you feel loved and valuable.

Opportunities to show kindness abound. If someone were to pay you 10 cents for every kindness you ever showed and would collect 5 cents for every unkind word or action, would you be rich or poor?

Flash a smile to those you meet on the street. William Arthur Ward believed, "A warm smile is the universal language of kindness."

Use the precious words "please" and "thank you" at every possible occasion. St. Ambrose suggested that "no duty is more urgent than that of returning thanks."

Show concern for those inflicted with little hurts and big ones. Allow others to go in front of you in the grocery line (that's a tough one for me). Make it possible for people to change lanes in heavy traffic. Open the door for someone entering the same building as you. Offer a warm greeting to people you meet walking in hotel hallways.

You might be saying, "Isn't this a bit simplistic?" You're right. But, remember what impressed Anne Morrow? It was a sensitive expression of concern for a bandaged finger that made a positive impression. Simple? Maybe. Effective?

When we remember our unkindness to friends who have passed beyond the veil, we wish we could have them back again, if only for a moment, so that we could go on our knees to them and say, "Have pity and forgive."
MARK TWAIN

No doubt. It's the consistency of our little acts of kindness that cause people to smell a pleasant aroma about us wherever we go.

"Spread your love everywhere you go," encouraged Mother Teresa. "First of all in your own house. Give love to your children, to your wife or husband, to a next-door neighbor . . . let no one ever come to you without leaving better and happier. Be the living expression of God's kindness; kindness in your face, kindness in your eyes, kindness in your smile, kindness in your warm greeting."

RANDOM ACTS OF KINDNESS

I read a story about a woman who answered the knock on her door to find a man with a sad expression.

"I'm sorry to disturb you," he said, "but I'm collecting money for an unfortunate family in the neighborhood. The husband is out of work, the kids are hungry, the shelves are bare, the utilities will soon be cut off, and worse, they're going to be kicked out of their apartment if they don't pay the rent by this afternoon."

"I'd be happy to help out," said the woman with great concern. "But who are you?"

"I'm the landlord," he replied.

Suffice it to say the landlord is not an enviable example of kindness. At the same time we can probably all relate to times when kindness was used to get our own way or to convince someone to do something that would benefit us. But pure kindness flows from pure motives.

Never lose sight of the fact that the most important yardstick of your success will be how you treat other people—your family, friends, and co-workers, and even strangers you meet along the way.

BARBARA BUSH

According to the Associated Press, Chuck Wall, a human-relations instructor at Bakersfield College in California, was watching a local news program one day when a cliché from a broadcaster caught his attention: "Another random act of senseless violence."

Wall got an idea. He gave an unusual and challenging assignment to his students. They were to do something out of the ordinary to help someone and then write an essay about it.

One thing led to another. Wall then dreamed up a bumper sticker that read, "Today, I will commit one random act of senseless KINDNESS . . . Will You?" Students sold the bumper stickers for one dollar each and donated the profits to a county Braille center.

An impressive variety of acts of kindness were performed. One student paid his mother's utility bills. Another student bought 30 blankets from the Salvation Army and took them to homeless people gathered under a bridge.

The idea expanded. Bumper stickers were slapped on all 113 county patrol cars. The message was trumpeted from the pulpits, in schools, and was endorsed by professional associations.

As Chuck Wall reflected on the success of his idea, he commented, "I had no idea our community was in such need of something positive."

It's not just Mr. Wall's community that needs random acts of kindness.

After Wausau, Wisconsin was featured as the subject of a negative story on *60 Minutes, The Wausau Daily Herald* talked area businesses into co-sponsoring a Random Acts of Kindness Week.

Courtesy is the one coin you can never have too much of or be stingy with.
JOHN WANAMAKER

Businesses, organizations, and individuals were encouraged to perform simple acts of kindness for people they knew or didn't know. The response was astronomical. Over 200 businesses and organizations participated. The employees of the newspaper went out wearing T-shirts bearing the Random Acts of Kindness slogan, and they performed good deeds.

Banks washed car windows in the drive-up lanes, church groups mowed lawns for people in the neighborhood, movie theaters gave out free passes to people waiting in line. One individual walked into a restaurant and bought a cup of coffee for every person in the place. The newspaper ran a hot line for people to phone in the acts of kindness they had witnessed. More than 500 calls were received. The response was so tremendous that *The Wausau Daily Herald* decided to repeat the event the next year.

How about creating a random-acts-of-kindness lifestyle. Your motto could be, "Everyday in some way I will show kindness to someone who is not in a position to repay me." You might be amazed at how the idea grows.

Friendship

A friend is someone we can count on for understanding, support, discretions, and, if we're lucky, insight, wisdom, and well-timed foolishness.

JOHN R. O'NEIL

PORTRAIT OF A FRIENDSHIP

Out of the *Book of Sunshine* came this portrait of a friendship:

Those who turn their radio dials to sports commentaries will perhaps have relished this human interest story of President Dwight Eisenhower.

It occurred in a little town in Kansas, where Dwight Eisenhower spent his boyhood days. He was a comely lad, strong and virile, filled with the spirit of an athlete. He chose boxing as his pastime, and his ambition and skilled technique soon made him the champion boxer of the town. There was none who dared challenge young Eisenhower's prowess.

But one day, there came to town another young man. He gave his name as Frankie Brown. Brown bore the reputation of a professional boxer, and he soon learned of the ambitious young Eisenhower. A match was arranged between the two young athletes. No one was ever able to tell who won the honors, but both fought so well that before the bout was over, the two were fast friends.

They retired to a restaurant following the affair, and there they discussed plans for their future. Eisenhower desired to go to college, but Brown wanted to pursue boxing as a professional career. Eisenhower sought to persuade Brown first to acquire the higher schooling. In the wee hours of the night, the two emerged, both determined to go to college.

Frankie Brown entered Notre Dame. The determination that led him to follow Dwight Eisenhower's advice also stood him in hand in becoming the noted and beloved football coach of Notre Dame—Knute Kenneth Rockne.

In a fateful hour on March 31, 1931, the airplane in which Knute Rockne was enroute to his old friend in Kansas crashed to earth, crushing a life that had matched the determination and friendship and prowess of an Eisenhower.

Once, while sitting in a restaurant, Henry Ford, Sr. was asked: "Who is your best friend?"

Ford thought for a moment, then took out his pencil and wrote in large letters on the tablecloth: "He is your best friend who brings out of you the best that is in you."

Rockne and Eisenhower's friendship exemplified this belief. They challenged each other, encouraged each other to raise the bar on their personal expectations, and built a relationship around mutual respect. That combination inspired Knute Rockne and Dwight Eisenhower to reach for their potential.

It's enjoyable having friends who make us laugh. I cherish those friends who offer sincere advice. Friends who want to understand what's important to me are so valuable. I deeply respect those friends who genuinely celebrate my successes and encourage me through the failures. I don't want to leave out those friends who help me maintain my childlike, fun spirit. But the friend who challenges me to be all God intended me to be can't be replaced. Everybody needs a friend like that.

The easiest kind of relationship for me is with ten thousand people. The hardest is with one.
JOAN BAEZ

ARE YOU FILLING PEOPLE UP OR SUCKING THEM DRY?

To do something, however small, to make others happier and better is the highest ambition, the most elevating hope, which can inspire a human being.
JOHN LUBBOCK

I'm more convinced than ever before that success and fulfillment in life are in direct proportion to the investment we make in people. If someone spent the whole day with you, how would they feel at the end of the day—filled up or sucked dry? Are you the kind of person who searches for ways to inject hope, encouragement, and goodwill, or do you tend to extract those necessities in your daily interaction?

The good news is that no one needs to live a minute longer extracting life out of people. We can all increase our building, filling, and replenishing habits and thereby make it possible for people to like themselves and their lives better when they're with us. Consider a few practical actions to put on your daily relationship agenda.

1. Remember the Basics. In 1860, the *Lady Elgin* collided with a lumber barge on a stormy night and sank, leaving 393 people stranded in the waters of Lake Michigan. Two hundred seventy-nine of these people drowned. A young college student named Edward Spencer plunged into the water again and again to rescue people. After he had pulled 17 people from the freezing water, he was overcome with exhaustion and collapsed, never to stand again. For the remainder of his life, Spencer was confined to a wheelchair. Years later, someone asked him his most vivid memory of that fateful night. "The fact that not one of the 17 ever returned to thank me," was his reply, according to a Chicago newspaper.

I'm sure you would agree that this is unthinkable. How could 17 people, who had their lives spared because of this young man, fail to show their gratitude? Before we judge them too harshly, it might be worth our time to evaluate our consistency in remembering life's basic manners. Smile. Say "please" and "thank you." Use people's first names when speaking with them. Greet people with a hearty "hello!" or "good morning!" Show interest in your coworkers' welfare. Maintain a positive, optimistic outlook on matters other people tend to scowl at. Think about how others feel. Be an advocate of dignity and respect for all people.

The value of these basics is often overlooked, taken for granted, or missed completely. These simple actions communicate the caring and compassionate attitude encouragers possess. Review the list and find ways to continually do the little acts of kindness that produce big dividends.

2. Honk an Encouraging Message. Have you ever noticed how some friendships, marriages, and parent–child relationships are vibrant and growing while others seem to be plagued with discouragement? It may be a difference in attitude. If people build up and encourage one another, the whole atmosphere is refreshing. But a critical, negative spirit breeds tension and conflict.

Bruce Larson, in his book *Wind and Fire,* illustrates the power of encouragement. Writing about sandhill cranes, he said, "These large birds who fly great distances across continents have three remarkable qualities. First, they rotate leadership. No one bird stays out in front all the time. Second, they choose leaders who can handle turbulence. And then (this is my favorite), all during the time one bird is leading, the rest are honking affirmation."

Conduct an attitude check. Are you critical of people, situations, and life in general? Do you complain about the job someone else is doing or should have done? Do you have a negative spirit? If so, work to become a positive honking friend, spouse, parent, and coworker. Negative sourpusses are energy suckers. Positive horn honkers inspire others to fly further and higher.

Isn't it amazing how applicable the unique habits of a sandhill crane are to us. When people consistently build up and encourage, the whole atmosphere of their relationship is nurturing. People feel safe, comfortable taking risks, and they experience healthier feelings about themselves. Virginia Arcastle said, "When people are made to feel secure, important, and appreciated, it will no longer be necessary for them to whittle down others in order to seem bigger in comparison."

Check your interactions. What kind of messages have you been honking lately?

3. *Believe in People.* Dale Carnegie said, "Tell a child, a husband, or an employee that he is stupid or dumb at a certain thing, that he has no gift for it, and that he is doing it all wrong and you have destroyed almost every incentive to try to improve. But use the opposite technique; be liberal with encouragement; make the thing seem easy to do; let the other person know that you have faith in his ability to do it, that he has an undeveloped flair for it—and he will practice until the dawn comes in at the window in order to excel."

According to a selection in the March 1992 *Homemade,* a young man in London wanted to be a writer, but the cards seemed stacked against him. He had only four years of school, and his father was in jail because he couldn't pay his debts. Just to survive the pain of hunger, the young man got a job pasting labels on bottles in a rat-infested warehouse. He slept in an attic with two other boys from the slums. With such little confidence in himself and in his ability to write, he secretly slipped out in the middle of the night to mail his first manuscript so nobody would laugh at his dream. That manuscript, along with countless others, was rejected. Finally, one story was accepted. He wasn't paid anything, but the editor praised him for his writing. That one little compliment caused him to wander aimlessly through the streets with tears rolling down his cheeks. The compliment inspired him to continue and improve. It also led to a brilliant career for Charles Dickens.

Donald Laird said, "Always help people increase their own self-esteem. Develop your skill in making other people feel important. There is hardly a higher compliment you can pay an individual than helping him be useful and to find satisfaction from his usefulness."

Expressing our belief and faith in people can provide the inspiration for people to pursue their dreams. Find the seed of achievement waiting for your nourishment. Help people believe in themselves more than they believe in themselves and watch them blossom.

4. Express Your Love. I fear too many of us might be represented by the guy who exclaimed to his wife, "Honey, when I think about how much I love you, I can hardly keep from telling you."

Telling someone how much they mean to you seems like a basic relationship action. And it should be. But it's not. We may want to tell others how much they mean to us, but we don't. We want to hear words of love and affection and are disappointed at how infrequent those messages touch our ears. By our very nature, our hearts respond to a message of love.

In his book *In the Arena,* former President Richard Nixon reflected on the depression he experienced following his resignation from the presidency and then undergoing surgery. At the depths of his discouragement, he told his wife, Pat, that he just wanted to die.

At Mr. Nixon's lowest point, a nurse entered the room, pulled open the drapes, and pointed to a small airplane flying back and forth. The plane was pulling a banner that read: GOD LOVES YOU AND SO DO WE. This powerful, uplifting expression of love was arranged by Ruth Graham, evangelist Billy Graham's wife. Nixon said this was a turning point. Realizing someone cared lifted his spirits and gave him the courage and desire to press on.

Somebody once said, "Appreciating others without telling them is like winking at someone in the dark. You know what you're doing, but nobody else does."

Don't just think about expressing your love and appreciation for those you care about. Take the initiative. Don't wait for the other person—the two of you could wait a long time. Never assume people know how you feel about them. Give someone close to you a hug, pat him on the back and say, "I love you," or "You mean a lot to me," or "I care about you."

It feels good.

Someone might say, "I'm not into this 'touchy-feely' stuff. I'm uncomfortable giving hugs or verbal praise." If you're saying "amen" to that, here's another option. Write a letter or send a note to brighten someone's day. Who could benefit from a note of appreciation, word of concern, or a card complimenting her for a job well done? Don't let the impulse slip by without taking action. Tread yourself a well-worn path to the mailbox.

5. *Uphold People's Self-Esteem.* I like Henry Ward Beecher's observation that "There are persons so radiant, so genial, so kind, so pleasure-bearing, that you instinctively feel good in their presence that they do you good, whose coming into a room is like bringing a lamp there."

I had the privilege of working several years as a volunteer with junior-high-age youth in a basketball program. It would be self-gratifying to say I was always the type of person Beecher described, but I wasn't. I did learn, however, that when I built young people's self-esteem, they were open to instruction.

Imagine 12-year-old Laurie struggling to get the little round ball through the round cylinder. She's zero for ten and you approach her saying, "Laurie, I like the way you put everything into your shot. I think you're going to make a good basketball player."

Laurie beams. She is receptive and eager to learn more. Laurie is all ears when you add, "Laurie, you tend to throw your elbow out and shoot off your palms. Let me show you the proper shooting method."

Sounds simple, doesn't it. The beauty is, upholding a person's self-esteem is simple, if our motives are right. Rather than being intent on correction, let your instruction be grounded in affirmation.

The following illustration from *Our Daily Bread* puts the finishing touches on the importance of upholding self-esteem. Benjamin West was just trying to be a good baby-sitter for his little sister, Sally. While his mother was out, Benjamin found some bottles of colored ink and proceeded to paint Sally's portrait. But by the time Mrs. West returned, ink blots stained the table, chairs, and floor. Benjamin's mother surveyed the mess without a word until she saw the picture. Picking it up she exclaimed, "Why, it's Sally!" And she bent down and kissed her young son.

In 1763, when he was 25 years old, Benjamin West was selected as history painter to England's King George III. He became one of the most celebrated artists of his day. Commenting on his start as an artist, he said, "My mother's kiss made me a painter."

Each of us yearns for someone to fill us, build us, and lift us up. We encounter plenty of people along the way intent on letting us know where we've failed, fallen short of expectations, or about what areas of our life are less than perfect. These energy suckers are a dime a dozen. We need people who make us feel valued and worthwhile just as we are.

Make it possible for people to say, "I like myself better when I'm with you."

Remember the basics, honk encouraging words, believe in people more than they believe in themselves, freely express your love, and uphold people's self-esteem.

Do not do unto others as you think they should do unto you. Their tastes may not be the same.

GEORGE BERNARD SHAW

YOU NEED A LITTLE SPACE

To keep the fire burning brightly, keep the two logs together, near enough to keep each other warm, and far enough apart—about a finger's breadth—for breathing room. Good fire, good marriage—same rule.

MARNIE REED CROWELL

Some married couples insist every moment of their lives be occupied with each other.

Relationship experts indicate that healthy marriages are interdependent, where couples are comfortable in situations requiring independence and where they even enjoy periodic dependency. Just as with any friendship, danger occurs when neither person has learned to be independent. Obsessive dependency can destroy relationships but can also inhibit the opportunity to learn self-sufficiency.

An article in the February 3, 1984 *Los Angeles Times* told of a couple in Vista, California, who took ill at the same time. The article tells how Harry and Cora Walker were inseparable in their 50 years of living together. When they took ill they went to the hospital and Harry was admitted into one room with pneumonia while Cora was admitted to another room with a kidney ailment. They visited each other daily, but within a few days Harry took a turn for the worse and died. Eight hours after her husband's passing, Cora was dead, too.

Marital interdependence is an outgrowth of a person's healthy independence. When we learn to seek the best within ourselves and our partner, there is joy in living whether together or apart.

A marriage is like a long trip in a tiny rowboat: If one passenger starts to rock the boat, the other has to steady it; otherwise, they will go to the bottom together.
DAVID REUBEN

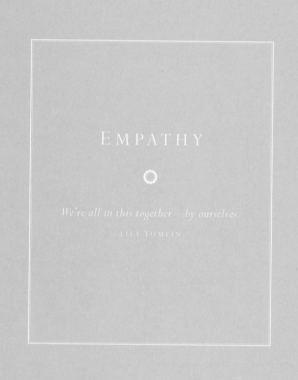

Empathy

We're all in this together—by ourselves.

LILY TOMLIN

A CURE FOR THE LONELY

The unfortunate truth in Lily Tomlin's comment came to life in October of 1993 when the major television networks covered a story from Worcester, Massachusetts. Police found a woman dead on her kitchen floor. Adele Gaboury died of natural causes at age 73—four years before she was found. No one missed her.

Warmth, kindness, and friendship are the most yearned for commodities in the world. The person who can provide them will never be lonely."
ANN LANDERS

How can this be? How can any human being go unmissed for four years? According to the Associated Press, neighbors had notified authorities years earlier when they noticed an unusual amount of accumulated mail and newspapers and that the lawn was virtually unkempt.

When the police notified Ms. Gaboury's brother, he indicated she had gone into a nursing home. Police notified the postal service to stop delivering mail. Neighbors stepped in to care for the yard and have the utility company shut off the water when a pipe froze, broke, and sent water flowing out under the door. No one suspected Ms. Gaboury's lifeless body was stretched out inside.

Loneliness is the prison of the human spirit.
JOHN POWELL, S.J.

One friend from the past commented, "She didn't want anyone bothering her at all. I guess she got her wish, but it's awfully sad."

According to newspaper reports, Adele lived in her house in this middle-class neighborhood for 40 years, but none of her neighbors knew her well. "My heart bleeds for her," a neighbor was quoted as saying, "but you can't blame a soul. If she saw you out there, she never said hello to you."

I have to believe Adele Gaboury lived in a lonely world. She was surrounded by people, yet alone. Although it appears she made little effort to reach out to those around her, it's evident few people showered her with attention.

This unfortunate scenario reminds us that giving and receiving are interdependent. They work together to form the natural laws that govern our relationships. What we give to others, we'll get. What we send out, comes back to us. What we sow, we reap. In other words, what goes around comes around. Simply put, when you reach out to meet the needs of other people, your needs will be met.

We can learn a valuable lesson from Adele Gaboury's experience. What if Adele and her neighbors had understood and lived out the natural laws? Smiled. Been friendly. Offered assistance. Performed kind deeds. Been generous. Been nice. Showed courtesy. Shared love. A multitude of other gestures would have produced a like response.

But we must be willing to share these expressions to receive them. A lonely life and unnoticed death are unnecessary. Be patient and persistent in seeking out opportunities to unselfishly give of yourself to meet the needs of others. Don't hesitate. "You cannot do a kindness too soon," said Ralph Waldo Emerson, "for you never know how soon it will be too late."

The most terrible poverty is loneliness and the feeling of being unwanted.

MOTHER TERESA

MAKE A DIFFERENCE IN PEOPLE'S LIVES

Doing nothing for others is the undoing of one's self. We must be purposely kind and generous or we miss the best part of existence. The heart that goes out of itself gets large and full of joy. This is the great secret of the inner life. We do ourselves the most good by doing something for others.

HORACE MANN

A wise and beloved shah once ruled the land of Persia. He cared deeply for his people and wanted only what was best for them. The Persians knew this shah took a personal interest in their affairs and tried to understand how his decisions affected their lives. Periodically he would disguise himself and wander through the streets, trying to see life from their perspective.

One day he disguised himself as a poor village man and went to visit the public baths. Many people were there enjoying the fellowship and relaxation. The water for the baths was heated by a furnace in the cellar, where one man was responsible for maintaining the comfort level of the water. The shah made his way to the basement to visit with the man who tirelessly tended the fire.

The two men shared a meal together, and the shah befriended this lonely man. Day after day, week in and week out, the ruler went to visit the fire tender. The stranger soon became attached to his visitor because he came to where he was. No other person had showed that kind of caring or concern.

One day the shah revealed his true identity. It was a risky move, for he feared the man would ask him for special favors or for a gift. Instead, the leader's new friend looked into his eyes and said, "You left your comfortable palace and your glory to sit with me in this dungeon of darkness. You ate my bitter food and genuinely showed you cared about what happens to me. On other people you might bestow rich gifts, but to me you have given the best gift of all. You have given yourself."

For thousands of years, people have been speculating on what constitutes quality human relationships. With all the philosophies, theories, and speculations, only one principle seems to stand strong. It is not new at all. In fact, it is almost as old as history itself. It was taught in Persia over three thousand years ago by Zoroaster to his fire worshipers. Confucius asserted the principle in China twenty-four centuries ago. In the Valley of Han lived the followers of Taoism. Their leader Lao-Tzu taught the principle incessantly. Five hundred years before Christ, Buddha taught it to his

If you wish others to respect you, you must show respect for them. . . . Everyone wants to feel that he counts for something and is important to someone. Invariably, people will give their love, respect and attention to the person who fills that need. Consideration for others generally reflects faith in self and faith in others.
ARI KIEV

disciples on the banks of the holy Ganges. The collections of Hinduism contained this principle over fifteen hundred years before Christ. Nineteen centuries ago, Jesus taught his disciples and followers much the same principle. He summed it up in one thought: "Do unto others as you would have them do unto you."

Unselfishly giving of ourselves probably wouldn't make it as a primary course of study in the school of success. Although we make a living by what we get, the true rewards are experienced because of what we give. You have not really lived a fulfilled day, even though you may be a success by societal standards, unless you have done something for someone who will never be able to repay you.

In the midst of your flurry of activities in this competitive, go-get-'em world, take a moment for the next several days to reflect on Rabbi Harold Kushner's thoughts: "The purpose of life is not to win. It is to grow and to share. You will get more satisfaction from the pleasure you have brought into other people's lives than you will from the times you outdid and defeated them."

A UNIQUE SPIN ON GETTING EVEN

During the days of the Berlin Wall, a few East Berliners decided to send their West Berlin neighbors a "gift." They proceeded to load a dump truck with undesirables including garbage, broken bricks, building material, and any other disgusting items they could find. They calmly drove across the border, received clearance, and delivered their present by dumping it on the West Berlin side.

You will find as you look back on life that the moments when you have really lived are the moments when you have done things in a spirit of love.
HENRY DRUMMOND

Needless to say, the West Berliners were irritated and intent on "getting even." People immediately began offering ideas on how to outdo the repulsive actions of their adversaries. A wise man interrupted their angry reactions and offered an entirely different approach. Surprisingly, people responded favorably to his suggestions and began loading a dump truck full of essential items scarce in East Berlin. Clothes, food, and medical supplies poured in. They drove the loaded truck across the border, carefully unloaded and

Shall we make a new rule of life from tonight: always to try to be a little kinder than is necessary.
JAMES M. BARRIE

stacked the precious commodities, and then left a sign that read, "Each gives according to his ability to give."

Imagine the reaction of those who saw the "payback" and powerful message on the sign. Shock. Embarrassment. Distrust. Disbelief. Maybe even a bit of regret.

What we give to others sends a loud message about who we are. How we respond to unkindness, unfairness, or ingratitude speaks a truckload about our true character.

INFLUENCE

There are little eyes upon you,
And they're watching night and day;
There are little ears that quickly
Take in every word you say;
There are little hands all eager
To do anything you do;
And a little boy who's dreaming
Of the day he'll be like you.

You're the little fellow's idol;
You're the wisest of the wise,
In his little mind about you,
No suspicions ever rise;
He believes in you devoutly,
Holds that all you say and do,
He will say and do, in your way
When he's a grown-up like you.

There's a wide-eyed little fellow,
Who believes you're always right,
And his ears are always open,
And he watches day and night;
You are setting an example
Every day in all you do,
For the little boy who's waiting
To grow up to be like you.

AUTHOR UNKNOWN

NEVER ASSUME YOU'RE PEDALING TOGETHER

We are born for co-operation, as are the feet, the hands, the eyelids and the upper and lower jaws. People need each other to make up for what each one does not have.
MARCUS AURELIUS

The definition of the word "cooperation" stems from two Latin words, *co*, meaning "with," and *opus*, meaning "work." So, quite literally, cooperation means working with others. Sounds simple, doesn't it.

For over 25 years the *Des Moines Register* newspaper has sponsored a summer RAGBRAI (Register's Annual Great Bike Ride Across Iowa). Bikers from all over the country emerge on the western side of Iowa determined to be one of hundreds of successful riders who invest a week of their life pedaling their way across the state.

One year RAGBRAI designated our community as a stopping point for the night. It was an incredible sight to watch the bikers swarm into town and set up camp. Young and old alike enjoyed the challenge, fellowship, and fun that accompanied this popular event.

As I walked through one of the camping areas, I overheard a conversation between two riders who were navigating the trail together on a tandem bike. The man was complaining about the difficulty of one of the hills they had to climb earlier in the day. "That was a struggle," he said. "I thought for sure we were going to have to push the bike up the hill on foot."

The purpose of life is to collaborate for a common cause; the problem is nobody seems to know what it is.
GERHARD GSCHWANDTNER

"It sure was a steep hill," his female companion responded, "and if I hadn't kept the brake on all the way, we would have rolled back down for sure."

There's practically no limit to what people can accomplish when they work cooperatively. However, if just one person drags her feet or continually applies the brake, everyone else suffers. Married couples, work departments, athletic teams, dancers, or the cast in a play need to understand where the team is going, how they will get there, what effort will be required by each person, and what they can do to help each other.

When you're on a tandem bike, you have to pedal together.

NO ONE IS AN ISLAND

A true friend never gets in your way unless you happen to be going down.
ARNOLD GLOSOW

A few years ago I conducted a seminar in Des Moines, Iowa in late October. I arose early in the morning to prepare for the program and was shocked when I turned on the television to see news reports of a premature heavy snowfall in progress. Electricity was out in various parts of the city, numerous traffic accidents had been reported, and no travel was advised.

Later in the day, the no-travel advisory had been lifted so I loaded my vehicle to attempt the trip home. On each side of the freeway that runs through Des Moines were trees loaded with the heavy white snow. I noticed in areas where evergreen trees were close together bowed branches from one tree were resting against the trunk of another, and each tree seemed to be supported by the branches or trunk of another tree.

Where trees stood alone, the heavy snow had caused tremendous damage. The branches were unable to handle the heavy weight and, without the support of other trees, they had snapped. Thousands of small and large branches painted the white landscape. Seedlings and strong mature trees were irreparably damaged.

We are not unlike those trees. When the premature, unexpected, or normal storms of life hit, we need the support of other people to withstand the weight of the burden. Human beings aren't designed to stand on their own, and the closer we grow together, the more mutual support we can provide.

FOOTSTEPS

A careful man I ought to be;
A little fellow follows me.
I do not dare to go astray
For fear he'll go the selfsame way.
Not once can I escape his eyes;
Whate'er he sees me do he tries.
Like me he says he's going to be—
That little chap who follows me.
I must remember as I go
Through summer sun and winter snow,
I'm molding for the years to be—
That little chap who follows me.

AUTHOR UNKNOWN

Love

There is little doubt that most of us
long for stronger, more creative and rewarding
ways of loving each other.

LEO F. BUSCAGLIA

GOOD ADVICE . . . . WRONG APPLICATION

A couple engaged to be married began experiencing difficulties in their relationship. The constant conflict caused them to question their wedding plans. The man, concerned he could lose the woman he loved, realized there were many unresolved issues he had no idea how to handle. So he sought the advice of a counselor who suggested the problems could be solved if he would take up biking. "I want for you to ride ten miles a day for the next two weeks and then check back with me." Two weeks went by and the man reported back to his counselor as requested. "So, how are you and your fiancee doing now?" the counselor inquired. "How should I know," the man replied, "I'm 140 miles away from home and haven't talked to her for 14 days."

There will always be challenges and problems in any relationship. No problem! Dr. Theodore Rubin advises in *One to One:* "The problem is not that there are problems. The problem is expecting otherwise and thinking that having problems is a problem."

I like long walks, especially when they are taken by people who annoy me.
Fred Allen

Abundant advice is available from assorted sources for anyone wishing to enrich his or her relationships. Unfortunately, none of that advice is worth a plugged nickel unless you're willing to step up your investment in people.

My advice: (1) Remember that creating and nourishing relationships is hard work; (2) there will always be problems; (3) relationships are worth every ounce of effort it takes to work through the unavoidable challenges.

This is good advice, if I must say so myself. Apply it—NOW.

CREATE YOUR EMOTIONS THROUGH YOUR MOTIONS

Dr. Joyce Brothers tells the story of a judge trying to change the mind of a woman filing for divorce. "You're 92," he said. "Your husband is 94. You've been married for 73 years. Why give up now?" "Our marriage has been on the rocks for quite a while," the woman explained, "but we decided to wait until the children died."

Happy marriages begin when we marry the ones we love, and they blossom when we love the ones we marry.
TOM MULLEN

Dr. Robert Taylor, author of the book *Couples: The Art of Staying Together,* said, "We're now living in the age of disposability: Use it once, and throw it away. Over the past decade, there has developed a feeling that relationships are equally disposable."

The throw-away culture in which we live seems intent on throwing out the principle that marriage is a commitment requiring effort.

According to a *U.S. News and World Report* study, the single biggest reason couples split up is the "inability to talk honestly with each other, to bare their souls, and to treat each other as each other's best friend." The same factors continue to rank high on the list of reasons for marriage breakups.

On the dance floor, as in life, you're only as good as your partner.
ROBIN MARANTZ HENIG IN *USA TODAY*

Here's a familiar scenario: Your spouse complains, "You never tell me you love me anymore." You take the hint and mumble, "Of course I love you." But inside you're thinking, "Silly, I wouldn't be living with you if I didn't love you. But if anything changes, you'll be among the first to know." Why don't we just respond with a warm kiss and then say, "I'm sorry I haven't told you lately how much I love you."

The great psychologist Dr. George W. Crane said in his famous book, *Applied Psychology,* "Remember, motions are the precursors of emotions. You can't control the latter directly but only through your choice of motions or actions. . . . To avoid this all too common tragedy (marital difficulties and misunderstandings) become aware of the true psychological facts. Go through the proper motions each day and you'll soon begin to feel the corresponding emotions! Just be sure you and your mate go through those motions of dates and kisses, the phrasing of sincere daily compliments, plus the many other little courtesies and you need not worry about the emotion of love. You can't act devoted for very long without feeling devoted."

When we treat our spouse as the most important person in our life, we will begin feeling it, believing it, and enjoying it. What can you do this week to turn "motions into emotions"?

TO MY GROWN-UP SON

My hands were busy through the day
I didn't have much time to play
The little games you asked me to.
I didn't have much time for you.
I'd wash your clothes, I'd sew and cook,
But when you'd bring your picture book
And ask me please to share your fun,
I'd say: "A little later, son."
I'd tuck you in all safe at night
And hear your prayers, turn out the light,
Then tiptoe softly to the door.
I wish I'd stayed a minute more.
For life is short, the years rush past.
A little boy grows up so fast.
No longer is he at your side,
His precious secrets to confide.
The picture books are put away,
There are no longer games to play,
No good-night kiss, no prayers to hear.
That all belongs to yesteryear.
My hands, once busy, now are still.
The days are long and hard to fill.
I wish I could go back and do
The little things you asked me to.

AUTHOR UNKNOWN

WHAT DOES LOVE LOOK LIKE?

What does love look like? It has the hand to help others. It has the feet to hasten to the poor and needy. It has the eyes to see misery and want. It has the ears to hear the sighs and sorrows of men. That is what love looks like.

SAINT AUGUSTINE

Much has been written "about" love but maybe we've been short-sighted in helping people understand "how to" love. I know this is elementary, but love is more than hugs, kisses, and affection. It also transcends the emotional feeling so many consider love. Love is demonstrated by an attitude of sensitivity and concern and is expressed through sincere actions. Then, the emotion of love surfaces and grows from there.

Let me make this simple. "You can't put a price tag on love," said Melanie Clark, "but you can on all its accessories." Activating the "accessories" of love requires us to eliminate the baggage of pettiness, jealousy, resentment, and judgment. Just love. Think and behave as if you love. By loving thinking and loving actions, we expand our ability to express authentic love. Remember, the emotional part of love is achieved when the thinking and acting are activated.

Maybe a few real-life examples will clarify the "how to" for loving and encourage you to show the accessories of love:

A Welsh gentleman fell in love with one of his neighbors and wanted to marry her. The couple got into an argument and she refused to forgive. The man was shy and hesitated to face his love. Instead, he slipped a love letter under her door every week.

Finally, after 42 years, he worked up the courage, knocked on her door, and asked her to become his wife. To his surprise, she said yes. The couple was married at age 74.

Although his approach was a bit unconventional, it was a determined display of persistent love. What are you doing every week to show those you love how much they mean to you?

I've enjoyed attending the entertaining musical play *Fiddler on the Roof* many times. In one scene, Tevye, seeing the example of his daughters, begins to think about love as a basis for marriage. So after years of marriage, he asks his wife, "Do you love me?" She replies, "For 25 years I washed your clothes, slept in your bed, bore your children, and fixed your meals. If that isn't love, what is?" But Tevye persists: "Do you love me?" After repeated requests, Tevye's wife was only able to respond, "I suppose I do."

"Do you love me?" In the ideal world, this question would be unnecessary. In the real world, countless people yearn to hear the words "I love you."

Ida Fay Oblesby, writing in the *P.E.O. Record* (January 1983), tells the story of an eight-year-old girl in a Pennsylvania orphanage who was shy, unattractive, and regarded as a problem. Two other asylums had her transferred, and now this director was seeking some pretext for getting rid of her. One day, someone noticed the little girl was writing a letter. An ironclad rule of the institution was that any communication from a child had to be approved before it was mailed. The next day, the director and her assistant watched the child steal out of the dormitory and slip down to the main gate. Just inside the gate was an old tree with roots showing above the ground. They followed and watched as the child hid the letter in one of the crevices of the root. Carefully looking around, the little girl scurried back to the dormitory.

The director took the note and tore it open. Then, without speaking, she passed the note to her assistant. It read, "To anybody who finds this: I love you."

What a powerful message from the hearts of those hungry to have someone to love and love them back.

Alvin Straight lived a few miles from me in Laurens, Iowa. His brother, age 80, lived several hundred miles away in Blue River, Wisconsin. According to local news reports, Alvin's brother had suffered a stroke, and Alvin wanted to see him, but had no transportation. Alvin's eyesight wasn't good enough to have a driver's license, and he refused to take a plane, train, or bus. So Alvin, at age 73, climbed aboard his 1966 John Deere tractor lawn mower and drove it all the way to Blue River, Wisconsin. Now that's devotion.

People's needs are not inconveniences, irritations, or a disruption to our comfortable lifestyles. Needs are opportunities to share a portion of ourselves, to stretch our ability to give, and to sharpen our ability to become others-minded.

The following appeared on the editorial page of the *Pasadena Star News* in November of 1985:

Just about everyone knows the Jim Brady story—the man who, only two months after becoming White House press secretary, was shot in the head during the attempted assassination of President Reagan, and how he has fought his way back from brain surgery and the crippling, enduring damage from the stray bullet. However, not many people know, however, about the ceaseless, selfless, devoted love of Bob Dahlgren . . . a man who loved Brady like himself.

A few months ago, Bob Dahlgren died in his sleep, at 52 years of age. It didn't even make the morning news. But during the long months following the shooting, it was

Dahlgren who kept the vigil with Brady's wife, Sarah, through the long series of brain operations.

It was Dahlgren and his wife, Suzie, who took Brady's young son Scott into their home through the early days of the ordeal. It was Dahlgren who arranged the happy hours with Brady's friends by his hospital bedside. As Brady recovered and returned to a semi-normal life, it was always Dahlgren who scouted out the advance arrangements, who helped load and unload his friend from the specially equipped van in which Brady did most of his traveling. It was Dahlgren who helped Sarah field the questions about Brady's health and spent endless hours keeping friends posted on his condition. It was Dahlgren who helped organize a foundation to assure financial support for the family.

For more than four and a half years after Brady was shot, Bob Dahlgren devoted virtually all his time to the man he loved. And he did so with little recognition and no hint of seeing anything in return. Never, ever did Dahlgren complain. Never did he hesitate when needed. Never did he stop looking for the needs or the response of love.

As Dr. Arthur Kobrine, the surgeon who lived through Brady's long ordeal with him, once said, "Everyone should have a friend like Bob Dahlgren."

I read a story in *Our Daily Bread* about a king who had a silver bell placed in a high tower of his palace early in his reign. He announced that he would ring the bell whenever he was happy so that his subjects would know of his joy.

The people listened for the sound of that silver bell, but it remained silent. Days turned into weeks, and weeks into months, and months into years. But no sound of the bell rang out to indicate that the king was happy.

The king grew old and gray, and eventually he lay on his deathbed in the palace. As some of his weeping subjects gathered around him, he discovered that he had really been loved by his people all through the years. At last the king was happy. Just before he died, he reached up and pulled the rope that rang the silver bell.

Think of it—a lifetime of unhappiness because he didn't know that he was warmly loved and accepted by his loyal subjects.

Many people live out their days without the joy of knowing or experiencing the love of others. This book is filled with ideas, illustrations, and inspiration for showing others what love looks like. Give them a try.

Love is like a beautiful flower which I may not touch, but whose fragrance makes the garden a place of delight just the same.

HELEN KELLER

THE FLIP SIDE OF LOVE

Our lives are shaped by those who love us—by those who refuse to love us.
JOHN POWELL, S.J.

I love to watch reruns of old television series such as the *Andy Griffith Show.* Unlike many of today's programs, the oldies seem to contain a practical, life-enhancing message. In one of the first segments, Sheriff Andy Taylor decides to invite his spinster Aunt Bee to come and live with Opie and him. Following the death of his wife, Andy thought Aunt Bee would add the missing feminine touch to their home.

Opie doesn't share Andy's sentiments and is skeptical of having Aunt Bee coming to "replace" his mother. Andy devises a plan to help Opie accept the idea. He invites Aunt Bee to go fishing and frog catching with them so that Opie will have a chance to get to know her and, it's hoped, bond with her. Unfortunately, Aunt Bee fails miserably at fishing, can't catch a frog, and later reveals her lack of football skills.

Late that night, after Opie is in bed, Aunt Bee talks Andy into taking her to the bus station. Opie hears her crying beneath his bedroom window and realizes she is probably leaving. He jumps out of bed, runs downstairs and out to the truck, exclaiming, "We can't let her go, Pa; she needs us. She can't even catch frogs, take fish off the hook, or throw a football. We've got to take care of her or she'll never make it."

Love springs to life when we realize the benefit of our relationships is not what we will receive from someone else. We need other people because of our weaknesses, and they need us to complement their lives by infusing our strengths with their weaknesses. The process for creating healthy, mutually beneficial relationships unveils a realization that love is best expressed when we fill in the void in someone's life and by doing so expand the value of our own lives.

Although Sheriff Taylor acted on a pure motive of wanting a feminine touch in their home, it was Opie who delivered the punch line, "We've got to take care of her or she'll never make it." Although love may not be reciprocated by those we give it to, our lives will not remain the same when we commit to filling the vacuum in others' lives. "Love cures people," said Karl Menninger, " both the ones who give it and the ones who receive it."

Love has nothing to do with what you are expecting to get—only what you are expecting to give—which is everything. What you will receive in return varies. But it really has no connection with what you give. You give because you love and cannot help giving. If you are very lucky, you may be loved back. That is delicious but it does not necessarily happen.

KATHARINE HEPBURN

Forgiveness

He that cannot forgive others
breaks the bridge over which he must pass himself;
for every man has need to be forgiven.

THOMAS FULLER

KEEP YOUR BRIDGES IN GOOD REPAIR

An army general once said to John Wesley, "I never forgive and I never forget." John Wesley answered, "Then, sir, I hope you never sin."

I feel sorry for this general. He probably never experienced the load-lifting action of forgiveness. To forgive someone means to let go. Once you forgive, the emotional baggage from tension, unresolved conflicts, or mistreatment is lifted. Robin Casarjian, author of *Forgiveness: A Bold Choice for a Peaceful Heart,* who managed to forgive the man who raped her, said, "Once you forgive, you are no longer emotionally handcuffed to the person who hurt you." What freedom!

"You have a tremendous advantage over the person who slanders you or does you a willful injustice," declared Napoleon Hill. "You have it within your power to forgive that person."

Are you angry with someone who has offended you? Let it go. The anger only pulls you down. Forgiveness provides you the power to get on with life.

Do you carry grudges? Grudges are simply a buildup of resentment produced by an unwillingness to genuinely forgive. We can't "bury the hatchet" with the handle sticking out.

Have you ever said, "I'll forgive but I can't forget?" That is only superficial forgiveness allowing us to continue wallowing in self-pity. The quickest way to forget is to quit dwelling on the wrong done to you.

The American Red Cross was founded by a pioneering woman named Clara Barton, who was widely known for her forgiving spirit. On one occasion a friend brought up an injustice done to her years before. When Barton failed to respond to the effort to relive this event, the friend persisted, "Don't you remember how much that person hurt you?"

"No," Clara Barton cheerfully responded. "I distinctly remember forgetting that."

To proactively forgive the past, quit dwelling on the hurt. By not reliving the situation over and over, you will gain peace and victory over the incident.

If you want to maintain the bridges that sustain relationships but sense some repair work is needed, consider these suggestions.

1. *Be the First to Ask Forgiveness.* Whether you have hurt someone or been mistreated, be the first to say, "Please forgive me if I've done anything to hurt our relationship." This action will allow you to let go and get on with your life.

2. *Rebuild Your Thoughts.* The mind is a marvelous mechanism. The thoughts we hold in this massive human computer will dominate our lives. Although not an easy task, discipline yourself not to dwell on the situation or the bitterness, blame, or hurt that can saturate the walls of your mind.

3. *Pray.* I am rarely capable of genuine forgiveness without divine intervention. Relying on God to help me deal with the pain, the person, and the process of healing replaces the human tendency of revenge with release.

4. *Write a Letter.* Expressing your feelings in writing, without placing judgment or blame, can be a significant bridge from pain to peace. Simply communicating your heart signals a desire to achieve resolution. Whether or not you ever send the letter, writing it contains its own value.

5. *Focus on the Future.* Wallowing in the mire of the past destroys the bridge to the future. Tomorrow can never be lived to the fullest when we are consumed with the uncontrollable past.

Elbert Hubbard wrote, "A retentive memory may be a good thing, but the ability to forget is the true token of greatness. Successful people forget. They know the past is irrevocable. They're running a race. They can't afford to look behind. Their eye is on the finish line. Magnanimous people forget. They're too big to let little things disturb them. They forget easily. If anyone does them wrong, they consider the source and keep cool. It's only the small people who cherish revenge. Be a good forgetter. Business dictates it, and success demands it."

Forgiveness allows you to be free from the nightmares of the past and to reclaim your dreams for the future.

6. *Replace Selfishness with Unconditional Love.* Old Pete was in bad health and death seemed imminent. For years there had been a thorn of bitterness with Joe, formerly one of his best friends. Wanting to clear the air, Pete sent word for Joe to come and see him.

When Joe arrived, Pete told him that he couldn't live another day or face eternity knowing their relationship had been destroyed. Pete painfully and reluctantly apologized for the hurtful things he had said and done. He also assured Joe that he forgave him for his actions. The two old friends shook hands and everything seemed fine until Joe turned to go. As he turned to leave, Pete said, "If I get better, none of this counts."

Ninety percent of the art of living consists of getting along with people you cannot stand.
SAMUEL GOLDWYN

Saying "I forgive you" and then placing conditions on our forgiveness equates with not forgiving at all. It's tough to remove our selfish motives and refrain from resurrecting past grievances when frictions arise.

I'm reminded of the lady who sought marriage counseling. The counselor asked her what seemed to be the source of their difficulty. "Whenever we get into an argument," the lady said, "my husband becomes historical."

"Don't you mean hysterical?" the counselor responded.

"No, I mean historical! He always brings up the past."

Emotional problems and relational stress will continue as long as forgiveness hinges on the past. Total forgiveness requires unconditional love.

I hope your relationships will continue to mature and reap positive results. A forgiving spirit is a basic requirement for that to occur. Forgiveness remains the bridge we must cross to enter brighter tomorrows. Remember the words of Martin Luther King, Jr.: "Forgiveness is not an occasional act; it is a permanent attitude."

In *The Essential Calvin Hobbes,* the cartoon character Calvin says to his tiger friend, Hobbes, "I feel bad that I called Susie names and hurt her feelings. I'm sorry I did it."

"Maybe you should apologize to her," Hobbes suggests.

Calvin ponders this for a moment and replies, "I keep hoping there's a less obvious solution."

There's no easy way of saying "I'm sorry, I was wrong." Do it anyway. Rather than allowing bitterness and resentment to surface, allow the sweet smell of harmony to be the trademark of your relationships.

PLACING PEOPLE IN PROPER PERSPECTIVE.

Barbara Bush was not Wellesley College's first choice as their 1990 graduation commencement speaker. Some of the seniors were hesitant about her appropriateness as a role model for the issues facing today's modern woman.

"To honor Barbara Bush as a commencement speaker," they protested, "is to honor a woman who has gained recognition through the achievements of her husband, which contradicts what we have been taught the past four years."

The first lady handled the accusations in her normal classy style and didn't allow the protests to either offend or intimidate her. Mrs. Bush spoke from her heart and the fulfillment she had experienced from her traditional values. She offered this advice in her commencement address:

"Cherish your human connections, your relationships with friends and family. For several years, you've had impressed upon you the importance to your career of dedication and hard work.

The primary joy of life is the acceptance, approval, sense of appreciation, and companionship of our human comrades. Many men do not understand that the need for fellowship is really as deep as the need for food, and so they go throughout life accepting many substitutes for genuine, warm, simple relatedness.

JOSH LIEBMAN

"This is true, but as important as your obligations as a doctor, lawyer, or business leader will be, you are a human being first and those human connections—with spouses, with children, with friends—are the most important investments you will ever make.

"At the end of your life, you will never regret not having passed one more test, not winning one more verdict, or not closing one more deal. You will regret time not spent with a husband, a friend, a child, or a parent."

The first lady addressed the heart of living. All of our personal and professional endeavors are made sweeter, richer, and more satisfying by sharing them with others. As Antoine de Saint-Exupery wrote, "There is no joy except in human relationships."

Too often, what should matter most in our lives receives the least attention. Battles with the almighty dollar, pursuing selfish interests, attaining that next promotion, or closing a deal are empty pursuits without the human element. It's easy to overlook that our relationships are what encourage the heart and nourish the soul.

Harold Kushner, writing in *When All You've Ever Wanted Isn't Enough,* said: "A life without people, without the same people day after day, people who belong to us, people who will be there for us, people who need us and whom we need in return, may be very rich in other things, but in human terms, it is no life at all."

A life without relationships limits the value of everything you do. Regardless of the pressures you feel to succeed in our what's-in-it-for-me society, don't make the mistake of placing value on only those activities and goals that enhance your paycheck. Make time to reach out to those who add meaning to your life. And when the ties have been broken by disagreement or misunderstanding, reach out with a spirit of forgiveness.

Only you can know how much you can give to every aspect of your life. Try to decide what is the most important. And if you do, then only occasionally will you resent or regret the demands of the marriage, the career, or the child, or the staying.

BARBARA WALTERS

BE WILLING TO SAY "I'M SORRY"

The most deadly of all sins is the mutilation of a child's spirit.
ERIK H. ERIKSON

After 15 years of being a parent, I think I'm finally realizing what I cherish most about my children: our relationship.

Oh, I admit it's nice when they score points in a basketball game or gracefully perform a dance routine. I'm pleased when their report cards reveal above-average performance or when I observe the sweat and effort put into a school project. And of course it's flattering when people comment how nice they look or how respectful they are.

But what really trips my trigger and renews my parental energy—after returning from a speaking trip, or working on a free-throw shot, playing taxi driver, or setting curfew—is a loving smile, a hug, a high five, and the four cherished words: "I love you, Dad."

I'm keenly aware how my actions, words, tone of voice, or nonverbals affect the loving, caring, and mutually respectful relationship we enjoy. And, I've failed at times as a father to uphold my end of the responsibility. There have been times when I crushed my children's spirit.

When my son was in the sixth grade, another dad and I agreed to coach a traveling basketball team. Along with our two sons, we invited ten other boys to enjoy the experience with us.

It didn't take long for me to realize that the definition of a father–coach is someone who expects his son to be everything he wasn't. I upheld high and sometimes unrealistic expectations. I even found it easy to justify my demands by attempting to motivate my son to be the best he could be. However, during one game I overstepped my parental privileges.

The game was already won. The boys fought courageously to overcome a major point deficit to hold a comfortable lead with 37 seconds left in the game. Out of nowhere Matt (my son) stole the ball, dribbled the length of the court, and MISSED an uncontested layup.

I chose to release my accumulated tension from the game on my son for missing that layup. The shot meant nothing. We had won the game and advanced to the finals. Matt played with heart and gave his all . . . yet he blew that simple layup. I let him know in no uncertain terms how disappointed I was and how ridiculous it was for him to miss such a simple shot.

The joy of winning drained from his face. He stood motionless and speechless as Dad continued to drain the power from his self-esteem battery. I knew I'd blown it but continued to justify my outburst and dig myself into a deeper hole.

It was a long and quiet few hours waiting for the championship game. Matt was hurting inside, and I was full of guilt. There was little question that I needed my son's forgiveness.

Sitting in our van outside the gymnasium, I slowly turned to look into Matt's fearful and discouraged face. "Matt, I was wrong," I began. "I'm sorry for blowing up at you. You worked hard in that game, and I failed to recognize you for all the good things you did. Please forgive me."

It was then Matt touched my heart and filled my eyes with tears. "It's okay, Dad. I know you love me."

Thanks to my son, I could walk into the championship game with a clear conscience, repaired heart, and softer spirit.

We lost the championship game by one point, but I came out of that tournament a winner. My son had forgiven me.

I realized in the van with Matt that day that I had admitted and he had acknowledged that I was human. Most important, Matt knew that I knew I was wrong and was willing to admit it.

The only way to heal a damaged spirit is to swallow the parental pride and say, "I'm sorry. I was wrong. Please forgive me." Failure to bring healing when you've been unfair or hurtful can breed anger for years to come.

If you were to ask what is the hardest task in the world, you might think of some muscular feat, some acrobatic challenge, some chore to be done on the battlefield or the playing field. Actually, there is nothing which we find more arduous than saying, "I was wrong."

SUNSHINE MAGAZINE

LET GO OF THE PAST

Forgiveness is the key that unlocks the door of resentment and the handcuffs of hate. It is a power that breaks the chains of bitterness and the shackles of selfishness.

WILLIAM ARTHUR WARD

I was fairly young when the movie *The Hiding Place* was released. The impact of this dramatic story detailing one family's efforts to hide Jews in Holland from the Nazis and their later suffering in a Nazi death camp remains with me many years later. Corrie ten Boom and her family were featured in the movie, and later she returned to that death camp in Germany to deliver a message of forgiveness to a group of German people. Little did she know that this experience would test her forgiving spirit.

In her book *Tramp for the Lord,* Corrie recalls, "The place was Ravensbruck and the man who was making his way forward had been a guard—one of the most cruel guards.

"Now he was in front of me, hand thrust out: 'A fine message, Fraulein! How good it is to know that, as you say, all our sins are at the bottom of the sea!'

"And I, who had spoken so glibly of forgiveness, fumbled in my pocketbook rather than take that hand. He would not remember me, of course—how could he remember one prisoner among those thousands of women?

"But I remember him and the leather crop swinging from his belt. I was face-to-face with one of my captors and my blood seemed to freeze.

"'You mentioned Ravensbruck in your talk,' he was saying. 'I was a guard there.' No, he did not remember me.

"'But since that time,' he went on, 'I have become a Christian. I know that God has forgiven me for the cruel things I did there, but I would like to hear it from your lips as well. Fraulein'—again the hand came out—'will you forgive me?'

"And I stood there—I whose sins had again and again to be forgiven—and could not forgive. Betsie [Corrie's sister] had died in that place—could he erase her slow terrible death simply for the asking?

"It could not have been many seconds that he stood there—hand held out—but to me it seemed hours as I wrestled with the most difficult thing I had ever had to do."

Visualize that scene in your mind. Try to feel what Corrie ten Boom felt, although I doubt that any of us can come close to the inner struggle she was experiencing. How could this man expect to be forgiven for the cruel and inhumane treatment he delivered? How could he have the audacity to suggest that Corrie offer him release from his past?

Mahatma Gandhi believed that "the weak can never forgive. Forgiveness is the attribute of the strong." Corrie ten Boom was a strong person, a gallant believer in the benefits of two-way forgiveness. She forgave. I believe Corrie ten Boom not only released that prison guard from a past of regret but made a critical leap forward in her own faith, inner healing, and ability to move forward.

We all experience various ups and downs in our relationships. Some of us have been hurt by those we love the most. Others live in a daily environment of put-downs and disrespect. There are people who dread the encounter of someone who has broken their spirit and still others who shudder every time they think about people who have destroyed their trust.

Hurt people are everywhere. Relationships are in shambles. Loneliness is rampant. Undeserved unfairness, injustice, or even abandonment happens. Isolation becomes the escape for many.

There are many people out there waiting to hear the words "I forgive you," while many victims are finding a way to pay them back or seek revenge. We've become a nation obsessed with getting even. How else can you explain the headlines in our newspapers? Neighbors threatening neighbors. Lawsuits (for the most ridiculous reasons). Shootings in schools. Grudges leading to beatings. Stalkings. Parents kidnapping their own children from the other parent. The list is depressing.

Ernest Hemingway, in his short story "The Capital of the World," tells the story of a father and his teenaged son living in Spain. Through a series of events, their relationship became strained and eventually shattered. The boy opted to flee from his home, and the father began a desperate search for his lost, rebellious, yet loved son.

Running out of options, the father resorted to placing an ad in the Madrid newspaper. His son's name was Paco, a common name in Spain. The ad simply read: "Dear Paco, meet me in front of the Madrid newspaper office tomorrow at noon. All is forgiven. I love you."

Hemingway then provides us with an incredible picture and message. The next day at noon in front of the newspaper office, there were 800 "Pacos" all seeking forgiveness.

There are countless people in this world waiting to be forgiven. There are just as many who could benefit from forgiving. Show me a person who lives in peace with himself or herself and with others and I'll show you a person who freely and sincerely forgives. Forgiveness is the bridge we all must cross to leave pain, heartache, despair, anger, and hurt behind. It takes tremendous courage, humility, and a willingness to risk to cross that bridge, but on the other side peace, joy, love, and comfort await us. To fully forgive allows us to fully live.

So often people dwell on past bitterness and present themselves as a martyr for having endured. Unfortunately, the feelings of anger, mistrust, and resentment seep into their other relationships and poison what could otherwise be a healthy experience. There is only one cure and that is to forgive and let it go. Brian Tracy suggests that we "issue a blanket pardon to everyone for everything that they have ever done to hurt you in any way."

I in no way want to suggest this will be easy. In fact, Laurence Sterne said, "Only the brave know how to forgive . . . a coward never forgave; it is not in his nature." I figure if Corrie ten Boom could muster the courage to forgive the man responsible for her torment, who am I to pass eternal judgment and harbor lifelong resentment for the comparatively insignificant abuses I've experienced.

A few years ago, our high school put on the play *Joseph and the Amazing Technicolor Dreamcoat.* In addition to the enjoyment of watching my son perform on stage, I was once again reminded how this young biblical character was mistreated and hated by his brothers. Joseph was a young visionary who often had dreams about the future. What really irked his brothers is that in one dream he saw himself as ruling over his family. The brothers didn't take kindly to that. The brothers were also a bit jealous about their father's visible favoritism toward Joseph, which included the gift of a multicolored coat. Joseph's brothers figured enough is enough so they grabbed him, tossed him into a pit, and sold him into slavery.

Doing an injury puts you below your enemy; revenging one makes you but even with him; forgiving it sets you above him.
BENJAMIN FRANKLIN

Joseph endured the rejection of his own blood, working for a wealthy Egyptian whose wife had a thing for Joseph and continually tried to seduce him. He was wrongly accused and imprisoned. Joseph was later released, gained favor with the king, offered power and privileges second only to the king, and was ultimately highly esteemed by others.

Here's where the story gets interesting. Years after his brothers' betrayal they came to Egypt during a time of famine looking for help from the government. Little did they know their little brother Joseph was in charge of those services. Joseph immediately recognized his brothers but it was clear to Joseph that they didn't recognize him. Joseph possessed the power to get sweet revenge, but what did he do? Joseph rose above past circumstances, refused to cast blame, and responded to his brothers in love, acceptance, and forgiveness.

Letting go of the past provides a springboard for our lives to move into the future. Corrie ten Boom did it, Joseph did it, Ronald Reagan did it, and so can you.

In *Angels Don't Die,* Patti Davis shares the impact of the attitude of her father, Ronald Reagan, had on her after the 1982 assassination attempt.

"The following day my father said he knew his physical healing was directly dependent on his ability to forgive John Hinckley. By showing me that forgiveness is the key to everything, including physical health and healing, he gave me an example of Christ-like thinking."

Acceptance

If you are losing a tug-of-war with a tiger, give him the rope before he gets to your arm. You can always buy a new rope.

MAX GUNTHER

MY WIFE IS ALWAYS RIGHT

A message on my desk indicated that my wife had called while I was in an early-morning meeting. The note stated I was to call her as soon as possible.

Marty rarely calls me at work. She's made it a habit not to interrupt my day unless there is an emergency or an issue needing immediate attention. As a result, I was a bit anxious returning her call.

"Hello, sweetheart," I said. "What's up?"

"A bad thing happened," she sheepishly replied. "You know, it's really noisy when you back your car into the garage door."

"Pardon me," I responded while quickly attempting to visualize the scene.

"It's your fault," she continued. "When you left for work this morning, you left your garage door open. I entered the garage through your open door, and the garage was so well lit from the outside light I didn't realize my door was closed."

"It's my fault?" I chuckled.

"Yes, and now the door is shattered."

Marty and I have laughed about that situation many times, and I, of course, continue to remind her that I was not the one in the driver's seat. However, I learned a few important things about potential conflicts, arguments, and marital disputes from this unfortunate incident. First, scratched bumpers and dented trunks can be fixed. They are not worth getting upset about, especially at the expense of harmony.

Second (and this is most important), I learned that my wife is always right. Now don't get me wrong here. I don't mean to say that I am always wrong, but I carefully choose the issues worth debating. I often recall the advice of Jonathan Kozol: "Pick battles big enough to matter, small enough to win." In other words, decide what issues are worth dying for and which ones you refuse to argue about.

The newspaper and magazine editor H. L. Mencken often drew letters of criticism and outrage for his critiques of American life. He answered every critical letter and handled each one the same way. Mencken simply wrote back, "You may be right." What a marvelous way to diffuse a potentially volatile situation.

For most of us the hardest thing to give is . . . "giving in." Wanting to win fuels the fire and often causes arguments to digress into a lose–lose situation. Maybe that's why Ben Franklin believed, "If you argue and rankle and contradict, you may achieve a victory sometimes; but it will be an empty victory because you will never get your opponent's good will."

Franklin's comment reminds me of the couple traveling down the highway in complete silence. An earlier argument left both unwilling to concede their positions. Passing a barnyard of mules, the husband sarcastically asked, "Are they relatives of yours?"

"Yes," his wife replied. "I married into the family." Ouch!

Sydney J. Harris submitted, "The most important thing in an argument, next to being right, is to leave an escape hatch for your opponent, so that he can gracefully swing over to your side without too much apparent loss of face." That's why I've adopted the attitude that my wife (and other potential opponents) are always right, even though in the long run my conviction might be proven right.

What's the benefit of taking such an approach? Isn't this a chicken way out? I suppose you could look at it like that.

Even though I know there are two sides to every issue—my side and the side that no informed, intelligent, clear-thinking, self-respecting person could possibly hold (only kidding)—any quarrel will not last long if we refuse to continue stirring it up by trying to prove others wrong.

The story is told about two guys, Jake and Sam, who were stuck together on a deserted island. They got along so well that not even a cross word passed between them. In fact, their passive behavior made life so harmonious that it became monotonous at times.

One day Jake came up with an idea to break the boredom. "Let's have a heated argument," he suggested, "like people back home often have." Sam responded, "But we don't have anything to argue about." Jake thought for a moment and then suggested, "Let's find a bottle that's washed up on shore and place it on the beach between us. I'll say, 'This bottle is mine!' And you'll say, 'No, it isn't, the bottle is mine!' That will surely get a good argument started."

So, finding a bottle and placing it on the sandy beach between them, Jake exclaimed, "This bottle is mine!" Sam, pausing a moment, responded meekly, "I think, my friend, that the bottle is mine." "Oh, really," Jake said agreeably, "if the bottle is yours, take it."

It is not humanly possible to carry on an argument between two people when one refuses to argue. So, here's a thought: Let people be right until the heat has subsided and you can discuss the situation rationally.

Two months after our car crashed into the garage door and we had purchased a minivan with a luggage carrier (don't get ahead of me), I got another call at work. "Glenn, you closed your door but my garage door didn't go up high enough so the luggage carrier hooked the garage door and shattered it. The luggage carrier isn't in such good shape either."

You can draw your own conclusions on how this conversation ended.

Over the years I've come to know that there are times when it is best to simply accept my wife's point of view, especially at times when emotions can run high (like after the second garage-door mishap). I know that I can always broach the subject later and rationally discuss the situation. What almost invariably happens is that later, when we're both feeling more rational, we're not interested in who was at fault. What seemed like a major issue earlier suddenly doesn't seem so important, and what may have ended in a disagreement is now a calm discussion without mention of who's wrong or right.

A married couple were involved in another round of repeated disagreements. The same issue had been bitterly discussed over and over. The wife finally blurted in desperation, "You're impossible!"

Not missing a beat, the husband retorted, "No, I'm next to impossible."

CREATING A RELATIONSHIP MASTERPIECE

A relationship is a living thing. It needs and benefits from the same attention to detail that an artist lavishes on his art.
DAVID VISCOTT

Let's carry David Viscott's artistic thought a bit further. Consider the following qualities present in relationship masterpieces.

Start with a blank canvas of acceptance. Permit people to be who they are—not what they could be, should be, or would be if only they listened to you. Accept the imperfections and celebrate each person's individuality. Acceptance affirms people's value, raises self-esteem, and makes them feel comfortable in your presence.

Artists are masters at the use of primary colors, which create the heart of the finished product. Mutual trust is one such primary ingredient. We live in an imperfect, messy world made up of imperfect people. Unfortunately, many of us are prone to trusting people when they prove themselves trustworthy. I tend to believe that if we trust people, they will prove themselves trustworthy. I know trust can be betrayed but it is essential for relationships to develop. Step out. Make an effort to believe in the intrinsic goodness of people. Sure you might be disappointed at times, but you will also be blessed.

Share yourself with others. There is a bit of risk here but withholding who we are places a permanent blemish on the relationship canvas. Open and honest communication stands out in any close friendship. Use discretion but share your hurts, fears, and failures. Throw the good stuff in there too. Just refrain from unnecessary critical, cheap shots or hurting comments that are better left unsaid.

I'm sure every artist has his or her favorite color that tends to find its way into each creation. My favorite relationship ingredient is improving the ability to see the good in people. Tell your friends, family, and coworkers what you like about them. Tell people how thankful you are for them. Recognize their talents, applaud their successes (one of the most difficult actions of human nature), and make others feel important about themselves. Expressing appreciation on every possible occasion is one of the surest ways to boost mutual respect and encourage positive behaviors.

A masterpiece stands out in the viewer's mind when the proper highlights are added. When it comes to relationships, you can move to the next level by:

Giving more than you get

Allowing people to have their space

Maintaining confidentiality

Giving supportive and positive advice

Being loyal

Listening

Treating others with dignity

Saying "please" and "thank you"

Being agreeable

Accepting others' opinions

Forgiving wrongs committed

Quality relationships are most fulfilling. Relationships don't fail to become a beautiful experience because they are wrong but because most people don't want to invest what it takes to create an original. To evaluate how effective you are in creating a relationship masterpiece, just ask yourself, "If I were my friend, would I enjoy the artistic strokes (qualities) I experience being with me?"

LOYALTY

I'm very loyal in a
relationship.
When I go out with my mom,
I don't look at other moms.
I don't go, "Oooh, I wonder
what her macaroni and cheese
tastes like."

GARY SHANDLING

SHE COULD HAVE MARRIED MOZART

At the heart of personality is the need to feel a sense of being lovable without having to qualify for that acceptance.
MAURICE WAGNER

Joe was a little shy in his teenage years, and even in college he found it difficult to ask girls out on dates. One night a buddy, Jake, who lived down the hall from Joe in the same dormitory presented an offer he couldn't refuse. "I've got great news," Jake began. "I've lined you up with a great date for Saturday night. Everything is set."

"Who is it?" Joe asked. It turned out to be a friend of Jake's girlfriend, who was going to be visiting for the weekend. Joe had never met her. "No, thank you," Joe said. "Blind dates aren't for me."

"No need to worry about this one," Jake reassured Joe. "Julie's a terrific girl. And trust me—she's a beauty."

"No," Joe repeated.

"This is a no-fail situation. I'll even give you an out."

Now he had Joe's attention. "How?" Joe asked.

"When we get to the dorm room to pick them up, wait for her to come to the door and check her out. If you like what you see, then great, we're off for a super evening. But if she's ugly, fake an asthma attack. Just go 'Aaahhhgggggg!' and grab your throat as if you're having trouble breathing. When she asks, 'What's wrong?' you say, 'It's my asthma.' And so we'll call off the date. Just like that. No questions asked. No problem."

Joe was hesitant, to say the least, but agreed to give it a try. What did he have to lose?

When they got to the door, Joe knocked and she came to the door. He took one look at her and couldn't believe his eyes. She was beautiful. How lucky could he get? He hardly knew what to say.

She took one look at Joe and went, "Aaahhhhgggggg!"

It seems they weren't the only ones with a foolproof plan. Most of us, at one time or another, have been rejected by someone because we weren't smart enough, tall enough, athletic enough, good looking enough, or whatever. It's tough to feel rejected.

When we unconditionally accept someone, we give them the freedom to be on the outside who they are on the inside. True acceptance will allow us to see the real value of a human being.

The young woman who was engaged to Mozart, before he rose to fame, could have benefited from a spirit of unconditional acceptance. Impressed by more handsome men, she became disenchanted with him because he was so short. She ultimately gave him up for someone tall and attractive. When the world began to recognize Mozart for his outstanding musical accomplishments, she regretted her decision. "I knew nothing of the greatness of his genius," she said. "I only saw him as a little man."

Acceptance communicates love and value and gives people the self-confidence to become all they can be. It also allows them to be who they are until they become what they are capable of becoming.

When Marty and I were dating, I knew we were going to have a wonderful future together. If she would only make a few changes that future could be even brighter. I'm not naive, so I certainly didn't bring up the issue during our dating and refrained from talking about it on our honeymoon.

Within a few weeks of settling into marital bliss, I decided it was time to bring my suggested changes to the surface. I was bold and stupid enough to verbalize my thoughts at supper one night. I gracefully, lovingly, and rather forthrightly stated my case. Wow, did I learn a ton about marriage that night. I also gleaned a valuable lesson about acceptance.

When we attempt to force people to be who we want them to be, the defensive, stubborn, and hurt qualities emerge. However, when you allow people to refuse to change, you give them the freedom to change.

Refrain from accepting people based on what they could be, should be, or would be if only they listened to you. Until we accept unconditionally, we will continually be looking through the filters of musts, shoulds, ought-to's, have-to's, and prejudices.

Eugene Kennedy suggests that, "When someone prizes us just as we are, he or she confirms our existence." After being married over 20 years I'm realizing the value of loving someone regardless of who they are or aren't, what they have or don't have, or for what they do or don't do.

I love the *Peanuts* cartoon where Lucy says to Snoopy:

"There are times when you really bug me, but I must admit there are also times when I feel like giving you a big hug."

Snoopy replies:

"That's the way I am . . . huggable and buggable."

Seems to me that might be an appropriate description for most people in this world . . . huggable and buggable. Love them anyway.

Here's a flash of insight from *Newsweek* magazine. According to reported research, the spotted owl's greatest threat may not be logging, but one of its relatives.

For the past several years, the barred owl has been rapidly migrating westward. Barred owls, which used to live exclusively east of the Mississippi, enjoy the same food as spotted owls but are more aggressive and adaptable.

Sometimes, even our relatives (whom we can't choose) cause us the most difficulty. It's then we need a good friend who won't fight us but will participate with us in the things we both enjoy.

I HAVE A PROPOSITION FOR YOU

In my senior year of college I took a class entitled "Marriage and the Family." I wasn't even dating anyone at the time but I figured why not prepare for future possibilities. The professor was an entertaining person and offered ample personal examples from his marriage to liven up the lecture. At the time, I questioned the validity of his stories but now that I've been married 25 years I understand how even the most outlandish ones could be true.

Whoever thinks marriage is a 50–50 proposition doesn't know the half of it.
FRANKLIN P. JONES

He began his lecture one day with this bold statement: "The secret of a successful marriage is this: Marriage is not a 50–50 proposition. A 50–50 proposition is one where nobody is giving anything.

"Rather, the secret of a happy marriage is 60–40. The husband gives in 60 percent of the time and expects his wife to give in 40 percent of the time. The wife gives in 60 percent of the time and expects her husband to give in 40 percent of the time. In a 60–40 proposition, you don't clash in the middle and say, 'Now, it's your turn.' Instead, you intersect and overlap, because you're each giving 60 percent."

I walked out of that classroom, along with 75 other students, and never thought about the 60–40 proposition again, except of course when it appeared on the final exam. I'm not sure there is any magic formula for successful marriage, but I remain intrigued by the concept of always giving a little more than the other person. There is some truth in the saying that "marriage is an empty box. It remains empty unless you put more in than you take out."

There are no doubt a multitude of attitudes, abilities, and opinions about what makes a marriage work. In fact, I've pulled together a few tidbits of marriage wisdom. I thought you might enjoy a wide spectrum of perspectives on the joys of tying the knot. Some of the ideas reflect marvelous wisdom while others are intended to offer a bit of levity.

The difference between a successful marriage and a mediocre one consists of leaving about three things a day unsaid.

MICHELLE GELMAN

The failure of modern marriage is, in large measure, accounted for by our failure to employ humor in the process of marital adjustment.

JULIUS GORDON

Only two things are necessary to keep one's wife happy. First is to let her think she's having her own way. Second is to let her have it.

LADY BIRD JOHNSON

Marriage is not just spiritual communion and passionate embraces; marriage is also three-meals-a-day and remembering to carry out the trash.

DR. JOYCE BROTHERS

A happy wife sometimes has the best husband, but more often makes the best of the husband she has.

MARK BELTAIRE

It takes a loose rein to keep a marriage tight.

JOHN STEVENSON

Marriage is popular because it combines the maximum of temptation with the maximum of opportunity.

GEORGE BERNARD SHAW

Marriage resembles a pair of shears, so joined that they cannot be separated; often moving in opposite directions, yet always punishing anyone who comes between them.

SYDNEY SMITH

Marriage should be a duet—when one sings, the other claps.

JOE MURRAY

I've never thought about divorce. I've thought about murder, but never divorce.

DR. JOYCE BROTHERS

Marriage is a lot like taking vitamins. It's a process that involves the supplementation of each other's minimum daily requirements.

PAUL NEWMAN

Sometimes I wonder if men and women really suit each other. Perhaps they should live next door and just visit now and then.

KATHARINE HEPBURN

One of the reasons I made the most important decision of my life—to marry George Bush—is because he made me laugh. It's true, sometimes we laugh through our tears, but that shared laughter has been one of our strongest bonds.

BARBARA BUSH

There is no more lovely, friendly and charming relationship, communion or company than a good marriage.

MARTIN LUTHER

People are always asking couples whose marriage has endured at least a quarter of a century for their secret for success. Actually, it is no secret at all. I am a forgiving woman. Long ago, I forgave my husband for not being Paul Newman.

ERMA BOMBECK

Lots of people have asked me what Gracie and I did to make our marriage work. It's simple—we didn't do anything. I think the trouble with a lot of people is that they work too hard at staying married. They make a business out of it. When you work too hard at a business, you get tired; and when you get tired, you get grouchy; and when you get grouchy, you start fighting; and when you start fighting, you're out of business.

GEORGE BURNS

An archaeologist is the best husband any woman can have. The older she gets, the more he is interested in her!

AGATHA CHRISTIE

Some people ask the secret of our long marriage. We take time to go to a restaurant two times a week. A little candlelight, dinner, soft music and dancing. She goes Tuesdays. I go Fridays.

HENNY YOUNGMAN

We have a picture of the perfect partner, but we marry an imperfect person. Then we have two options. Tear up the picture and accept the person, or tear up the person and accept the picture.

J. GRANT HOWARD, JR.

It destroys one's nerves to be amiable every day to the same human being.

BENJAMIN DISRAELI

Familiarity breeds contempt—and children.

MARK TWAIN

The most important thing a father can do for his children is to love their mother.

REV. THEODORE HESBURGH

More marriages might survive if the partners realized that sometimes the better comes after the worse.

DOUG LARSON

After winning an argument with his wife, the wisest thing a man can do is apologize.

ANN LANDERS

We sleep in separate rooms; we have dinner apart; we take separate vacations—we're doing everything we can to keep our marriage together.

RODNEY DANGERFIELD

And finally from the 1763 King of Poland, Stanislaus Leszcynski:

In marrying, you vow to love one another. Would it not be better for your happiness if you vowed to please one another.

UNDERSTANDING

If I can listen to what he tells me, if I can understand how it seems to him, if I can sense the emotional flavor which it has for him, then I will be releasing potent forces of change within him.

CARL ROGERS

WHOSE LANGUAGE ARE YOU SPEAKING?

Dr. Robert Schuller, in his book *Reach Out for New Life,* tells a story about an incident that occurred many years ago in England. The character at the heart of the story was the most famous elephant in the circus world named Bozo.

Bozo was a beautiful beast—a great big tender hunk of gentleness. Children would come to the circus and extend their open palms, filled with peanuts, through the gate. The elephant would extend his trunk to pick the peanuts out of their hands and then curl his trunk and feed himself. He seemed to smile as he swallowed the gifts. Everyone loved Bozo.

Then one day something happened that changed his personality from positive to negative almost overnight. He almost stampeded, threatening to crush the man who was cleaning his cage. Then he began to charge the children. The circus owner knew the elephant was now dangerous and that the problem had to be faced. He came to the conclusion that he would have to exterminate this big old beast. This decision hurt him, first, because he loved the elephant; second, because it was the only elephant he had. Bozo had been imported from India, and it would cost him thousands of dollars to replace him.

Then he had an idea. This desperate and crude man decided that he would sell tickets to view the execution of Bozo. At least he would be able to raise the money to replace him.

The story spread, tickets were sold out, and the place was jammed. There, on the appointed date, was Bozo in his cage, as three men with high-powered rifles rose to take aim at the great beast's head.

Just before the signal to shoot, a little stubby man with a brown derby hat stepped out of the crowd, walked over to the owner, and said, "Sir, this is not necessary. This is not a bad elephant." The owner said, "But it is. We must kill him before he kills someone." The little man with the derby hat said, "Sir, give me two minutes alone in his cage, and I'll prove that you are wrong. He is not a bad elephant."

The circus owner thought for a moment, wrung his hands and said, "All right. But first you must sign a note absolving me of all responsibility if you get killed."

The little man scribbled on a piece of paper the words "I absolve you of all guilt," signed his name, folded the paper, and handed it to the circus owner. The owner opened the door to the cage. The little man threw his brown derby hat on the ground and stepped into the cage. As soon as he was inside, the door was locked behind him. The elephant raised his trunk and bellowed and trumpeted loudly.

But before the elephant could charge, the little man began talking to him, looking him straight in the eye. The people close by could hear the little man talking, but they couldn't understand what he was saying. It seemed as if he were speaking in an unknown tongue. The elephant still trembled, but hearing these strange words from this little man he began to whine, cry, and wave his head back and forth. The stranger walked up to Bozo and began to stroke his trunk. The now gentle beast tenderly wrapped his trunk around the feet of the little man, lifted him up, carried him around his cage, and cautiously put him back down at the door. Everyone applauded.

As he walked out of the cage, the little man said to the keeper, "You see? He is a good elephant. His only problem is that he is an Indian elephant, and he only understands

One learns people through the heart, not the eyes or the intellect.
MARK TWAIN

Hindustani. He was homesick for someone who could understand him. I suggest, sir, that you find someone in London who speaks Hindustani and have him come in and just talk to the elephant. You'll have no problems."

As the man picked up his derby and walked away, the circus owner looked at the note and read the signature of the man who had signed it. The man with the little brown derby was Rudyard Kipling.

Dr. Schuller said, "People also become frustrated, angry, and defeated when no one understands them." Could it be the person you are having a difficult time with just needs someone to understand their situation, to speak their language.

John Luther believed, "Natural talent, intelligence, a wonderful education—none of these guarantees success. Something else is needed: The sensitivity to understand what other people want and the willingness to give it to them."

PEOPLE DO THINGS FOR THEIR REASONS

I think Mark Twain must have had a bad day when this quote was recorded. Although there is good reason for the common theory that a dog is man's best friend, even a dog can become disillusioned if the relationship is a one-way affair. Let me explain what I mean.

If you pick up a starving dog and make him prosperous, he will not bite you. This is the principal difference between a man and a dog.
MARK TWAIN

Ralph Waldo Emerson was a great historian, poet, and philosopher, but he didn't know much about getting a stubborn calf through a barn door. One day, Emerson and his son were involved in such a challenge. Can't you just see the son with his arms around the calf's neck and Emerson in the rear braced to push with all his might? As they pushed and pulled repeatedly, the calf braced itself by locking her knees and digging her feet into the ground determined not to comply.

Drenched with sweat, full of bovine smell, and frustrated to the point of exasperation, Emerson stood helpless over the calf. An Irish servant girl who had observed the comical pursuit approached Emerson and asked if she could be of assistance. She walked around to the front of the calf and thrust her finger in the calf's mouth, and the calf peacefully followed the girl into the barn.

Bob Conklin, in *How to Get People to Do Things,* said, "People are like that calf. You can poke them, prod them, push them, and they don't move. But give them a good reason—one of their reasons—a way in which they will benefit, and they will follow gently along. People will do things for *their* reasons. Not *your* reasons. And those reasons are emotional, aroused by the way they feel."

People do things for their reasons, not your reasons. This is one of the greatest and yet simplest principles of human relations. People do things because they want to, not because you want them to. As Lord Chesterfield advised, "If you will please people, you must please them in their own way."

Once we understand that relationships evolve around people's needs and expectations, it's more natural to create an environment where mutual warmth and love exist.

What do people need? What are the reasons people do things? What are the qualities we display that cause people to want to pursue and maintain a relationship with us?

Don't make this too philosophical or difficult. In many ways, Anthony Robbins's comment that "When people are like each other, they tend to like each other" provides us a hint to the answers we're looking for. The same things that cause you to be drawn to someone oftentimes open the door for others to feel comfortable with you.

Needing someone is like needing a parachute. If he isn't there the first time you need him, chances are you won't be needing him again.
DILBERT'S *WORDS OF WISDOM*

Make a list of the qualities, actions, and attitudes of people you enjoy being around. Endeavor to sharpen and refine those attributes in your life. There is no shortcut to nourishing relationships, but understanding what people need is the shortest way between where you are and where you want your relationships to be.

To counter Mark Twain's cynical comparison between people and dogs, perhaps we should consider that oftentimes we give more thought and energy to what our dog wants and likes than we do to our spouse, children, and friends.

COULD YOU JUST LISTEN?

Most of the successful people I've known are ones who do more listening than talking. If you choose your company carefully, it's worth listening to what they have to say. You don't have to blow out the other fellow's light to let your own shine.
BERNARD M. BARUCH

It happens about once a week. My wife and I have a nice conversation about a favorite topic, or she will fill me in on the details of an upcoming event. A little while later I ask a question that she already addressed in our conversation. Marty then looks at me and says, "You never listen to me." Ouch. I do listen, I think, but for some reason a portion of the information just seems to leak from my memory. Although I think I know how to listen, my actions often prove otherwise.

John Maxwell tells a delightful story about an 89-year-old woman with hearing problems. She visited her doctor, and after examining her, he said, "We now have a procedure that can correct your hearing problem. When would you like to schedule the operation?"

"There won't be any operation because I don't want my hearing corrected," said the woman. "I'm 89 years old, and I've heard enough!"

There are times, at any age, where we might think "I've heard enough and don't care to listen anymore." Karl

Menninger believes, "The friends who listen to us are the ones we move toward, and we want to sit in their radius." If a relationship is important to us, it's wise to remember that the difference between someone feeling comfortable with us or avoiding us often depends on our willingness to listen.

The following poem reveals the feelings of someone who badly wants to be heard.

When I ask you to listen to me
and you start giving me advice,
you have not done what I asked.

When I ask you to listen to me
and you tell me I shouldn't feel that way,
you are trampling on my feelings.

When I ask you to listen to me
and you try to solve my problems for me,
you have failed me.

Listen! All I asked was that you listen,
not talk to or do—
just hear me.

Advice is cheap;
the price of a newspaper will get you both
Dear Abby and Billy Graham.

I can do for myself; I'm not helpless—
maybe discouraged and faltering
but not helpless.

So please listen and just hear me.

And if you want to talk,
wait a minute for your turn—
and I'll listen to you.

AUTHOR UNKNOWN

This unknown writer was expressing a frustration experienced by a multitude of people everyday. From the corporate office to the school playground, from the hospital room to the bedroom, and from the subway to the carpool you will find people who genuinely feel no one is interested in their life. Paul Tournier addressed this universal need. "It is impossible," he said, "to overemphasize the immense need humans have to be really listened to, to be taken seriously, to be understood. No one can develop freely in this world and find their life full, without feeling understood by at least one person. . . Listen to all the conversations of our world, between nations as well as between couples. They are for the most part, dialogues of the deaf."

Studies indicate that we spend 30 percent of a normal business day speaking, 16 percent reading, 9 percent writing, and 45 percent, the majority of our time, listening. Yet, very few people have studied or mastered listening techniques even though close to half of our day is spent in such activity.

An unofficial listening study offers this perspective: "We hear half of what is being said, listen to half of what we hear, understand half of it, believe half of that and remember only half of that." If you translate those assumptions into an eight-hour workday, it means that:

You spend about four hours in listening activities;

You hear about two hours' worth;

You actually listen to an hour's worth;

You understand 30 minutes of that hour;

You believe only 15 minutes' worth; and

You remember just under 8 minutes' worth.

Listening is primarily an activity of the mind, not the ear. When the mind is not actively involved in the process, it should be called hearing, not listening.
MORTIMER ADLER

Statistics indicate the importance and difficulty of listening as well as the widespread listening incompetence most people display. The world needs people who aspire to be listeners. Ironically, they not only enhance others' lives but their own as well. It is a win–win affair. And, the benefits of acquiring this important skill are enjoyed throughout our lives.

PLEASE UNDERSTAND ME

A few weeks into my daughter's freshman year of high school, she became frustrated. Although a normally happy, vivacious young lady, the pressures of school, conflict with friends, teacher expectations, and the time demands of extracurricular activities were a bit overwhelming. As Katy shared her traumatic experiences with me, I tried to console her by telling her everything would be okay and that she need not be distressed by these minor difficulties.

To love you as I love myself is to seek to hear you as I want to be heard and understand you as I long to be understood.
DAVID AUGSBURGER

"That's easy for you to say, Dad," she responded. "You have all your problems over with."

From a teenager's perspective adults are all through with their problems and life is one continuous party. Even more important, I think Katy was trying to tell me she could use a little empathy. She wanted me to understand what it feels like to be a freshman. I gave my daughter sound, practical, and realistic advice when all she really wanted was an understanding heart. This could have been a magical father–daughter moment. Instead, it was just another conversation.

Poet Shel Silverstein wrote a heart-touching verse entitled "The Little Boy and the Old Man." In it he portrays a young boy talking to an elderly gentleman.

The boy says, "Sometimes I drop my spoon." "I do that too," replies the old man.

"I often cry," continues the boy. The old man nods, "So do I."

"But worst of all," says the boy, "it seems grownups don't pay attention to me." Just then the boy feels "the warmth of a wrinkled hand." "I know what you mean," says the little old man.

Most people think they see the world as it is. Unfortunately, we really see the world as we are.

I saw my daughter's difficulties through the eyes of a grownup, not a high school freshman. The little boy saw the world through his eyes, which he learned were much like the eyes of the old man. In a world obsessed with "me" there is a tremendous opportunity to touch people's lives by focusing on what's important to them.

John Powell wrote, "Sometimes I think that the main obstacle to empathy is our persistent belief that everybody is exactly like us." I know that doesn't sound too profound but the significance of that statement is an entryway to people's hearts. To realize others don't necessarily think like me, act like me, feel as I feel, or respond to every situation as I would respond prepares me to gain valuable insights that might otherwise have been overlooked.

The ability to truly understand other people is a valuable asset. It involves opening your mind and heart with an insatiable desire to help people feel understood. A sincere attempt is made in every conversation to think how others think and feel what others are feeling. If every conversation began and evolved around this intent, I wonder how many conflicts could be avoided.

Sometimes you can defuse a difficult situation simply by being willing to understand the other person. Often all that people need is to know that someone else cares about how they feel and is attempting to understand their position.
BRIAN TRACY

Are your daily conversations motivated by a desire to get people to understand you, or are you committed in every conversation to put yourself in the other person's world? See her world, experiences, hopes, fears, and dreams as she sees them. The benefits are immeasurable because for every person we sincerely seek to understand, there will be someone who wants to do the same for us.

Make it possible for someone today to say, "When I'm with you, I feel understood."

ENCOURAGEMENT

You can't make the other fellow feel important in your presence if you secretly feel that he is a nobody.

LES GIBLIN

HOW GOOD CAN PEOPLE BE?

I read about a young football coach at Louisiana State University who knew how to capitalize on high expectations. Paul Dietzel's 1958 football team was picked to finish near the bottom of the Southeastern Conference. Of his top 30 players, none of them weighed over 210 pounds and their abilities were far from impressive. Dietzel eliminated the customary first-, second-, and third-team concept and, instead, broke his squad into three units and named them the White Team, Go Team, and Chinese Bandits. The Chinese Bandit squad would customarily be known as benchwarmers. However, Dietzel convinced them they were defensive specialists and challenged them to live up to their name.

Throughout the season, the Chinese Bandits were called upon to display their tough and aggressive defensive tactics that frequently spelled the difference between winning and losing. That year, L.S.U. defied all odds by going undefeated

The only person who behaves sensibly is my tailor. He takes new measurements every time he sees me. All the rest go on with their old measurements.
GEORGE BERNARD SHAW

and being named the number-one team in both the Associated Press and United Press polls.

The 1958 L.S.U. football team wasn't technically very good, but Dietzel never let them know it. He wasn't like the football coach who told his team, "We are undefeated and untied. Nobody has scored on us. Enjoy it because we now have to play our first game." Dietzel instilled a belief in his players that they could succeed and that belief produced the power to live up to his expectations.

How good would you be if you didn't know how good you were? How good would your team be if they didn't know how good they were? How good could those around you become if you raised your expectations of them?

Create high expectations for people and let them know you believe in them more than they believe in themselves. People succeed if someone they respect thinks they can.

OFFER A SHOULDER TO LEAN ON

The 1992 Olympics in Barcelona, Spain provided spectators with a multitude of great moments. Reruns of one track-and-field event live in my memory.

Few things in the world are more powerful than a positive push. A smile. A word of optimism and hope. A 'you can do it' when things are tough.
RICHARD M. DEVOS

Britain's Derek Redmond had a lifelong dream of winning a gold medal in the 400-meter race. His chances of achieving that dream increased when the gun sounded to begin the semifinals in Barcelona. Redmond was running a great race, and the finish line was clearly in sight as he rounded the turn in the backstretch. Then disaster struck. A sharp pain shot up the back of his leg. He fell face-first onto the track with a torn right hamstring.

Sports Illustrated provided this account of the events that followed:

As the medical attendants were approaching, Redmond fought to his feet. "It was animal instinct," he would say later. He set out hopping, in a crazed attempt to finish the race.

When he reached the stretch, a large man in a T-shirt came out of the stands, hurled aside a security guard and ran to Redmond, embracing him. It was Jim Redmond, Derek's father. "You don't have to do this," he told his weeping son. "Yes, I do," said Derek. "Well, then," said Jim, "we're going to finish this together."

And they did. Fighting off security men, the son's head sometimes buried in his father's shoulder, they stayed in Derek's lane all the way to the end, as the crowd gaped, then rose and howled and wept.

What a dramatic sight! Derek Redmond failed to capture a gold medal, but he left Barcelona with an incredible memory of a father who left the crowd to share his son's pain. Together, they limped to the finish.

There isn't a person alive who hasn't experienced the disappointment of unmet expectations. Things don't always go as planned in the pursuit of our dreams. Unexpected obstacles, unplanned events, or the onset of circumstances beyond our control can burst our bubble. It is amazing how quickly our hopes can vanish followed by the pangs of failure, embarrassment, and discouragement.

A word of encouragement during a failure is worth more than a whole load of praise after a success. Orison Swett

Marden said, "There is no medicine like hope, no incentive so great, and no tonics so powerful as expectation of something better tomorrow." You can be the distributor of hope that propels someone past the present burden and into future possibilities.

The worst part of success is trying to find someone who is happy for you.
BETTE MIDLER

Understanding how quickly momentum can be brought to an abrupt halt increases our sensitivity to how others feel when disappointments sabotage their dreams. It's then that people need someone who cares enough about them to come out of the crowd and on to the track. Let them know you are there for them. Offer a shoulder to lean on to help carry them through the pain. They may not attain the level of success they aspired to, but they'll never forget the person who lifted them up when they felt let down.

HELP PEOPLE BELIEVE IN THEMSELVES

Those who believe in our ability do more than stimulate us. They create for us an atmosphere in which it becomes easier to succeed.
JOHN H. SPALDING

Yogi Berra was asked whether he thought Don Mattingly's performance in 1984 exceeded his expectations. Yogi responded, "No, but he did a lot better than I thought he would."

Yogi Berra is a master of confusing messages. Yet, our message concerning what we expect of others is normally received loud and clear.

Tommy was having a difficult time in school. He was full of questions and tended to fall behind on class assignments. Tommy's teacher became frustrated with his performance and told his mother Tommy had little chance for academic achievement or life success.

Tommy's mother believed differently. She removed Tommy from the low-expectation environment and taught him herself. She nurtured his inquisitive nature and encouraged him to use failure as a signal to find another way.

Tommy did all right for himself. He became an inventor, recording more than a thousand patents. We can thank him for the lights in our homes and countless other electronic inventions. Thomas Edison thrived on the hope created by his mother's positive expectations.

Our mission in relationships should not be to impress others but to get people to believe in themselves. When we express faith, the door is opened for people to think higher of themselves. That confidence in themselves creates an environment in which people feel safe to risk going beyond where they are. Every time you express positive expectations in someone, you're providing life-sustaining nutrition.

Rent the movie *Stand and Deliver.* Watch how calculus teacher Jaime Escalante works with high-school students in East Los Angeles. Keep in mind this is a part of the country where high expectations are virtually nonexistent, and the idea of quality education is a hopeless pursuit.

Escalante endeavors to work with his students to exceed all previous societal and self-imposed limitations. He's committed to offering them an opportunity to believe in themselves and create hope for the future. The kids respond.

Keep away from people who try to belittle your ambitions. Small people always do that, but the really great make you feel that you, too, can become great.
MARK TWAIN

I smiled when the Educational Testing Service voiced their skepticism about the results earned by Escalante's students. The ETS investigates the class for cheating. Ultimately, the service provider had to admit that Escalante's students had honorably achieved their scores. This great teacher challenged their minds and instilled a belief in themselves.

In order for us to get people to feel important, we must see their value. What we look for in people, we can see. What we see, we communicate. What we communicate stimulates people to respond accordingly. What do you see in and expect of others?

REDUCING THE STING OF CRITICISM

Face it, some people have photographic memories. They remember all the negatives about the people around them. You have probably encountered such a person somewhere in your life and have scrambled to avoid his or her crushing blows. Although it's true that criticism won't kill you, its sting can have a lasting impact.

A successful man is one who can lay a firm foundation with the bricks that others throw at him.
DAVID BRINKLEY

It's difficult to live out the wisdom of Charles Spurgeon, who said, "Insults are like bad coins; we cannot help their being offered to us, but we need not take them." Easier said than done. Criticism seems to immediately cut its way to our emotional center and leave undesirable scars.

We do have a choice in how we deal with the insults we encounter, and we must realize that no matter how small or large the issue might be, it can be made worse or better by our reaction. When I am criticized, I have a tendency to overreact and become defensive. I dwell on the comment, running it through my mind over and over attempting to justify my actions or prove mentally how wrong the other person was. Incredible energy is wasted in this spiraling, unproductive activity.

The next time you find yourself in the path of critical bricks hurled your way, learn to desensitize the impact of accusations rather than stand defenseless.

1. Consider the Source. Normally it is the person who can't dance who complains about the unevenness of the floor. Likewise, people who criticize other people are frequently hurting themselves. Out of their frustration with life, they find someone else to blame. Don't take their criticism personally.

While driving along a desolate highway on a hot summer afternoon, I noticed vultures soaring high overhead, swooping down, then rising up again. Their motives were undoubtedly selfish as I watched a small group of them tear apart and devour the remains of a small animal on the side of the road. That's their lifestyle—continually on the lookout for some creature they can take advantage of. Much like the vultures, critical people tend to look for unsuspecting, vulnerable victims they can tear apart and devour. Consider the source before deciding to take seriously what has been said.

2. Smile. Have you ever tried arguing with someone who is smiling at you? If you want to disarm an attacker, take a deep breath, smile, and say, "Thank you." O. A. Bautista says, "One of the surest marks of good character is a person's ability to accept criticism without malice to the one who gives it." I might add that it takes an equally strong character to neutralize criticism before it damages yourself or the relationship. I'm not suggesting that this is easy, but you will find it helpful in keeping critical comments in perspective.

Along with your smile, keep your sense of humor intact. Humor is a marvelous tool for neutralizing the sting of criticism and disapproval. It will divert your attention and diminish the effects.

I love the story of the lady who took her overworked husband to the family physician for a checkup. The physician took the wife aside and whispered: "I don't like the way your husband looks."

"I don't either," she replied, "but he's always been a good provider."

3. Expect It but Don't Accept It. Epictetus provided us an ideal approach to dealing with all those people with photographic memories. "If someone criticizes you, agree at once. Mention that if only the other person knew you well, there would be more to criticize than that." Arguing with one who criticizes is a no-win battle, so Epictetus believed the best way to silence your critics and not waste energy is to agree with them and get on with life.

Someone once said that there are only two critical people in the whole world . . . they just move around a lot and seem to pull down the masses with their criticism. "Nothing takes a greater toll on us than to be around a pessimist—a person always finding fault and criticizing others," said Cavett Robert. "We've all seen the type. He has mental B.O. He's a one-man grievance committee, always in session." Actually, criticism has become a national pastime and sooner or later you will be the target of someone's mental B.O. Not everything everybody says about you is true. It is important that you immediately and objectively weigh the value of the other's comment. Learn what you can from the criticism. If the person is right, make changes. If he or she is wrong, don't spend another moment focused on the accusations.

4. Don't Take It Personally. Abraham Lincoln would never have achieved all he did had he not learned to duck or build on the massive criticism he encountered. His insight is worth your consideration: "If I were to try to read, much less to answer, all the attacks made on me, this shop might as well be closed for any other business," Lincoln said. "I do the very best I know how—the very best I can; and I mean to keep doing so until the end. If the end brings me out all right, then what is said against me won't matter. If the end brings me out wrong, then ten angels swearing I was right would make no difference."

Colonel George Washington Goethals faced enormous opposition as the supervisor responsible for building the Panama Canal. Not only did his builders face incredible challenges with geography, climate, and disease, but people back home predicted they would never complete the "impossible task." The great engineer kept the faith and was resolute in steadily moving forward to complete the project without responding to his opposition.

At one point a frustrated coworker asked, "Aren't you going to answer your critics?" "In time," Goethals replied. "How?" the man asked. The colonel smiled and said, "With the canal!" That answer materialized on August 15, 1914, when the canal opened to traffic for the first time.

Pressing forward. Not getting caught up in verbal warfare. Producing results. Those are often the best ways to counteract ridicule. Expect it. Don't accept it. Press on.

5. *Ponder the Benefits.* When the legendary Knute Rockne was head football coach at Notre Dame, a column appeared in the school paper with no indication as to who wrote it, other than the signature "Old Bearskin." The columnist picked apart

each player, pointing out his individual weaknesses and lambasting his shortcomings and inept performance.

Word spread quickly across campus, and players complained to Rockne that they were being unfairly criticized. Rockne would empathize with their position and encourage them to get out on the field and prove their critic wrong.

The writer of that column was never identified—that is, until after Rockne died. And guess what? "Old Bearskin" was actually the players' best friend and their coach. Yes, Rockne penned the article. He was aware of what happened to football legends whose success on the field went to their heads. As "Old Bearskin," his criticisms were an attempt to help them avoid the pitfalls of pride and strive continually to achieve new levels of performance.

As unfair as criticism might be, it can also be a helpful guardian against the snares of success. Corrie ten Boom believes, "Our critics are the unpaid guardians of our souls." That may be a bit difficult to swallow, but with an open mind the perceptions of others can actually assist us in keeping our talents fine-tuned. The master retailer Marshall Field maintained a healthy attitude about criticism. He said, "Those who enter to buy, support me. Those who come to flatter, please me. Those who complain, teach me how I may please others so that more will come. Only those hurt me who are displeased but do not complain. They refuse me permission to correct my errors and thus improve my service."

I had the unfortunate experience of going to the doctor to determine the source of severe stomach pain. As I lay on the examination table he began to poke, prod, and push in various areas, all the while asking, "Does this hurt? How about this?" It was an unpleasant experience.

When I flinched with pain each time he pressed a certain area, it was evident that he was either pressing too hard, without the right sensitivity, or it was a problem area. In my case, additional tests were required resulting in the diagnosis of an infection and the need for treatment.

So it is with criticism. When you cry out with discomfort, that might be an indication there is need for additional attention. Maybe someone is just pushing a hot button and is not so sensitive as he or she should be. You can't control the critical people in your life. But what you do with criticism is your decision. And you can control the way in which you dish out criticism. Do you do it with kindness and use it to encourage others, or do you wield it as a weapon of destruction? The next time you have criticism of another that you feel you should give, be sure that the ultimate message is one of encouragement.

I can please only one person per day. Today is not your day. Tomorrow isn't looking good either.

DILBERT'S *WORDS OF WISDOM*

Communication

The reason you don't understand me is because
I'm talkin' to you in English and
you're listenin' in dingbat.

ARCHIE BUNKER

FOR MEN ONLY

Dr. Paul Faulkner believes there is a distinct difference in the listening ability between men and women. In his book *Making Things Right,* Dr. Faulkner suggests that women are wired for 440 volts! They have little emotional wires sticking out from them in all directions. They are wired for sound and two-way communication. They talk and receive. They hook into another person's emotions and needs.

On the other hand, men are wired for 12 volts. That's all. We have two little wires sticking out, and they're both bent. Our speakers are usually hooked up, but our receivers are dead. So we have to work a lot harder to listen than the women do. We're just wired differently. We men are like two tin cans and a waxed string. But the women are hooked up like Ma Bell.

Archie and Edith Bunker's communication difficulties probably had little to do with one speaking English and other communicating in "dingbat." Dr. Faulkner might suggest that Archie Bunker give some serious attention to his bent wires and dead receiver.

Now that I think about it, I'm going to put additional effort into my own 12-volt wiring system to improve my reception. What about you?

Before a marriage, a man will lie awake all night thinking about something you said; after marriage, he'll fall asleep before you finish saying it.

HELEN ROWLAND

MASTER A RARE SECRET TO SUCCESS

You ain't learnin' nothin' when you're talkin'.
LYNDON B. JOHNSON

Henry Ford suggested, "If there is any one secret to success it lies in the ability to get the other person's point of view and see things from his angle as well as your own." Effective listening plays a major role in our ability to understand situations from another person's perspective, thereby ensuring a mutual understanding. Henry Ford considered this ability so important that he promoted it as a secret to success. Consider these four major principles for successful listening. These practical and proven techniques will increase your impact on people dramatically.

1. *Develop a Willingness to Listen.* Your heart, not your ears, determines your listening efficiency. It has been said that "when the heart is willing it will find a thousand ways, but when the heart is weak it will find a thousand excuses."

A man approached his farmer neighbor one day asking to borrow his rope. "Can't do it," the farmer replied, "I'm using it to tie up my milk."

"You can't tie up your milk with a rope," the borrower responded.

"I know," the farmer replied, "but when you don't want to do something, one excuse is as good as another."

How true! Listening is a desire, an attitude that wants to hear what others are saying. Dick Cavett explained why this attitude is so important. He said, "It's a rare person who wants to hear what he doesn't want to hear." Developing an attitude or wanting to hear is an inside job. You can read all the books, take an array of classes, or indulge yourself with other learning sources but the prerequisite to becoming an effective leader is developing a willingness to listen.

2. Be Open-Minded. "Real communication," wrote Carl Rogers, "takes place when we listen with understanding; that is, see the speaker's idea from his or her viewpoint, sense how they feel about it, and realize why they're talking about it." People can be distracted from achieving this level of communication when they jump to conclusions, find fault with the message, react to emotionally charged words, or allow their prejudices to interfere with what is being said.

I rarely travel in my car without the entertainment of a motivational or educational cassette message playing. Rarely do I argue, interrupt, or yell at my cassette player. Instead, I carefully listen to the speaker's entire message, take a few written notes, and then reflect on what has been said. In other words, even though I might not agree with everything I hear, it is not an option to listen selectively, pay attention only to what I agree with, or block out topics that fail to be appealing. It's critical to hear the whole message without making assumptions that block our ability to understand the other person's perspective.

The word "communication" comes from the Latin root which means "to have in common." When you listen, be open-minded enough to look for common ground. This open-minded approach to listening will increase your comprehension and ability to understand the ideas and feelings being shared.

I fear that far too often our listening minds are like the seasoned consultant. An aspiring management consultant was learning the ropes from an experienced senior partner. As the novice shadowed his model, he noticed how several times a day people would dump their problems on the other man. The experienced consultant would maintain eye contact, nod, and smile warmly. Then it was on to another department where the same scenario would be repeated. Day in and day out the seasoned consultant seemed to patiently listen to everyone's moans and groans.

Finally, the young man could restrain himself no longer. "I don't see how you can do it. How do you put up with listening to everyone's problems all of the time and still remain so positive?"

The older consultant flashed a wry smile and said, "Who listens?"

3. Be Attentive. President Abraham Lincoln said, "When I'm getting ready to reason with a man, I spend one third of my time thinking about myself and what I am going to say—and two thirds thinking about him and what he is going to say." Lincoln, the master communicator, knew how important it was to be attentive to those he was communicating with.

Attentive listening is difficult partly because the normal person can listen at 400–600 words per minute, while the average speaking rate is 200–300 words per minute. That leaves a substantial amount of time for the mind to wander.

Maybe this explains why the normal listener retains only 50 percent of what he or she hears; after 48 hours, retains only 25 percent; and after one week, 10 percent.

In addition, we listen at about a 25 percent efficiency rate. That means that we ignore, misunderstand, or distort a majority of what we hear.

So, how can we increase our attention quotient? Become a sponge. Soak in everything the other person is saying. Soak it up. Everything. Shut out all distractions. Remember, your mind is working at 400–600 words a minute. Therefore, to give someone your undivided attention and soak up the entire message:

Maintain comfortable eye contact. Don't stare.

Don't jump to conclusions and guess what the person is going to say next.

Refrain from interrupting. Let the person finish.

Be patient.

Listen for the spoken and unspoken message.

Don't tune people out. Keep an open mind.

Be silent. Juggle the letters in listen and "silent" emerges.

Take a few notes.

Wait to prepare your reply until the person has finished.

Nod, smile, agree with what is being said, lean slightly forward. Actively participate in the conversation.

Ask questions to clarify.

Don't allow how people say something to distract you from what they say.

Paraphrase what's been said. Make sure you have an accurate picture of the message.

These strategies take tremendous discipline and self-control. You can do it. Commit yourself and avoid the temptation to be distracted. You will pay people the utmost compliment by giving them your undivided attention.

4. Make People Glad That They Talk to You. So often I assume people talk to me because they are looking for advice. More often than not, advice is the last thing they seek. People want a sympathetic ear, one that will sincerely attempt to experience what they are feeling and accept them for it. "After 36 years," said Ann Landers, "I realize that many people who write to me don't want advice. They just need someone who will listen."

A particularly heart-warming story concerning the value of listening involves a young woman asked out on two dates. The first night she went to dinner with William E. Gladstone, the distinguished British diplomat. Upon arriving home, she was asked her opinion of the evening. "Oh," she responded, "William Gladstone is the cleverest man in England."

When her evening with the equally distinguished Benjamin Disraeli was over, the same question was posed to her. She replied thoughtfully, "Benjamin Disraeli made me feel like the cleverest woman in England."

What was the difference? It has been said that listening to someone is the highest form of compliment you can pay. That person will feel valued by your attention to them and what they have to say. Disraeli was known for his listening skills and it only followed that an evening spent with him would make anyone feel important.

George and Nikki Kochler mirror the importance of affirming people through listening: "When you and I listen to another person we are conveying the thought that 'I'm interested in you as a person, and I think that what you feel is important. I respect your thoughts, even if I don't agree with them. I know that they are valid for you. I feel sure that you have a contribution to make. I'm not trying to change you or evaluate you. I just want to understand you. I think you're worth listening to, and I want you to know that I'm the kind of person that you can talk to.'"

Is that the attitude that permeates your conversations? A credible way to evaluate that question is to answer this one: How important do people feel after spending time with me?

One often reads about the art of conversation—how it's dying or what's needed to make it flourish, or how rare good ones are. But wouldn't you agree that the infinitely more valuable rara avis *is a good listener?*

MALCOLM FORBES

UNTANGLE YOUR HORNS

For some of the large indignities of life, the best remedy is direct action. For the small indignities, the best remedy is a Charlie Chaplin movie. The hard part is knowing the difference.
CAROL TAVRIS

I am told that displayed in an old monastery near Babenhausen, Germany are two pairs of deer antlers permanently interlocked. Apparently they were found in that position many years ago. Legend has it the animals had been fighting fiercely, and their horns became so entangled they were unable to free themselves. As a result, both deer perished from hunger.

Imagine those entangled horns. They represent the frozen condition conflict can create. When we are determined to have our own way, win every argument, or demand our rights, we risk becoming entangled to the degree that we starve a relationship. Unresolved conflict threatens to dissolve relationships.

Heightened negative emotions can also spread to those outside the initial conflict. That's what happened in the spring of 1894 when the Baltimore Orioles arrived in Boston to play a regular season, a routine baseball game. The game became anything but routine when a clash occurred between two players.

The Orioles' John McGraw got into a fight with the Boston third baseman. Within minutes both benches emptied to join the brawl. People in the grandstands decided to get involved and the conflict between fans erupted. Someone set fire to the stands, and eventually the entire ballpark burned to the ground. To make matters worse, the fire spread to 107 other Boston buildings. This unnecessary conflict turned into a community disaster.

Conflicts are inevitable, but such devastating effects can be avoided. We bring different backgrounds, experiences, opinions, and emotions into our relationships. Whenever two people interact on an ongoing basis there is bound to be some discord. Having conflict need not be perceived as abnormal. The real issue is whether or not we get it resolved.

Past experiences certainly affect our present approaches to conflict. When I was growing up my two brothers and I would periodically get into a wing-ding of an argument. My mother would immediately intercede, separate us, and tell us each to go to our rooms until we could learn to get along. But think about that a minute. It is impossible to learn how to get along with people when you are separated from them. At any rate, when I encounter conflict today, my first reaction is to go to my room (or someplace else where I can be alone).

Unfortunately, when I come out of my room the conflict is still waiting for me.

There's no magic solution for resolving conflict. There are, however, a number of actions we can take to diffuse tense situations and move toward resolving the issues.

1. Strive for Mutual Benefit. The ridiculousness of selfish, unsettled disputes was exhibited by a man in Cresco, Iowa a few years ago. He made a half-car garage out of a one-car garage by hiring a contractor to saw the structure in half. The sawing was the climax to a property-line dispute between Halsted and the owner of a small adjoining lot. When it was learned that Halsted's garage straddled the line between the two properties, negotiations over his use of the garage broke down, and he had the half not on his property cut down.

There is no use pursuing resolution to any conflict unless you are willing to seek an agreement that is mutually beneficial. It's imperative for people to focus on *what's* right for people, not *who's* right. I learned a long time ago that supposed winners in a conflict don't learn anything and losers never forget who stepped on them to get their way.

2. Seek Understanding. I am working on an invention that will revolutionize the world of negotiations. Once perfected, I predict this invention will eliminate conflict. What is it? An

Ego Enema. Countless relationship struggles would be solved if we could eliminate egos from the formula.

"If you don't agree with me," Sam Markewich said, "it means you haven't been listening." His comment would indicate that there are basically two sides to any argument—our side and the side that no intelligent, informed, breathing, sane, or self-respecting person could possibly hold. See what I mean about needing an Ego Enema?

Most people think they see the world as it is, but they don't. They see the world as they are. We perceive situations based on who we are, not on other people's perspectives. Try to see the world the way they see it. Be sensitive to others' emotions. Emotions are neither right nor wrong. Accept people and their opinions. Attempt to understand their perspective concerning the issues. Realize their priorities may not be yours, and the reasons behind their convictions could shed valuable light on the entire situation. Maintain calmness and patience as you listen to others talk. Accept your personal differences and move on.

3. Focus on the Problem. Get the facts. Don't rely on assumptions. Any time a conflict occurs, it is wise to make sure both parties are reading the same page. Refrain from attacking people and stay clear of arguing. Avoid fighting, battling, or trying to overcome another's opinions or behavior. Insults, accusations, and blaming are dead-end strategies.

Aristotle had a good point. "How many a dispute could have been deflated into a single paragraph," he said, "if the disputants had dared to define their terms." Resolution isn't possible by dealing with symptoms. Define your terms by first defining the problem. Please make sure you agree on what the REAL problem is.

4. Find a Point of Agreement. You've heard it said that sometimes people just need to learn to agree to disagree. That might be true, but I much prefer a different approach before resigning myself to that conclusion. Cullen Hightower said: "There's too much said for the sake of argument and too little said for the sake of agreement." I like being around agreeable people with whom I can freely and openly discuss issues, concerns, or topics that we don't necessarily agree on. Being agreeable involves the ability to smile, nod, and express respect for another person's position.

Whenever you are intent on being disagreeable, other people will feel challenged and their intelligence will be questioned. Telling someone they are flat-out wrong will immediately raise the defenses, heighten their stubbornness, and cause them to be more adamant about their position.

How about agreeing to find out what we can agree on and committing our efforts to building on the things we can agree on and moving beyond the disagreements?

There is an old saying that goes, "Agree with thine adversary quickly." Help others be right about as many things as possible and you'll be amazed at how quickly the resistance will subside on other things.

5. *Generate Solutions.* Don't get stuck dwelling on the problem—just agree on it and then move on to the creatively stimulating process of generating solutions. "You cannot shake hands," said Golda Meir, "with a clenched fist." Neither can you generate solutions to a disagreement with a one-track mind or private agenda. What are ALL of the possible solutions that will produce a mutual benefit?

6. *Determine a Win–Win Plan of Action.* The motivation behind every conflict discussion should be to reach a point where we can genuinely agree on a solution that benefits each of us. Give way on the minor points of disagreement that have become a thorn in the flesh. Look for major points of agreement that will be mutually beneficial. Find ways to nurture the other person's self-esteem. Be likable, respectful, and considerate rather than being intimidating and demanding—you'll get much further. Try to love that person

There comes a time in the affairs of (people) when you must take the bull by the tail and face the situation.
W. C. FIELDS

on the other end as you accept differences and capitalize on agreements.

Too often people approach arguments like the man who said to his coworker: "OK, I'll meet you halfway. I will admit I'm right if you'll admit you're wrong."

In an issue of *Pulpit Helps* a humorous tale appeared about a hunter who had his gun aimed at a large bear and was ready to pull the trigger. Just then the bear spoke in a soft, soothing voice, saying, "Isn't it better to talk than to shoot? Why don't we negotiate the matter? What is it you want?" The hunter lowered his rifle and answered, "I would like a fur coat." "That's good," said the bear. "I think that's something we can talk about. All I want is a full stomach; maybe we can reach a compromise." So they sat down to talk it over. A little while later the bear walked away alone. The negotiations had been successful—the bear had a full stomach, and the hunter had a fur coat!

This far-fetched fable embodies healthy advice for arriving at win–win solutions (although had I been the hunter I believe I would have spent a bit more time in the generating-solutions stage). A great way to keep our horns unlocked is to start and end any discussion with these questions: "What is it the other person wants? How can both of our needs be met?"

WORK THROUGH IT

A husband and wife who were having problems in their marriage asked their pastor for counsel. After a rather lengthy session with them, he realized that he wasn't making any progress in resolving their conflicts. Noticing a cat and a dog lying side by side in front of the fireplace, he said, "Look at how peaceful they are. They certainly don't see eye to eye on everything." The husband commented, "Yes, but just tie them together and see what happens!"

Marriage is a mutual admiration society in which one person is always right, and the other is always the husband.

MARY MARTIN

"A marriage without conflicts," says Andre Maurois, "is almost as inconceivable as a nation without crises."

Maurois's comment reminded me of a judge in a divorce case who asked the husband, "Can you tell the court what passed between you and your wife during your heated argument that prompted the two of you to seek this separation?"

"I sure can, your honor," the man nervously responded, "there was a toaster, two knives, and a set of crystal."

Although amusing, this incident reminds us that conflict is normal; marital wars are dangerous.

Face it: The unique union of a man and woman is bound to create some issues of incompatibility. The transition from a casual to a formal relationship makes George Levinger's advice especially important. He said, "What counts in making a happy marriage is not so much how compatible you are, but how you deal with incompatibility. Differences that existed before marriage are intensified when we live with them. We come from different backgrounds, possess our own personality, see the world from unique perspectives, and are the unfortunate owners of irritating habits. We don't think alike, respond to life alike, or act alike. It can be frustrating. Rather than allowing the relationship to get tied up in knots, learn to loosen the noose a bit."

Author Charles Swindoll, writing in *Commitment: The Key to Marriage,* discusses the reality of conflict in marriage.

"There is no such thing as a home completely without conflicts. The last couple to live 'happily ever after' was Snow White and Prince Charming. Even though you are committed to your mate, there will still be times of tension, tears, struggle, disagreement, and impatience. Commitment doesn't erase our humanity! That's bad news, but it's realistic."

Although normal, work through conflict. Don't allow your behaviors to elevate it.

Ogden Nash suggested: "To keep your marriage brimming, with love in the loving cup, when you're wrong, admit it. When you're right, shut up."

There will always be a battle between the sexes because men and women want different things. Men want women and women want men.
GEORGE BURNS

A DIFFERENCE OF OPINION

In every house of marriage there is room for an interpreter.
STANLEY KUNITZ

Our monthly card club tended to stray from the bridge game we came to play to conversations about local news, our children's activities, and sports events. One Saturday night a discussion ensued about marriage, men's irritating habits (from the women's perspective), and women's misconceptions about men (from the men's viewpoint). It was a lighthearted, give-and-take debate that digressed into a competition to see who could share the most cynical philosophy.

My favorite bantering came from a happily married couple with a great sense of humor.

The husband explained the key to their model marriage: "My wife and I understand each other. I don't try to run her life, and I don't try to run mine."

Not to be outdone, his wife responded, "The real secret to us staying married such a long time is simple, one of us talks, and the other doesn't listen."

AN IRISH PRAYER

May those who love us, love us;
And those who don't love us,
May God turn their hearts,
And if He doesn't turn their hearts,
May He turn their ankles,
So we'll know them by their limping.

Gratitude

Husbands, take your wife on at least one date a week. It doesn't have to be expensive (or fancy) but one that calls for dressing up a little for each other and providing undisturbed time together.

RALPH L. BYRON

KEEP THOSE FIRES BURNING

It's no secret that romantic gratification or the lack of it are factors in every marriage. The idea of having one date together a week is a great way to keep the romantic fires burning. Undisturbed private time allows you to be continually reacquainted and in tune with each other's needs.

The following story provides a humorous look at one person's experience:

Mr. Smith came home from work early and found his wife in bed with a handsome young man. Just as Mr. Smith was about to storm out, she stopped him and said, "Before you leave, I'd like you to know how this happened.

"When I was driving home from shopping this afternoon, I hit a hole in the pavement. The hole was filled with water. Great blobs of mud spattered all over this man. Without a trace of anger, he looked at me and said, 'What rotten luck. I have a very important meeting this afternoon and just look at me!'

"I told him that I was terribly sorry and offered to clean him up. He seemed grateful, and I brought him home.

"He undressed in the bathroom, and I handed him the bathrobe I bought you for Christmas a few years ago. It no longer closes in front because of your pot belly.

"While his clothes were drying, I gave him lunch—the casserole you missed last night because you decided to go out with the guys after work. He said it was the best home-cooked meal he had had in months. I told him it was the first compliment I had received about my cooking in years.

"We talked while I pressed his shirt, and it was wonderful to have a conversation with a man who seemed interested in what I had to say. Suddenly he noticed the ironing board was wobbly. I had asked you a dozen times to fix it, but you were always too busy. The man fixed the ironing board in ten minutes, and then he actually put the tools away.

"As he was about to leave, he asked with a smile, 'Is there anything else your husband has neglected lately?' And that is the end of my story!"

James C. Dobson equals this story with one of his own. Dobson claims he knows an obstetrician who is deaf and blind in the same way. It seems the obstetrician called a physician friend of Dobson's, asking for a favor.

"My wife has been having some abdominal problems and she's in particular discomfort this afternoon," he said. "I don't want to treat my own wife and wonder if you'd see her for me?"

The physician invited the doctor to bring his wife for an examination, whereupon he discovered (are you ready for this?) that she was five months pregnant! Her obstetrician husband was so busy caring for other patients that he hadn't even noticed his wife's burgeoning pregnancy. "I must admit wondering," comments Dobson, "how in the world this woman ever got his attention long enough to conceive!"

James Smith wrote, "The tragedy of western marriages is that most of us quit courting once we're married."

Have you been taking your spouse for granted? What are you waiting for? Set the time now for your next date, and plan something unexpected to show your spouse that he or she is truly valued in your life.

The difference between courtship and marriage is the difference between the pictures in the seed catalog and what comes up.
AUTHOR UNKNOWN

HERE'S HOW TO PHRASE IT WHEN YOU WANT TO PRAISE IT

In spite of our supersonic generation, high-tech wizardry, and computer gadgetry, there is no technical tool equal to praise.
JERRY D. TWENTIER

Upon accepting an award, Jack Benny once remarked, "I really don't deserve this. But I have arthritis and I don't deserve that either."

Wouldn't it be great if appreciation would become as natural to give as undesirable life experiences were to contract? Yet how many times do small, seemingly insignificant actions go unnoticed? The doers of such tasks feel they would be better off getting attention in unacceptable ways.

Consider the employee who comes in late one morning only to be greeted by his supervisor who says, "Sam, you're late!"

Sam goes about his duties thinking, "So that's what I need to do to get noticed. Day in and day out I do my job without anyone paying any attention. Come in late and, finally, they know I'm working here."

People want to believe their efforts deserve praise, and they are willing to go to great lengths to receive it. Yet, expressing appreciation is one of the most neglected acts in relationships. When you observe people doing good things, let them know you recognized it. How? Glad you asked. Here are some simple phrases that will help you praise people and encourage them to repeat their positive behavior:

"I appreciate the way you . . ."

"I'm impressed with . . ."

"You're terrific because . . ."

"Thanks for going all out when you . . ."

"One of the things I enjoy most about you is . . ."

"I admire your . . ."

"Great job with . . ."

"I really enjoy working with you because . . ."

"Our team couldn't be successful without your . . ."

"Thank you for your . . ."

"You made my day when . . ."

"You can be proud of your . . ."

"You did an outstanding job of . . ."

"It's evident you have the ability to . . ."

"I like your . . ."

"You deserve a pat on the back for . . ."

"You should be proud of yourself for . . ."

"I admire the way you take the time to . . ."

"You're really good at . . ."
"You've got my support with . . ."
"What a great idea!"
"It's evident you have a special knack of . . ."
"You were a great help when . . ."
"You have a special gift for . . ."
"I enjoy being with you because you . . ."
"You're doing a top-notch job of . . ."
"It's fun watching you . . ."
"I know you can do it!"
"I believe in you."
"Your commitment to ______________ is appreciated!"

The power of positive praise is limited only by its lack of use. How many people do you know who could benefit from a sincere "congratulations" or "great job" or possibly even "you're the best"? Silent appreciation doesn't mean much. Let others know you value them. They'll live up to your expectations.

Samuel Goldwyn said, "When someone does something good, applaud! You will make two people happy." I've provided a sampling of phrases you can use to applaud people. Use them frequently. Find additional ways to praise and increase people's good feelings about themselves. You'll be happy you did.

I believe that you should praise people whenever you can; it causes them to respond as a thirsty plant responds to water.
MARY KAY ASH

VALUE YOUR FRIENDS

Friendship is a strong habitual inclination in two persons to promote the good and happiness of one another.

EUSTACE BUDGELL

Socrates once asked an elderly man what he was most thankful for. The man replied, "That being such as I am, I have had the friends I have had."

When we count up the truly valuable treasures of life, friendships certainly ought to be toward the top of the list. As all other tangible life rewards drift away, our friendships warrant whatever energy it takes to keep them alive and healthy. Consider the wisdom offered throughout history on ways to maintain, value, and enrich our friendships.

Friendship is built upon the commitment to be a friend, not upon the desire to have a friend.

AUTHOR UNKNOWN

If the people around you don't believe in you, if they don't encourage you, then you need to find some people who do.

JOHN MAXWELL

Do not use a hatchet to remove a fly from your friend's forehead.

CHINESE PROVERB

Any one who has had a long life of experience is worth listening to, worth emulating, and worth trying to have as a friend.

GEORGE MATTHEW ADAMS

The proper office of a friend is to side with you when you are in the wrong. Nearly anybody will side with you when you are right.

MARK TWAIN

A loyal friend laughs at your jokes when they're not so good, and sympathizes with your problems when they are not so bad.

ARNOLD H. GLASOW

The glory of friendship is not in the outstretched hand, nor the kindly smile, nor the joy of companionship; it is in the spiritual inspiration that comes to one when he discovers that someone else believes in him and is willing to trust him.

RALPH WALDO EMERSON

A true friend is one who hears and understands when you share your deepest feelings. He supports you when you are struggling; he corrects you, gently and with love, when you err; and he forgives you when you fail. A true friend prods you to personal growth, stretches you to your full potential. And most amazing of all, he celebrates your successes as if they were his own.

RICHARD EXLEY

Be careful the environment you choose for it will shape you; be careful the friends you choose for you will become like them.

W. CLEMENT STONE

Friend: One who knows all about you and loves you just the same.

ELBERT HUBBARD

You can always tell a real friend. When you've made a fool of yourself, he doesn't feel you've done a permanent job.

AUTHOR UNKNOWN

PRAISE FOR
DAUGHTER OF FORTUNE

"The Chilean novelist possesses the eyes, ears, mind, heart, and pluck to manufacture generous and feisty fiction. . . . [A] rambunctious picaresque about love and obsession."

—*Miami Herald*

"Allende interweaves a densely layered tale of passion with the stuff of history and legend." —*San Diego Union-Tribune*

"Allende details her plot and settings richly."

—*Entertainment Weekly*

"A fast-pased adventure story." —*San Francisco Chronicle*

"Allende projects a woman's point of view with confidence, control, and an expansive definition of romance as a fact of life."

—*Time*

"*Daughter of Fortune* is full of energy and vivacity. It holds out a promise of happiness." —*Vogue* (Australia)

Daughter of Fortune

BOOKS BY ISABEL ALLENDE

The House of the Spirits

Of Love and Shadows

Eva Luna

The Stories of Eva Luna

The Infinite Plan

Paula

Aphrodite: A Memoir of the Senses

Daughter of Fortune

ISABEL ALLENDE

Daughter of Fortune

A NOVEL

Translated from the Spanish
by Margaret Sayers Peden

HARPER PERENNIAL

HARPER PERENNIAL

A hardcover edition of this book was published in 1999 by HarperCollins Publishers.

HarperCollins books may be purchased for educational, business, or sales promotional use. For information please write: Special Markets Department, HarperCollins Publishers Inc., 10 East 53rd Street, New York, NY 10022.

First Perennial edition published 2000.

Designed by Barbara DuPree Knowles, BDK Books

Map copyright © 1999 by Anita Karl & Jim Kemp

The Library of Congress has catalogued the hardcover edition as follows:

Allende, Isabel.
[Hija de la fortuna. English]
Daughter of Fortune : a novel / Isabel Allende
p. cm.
ISBN 0-06-019491-X
I. Title.
PQ8098.1.L54H5513 1999
863—dc21 99-26021

ISBN 0-06-093275-9 (pbk.) ISBN 978-0-06-093275-6

05 ❖/RRD 30 29 28 27 26 25 24 23 22

Contents

Contents

PART THREE

1850–1853

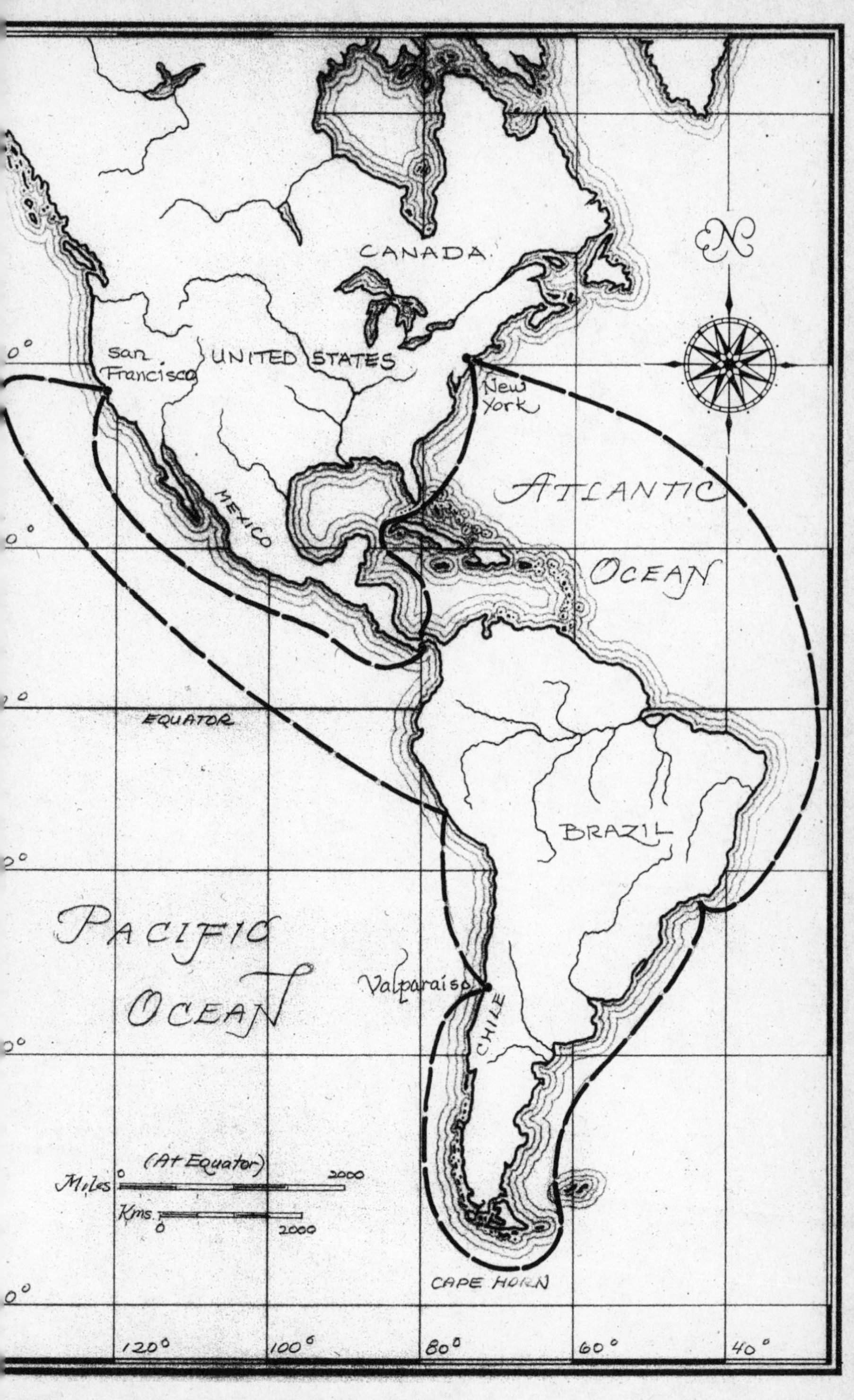

CANADA
UNITED STATES
San Francisco
New York
ATLANTIC
OCEAN
MEXICO
EQUATOR
BRAZIL
PACIFIC
OCEAN
Valparaiso
CHILE
CAPE HORN
(At Equator)
Miles 0 2000
Kms. 0 2000
120°
100°
80°
60°
40°

Daughter of Fortune

PART ONE

1843–1848

Eliza

Everyone is born with some special talent, and Eliza Sommers discovered early on that she had two: a good sense of smell and a good memory. She used the first to earn a living and the second to recall her life—if not in precise detail, at least with an astrologer's poetic vagueness. The things we forget may as well never have happened, but she had many memories, both real and illusory, and that was like living twice. She used to tell her faithful friend, the sage Tao Chi'en, that her memory was like the hold of the ship where they had come to know one another: vast and somber, bursting with boxes, barrels, and sacks in which all the events of her life were jammed. Awake it was difficult to find anything in that chaotic clutter, but asleep she could, just as Mama Fresia had taught her in the gentle nights of her childhood, when the contours of reality were as faint as a tracery of pale ink. She entered the place of her dreams along a much traveled path and returned treading very carefully in order not to shatter the tenuous visions against the harsh light of consciousness. She put as much store in that process as others put in numbers, and she so refined the art of remembering that she could see Miss Rose bent over the crate of Marseilles soap that was her first cradle.

"You cannot possibly remember that, Eliza. Newborns are like cats, they have no emotions and no memory," Miss Rose insisted the few times the subject arose.

Possible or not, that woman peering down at her, her topaz-colored dress, the loose strands from her bun stirring in the breeze were engraved in Eliza's mind, and she could never accept the other explanation of her origins.

"You have English blood, like us," Miss Rose assured Eliza when she was old enough to understand. "Only someone from the British colony would have thought to leave you in a basket on the doorstep of the British Import and Export Company, Limited. I am sure they knew how good-hearted my brother Jeremy is, and felt sure he would take you in. In those days I was longing to have a child, and you fell into my arms, sent by God to be brought up in the solid principles of the Protestant faith and the English language."

"You, English? Don't get any ideas, child. You have Indian hair, like mine," Mama Fresia rebutted behind her *patrona*'s back.

But Eliza's birth was a forbidden subject in that house, and the child grew accustomed to the mystery. It, along with other delicate matters, was never mentioned between Rose and Jeremy Sommers, but it was aired in whispers in the kitchen with Mama Fresia, who never wavered in her description of the soap crate, while Miss Rose's version was, with the years, embroidered into a fairy tale. According to her, the basket they had found at the office door was woven of the finest wicker and lined in batiste; Eliza's nightgown was worked with French knots and the sheets edged with Brussels lace, and topping everything was a mink coverlet, an extravagance never seen in Chile. Over time, other details were added: six gold coins tied up in a silk handkerchief and a note in English explaining that the baby, though illegitimate, was of good stock—although Eliza never set eyes on any of that. The mink, the coins, and the note conveniently disappeared, erasing any trace of her birth. Closer to Eliza's memories was Mama Fresia's explanation: when she opened the door one morning at the end of summer, she had found a naked baby girl in a crate.

"No mink coverlet, no gold coins. I was there and I remember very well. You were shivering and bundled up in a man's sweater. They hadn't even put a diaper on you, and you were covered with your own caca. Your nose was running and you were red as a boiled lobster, with a head full of fuzz like corn silk. That's how it was. Don't get any ideas," she repeated stoutly. "You weren't born to be a princess and if your hair had been as black as it is now, Miss Rose and her brother would have tossed the crate in the trash."

At least everyone agreed that the baby came into their lives on March 15, 1832, a year and a half after the Sommers arrived in Chile, and they adopted that date as her birthday. Everything else was always a tangle of contradictions, and Eliza decided finally that it wasn't worth the effort to keep going over it, because whatever the truth was, she could do nothing to change it. What matters is what you do in this world, not how you come into it, she used to say to Tao Chi'en during the many years of their splendid friendship; he, however, did not agree. It was impossible for him to imagine his own life apart from the long chain of his ancestors, who not only had given him his physical and mental characteristics but bequeathed him his karma. His fate, he believed, had been determined by the acts of his family before him, which was why he had to honor them with daily prayers and fear them when they appeared in their spectral robes to claim their due. Tao Chi'en could recite the names of all his ancestors, back to the most remote and venerable great-great-grandparents dead now for more than a century. His primary concern during the gold madness was to go home in time to die in his village in China and be buried beside his ancestors; if not, his soul would forever wander aimlessly in a foreign land. Eliza, naturally, was drawn to the story of the exquisite basket—no one in her right mind would want to have begun life in a common soap crate—but out of respect for the truth, she could not accept it. Her bloodhound nose remembered very well the first scents of her life, which were not clean batiste sheets but wool, male sweat, and tobacco. The next smell she remembered was the monumental stench of a goat.

Eliza grew up watching the Pacific Ocean from the balcony of her adoptive parents' home. Perched on the slopes of a hill overlooking the port of Valparaíso, the house was meant to imitate a style then in vogue in London, but the exigencies of landscape, climate, and life in Chile had forced substantial changes and the result was an unfortunate hodgepodge. At the rear of the patio, springing up like organic tumors, were various windowless rooms with dungeonlike doors where Jeremy Sommers stored his company's most precious cargo, which tended to disappear from the warehouses in the port.

"This is a land of thieves. Nowhere else in the world does the company spend so much on safeguarding the merchandise as here. Everything gets stolen, and everything we save from the rabble is soaked by winter floods, scorched in summer, or smashed during one of their ungodly earthquakes," he said every time the mules brought new bundles to be unloaded in the patio of his home.

From sitting so long at the window overlooking the sea to count the ships and the whales on the horizon, Eliza convinced herself that she was the child of a shipwreck and not of an unnatural mother capable of abandoning her and leaving her exposed to the uncertainty of a March day. She wrote in her diary that a fisherman had found her on the beach amid the debris of a beached ship, wrapped her in his sweater, and left her at the finest house in the English colony. As time passed she concluded that this story wasn't bad at all: there is a certain poetry and mystery about what the sea washes up. If the ocean should draw back, the exposed sand would be a vast, damp desert strewn with sirens and dying fish, John Sommers used to say. He was the brother of Jeremy and Rose and had sailed all the seas of the world, and he would vividly describe how the water gathered itself in sepulchral silence and roared back in a single monstrous wave, sweeping away everything before it. Horrible, he maintained, although at least that gave you time to run toward the hills, while with earthquakes the church bells clanged, announcing the catastrophe as everyone was scrambling through the rubble.

At the time the baby appeared, Jeremy Sommers was thirty years old and was beginning to forge a brilliant future with the British Import and Export Company, Ltd. In commercial and banking circles he was known as an honorable man: his word and a handshake were as good as a signed contract, an indispensable virtue in a transaction, since letters of credit took months to cross the ocean. For Jeremy Sommers, lacking a fortune, his good name was more important than life itself. With sacrifice, he had achieved a solid position in the remote port of Valparaíso, and the last thing he wanted in his well-organized life was a tiny baby to disturb his routine, but when Eliza turned up on their doorstep he had to take her in because his resolve crumbled when he saw his sister, Rose, clinging to the babe as if its mother.

Rose was only twenty, but she was already a woman with a past, and her chances for making a good marriage were minimal. In addition, she had totted up her possibilities and had decided that marriage, even in the best of cases, was a dreary business. With her brother Jeremy she enjoyed the independence she would never have with a husband. She had her life in order and she was not daunted by the stigma attached to spinsterhood; just the opposite, she was determined to be the envy of all wives despite the current theory that when women deviated from their role as mothers and wives they grew a mustache, like the suffragettes; but she had no children and that was the one affliction she could not transform into a triumph through the disciplined exercise of imagination. Sometimes she dreamed that the walls of her room were covered with blood, that blood soaked the carpet, spattered the walls up to the ceiling, and that she was sprawled in the center, naked and as wild-haired as a madwoman, giving birth to a salamander. She would awake screaming and spend the rest of the day disoriented, unable to rid herself of the nightmare. Jeremy watched her, worrying about her nerves and feeling guilty for having dragged her so far from England, although he could not avoid a certain smug satisfaction with their mutual arrangement. As the idea of matrimony had never passed through his heart, Rose's presence solved all his domestic and social problems, two important aspects of his career. His sister compensated for his introverted and solitary nature, and that was why he bore her shifts of mood and unnecessary expenditures with good humor. When Eliza appeared and Rose insisted on keeping her, Jeremy did not dare oppose her or express niggardly doubts, and he gallantly lost all his battles to keep the baby at arm's length, beginning with the first: giving her a name.

"We will call her Eliza, after our mother, and she will have our family name," Rose decided almost as soon as she had fed, bathed, then wrapped the baby in her own little blanket.

"We will do no such thing, Rose! Whatever would people say?"

"I'll take responsibility for that. People will say you are a saint for taking in a poor little orphan, Jeremy. There is no worse fate than not having a family. Where should I be without a brother like you?" she replied, conscious of her brother's horror of the least hint of sentimentality.

Gossip was inevitable, but Jeremy Sommers had to resign himself even to that, just as he accepted that the baby would have his mother's name, sleep all her early years in his sister's bedroom, and create an uproar in the house. Rose spread the implausible story of the lavish basket left anonymously at the office of the British Import and Export Company, Ltd., and no one swallowed it, but since they could not accuse her of a misstep—they saw her every Sunday of her life singing in the Anglican service and her tiny waist was a challenge to the laws of anatomy—they said that the baby was the product of Jeremy's relation with some loose woman and that was why they were bringing Eliza up as one of the family. Jeremy made no effort to defend himself against the malicious rumors. Children's irrationality in general upset him, but Eliza managed to enchant him. Although he would not admit it, he liked watching her play at his feet in the evenings when he sat down in his easy chair to read the newspaper. There were no demonstrations of affection between them; Jeremy went stiff just shaking a human hand, and the thought of more intimate contact sent him into a panic.

When the tiny newborn appeared at the Sommers' home that March fifteenth, Mama Fresia, who served them as cook and housekeeper, argued against keeping her.

"If her own mother abandoned her, it's because she is cursed, better not to touch her," she said, but she could do nothing to dent her *patrona*'s determination.

The minute Miss Rose picked up the baby, Eliza started screeching at the top of her lungs, shaking the house and grating on the nerves of everyone in it. Unable to get the infant to stop crying, Miss Rose improvised a cradle in a dresser drawer and pulled a cover over her while she rushed out to look for a wet nurse. She soon returned with a woman she had found in the market. It had never occurred to Miss Rose to examine her find close up; all she had needed to engage the woman on the spot was one glimpse of huge breasts straining to escape a billowing blouse. She turned out to be a rather dull-witted campesina who brought her baby with her, a poor creature as begrimed as she was. They had to soak that child a long time in warm water to loosen the filth on his bottom and dip the woman's head in a bucket of water with lye to get rid of her lice. The two babies, Eliza and the wet nurse's, came down with colic and a bilious diarrhea that rendered the family's physician and the German pharmacist helpless. Done in by the babies' howling, which was pain and misery added to hunger, Miss Rose wept, too. Finally, on the third day, Mama Fresia reluctantly intervened.

"Can't you see that woman has sour breasts?" she grumbled. "Buy a she-goat to feed your baby and dose her with cinnamon tea, because if you don't she'll be gone before Friday."

At that time Miss Rose barely stumbled through a little Spanish, but she understood the word "she-goat"; she sent the coachman to fetch one and dismissed the wet nurse. The minute the coachman brought the goat, Mama Fresia lay Eliza directly beneath its swollen udders—to the horror of Miss Rose, who had never seen such a revolting spectacle. The warm milk and cinnamon infusions promptly addressed the situation, however; the baby stopped crying, slept seven hours in a row, and awoke making frantic sucking sounds. After a few days she had the placid expression of a healthy infant and it was evident that she was gaining weight. Miss Rose bought a baby bottle when she realized that when the she-goat bleated in the patio, Eliza began sniffing, looking for the teat. Rose did not want to see the child grow up with the bizarre notion that the animal was her mother. That colic was one of the few upsets Eliza suffered in her infancy; the others were headed off at the first symptoms by Mama Fresia's herbs and incantations, including the fierce epidemic of African measles carried to Valparaíso by a Greek sailor. As long as that danger lasted, Mama Fresia placed a piece of raw meat on Eliza's navel every night and bound it with a strip of red flannel, nature's secret for preventing contagion.

In the following years, Miss Rose made Eliza her play toy. She spent happy hours teaching her to sing and dance, reciting verses her charge memorized with no effort, braiding her hair and dressing her up, but the minute she found another diversion or was felled by a headache, she sent the child to the kitchen with Mama Fresia. Eliza grew up between Miss Rose's sewing room and the back patios, speaking English in one part of the house and a mixture of Spanish and Mapuche, her nana's native tongue, in the other, one day dressed and shod like a duchess and the next playing with hens and dogs, barefoot and barely covered by an orphan's smock. Miss Rose presented her at her musical evenings, and took her out in the coach to go shopping, or to visit the ships at the dock, or to stop at the finest pastry shop for hot chocolate, but she could just as easily spend days at a time writing in her mysterious notebooks or reading a novel without a thought for her protégée. When she did remember her, she would run repentently to look for her, cover her with kisses, shower her with treats, and dress her up like a doll and take her out for a ride. She devoted herself to giving Eliza the broadest possible education, not overlooking the skills appropriate for a young lady. The day Eliza threw a tantrum because she didn't want to practice the piano, Miss Rose grabbed her by an arm and without waiting for the coachman dragged Eliza twelve blocks downhill to a convent. On the adobe wall, above a heavy oak door with iron studs, you could read in letters faded by the salt air: "Foundling Home."

"Be thankful that my brother and I took you under our wing. This is where little bastards and abandoned children end up. Is this what you want?"

Speechless, the girl shook her head.

"Then you would do well to learn to play the piano like a little lady. Do you understand me?"

Eliza learned to play without either talent or grace, but through dint of strict discipline could by the time she was twelve accompany Miss Rose at her musical evenings. She never lost that skill, despite long periods without playing, and several years later she was able to earn her daily bread in a traveling brothel, an application that had never crossed Miss Rose's mind when she had insisted on teaching her ward the sublime art of music.

Many years later, on a tranquil evening as she drank tea and chatted with her friend Tao Chi'en in the delicate garden they both tended, Eliza concluded that the erratic Englishwoman had been a very good mother and that she was grateful to her for the large spaces of internal freedom she had given her. Mama Fresia was the second pillar of Eliza's childhood. She clung to her full black skirts, followed her around while she did her chores, and in the meantime drove her crazy with questions. That was how Eliza learned Indian legends and myths, how to read signs of the animals and the sea, how to recognize the habits of the spirits, and the messages in dreams, and also how to cook. With her prodigious nose, she was able to identify herbs, spices, and other ingredients with her eyes closed, and just the way she memorized poems, she remembered how to combine them. Soon Mama Fresia's complicated Chilean dishes and Miss Rose's delicate pastries lost all their mysteries for her. She had a rare culinary gift; at seven, without turning a hair, she could skin a beef tongue, dress a hen, make twenty empanadas without drawing a breath, and spend hours on end shelling beans while she listened openmouthed to Mama Fresia's cruel Indian legends and her colorful versions of the lives of the saints.

Rose and her brother John had been inseparable since they were children. In the wintertime she entertained herself by knitting sweaters and socks for the captain and he took great pains every voyage to bring her suitcases filled with gifts and huge boxes of books, several of which ended up under lock and key in Rose's armoire. Jeremy, as master of the house and head of the family, had the right to open his sister's correspondence, read her private diary, and demand a copy of the keys to her furniture, but he never showed any inclination to do it. Jeremy and Rose had a no-nonsense domestic relationship but had little in common except the mutual dependence that sometimes seemed closer to a hidden form of hatred. Jeremy paid for Rose's necessities, but he financed none of her whims and never asked where she got the money for things she wanted, simply assuming that John gave it to her. In exchange, she managed the house efficiently and with style, kept impeccable accounts, and never bothered him with minutiae. She had good taste and effortless grace, she put a polish on both their lives, and her presence was a check to the belief, widely held on these shores, that a man without a family was a potential malefactor.

"It is man's nature to be savage; it is woman's destiny to preserve moral values and good conduct," Jeremy Sommers pontificated.

"Really, brother. You and I both know that my nature is more savage than yours," Rose would joke.

Jacob Todd, a charismatic redhead with the most beautiful preacher's voice ever heard on those shores, disembarked in Valparaíso in 1843 with three hundred copies of the Bible in Spanish. No one was surprised to see him: he was just one more missionary among the many wandering all over preaching the Protestant faith. In his case, however, the voyage was not the result of religious fervor but an adventurer's curiosity. With the braggadocio of a high-living man with too much beer in his belly, he had bet at a gaming table in his London club that he could sell Bibles anywhere on the planet. Todd's friends had blindfolded him, spun a globe, and his finger had landed on a colony of the king of Spain lost at the bottom of the world where none of his merry cronies had suspected there was life. He soon found that the map was out-of-date; the colony had gained its independence more than thirty years before and was now the proud Republic of Chile, a Catholic country where Protestant ideas had little foothold, but the bet had been made and he was not disposed to turn back. He was a bachelor with no emotional or professional ties and the outlandishness of such a voyage attracted him immediately. Considering the three months over and another three back, sailing across two oceans, the project turned out to be a protracted one. Cheered by his friends, who predicted a tragic end at the hands of Papists in that unknown and barbarous country, and with the financial aid of the British and Foreign Bible Society, which provided him with the books and arranged his passage, he began the long crossing on a ship bound for the port of Valparaíso. The challenge was to sell the Bibles and return within a year's time with a signed receipt for each sale. In the archives of the British Museum he read the letters of illustrious men, sailors and merchants, who had been in Chile. They described a mestizo people of a little more than a million souls and a wild geography of imposing mountains, cliff-lined coasts, fertile valleys, ancient forests, and eternal ice. Chile, he was assured by those who had visited it, had a reputation for being the most intolerant country in religious matters of any on the American continent. Despite that hindrance, virtuous missionaries were determined to broadcast their Protestant faith, and without speaking a word of Spanish or a syllable of the Indians' tongue, they traveled south to where terra firma broke up into islands like a string of beads. Several died of hunger, cold, or, it was suspected, were devoured by their own flock. They had no better luck in the cities. The Chileans' sacred sense of hospitality was stronger than their religious intolerance and out of courtesy they allowed the missionaries to preach, but gave them little consideration. When they attended the meetings of the occasional Protestant pastor, it was with the demeanor of someone witnessing a spectacle, amused by the peculiar notion that they were thought of as heretics. None of this, however, disheartened Jacob Todd, because he had come as a Bible salesman, not a missionary.

In those same library archives he discovered that since its independence in 1810 Chile had opened its doors to immigrants, who had come by the hundreds and settled in that long and narrow land bathed top to tail by the Pacific Ocean. The English quickly made fortunes as merchants and ships' outfitters; many brought their families and stayed to live. They formed a small nation within the country, with their own customs, cults, newspapers, clubs, schools, and hospitals, but they did it with such refined manners that, far from arousing suspicion, they were considered an example of civility. The British harbored their fleet in Valparaíso to control the Pacific maritime traffic, and thus from a rude hamlet with no future at the beginnings of the republic Valparaíso had in less than twenty years become an important port where the ships that sailed across the Atlantic and around Cape Horn, and later those that steamed through the Straits of Magellan, came to anchor.

Valparaíso was a surprise to the weary voyager. There before his eyes was a port with a hundred ships flying the flags of half the world. The snow-capped mountains seemed so close they gave the impression of emerging directly from the sea, and from the inky-blue water rose the impossible fragrance of sirens. Jacob Todd never knew that beneath that peaceful-looking surface lay an entire city of sunken Spanish sailing ships and skeletons of patriots with quarry stones tied to their ankles, consigned to the deep by the soldiers of the captain general. The ship dropped anchor in the bay amid the thousands of gulls shattering the air with their tremendous wings and ravenous screeches. Countless small boats bobbed on the waves, some filled with huge live conger eels and sea bass flopping desperately for oxygen. Valparaíso, Todd was told, was the commercial emporium of the Pacific; in its warehouses were stored metals, sheep and alpaca wool, grains, and hides for the world's markets. Several landing boats ferried the passengers and cargo from the sailing ship to dry land. Todd stepped onto the dock amid sailors, stevedores, passengers, visitors, burros, and carts and found himself in a city boxed into an amphitheater ringed by steep hills, a city as populous and filthy as many famous in Europe, an architectural blunder with narrow streets of adobe and wood houses that fire could turn to ashes in a few hours' time. A coach drawn by two badly abused horses carried him and his trunks and boxes to the Hotel Inglés. They passed sturdy buildings set around a plaza, several rather unfinished-looking churches, and one-story residences surrounded by large gardens and orchards. He at first estimated an area of about a hundred blocks, but soon learned that the city was deceptive; it was a labyrinth of alleys and passageways. In the distance he glimpsed a fishing community where shacks were exposed to the wind off the ocean and nets stretched like enormous spiderwebs, and beyond them, fertile fields planted with vegetables and fruit trees. He saw coaches as modern as any in London, barouches, fiacres, and calashes, but also teams of mules driven by ragged children and carts drawn by oxen in the very center of the city. On street corners, priests and nuns begged for charity for the poor, surrounded by a sea of stray dogs and befuddled chickens. He saw women carrying bundles and baskets, children clinging to their skirt tails, barefoot but with black mantles over their heads, and quantities of idle men in cone-shaped hats sitting in doorways or talking in groups.

An hour after getting off the ship, Jacob Todd was sitting in the elegant salon of the Hotel Inglés, smoking black cigarettes imported from Cairo and thumbing through a British magazine long out of date. He sighed with pleasure. It seemed he would have no problems in adapting, and if he managed his funds carefully he could live here almost as comfortably as he did in London. As he was waiting for someone to come serve him—apparently no one hurried in this country—he was approached by John Sommers, the captain of the ship he had sailed on. Sommers was a large man with dark hair and skin tanned like shoe leather who took pride in his reputation as a hard drinker, woman chaser, and inexhaustible devotee of cards and dice. They had struck up a good friendship, and playing cards had entertained them through endless nights on the high seas and stormy, icy days rounding Cape Horn at the southern tip of the world. John Sommers was accompanied by a pale man dressed in black from head to toe and sporting a newly trimmed beard; although the captain introduced the man as his brother, Jeremy, it would be difficult to find two more different human beings. John was the image of good health and strength, open, loud, and likable, while his brother had the air of a ghost trapped in eternal winter. He was one of those persons who never seems to be entirely *there,* thought Jacob Todd, the kind it is difficult to remember because they have no outstanding features. Without waiting for an invitation, the two men joined him at his table with that familiarity of compatriots in a foreign land. Finally a waitress showed up and Captain John Sommers ordered a bottle of whiskey, while his brother asked for tea in the lingo invented by Britons to communicate with servants.

"How are things Back Home?" Jeremy inquired. He spoke in a low voice, almost a murmur, barely moving his lips, his accent rather affected.

"Nothing has happened in England for the last three hundred years," the captain answered.

"Forgive my curiosity, Mr. Todd, but I saw you arrive at the hotel and could not help but notice your luggage. I thought I saw you had several boxes labeled 'Bibles.' Was I in error?" asked Jeremy Sommers.

"No, they are Bibles."

"No one advised us they were sending another pastor—"

"We were three months together in that nutshell and I never made you out to be a pastor, Mr. Todd," the captain exclaimed.

"I confess I am not," Todd replied, hiding his discomfort behind a mouthful of cigarette smoke.

"A missionary, then. I suppose you are planning to go down to Tierra del Fuego. The Indians of Patagonia are ripe to be evangelized. Forget the Araucans, old boy, the Catholics have already reeled them in," Jeremy Sommers commented.

"There are probably no more than a dozen Araucans left," his brother added. "Those people have a mania for letting themselves be massacred."

"They were the most savage Indians in America, Mr. Todd. Most of them died fighting the Spanish. They were cannibals."

"They hacked pieces of flesh off living prisoners," the captain elaborated, "they preferred their meat fresh. But then, you and I would do no less if someone slaughtered our family, burned our village, and stole our land."

"Excellent, John! Now you are defending cannibalism," his brother replied, annoyed. "In any case, Mr. Todd, I must warn you not to tread on the toes of our Catholic friends. We must not provoke the natives. These people are extremely superstitious."

"Interesting that the beliefs of others are labeled mere superstitions, Mr. Todd. Ours we call religion. Did you know that the Indians of Tierra del Fuego, the Patagonians, are very different from the Araucans?"

"Equally savage, John. Why, they go about stark naked in an insupportable climate," said Jeremy.

"Take them your religion, Mr. Todd. Let's see if at least you can teach them to wear britches." The captain laughed.

Todd had not heard the bad reports about those Indians, and the last thing he wanted to do was to preach something he himself did not believe in, but he didn't dare confess that his voyage was the consequence of a drunken bet. He replied vaguely that he was thinking of forming a missionary expedition but that he still hadn't decided how to finance it.

"Had I known, Mr. Todd, that you were coming to preach the designs of a tyrannical god among those good people, I would have thrown you overboard in the middle of the Atlantic."

The waitress interrupted them, bringing their whiskey and tea. She was a young girl who deliciously filled out the black uniform with its starched coif and apron. When she bent down with the tray, she left a perturbing scent of crushed flowers and hot flat iron on the air. It had been weeks since Jacob Todd had seen a woman, and he sat staring at her with a stab of loneliness. John Sommers waited until the girl had left.

"Careful, my friend, Chilean women are fatal," he said.

"They do not seem so to me. They are short, broad through the posterior, and they have most unpleasant voices," said Jeremy Sommers, balancing his cup of tea.

"Sailors desert their ships for them!" the captain exclaimed.

"I admit I am no authority when it comes to women. I do not have time for that sort of thing. I must look after my business and our sister, or had you forgotten?"

"Not for a minute; you always remind me. You see, Mr. Todd, I am the black sheep of the family, a waster. If it were not for our good Jeremy here—"

"That girl looks Spanish," interrupted Jacob Todd, his eyes still on the waitress, who was now at another table. "I lived two months in Madrid, and I saw many like her."

"Here everyone has a touch of Indian blood, even those of the upper classes. They do not admit it, of course. Indian blood is hidden like the plague. I cannot say I blame them. Indians have a reputation for being filthy, drunken, and lazy. The government is trying to improve the race by importing European immigrants. Did you know, Mr. Todd, that in the south they are giving away land to colonists?"

"The favorite sport is killing Indians to take away their lands."

"You exaggerate, John."

"You don't always have to shoot them, giving them alcohol will do it. But killing them is much more entertaining, of course. In any case, we English do not indulge in that pastime, Mr. Todd. We are not interested in land. Why plant potatoes if we can make a fortune without taking off our gloves?"

"There is no dearth of opportunities here for an enterprising man. There is much to be done in this country. If you want to prosper, dear fellow, head north. There you find silver, copper, nitrates, guano—"

"Guano?"

"Bird shit, Mr. Todd," laughed the captain.

"I know nothing about that, Mr. Sommers."

"Mr. Todd is not interested in making a fortune, Jeremy. His interest is the Christian faith, right?"

"The Protestant colony here is large, and prosperous; they will help you. Come to my home tomorrow. On Wednesdays my sister Rose organizes a little musicale; it will be a good opportunity for you to meet the right people. I shall send my coach to pick you up at five in the evening. You will enjoy it," said Jeremy Sommers, excusing himself.

The next day, refreshed by a night free of dreams and a long bath that removed the coating of salt clinging to his soul but not the weaving step of the ocean traveler, Jacob Todd went out to stroll through the port. He walked slowly along the main street, which was parallel to the ocean and so close to the shore that it was splashed by the waves, had a few drinks in a cafe, and ate in a tavern in the market. He had left England in the middle of an icy February winter and, after crossing an endless desert of water and stars in which he was embroiled even in the count of his lost loves, had reached the Southern Hemisphere at the beginning of June and another merciless winter. Before he left it had not occurred to him to inquire about the climate. He imagined a Chile as warm and humid as India, because that was what one expected of poor countries; instead he found himself at the mercy of an icy wind that blasted his bones and lifted whirlwinds of sand and trash. He got lost more than once in twisting streets, and made turn after turn to get back to where he had begun. He climbed infinite stairs up tortuous alleyways bordered with houses absurdly suspended in midair, trying politely not to stare through windows and invade the privacy of others. He stumbled upon romantic plazas reminiscent of Europe, with bandstands where military ensembles were playing music for lovers, and walked through modest gardens trampled by burros. Lordly trees grew at the edge of the principal streets, nourished by fetid waters that poured down from the hills in open ditches. In the commercial zone the presence of the British was so evident that one breathed an illusory air of other latitudes. Signs on several shops were in English and he passed compatriots dressed in the mode of London fashion, even to the same black undertakers' umbrellas. The moment he was out of the center, poverty met him like a slap in the face; people looked undernourished, sleepy; he saw soldiers in threadbare uniforms and beggars in the doorways of the churches. At noon all the church bells began to chime in unison and instantly the tumult quieted; people in the street stopped; men removed their hats, the few women about knelt, and everyone crossed himself. This vision lasted as the bells tolled twelve times, then the activity was renewed as if nothing had happened.

The English

The fiacre sent by Sommers arrived at the hotel a half hour late. The coachman had more than a bit of alcohol under his belt, but Jacob Todd was in no position to be choosy. The driver started off toward the south. It had rained for a couple of hours, and in some sections mud puddles masked fatal traps that could swallow a distracted horse. Children waited on either side of the street with teams of oxen, ready to rescue bogged-down coaches in exchange for a coin, but even in his cups the driver somehow avoided most of the potholes and they soon began climbing uphill. As soon as they reached Cerro Alegre, where most of the foreign colony lived, the look of the city changed abruptly; the shacks and crowded dwellings he'd seen below disappeared. The coach stopped before an estate of generous proportions but tortuous design, a mishmash of pretentious towers and useless stairways straddling various ground levels and lighted with so many torches that night was in full retreat. An Indian servant came to the door, wearing livery that was much too large for him. He took Todd's overcoat and hat and led him to a spacious drawing room furnished with good furniture and somewhat theatrical green velvet drapes; the room was crammed with knickknacks and there was not an inch of wall space on which to rest the eyes. He assumed that in Chile, as in Europe, a bare wall was considered a sign of poverty; it was only later, when he visited the somber homes of the Chileans, that he learned better. Paintings leaned outward from the wall so they might be better appreciated, and much of the room was lost in the shadow of the high ceilings. Huge logs were blazing in the fireplace and several charcoal braziers dispensed an uneven warmth that left his feet icy and his head feverish. Over a dozen people dressed in the European mode were standing around as uniformed maids passed trays. Jeremy and John Sommers came forward to meet him.

"I want you to meet my sister, Rose," said Jeremy, leading him to the back of the drawing room.

At that moment, sitting to the right of the fireplace, Jacob Todd saw the woman who would destroy his peace of heart. Rose Sommers dazzled him instantly, not so much for her beauty as for her self-assurance and good cheer. She had none of the captain's gross exuberance nor the fastidious solemnity of her brother Jeremy; she was a woman with a sparkling expression who seemed always about to break into flirtatious laughter. When she did, a network of fine lines crinkled around her eyes, and for some reason that was what most attracted Jacob Todd. He could not judge her age—he thought somewhere between twenty and thirty—but he imagined that in ten years she would look the same because she had good bones and a queenly bearing. She was wearing a peach-colored taffeta dress and no adornment but a simple pair of coral earrings. The most elementary courtesy demanded that he do no more than simulate the gesture of kissing her hand, not actually touching it with his lips, but he was so overcome that unintentionally he planted a full kiss on her hand. That greeting was so inappropriate that for an eternal moment they both stood frozen in uncertainty, he clutching her hand the way you grip a sword, and she regarding the trace of his saliva, not daring to wipe it off for fear of embarrassing the visitor, until they were interrupted by a little girl dressed like a princess. Todd shook off his anguish, and as he straightened up intercepted a slightly mocking glance exchanged between the Sommers. Trying to smooth over his gaffe, he turned to the child with exaggerated attention, determined to win her over.

"This is Eliza, our protégée," said Jeremy Sommers.

Jacob Todd committed his second blunder.

"Protégée? I'm not sure I follow you." he said.

"It means that I do not belong to this family," Eliza explained patiently, in the tone of someone speaking to an idiot.

"No?"

"If I do not behave, they will send me off to the Papist nuns."

"What are you saying, Eliza! Pay no attention to her, Mr. Todd. Children get strange ideas. Of course Eliza belongs to our family," Miss Rose burst out, rising to her feet.

Eliza had spent the day with Mama Fresia, preparing dinner. The kitchen was at the back of the patio, but Miss Rose had had it joined to the house with a walkway to avoid being embarrassed by serving dishes that were either cold or splattered with dove droppings. That room blackened by grease and soot was the indisputable kingdom of Mama Fresia. Cats, dogs, geese, and hens wandered at will across the floor of rough unwaxed bricks. There the goat that had nursed Eliza ruminated through the winter; by now it was very ancient, but no one would think of sacrificing it, for that would be like murdering one's mother. The child loved the aroma of the dough in the pans as the yeast sighed and worked the mysterious process of leavening; the smell of caramel beaten to frost cakes; the fragrance of mounds of chocolate melting in milk. On Miss Rose's musical Wednesdays the serving girls—two Indian adolescents who lived in the house and worked in exchange for food—polished silver, ironed tablecloths, and made the crystal sparkle. At noon they sent the coachman to the pastry shop to buy sweets prepared with recipes jealously guarded since the times of the colonies. Mama Fresia always used the occasion to hang a leather bag of fresh milk to the horses' harness, and on the trip back and forth it was churned into butter.

At three in the afternoon, Miss Rose called Eliza to her bedroom, where the coachman and the valet installed a lion's paw–footed bronze bathtub that the chambermaids then lined with a sheet and filled with hot water perfumed with mint leaves and rosemary. Rose and Eliza splashed around in the tub like children until the water grew cool and the maidservants returned with armfuls of clothes and helped them into stockings and boots, underdrawers to the knees, batiste camisoles, contrivances with padding over the hips to accentuate a slim waist, then three starched petticoats and finally a dress, which covered the body completely, leaving only head and hands exposed. Miss Rose also wore a corset stiffened with whalebone and so tight that she could not take a deep breath or lift her arms higher than her shoulders. Neither could she get dressed without help nor bend from the waist because the whalebone would break and poke into her body like a knitting needle. That was the one bath of the week, a ceremony comparable only to Saturday's hair washing, which could be canceled on the least pretext since it was considered dangerous for the health. During the week, Miss Rose used soap with caution; she preferred to scrub herself with a sponge dampened in milk and to freshen up with a vanilla-scented *eau de toilette* that she was informed had been in fashion in France since the time of Madame Pompadour. With eyes closed, Eliza could pick Miss Rose out in a crowd by her peculiar fragrance of vanilla pudding. Although over thirty, she had not lost that transparent, delicate skin some Englishwomen have before the glare of the world and their own arrogance turns it to parchment. She cared for her looks, using rose and lemon water to blanch her skin, witch hazel blossom honey to keep it soft, chamomile to bring out the shine in her hair, and a collection of exotic balms and lotions her brother John brought her from the Far East, where, he said, the women were more beautiful than anywhere else in the universe. She designed dresses inspired by her magazines from London and stitched them herself in the sewing room; calling on intuition and cleverness she modified her wardrobe with the same ribbons, flowers, and feathers she had worn for years and yet never looked bedraggled. She did not, like Chilean women, wear a black mantle over her head when she went out, a custom she considered an aberration; she preferred short capes and assorted bonnets, even though people stared at her in the street as if she were a courtesan.

Enchanted to see a new face at the weekly gathering, Miss Rose forgave Jacob Todd his impertinent kiss and, taking his arm, led him to a round table in a far corner of the room. She invited him to choose among various liqueurs, insisting that he try her *mistela*, a strange beverage of cinnamon, alcohol, and sugar that he could not get past his lips and later surreptitiously poured into a flowerpot. Then she introduced him to the other guests: Mr. Appelgreen, a furniture manufacturer who was accompanied by his daughter, a pallid, timid girl; Madame Colbert, headmistress of an English school for girls; Mr. Ebeling, proprietor of the best gentlemen's haberdashery in town, and his wife, who latched on to Todd, pressing him for news of the English royal family as if they were her relatives. He also met two surgeons: Page and Poett.

"These gentlemen use chloroform in their operations," Miss Rose announced with admiration.

"It is still a novelty here, but in Europe it has revolutionized the practice of medicine," one of the surgeons clarified.

"I understand that in England it is sometimes employed in obstetric practice. Did not Queen Victoria use it?" Todd added, merely to have something to say, since he knew nothing about the subject.

"Here we encounter major opposition on the part of the Catholics. The biblical curse on women is that they bring forth children with pain, Mr. Todd."

"Does that not seem unjust, gentlemen? Man's curse is to toil with the sweat of his brow, but the men in this room—without having to go any farther—earn their living from the sweat of others' brows," Miss Rose rejoined, turning red as a beet.

The surgeons smiled with discomfort, but Todd was captivated. He would have stayed by her side the entire evening, even though, as he remembered, correct behavior at a London soirée dictated a stay of no more than half an hour. He noted, however, that in this gathering people seemed disposed to stay, and he imagined that social life must be quite limited and that perhaps the only occasion of the week was this one hosted by the Sommers. He was mulling this over when Miss Rose announced the musical entertainment. The maids brought more candelabras, making the room bright as day, and arranged chairs around a piano, a guitar, and a harp. The women were seated in a semicircle, and the men remained standing behind their chairs. A chubby-cheeked gentleman took his place at the piano and from his butcher's fingers flowed a delightful melody as the furniture manufacturer's daughter interpreted an old Scots ballad in a voice so sweet that Todd quite forgot she had a face like a frightened mouse. The headmistress of the school for girls recited a heroic poem, unnecessarily long; Rose sang a couple of raffish songs in a duet with her brother John, despite Jeremy Sommers' evident disapproval; and then Rose demanded that Jacob Todd give them the pleasure of a number from his repertoire, which allowed the visitor the opportunity to show off his fine voice.

"You are a true find, Mr. Todd! We shall not let you escape. You are sentenced to come here every Wednesday!" Rose exclaimed when the applause died down, ignoring the bewitched expression on her visitor's face.

Todd felt as if his teeth were sugarcoated, and his head was whirling, whether from his admiration for Rose Sommers or the liqueurs he had imbibed and the potent Cuban cigar he had smoked in the company of Captain Sommers, he didn't know. In that house no one could refuse a dish or a refreshment without causing offense; soon he would discover that this was a national characteristic in Chile, where hospitality was manifested by forcing one's guests to drink and eat beyond the bounds of human endurance. At nine, dinner was announced, and everyone paraded into the dining room where a new series of overly generous entrées and desserts awaited. It was near midnight when the women got up and continued their conversation in the drawing room while the men drank brandy and smoked in the dining room. Finally, when Todd felt he was on the verge of passing out, the guests began to ask for their overcoats and their coaches. The Ebelings, vitally interested in Todd's purported evangelizing mission in Tierra del Fuego, offered to take him back to his hotel and he immediately accepted, terrified at the idea of being driven through nightmarish streets in the black of night by the Sommers' drunken coachman. He thought the ride to the hotel would never end; he felt incapable of concentrating on the conversation, he was dizzy and his stomach was churning.

"My wife was born in Africa; she is the daughter of missionaries who preached the true faith in those lands; we know the sacrifices that entails, Mr. Todd. We do hope that you will allow us the privilege of assisting you in your noble endeavors among the natives," Mr. Ebeling said with great solemnity as they bid one another good evening.

That night Jacob Todd could not sleep. The vision of Rose Sommers assailed him repeatedly, and before day dawned he had made the decision to court her in earnest. He knew nothing about her, but he didn't care; perhaps it was his destiny to lose a bet and travel to Chile in order to meet his future wife. He would have begun his courtship the very next day but he was unable to crawl out of bed, having been felled by a violent griping of the bowels. He lay there a day and a night, at some moments unconscious and at others thinking he was dying, until he could summon enough strength to put his head out the door and call for help. At his request, the hotel manager advised the Sommers, his only acquaintances in the city, and called a boy to clean up the room, which stank like a dung heap. Jeremy Sommers arrived at the hotel at midday, accompanied by the best bloodletter in Valparaíso, who fortunately had a smattering of English and who, after bleeding Jacob Todd's legs and arms until he was nearly lifeless, explained to him that all newcomers fell ill when first they visited Chile.

"There's no reason to be alarmed, that I know of; very few die," he said to reassure Todd.

He left small rice-paper packets of quinine, but the suffering Englishman, doubled over with stomach cramps, could not get them down. He had been in India and he recognized the symptoms of malaria and other tropical illnesses treated with quinine, but his sickness did not resemble them even remotely. As soon as the phlebotomist left, the boy returned to take away the rags and wash down the room again. Jeremy Sommers had left the address of the doctors Page and Poett, but Todd did not get around to calling them because two hours later a formidable woman appeared at the hotel and demanded to see the sick man. She had by the hand a little girl dressed in blue velvet, white high-button shoes, and a bonnet embroidered with flowers, like a picture in a storybook. They were Mama Fresia and Eliza, whom Rose Sommers had sent because she had very little faith in bloodletting. They marched into Todd's room with such assurance that the weakened man did not dare protest. The woman had come in the guise of healer, and the little girl as translator.

"My mamita says that she is going to take off your pajamas. I will not look," the child explained, and turned her face to the wall while the Indian woman stripped off his clothes in a thrice and proceeded to scrub his entire body with strong liquor.

She placed hot bricks in Todd's bed, wrapped him in blankets, and fed him teaspoons of a honey-sweetened bitter herb tea to ease his stomach pain.

"Now my mamita is going to *romance* your sickness," the girl said.

"What is that?"

"Don't worry, it doesn't hurt."

Mama Fresia closed her eyes and began to pass her hands over Jacob Todd's torso and stomach as she whispered incantations in her Mapuche tongue. He felt a delicious drowsiness creep over him; even before the woman finished, he was sound asleep, unaware of when his two nurses left. He slept eighteen hours and awakened bathed in sweat. The next morning Mama Fresia and Eliza returned to administer another vigorous rubdown and feed him a bowl of chicken soup.

"My mamita says not to drink any more water. Take steaming-hot tea, and don't eat fruit, or else you will feel like you want to die again," the girl translated.

Within a week, when he could stand and look at himself in the mirror, Jacob Todd realized that he could not show himself before Miss Rose looking the way he did: he had lost several pounds and was so weak he could not take two steps without falling panting into a chair. When he was up to sending a note to thank Rose for saving his life, along with chocolates for Mama Fresia and Eliza, he learned that she had left with a friend and her chambermaid for Santiago, a perilous journey given the bad conditions of the road and the weather. Miss Sommers made the thirty-four-league trip once a year, usually at the beginning of autumn or in mid-spring, for the purpose of attending the theater, hearing good music, and making her yearly purchases in the Gran Almacén Japonés, an emporium perfumed with jasmine and lighted by gas lamps with rose-colored glass shades, where she purchased the bagatelles difficult to come by in the port. This year, however, there was good reason for going during the winter: she was to sit for a portrait. A famous French painter named Monvoisin had arrived in Chile, invited by the government to establish a school among the nation's artists. The maestro painted only the head, the rest was done by his assistants, and to save time lace might be applied directly onto the canvas. Despite such ignoble devices, however, nothing was as prestigious as a portrait signed by the French master. Jeremy Sommers insisted on having one of his sister to preside over the drawing room. The painting cost six ounces of gold, plus an additional ounce for each hand, but this was no time to try to save money. The opportunity to have an authentic work by the great Monvoisin did not present itself twice in the same lifetime, as his clients were wont to say.

"If expense is no problem, I want him to paint me with three hands. It will be his most famous painting, and someday will end up in a museum rather than over our fireplace," was Miss Rose's comment.

That was the year of the floods, which were immortalized in schoolchildren's textbooks and in their grandparents' memories. The deluge swept away hundreds of dwellings, and when finally the storm abated and the waters began to recede, a series of minor temblors, which came like God's wrath, finished destroying everything that had been softened by the pouring rain. Ruffians scrabbled through the rubble, taking advantage of the confusion to pillage ruined houses, and soldiers were issued orders to summarily execute anyone they surprised in such barbaric acts. Overly zealous in their duties, however, these same protectors began swinging away for the pleasure of hearing their victims yell and the order was revoked before they began slaughtering innocents. Jacob Todd, tucked in his hotel nursing a cold and still weak from his illness, spent hours despairing of the incessant tolling of church bells calling for repentance, reading old newspapers, and looking for a partner at cards. He made one trip to a pharmacy, looking for a tonic to settle his stomach, but the shop was a jumble of dusty blue and green glass bottles where a Teutonic clerk tried to sell him scorpion oil and pinworm liqueur. For the first time, Todd lamented being so far from London.

At night he was scarcely able to sleep because of drunken parties and quarrels, and because of the daily burials, which took place between twelve midnight and three in the morning. The new cemetery was high on a hill overlooking the city. The storm washed open graves and coffins rolled down the slopes in a muddle of bones that equalized all the dead in the same indignity. Many commented that the dead were better off ten years ago, when decent people were buried in the churchyard, the poor in the ravines, and foreigners on the beach. This is a truly eccentric country, concluded Todd, who kept a handkerchief tied around his face because of the sickening windborne stench of misfortune, which the authorities fought with great bonfires of eucalyptus branches. As soon as he felt a little better, he went out to watch the processions. Ordinarily they did not draw a crowd, since they were repeated every year during the seven days of Holy Week and on other religious holidays, but on this occasion they had become massive rallies imploring heaven to bring an end to the storms. Long lines of the faithful poured out of the churches, led by the associations of black-clad caballeros, each group carrying a platform bearing the statue of a saint in magnificent robes embroidered with gold thread and precious stones. One column bore a crucified

Christ whose crown of thorns lay around his neck. Someone explained to Todd that this was the Cristo de Mayo, the May Christ, which had been brought from Santiago especially for the procession because it was the most miraculous image in the world, the only one capable of changing the weather. Two hundred years before, a devastating earthquake had leveled the capital, completely destroying the church of San Agustín except for the altar that held this Christ. His crown had slipped from his head to around his neck, where it stayed, because every time they tried to put it back where it belonged the earth began to tremble. The festivities brought together hundreds of monks and nuns, pious women faint from fasting, humble people praying and singing at the top of their lungs, penitents in coarse robes, and flagellants flaying their naked backs with scourges of leather strips tipped with sharp metal rosettes. Some swooned and were attended by women who cleaned their open wounds and gave them cooling drinks, but as soon as they recovered they pushed their way back into the procession. Lines of Indians filed by, punishing themselves with demented fervor, followed by bands of musicians playing religious hymns. Mourners' prayers roared like a rushing stream, and the humid air was heavy with incense and sweat. There were processions of aristocrats, richly clad but all in black and stripped of jewelry, and others of the ragged, barefoot, down-and-out, all of whom crisscrossed the plaza without touching or mixing. The more who crowded in, the greater the uproar and the more intense the displays of piety: the faithful lifted their voices begging forgiveness for their sins, convinced that the bad weather was divine punishment for their failings. The repentant came in swarms, overflowing the churches, and rows of priests were installed beneath tents and umbrellas to hear confessions. The Englishman found the spectacle fascinating; he had seen nothing in any of his voyages to compare to such exoticism and gloom. Accustomed to Protestant sobriety, he felt he had awakened in the Middle Ages; his friends in London would never believe him. Even at a prudent distance he could sense the primitive shiver of animal suffering that swept in waves through the masses of humanity. With no little effort, he climbed upon the base of a monument in the church plaza facing the Iglesia de la Matriz, where he could enjoy a panoramic view. Suddenly he felt someone tugging at his pants leg; he looked down and saw a frightened little girl with a black mantle over her head, her face streaked with blood and tears. He jerked his leg away, but too late; his trousers were already stained. He swore and tried to shoo her away with gestures, since he could not remember the words to do it in Spanish. He was astounded when the child replied in perfect English that she was lost and that maybe he could take her home. He took a better look.

"I am Eliza Sommers. Do you remember me?" the child murmured.

Knowing that Miss Rose was in Santiago posing for her portrait and that Jeremy Sommers had scarcely been home because his warehouse was flooded, Eliza had seized the moment and nagged Mama Fresia to take her to the procession until the woman finally gave in. Her *patrones* had forbidden her to mention any Catholic or Indian rituals in front of the girl, much less expose her to them, but she herself was dying to see the Cristo de Mayo at least once in her life. The Sommers would never find out, she concluded. So the two stole out of the house, walked down the hill, and climbed onto a cart that took them close to the plaza, where they joined a column of Indian penitents. Everything would have worked out fine if in the tumult and fervor of the day Eliza had not let loose of Mama Fresia's hand, Mama Fresia being so caught up in the collective hysteria that she failed to notice. Eliza shouted to her, but her voice was lost in the clamor of the prayers and the mournful drums of the brotherhoods. She began running around, calling for her nana, but all the women looked the same beneath their dark mantles, and she kept slipping on cobbles slick with mud, candle wax, and blood. Eventually the many columns blended together into a single mass that dragged along like a wounded animal as bells pealed madly and the horns of the ships in the port blared. Eliza had no way of knowing how long she was paralyzed with terror until gradually she began to think clearly. In the meantime, the procession itself had grown quiet, everyone was kneeling, and on a platform in front of the church the bishop, in person, was celebrating mass. Eliza thought of just starting off toward Cerro Alegre, but she was afraid that she would be overtaken by darkness before she found her house; she had never been out alone and did not know which way to go. She decided not to move until the crowd thinned out; maybe then Mama Fresia would find her. That was when she spied the tall red-haired man clinging to the monument in the plaza and recognized the sick man she had helped her nana take care of. Without a moment's hesitation, she made a beeline straight for him.

"What are you doing here! Are you hurt?" he exclaimed.

"I'm lost. Can you take me to my house?"

Jacob Todd wiped Eliza's face with his handkerchief and checked her over quickly, satisfying himself that there was no visible harm. He concluded that the blood must have come from one of the flagellants.

"I will take you to Mr. Sommers' office."

She begged him not to do that, because if her guardian found out she had come to see the procession he would send Mama Fresia away. Todd set out to find a carriage for hire, not an easy task at that moment, while the girl trotted along, saying nothing but also not letting go of his hand. For the first time in his life, the Englishman felt a quiver of tenderness as he felt that tiny warm hand grasping his. Occasionally he glanced at her out of the corner of his eye, moved by the childish face with its almond-shaped black eyes.

Finally they came upon a small cart pulled by two mules and the driver agreed to carry them up the hill for double the usual fare. They made the journey in silence, and an hour later Todd dropped Eliza in front of her house. She thanked him as she said good-bye but did not invite him in. He watched her walk away, small and unbearably fragile, covered from head to toe in her black mantle. Suddenly she turned, ran back to him, threw her arms around his neck, and planted a kiss on his cheek. "Thank you," she said again. Jacob Todd returned to his hotel in the same cart. Occasionally he touched his cheek, surprised by the sweet yet sad feelings the child had aroused in him.

The processions had the effect of heightening collective repentance, but also, as Jacob Todd himself had witnessed, of ending the rains, justifying once again the splendid reputation of the Cristo de Mayo. In less than forty-eight hours the skies cleared and a timid sun peeked out, playing an optimistic note in the concert of current catastrophes. Owing to the storms and epidemics, nine whole weeks passed before the Wednesday gatherings in the Sommers' home were resumed, and several more before Jacob Todd dared hint to Miss Rose of his romantic feelings. When finally he did so, she pretended not to hear him, but when he persisted she came out with a crushing response.

"The only good thing about marriage is becoming a widow," she said.

"A husband, no matter how stupid, always makes a woman look good," he replied without losing his good humor.

"Not me. A husband would be an impediment, and he could not give me anything I do not already have."

"What about children?"

"But how old do you think I am, Mr. Todd?"

"No more than seventeen!"

"Do not tease me. It is my good fortune that I have Eliza."

"I am stubborn, Miss Rose, I will never give up."

"I am grateful to you, Mr. Todd. However, it isn't a husband who makes a woman look good, but many suitors."

In any case, Rose was the reason why Jacob Todd remained in Chile much longer than the three months designated for selling his Bibles. The Sommers were the perfect social contact; thanks to them, the doors of the prosperous foreign colony were thrown wide open to him, and all the English were ready to help him in his proposed religious mission in Tierra del Fuego. He set himself the task of learning something about the Patagonian Indians, but after a few half-hearted sweeps through some heavy tomes in the library, he understood that it made little matter what he knew or didn't know, since ignorance on the subject was universal. All he had to do was say what people wanted to hear, and for that he could rely on his golden tongue. To unload his Bibles among Chilean clients, however, he would have to improve his rudimentary Spanish. With the two months he had lived in Spain, and his good ear, he learned more quickly, certainly, and also more comprehensively than many of the British who had come to the country twenty years before him. At first, he concealed his too liberal political ideas, but soon he noticed that in every social gathering he was besieged with questions and always surrounded by a group of astonished listeners. His abolitionist, egalitarian, and democratic discourses shook those good people from their fog; they were the source of endless discussion among the men and horrified exclamations among the mature ladies, though inevitably they attracted the younger ones. He was catalogued in general opinion as a kind of harmless lunatic, and his incendiary ideas were considered entertaining; on the other hand, his mockery of the British royal family was badly received among members of the English colony for whom Queen Victoria, like God and Empire, was untouchable. His income—modest, though not to be sneezed at—allowed him to live with a certain ease without ever really having to work for a living, and that classified him as a gentleman. As soon as it was established that he was unattached there was no shortage of marriageable girls intent on capturing him, but after he met Rose Sommers he had no eyes for other women. He asked himself a thousand times why she had never married and all that occurred to that rationalist agnostic was that heaven intended her for him.

"How long are you going to go on tormenting me, Miss Rose? Aren't you afraid I may get tired of chasing you?" he teased her.

"You won't tire, Mr. Todd. Pursuing the cat is much more entertaining than catching it," she replied.

The bogus missionary's eloquence was a novelty in those surroundings, and as soon as it was learned that he had conscientiously studied Holy Scripture, he was invited to speak. There was a small Anglican church, frowned upon by the Catholic powers-that-be, but the Protestant community also met in private homes. "Whoever heard of a church without virgins and devils? Those English folks are all heretics; they don't believe in the Pope, they don't know how to pray, they spend most of their time singing, and they don't even take communion," a scandalized Mama Fresia would grumble when it was the Sommers' turn to hold Sunday service in their home. Todd planned to read briefly about the exodus of the Jews from Egypt and then refer to the situation of immigrants who, like the biblical Jews, had to adapt to a strange land, but Jeremy Sommers introduced him to the congregation as a missionary and asked him to speak about the Indians in Tierra del Fuego. Jacob Todd could not have found Tierra del Fuego on the map, or told why it had the intriguing name Land of Fire, but he succeeded in moving his audience to tears with the story of three savages captured by a British captain and taken to England. In less than three years those unfortunate individuals, who lived naked in glacial cold and from time to time practiced cannibalism, he said, went about properly dressed, had become good Christians and learned civilized customs, including a tolerance for English food. He failed to mention, however, that as soon as they were repatriated they had returned to their old ways, as if they had never been touched by England or the word of Jesus. At Jeremy Sommers' suggestion, a collection was taken up right there for Todd's plan to spread the faith, with such fine results that the following day Jacob Todd opened an account in the Valparaíso branch of the Bank of London. The account was nourished weekly with contributions from the Protestants and grew despite the frequent drafts Todd drew to finance personal expenses when his income did not stretch to cover them. The more money that came in, the more the obstacles and pretexts for postponing the evangelical mission multiplied. And in that manner two years went by.

Jacob Todd came to feel as comfortable in Valparaíso as if he had been born there. Chileans and English shared a number of character traits: they resolved everything with solicitors and barristers; they had an absurd fondness for tradition, patriotic symbols, and routine; they prided themselves on being individualists and enemies of ostentation, which they scorned as a sin of social climbing; they seemed amiable and self-controlled but were capable of great cruelty. However, unlike the English, Chileans were horrified by eccentricity and feared nothing so much as ridicule. If only I spoke Spanish well, thought Jacob Todd, I would feel entirely at home. He had moved into the boardinghouse of an English widow woman who took in stray cats and baked the most famous pastries in the port. He slept with four felines on his bed, better company than he had ever had, and breakfasted daily on his hostess's tempting tarts. He connected with Chileans of every class, from the most humble, whom he met in his wanderings through the poor neighborhoods of the port, to the high-and-mightiest. Jeremy Sommers introduced him into the Club de la Unión, where he was accepted as an invited member. Only foreigners of recognized social status could boast of such privilege, since the club was an enclave of landowners and political conservatives whose members' worth was determined by family name. Doors opened to him because of his skill with cards and dice; he lost with such grace that very few realized how much he won. It was there that he became a friend of Agustín del Valle, the owner of agricultural holdings in that area and flocks of sheep in the south, where del Valle had never thought of going since that was precisely why he had imported stewards from Scotland. That new friendship gave Todd occasion to visit the austere mansions of aristocratic Chilean families, dark, square edifices with huge, nearly empty rooms decorated with little refinement: heavy furniture, funereal candelabra, and a court of bloody, crucified Christs, plaster virgins, and saints dressed in the mode of ancient Spanish noblemen. These were houses that turned inward, closed to the street by tall iron railings, graceless and uncomfortable but relieved by cool colonnades and interior patios filled with jasmine, orange trees, and roses.

With the first signs of spring, Agustín del Valle invited the Sommers and Jacob Todd to one of his country estates. The road was a nightmare: a lone horseman could make it in four or five hours, but the caravan of family and guests started at dawn and did not arrive until late at night. The del Valles traveled in oxcarts laden with tables and plush sofas. Behind them came a mule team with the luggage, along with peasants on horseback armed with primitive blunderbusses to defend against the highwaymen who all too often awaited around the curve of the hill. Added to the maddening pace of the animals were the washed-out track where carts sank to their axles and the frequent rest stops during which the servants served refreshments amid clouds of flies. Todd knew nothing about agriculture, but he needed only a look to realize how abundantly things grew in that fertile soil: fruit fell from the trees and rotted on the ground because no one made the effort to gather it. At the hacienda he encountered the same style of life he had observed years before in Spain: a large family united by intricate bloodlines and an inflexible code of honor. His host was a powerful and feudal patriarch who held the destinies of his descendants in his iron fist and made much of a family tree he could trace back to the first Spanish conquistadors. My ancestors, he would say, walked more than a thousand kilometers weighed down in heavy iron armor; they crossed mountains, rivers, and the world's most arid desert to found the city of Santiago. Among his peers del Valle was a symbol of authority and decency, but outside his class he was known as a rake. He had untold bastards and a reputation for having killed more than one of his tenants in a legendary fit of temper, but those deaths, along with many other sins, were never mentioned. His wife was in her forties but she looked like an old woman, tremulous and hangdog, always dressed in mourning for the children who died in infancy and squeezed breathless by the pressure of her corset, her religion, and the husband fate had dealt her. Male offspring idled away the days in masses, outings, siestas, gambling, and carousing, while the girls floated like mysterious nymphs through the house and gardens in whispering petticoats, always beneath the vigilant eye of their chaperones. They had been trained since early childhood for a life of virtue, faith, and abnegation; their fate was a marriage of convenience and motherhood.

In the country, the party attended a bullfight that did not even remotely resemble the brilliant Spanish spectacle of courage and death: no suit of lights, no fanfare, no passion or glory, only a handful of reckless drunks tormenting an animal with spears and insults, then tossed into the dust to the tune of curses and guffaws. The most dangerous part of the fight was getting the enraged and ill-treated, but still unharmed, beast from the ring. Todd was grateful that they spared it the ultimate indignity of public execution, for in his good English heart he would rather have seen the bullfighter die than the bull. In the afternoons the men played ombre and *rocambor*, waited on like princes by a true army of humble, dark-skinned servants who never lifted their eyes from the ground or their voices above a murmur. They weren't slaves but may as well have been. They worked in exchange for protection, a roof over their heads, and a portion of the harvest; in theory they were free but they stayed with the *patron*, however despotic he might be or however harsh their conditions, since they had nowhere else to go. Slavery had been quietly abolished ten years before. The African slave trade had never been profitable in these lands because there were no large plantations—although no one mentioned the fate of the Indians who had been deprived of their lands and reduced to penury, or the tenants in the fields who were sold or inherited with the property, like the animals. Neither was there any reference to the shiploads of Chinese and Polynesian slaves destined for the guano deposits of the Chincha Islands. As long as they didn't leave the ship there was no problem: the law prohibited slavery on dry land but said nothing about the sea. While the men played cards, Miss Rose grew discreetly bored in the company of Señora del Valle and her many daughters. Eliza, in contrast, raced through the open fields with Paulina, the one daughter of Agustín del Valle who had escaped the languid pattern of the women of that family. She was several years older than Eliza, but that day she romped and played as if they were the same age, faces bare to the sun, their hair blowing loose in the wind as they whipped their horses on.

Señoritas

Eliza Sommers was a small, slender girl with features as delicate as a quill drawing. In 1845, when she was thirteen and beginning to show signs of breasts and a waist, she still looked like a child, although one with glimpses of the grace that would be her greatest attribute in beauty. Thanks to the implacable vigilance of Miss Rose—who made her charge sit with a metal rod strapped to her backbone through interminable hours of piano exercises and embroidery—Eliza stood straight as a spear. She did not grow much, and with the years kept the same deceptively youthful look that would save her life more than once. She was so much a little girl at heart that when she reached puberty she continued to sleep curled up in a ball in her childhood bed, surrounded by her dolls and sucking her thumb. She imitated Jeremy Sommers' air of ennui because she thought it was a sign of internal strength. As she got older she tired of pretending to be bored, but that training helped her tame her nature. She helped in the servants' chores: one day making bread, another grinding maize, one maybe sunning feather beds, yet another boiling the white clothes. She spent hours huddled behind the drapes in the living room, devouring the classics in Jeremy Sommers' library one by one, along with Miss Rose's romantic novels, out-of-date newspapers—anything that fell into her hands, however dull. She got Jacob Todd to give her one of his Bibles in Spanish, and set about deciphering it—with enormous patience, since all her schooling had been in English. She soaked up the Old Testament with a morbid fascination for the vices and passions of kings who seduced other men's wives, prophets who dealt out punishment with terrible lightning bolts, and parents who fathered children on their own daughters. In the storeroom where they kept castoffs, she found her uncle John's old maps, travel books, and logs, which gave her a feel for the shape of the world. Instructors hired by Miss Rose taught her French, writing, history, geography, and a little Latin, considerably more than was doled out in the best girls' schools in the capital, where, after all was said and done, all that was learned were prayers and good manners. Eliza's random reading, as well as Captain Sommers' tales, gave wing to her imagination. That world-traveling uncle would appear with his load of gifts, stirring her fantasy with his extraordinary stories of black emperors on thrones of pure gold, Malaysian pirates who collected human eyeballs in little mother-of-pearl boxes, and princesses immolated on the funeral pyres of aged husbands. On each of his visits everything was set aside, from school lessons to piano lessons. The year went by in waiting for him and putting pins in the map, imagining the point on the high seas where his ship was sailing. Eliza had little contact with other girls her age; she lived in the closed world of her benefactors' home, in the eternal illusion of being in England rather than Valparaíso. Jeremy Sommers ordered everything from a catalogue, from soap to shoes, and wore light clothing in the winter and an overcoat in the summer because he followed the calendar of the Northern Hemisphere. The little girl listened and observed attentively; she had a happy and independent temperament, she never asked for help, and she had the rare gift of making herself invisible at will, blending into the furniture, curtains, and flowered wallpaper. The day she waked to find her nightgown stained with red she went to Miss Rose to tell her she was bleeding "down there."

"Do not discuss this with anyone, it is very private. This means you are a woman now and you must conduct yourself as such; your days as a child are over. It is time for you to attend Madame Colbert's school for girls." That was her adoptive mother's complete explanation, blurted out in one breath and without meeting Eliza's eyes, as from her armoire she produced a dozen small towels she herself had hemmed.

"You're in for it now, child. Your body will change, your thoughts will be jumbled, and any man will be able to do what he wants with you," Eliza was advised by Mama Fresia, from whom she could not hide her new state.

The Indian knew of plants that would stop the menstrual flow permanently, but she did not give them to Eliza for fear of her *patrones*. Eliza took her nana's warning seriously and decided to be on the watch to keep those things from happening. She bound her chest tightly with a silk sash, sure that if that method had worked for centuries with the feet of Chinese women, as her uncle John had told her, there was no reason it would not do the same with her breasts. She also decided to write. For years she had seen Miss Rose writing in her notebooks and she supposed that she did it to combat the curse of jumbled ideas. As for the last part of the prophecy—that any man would be able to do what he wanted with her—she attached less importance to that because she was incapable of imagining a case in which there would be men in her future. They were all tired and old, at least twenty; the world was void of boys of her generation and the only men she would like for a husband, Captain John Sommers and Jacob Todd, were out of bounds because the first was her uncle and the second was in love with Miss Rose, as all Valparaíso could testify.

Years later, remembering her childhood and youth, Eliza thought that Miss Rose and Mr. Todd would have made a good couple; Rose would have softened Mr. Todd's harsh edges and he would have rescued her from boredom, but things had worked out differently. In their later years, when both were combing the gray in their hair and they had the long habit of solitude, they would meet in California under strange circumstances; then he would court her again with the same intensity and she would reject him with equal determination. But all that would come much later.

Jacob Todd lost no opportunity to be near the Sommers; there was no more faithful or punctual visitor at their musical evenings, no one more attentive to Miss Rose's impassioned trills or more disposed to appreciate her wit, including the slightly cruel remarks she tormented him with. She was a person filled with contradictions, but was that not true of him as well? Was he not an atheist selling Bibles and deluding half the world with the story of a purported evangelizing mission? He often asked himself why such an attractive woman had never married; a single woman of her age had no future in society. Among the foreign colony there were whispers of a certain scandal in England, years ago; that would explain her presence in Chile, where she acted as chatelaine for her brother, but he never tried to learn the details, preferring mystery to the knowledge of something he might not have been able to bear. The past didn't matter, he told himself. It took only one error in discretion or calculation to stain a woman's reputation and prevent her from making a good marriage. He would have given years of his life to have her love, but she gave no indication of yielding to his siege, although neither did she try to discourage him; she enjoyed the game of giving him rope only to rein him back in.

"Mr. Todd is a bird of ill omen; he has bizarre ideas, teeth like a horse, and his hands perspire. I would never marry him, even if he were the last bachelor in the universe," Miss Rose confessed to Eliza, laughing.

The girl was sorry to hear that. She was indebted to Jacob Todd, not only for having rescued her at the procession of the Cristo de Mayo, but also because he acted as if it had never happened. She was fond of her strange ally; both he and her uncle John smelled like big dogs. The good impression she had of him turned into loyal affection the day that, hidden behind heavy velvet drapes in the drawing room, she overheard a conversation between him and Jeremy Sommers.

"I must make some decision regarding Eliza, Jacob. She hasn't the least notion of her place in society. People are beginning to ask questions and Eliza surely imagines a future that does not befit her. Nothing as perilous, you know, as the demon of fantasy embedded in every female heart."

"Don't exaggerate, my friend. Eliza is still a little girl, but she is intelligent and surely she will find her place."

"Intelligence is a drawback in a woman. Rose wants to send her to Madame Colbert's school, but I am not in favor of that much schooling for girls; it makes them unmanageable. 'Let us always know our proper stations,' that is my motto."

"The world is changing, Jeremy. In the United States free men are equal before the law. Social classes have been abolished."

"We are speaking of women, old boy, not men. As for the rest, the United States is a country of merchants and pioneers, totally lacking in tradition or a sense of history. Equality does not exist anywhere, not even among animals, and much less in Chile."

"But we are foreigners, Jeremy, we speak scarcely a word of Spanish. What do Chilean social classes matter to us? This will never be our country."

"We must set a good example. If we British are incapable of keeping our own house in order, what can we expect of others?"

"Eliza has grown up in this family. I don't think that Miss Rose would agree to deprive her simply because she is growing up."

And she did not. Rose defied her brother, calling upon a full repertory of ills. First it was stomach upset and then an alarming headache that struck her blind overnight. For several days the entire house was cloaked in silence: drapes were closed, people walked on tiptoe and talked in whispers. Nothing was cooked because the smell of food exacerbated the symptoms. Jeremy Sommers ate at the club and returned home with the worried and timid attitude of someone visiting a hospital. Rose's peculiar blindness and many ailments, added to the stubborn silence of the household servants, quickly undermined Jeremy's resolve. As the last straw, Mama Fresia, mysteriously acquainted with the private discussions between brother and sister, became a formidable ally of her *patrona*. Jeremy Sommers thought of himself as a civilized and pragmatic man, invulnerable to intimidation by a superstitious witch like Mama Fresia, but when the Indian lighted black candles and fanned smoke from burning sage everywhere, under the pretext of driving off mosquitoes, he closed himself in the library, wavering between fear and fury. At night he could hear the swish of her bare feet outside his door, her low voice quietly singing psalms and curses. The Wednesday he found a dead lizard in his bottle of brandy he decided to act once and for all. For the first time ever, he knocked at his sister's door and was admitted into that sanctuary of feminine mysteries he preferred to know nothing of, just as alien to him as the sewing room, the kitchen, the laundry, and the dark corners of the attic where the maidservants lived, to say nothing of Mama Fresia's dark domain at the rear of the patio: he lived his world in the drawing rooms, the library with its waxed mahogany shelves and his collection of engravings of the hunt, the billiards room with its ornately carved table, his bedroom furnished in Spartan simplicity, and a small dressing room with Italian tile where someday he planned to install a modern toilet like those he had seen in catalogues from New York, because he had read that the system of chamber pots and of collecting human excrement in buckets to use as fertilizer was a breeding ground for epidemics. He had to wait for his eyes to adjust to the darkness, as he uneasily breathed in the combined scents of medicines and a persistent tone of vanilla. Rose was barely visible, wan and suffering, flat on her back in the bed, with no pillow, her arms folded across her breast as if practicing for her death. Beside her, Eliza was wringing a cloth dipped in a brew of green tea to place over Rose's eyes.

"Leave us, child," said Jeremy Sommers, taking a chair beside the bed.

Eliza bobbed her head and left, but she knew every last crack and chink of the house, and with her ear pressed to the thin dividing wall she could hear the conversation that later she repeated to Mama Fresia and wrote down in her diary.

"Very well, Rose. We cannot continue this warfare. Let us reach an accord. What is it you want?" asked Jeremy, conquered before he began.

"Nothing, Jeremy," Rose sighed in a barely audible voice.

"They will never accept Eliza in Madame Colbert's academy. Only proper girls go there, girls from well-to-do families. Everyone knows that Eliza is adopted."

"I shall make it my business to see that she is accepted!" Rose exclaimed with a passion unexpected in a dying woman.

"Listen to me, Rose, Eliza has no need for further education. She needs to learn a skill that will enable her to earn her living. What will become of her when you and I are not here to protect her?"

"If she has an education, she will make a good marriage," said Rose, tossing aside the compress of green tea and sitting up in the bed.

"Eliza is not exactly a beauty, Rose."

"You haven't truly looked, Jeremy. She is improving day by day, she will be winsome, I promise you. She will have more suitors than she can count!"

"An orphan, and without a dowry?"

"She shall have a dowry," Miss Rose exclaimed, stumbling from her bed, hair uncombed, barefoot, and feeling her way like a blind woman.

"How so? We have never spoken of that subject."

"Because it was not the moment, Jeremy. A marriageable girl must have jewels, a trousseau with enough clothing to last her several years, and everything she needs for her home, as well as a tidy nest egg that will help establish her and her husband in the world."

"And may I know what the groom's contribution is to be?"

"The house . . . and besides, he will have to support the woman for the rest of her life. In any case, it is still a number of years until Eliza is old enough to marry, and by then she will have a dowry. John and I will take charge of providing that, we shall not ask you for a penny . . . but it is pointless to waste time speaking of this now. You must think of Eliza as your daughter."

"She is not my daughter, Rose."

"Then treat her as if she were mine. Can you agree to do at least that?"

"Yes, I will do that," Jeremy Sommers conceded.

The tea-soaked cloths seemed to work miracles. The ailing Miss Rose recovered completely and within forty-eight hours had regained her sight and was radiant. She devoted herself to her brother's care with endearing solicitude: she had never been sweeter and sunnier. The house returned to its normal rhythm, and from kitchen to dining room flowed Mama Fresia's delicious Chilean dishes and Eliza's mouthwatering breads and fine pastries, which had contributed so greatly to the Sommers' reputation as good hosts. From that moment, Miss Rose drastically modified her erratic tutelage of Eliza and outdid herself in a never before demonstrated maternal dedication, preparing her for school while at the same time mounting a relentless offensive aimed at Madame Colbert. Miss Rose had decided that Eliza would have learning, dowry, and fame as a beauty even if she was not one, because it was her view that beauty is a question of style. Any woman who conducts herself with the queenly assurance of a belle, she maintained, will convince everyone that she is beautiful. The first step toward emancipating Eliza would be a good marriage, seeing that the girl could not count on an older brother to shield her as her own had done. She herself could not see the advantages of marriage; a wife was the husband's property, with fewer rights than those of a servant or a child; on the other hand, a woman alone and without a fortune was at the mercy of the worst abuses. A married woman, if she was clever, could at least manage her husband, and with a bit of luck could even be widowed young.

"I would happily give half my life to have the freedom a man has, Eliza. But we are women, and that is our cross. All we can do is try to get the best from the little we have."

Miss Rose did not tell Eliza that the one time she had tried to fly on her own she had crashed head-on into reality; she did not want to plant any subversive ideas in the girl's mind. She was determined that Eliza would have a better fate than her own; she would school the child in the arts of dissembling, manipulation, and cunning, which, she had no doubt, were more useful than candor. She spent three hours in the morning with Eliza and another three in the afternoon, studying schoolbooks imported from England. She entrusted the French lessons to a professor because no well-educated girl could be ignorant of that language. The rest of the time she personally supervised every stitch Eliza made for her trousseau: sheets, towels, table linens, and profusely embroidered undergarments, which Rose then wrapped in linen, perfumed with lavender, and stored in trunks. Every three months she took everything from the trunks and laid them in the sun to prevent the ravages of humidity and moths during the years leading up to a marriage. She bought a coffer for the jewels of Eliza's dowry and charged her brother John with filling it with gifts from his travels. Sapphires from India were added to emeralds and amethysts from Brazil, necklaces and bracelets of Venetian gold, and even a small diamond brooch. Jeremy Sommers knew nothing of these details, and was completely innocent of how his brother and sister financed such extravagances.

The piano lessons—now with a professor newly arrived from Belgium who used a ferule to rap the clumsy fingers of his students—became a daily martyrdom for Eliza. She also attended an academy of ballroom dancing, and at the master's suggestion Miss Rose obliged her to walk for hours balancing a book on her head, the purpose of which was to teach her to stand up straight. Eliza did all her assignments, practiced her piano lessons, and walked straight as a candle, even without a book on her head, but at night she slipped barefoot down to the servants' patio and often the dawn found her sleeping on a pallet with her arms around Mama Fresia.

Two years after the floods, things took a turn for the better and the country basked in good weather, political tranquility, and an economic boom. Chileans treaded warily; they were accustomed to natural disasters and such a bonanza could be the preparation for a major cataclysm. To top it off, rich veins of silver and gold were discovered in the north. During the Conquest, when the Spaniards wandered America seeking those ores and bearing off everything they found, Chile had been considered the backside of the world because, compared with the riches of the rest of the continent, it had very little to offer. The forced march across its towering mountains and the lunar desert of the north dried up the greed in the hearts of those conquistadors, and if any remained, unconquerable Indians made them rue it. The captains, exhausted and impoverished, cursed the land that gave them no choice but to plant their flags and lie down to die because to return without glory was worse. Three hundred years later those mines, hidden from the eyes of the ambitious soldiers of Spain and now suddenly, magically, exposed, were an unexpected prize for their descendants. New fortunes were formed, augmented by others from industry and commerce. The ancient landed aristocracy, which had always had the upper hand in the country, felt its privileges threatened, and new wealth became a social stigma.

One of those filthy-rich upstarts fell in love with Paulina del Valle. His name was Feliciano Rodríguez de Santa Cruz, and in a few years' time he had made a fortune in a gold mine he had developed with his brother. Little was known of their origins, except that it was suspected that their ancestors were converted Jews and had adopted that sonorous Christian family name to save their skins during the Inquisition, more than enough reason to be flatly rejected by the proud del Valles. Of Agustín's five daughters, Jacob Todd liked Paulina best because her dashing, happy nature reminded him of Miss Rose. The girl had an open way of laughing that contrasted with her sisters' simpers hidden behind fans and mantillas. When Jacob Todd learned of her father's plan to banish Paulina to a convent to foil her love affair, he decided, against his better judgment, to help her. Before she was taken away, he managed to steal a few words with her in a moment when her chaperone's attention was wandering. Aware that there was no time for explanations, Paulina pulled from her bodice a letter so folded and wadded up it looked like a weathered rock and begged Todd to take it to her beloved. The next day the girl, closely guarded by her father, was taken on a journey of several days over nearly impassable roads to Concepción, a city in the south near Indian reservations, where nuns would undertake the chore of bringing her to her senses with prayers and fasting. To rid her of the foolhardy notion that she might rebel or escape, del Valle had ordered her head to be shaved. Her mother collected Paulina's cut-off locks, wrapped them in an embroidered batiste cloth, and took them as a gift to the charitable women of the Iglesia de la Matriz to make wigs for the saints. Meanwhile, Todd not only succeeded in delivering Paulina's missive, he also learned the exact location of the convent from her brothers and passed on that information to a greatly distressed Feliciano Rodríguez de Santa Cruz. In gratitude, the suitor took out his pocket watch and pure-gold chain and insisted on giving them to his love's sainted spy, who refused them, offended.

"I have no way to repay you for what you have done," Feliciano murmured, nonplussed.

"You have no reason to do so."

For some time Jacob Todd heard nothing about the beleaguered pair, but after a couple of months the delicious tale of the girl's flight was the tidbit of every social gathering and there was nothing the haughty Agustín del Valle could do to prevent the addition of colorful details that made him the butt of ridicule. The version Paulina told Jacob Todd months later was that one June evening, one of those wintry twilights with a fine rain and early nightfall, she had managed to escape her keepers' vigilance and flee the convent dressed in a novice's habit, taking with her two silver candelabra from the main altar. Thanks to Jacob Todd's information, Feliciano Rodríguez de Santa Cruz had journeyed south, where he had been in secret contact with Paulina from the beginning, prepared to meet her at the first opportunity. That evening he was waiting a short distance from the convent, although when he saw her it was several seconds before he recognized the half-bald novice who melted into his arms, still clutching the candelabras.

"Don't look at me like that, Feliciano, hair grows," she said, kissing him smack on the lips.

Feliciano took Paulina back to Valparaíso in a closed carriage and temporarily installed her in his widowed mother's home, the most respectable hiding place he could think of, doing his best to protect her honor although aware that there was no way to keep her reputation from being tarred by the scandal. Agustín's first thought was to challenge his daughter's seducer to a duel, but when he acted on that impulse he learned that Feliciano was on a business trip in Santiago. He turned his attention instead to finding Paulina, assisted by armed sons and nephews preoccupied with avenging the honor of the family, while the mother and a chorus of sisters prayed a rosary for their misguided Paulina. The ecclesiastical uncle who had recommended sending Paulina to the nuns tried to instill a little sanity in the male del Valles, but those chauvinists were in no mood for that good Christian's sermonizing. Feliciano's trip was part of the strategy he had planned with his brother and Jacob Todd. He left without fanfare for the capital while the other two men set into action the Valparaíso portion of the plan, publishing in a liberal newspaper news of the disappearance of Señorita Paulina del Valle, word that the family had tried very hard to suppress. That saved the lovers' lives.

Finally Agustín del Valle accepted the fact that this was not the time to defy the law and that a public wedding would go farther than a double murder to cleanse the family honor. They set the guidelines for a negotiated peace and a week later, when everything was ready, Feliciano returned. The fugitives presented themselves at the del Valles' home, accompanied by the groom's brother, a lawyer, and the bishop. Jacob Todd was discreetly absent. Paulina wore a very simple dress, but when she took off her mantle she defiantly displayed a queen's diadem. She entered on the arm of her future mother-in-law, who was prepared to speak for her virtue but was not given the opportunity. The last thing the family wanted was a second story in the newspaper, so Agustín del Valle had no choice but to receive his rebellious daughter and her undesirable suitor. He did so surrounded by his sons and nephews in the dining room, which had been converted into a tribunal for the occasion, while the women of the family, secluded at the opposite end of the house, learned the details from the maidservants, who listened behind doors and then ran to them with every word. They reported that the girl had shown up with diamonds glittering in her bristly new hair and had faced her father without a trace of shyness or fear, announcing that she still had the candelabras, and, in fact, had taken them only to gall the nuns. Agustín del Valle raised his riding crop but Feliciano stepped forward to receive the punishment. Then the bishop, very weary but with the weight of his authority intact, intervened with the irrefutable argument that there could be no public marriage to still the gossip if the bride and groom showed up with bruised faces.

"Ask them to bring us hot chocolate, Agustín, and let us sit down and converse like decent people," this officer of the Church proposed.

And so they did. They ordered Paulina and the widow Rodríguez de Santa Cruz to wait outside the room because this was a man's affair, and after consuming several pots of foaming chocolate they reached an agreement. They dictated a document in which the economic terms were set out clearly and the honor of both parties saved, signed it before a notary, and proceeded to plan the details of the wedding. One month later Jacob Todd attended an unforgettable ball in which the prodigal hospitality of the del Valle family reached new heights:

the dancing, singing, and feasting lasted into the following morning and the guests all commented on the beauty of the bride, the happiness of the groom, and the good fortune of the del Valles, who had wed their daughter to a solid, if brand-new, fortune. The couple immediately left for the north.

A Ruined Reputation

Jacob Todd was sorry to see Feliciano and Paulina go; he had become good friends with the mining millionaire and his spunky wife. He felt as much at ease with the young impresarios as he began to feel ill at ease among the members of the Club de la Unión. Like him, the new industrialists were imbued with European ideas, they were modern and liberal, unlike the old Chilean oligarchy which at midcentury was decades behind the times. He still had one hundred and seventy Bibles stacked beneath his bed, which by now he had forgotten because he had long ago lost his bet. He had enough command of Spanish to manage on his own and, though it was not returned, he had never stopped loving Rose Sommers: two good reasons for staying in Chile. Her unfailing rebuffs had become a pleasant habit and no longer humiliated him. He learned to deflect them with irony and return them without malice, like a game of catch whose mysterious rules only they knew. He was acquainted with a few intellectuals and spent entire nights discussing French and German philosophers, along with scientific discoveries that were opening new horizons on human knowledge. He had long hours in which to think, read, and debate. He distilled ideas that he noted down in a thick notebook worn with use and spent a major part of his pension on books ordered from London and others he bought in the Santos Tornero bookstore in El Almendral, the district where the French lived and where all the best brothels in Valparaíso were located. The bookshop was a meeting place for intellectuals and aspiring writers. Todd sometimes spent whole days reading; later he passed his books on to his comrades, who translated them and published them in small, inexpensive pamphlets circulated from hand to hand.

Among the group of intellectuals, the youngest was one Joaquín Andieta, who was barely eighteen but who made up for lack of experience with the qualities of a natural leader. His electrifying personality was even more notable given his youth and poverty. This Joaquín was not a man of many words, but of action, one of the few with enough clearmindedness and courage to transform ideas from books into revolutionary impulses; the others would rather argue forever around a bottle in the back room of the bookstore. Todd had picked Andieta out from the beginning; there was something disquieting and pathetic about him that drew him like an abyss. Todd had noticed Andieta's scuffed satchel and threadbare suit, transparent and brittle as onion skin. To hide the holes in the soles of his boots, Andieta never crossed his legs, and Todd suspected that he did not remove his jacket because his shirt was mended and patched. He didn't own a decent overcoat, but in winter he was the first to get up early to hand out pamphlets and paste up posters calling workers to rebel against employers' abuses, or sailors against captains and ship companies, an often futile labor since most of those to whom the notices were directed were illiterate. His calls for justice were lost at the mercy of the wind and human indifference.

Through discreet inquiries Jacob Todd discovered that his friend was employed by the British Import and Export Company, Ltd. In return for a miserly salary and exhausting work schedule he kept an accounting of the goods that passed through the port office. He was also expected to wear a starched collar and shined shoes. He spent his days in a badly lit, badly ventilated room in which the desks were lined up one after the other to infinity and piled with dusty files and ledgers that no one had looked at in years. Todd asked Jeremy Sommers about the boy but he could not place him. He must see him every day, he said, but he had no personal interchange with his subordinates and could barely recognize their names. Through other sources, Todd learned that Andieta lived with his mother, but could find out nothing about his father. He imagined that he had been a sailor passing through the port and the mother one of those luckless women who did not fit into any social category, perhaps illegitimate or renounced by her family. Joaquín Andieta had Andalusian features and the virile grace of a young toreador; everything about him suggested firmness, athleticism, control; his movements were precise, his gaze intense, his pride touching. To Todd's Utopian idealism he posed a rock-hard realism. Todd preached the creation of a communal society without priests or police, governed democratically under a unique and flexible moral law.

"You live in the clouds, Mr. Todd. We have much to do, we can't waste time discussing fantasies," interrupted Joaquín Andieta.

"But if we don't begin by imagining the perfect society, how shall we create one?" Todd responded, waving his constantly growing notebook, to which he had added plans of ideal cities in which each citizen cultivated his food and children grew up healthy and happy, cared for by the community, for since there was no private property neither could one claim possession of children.

"We must improve the disaster of the here and now. The first thing is to organize the workers, the poor, and the Indians, give land to the campesinos and seize power from the priests. We must change the constitution, Mr. Todd. Here only property owners vote, which means the rich govern. The poor don't count."

At first, Jacob Todd sought ways to help his friend, but soon he had to give that up because his attempts were taken as offense by him. He assigned Andieta little jobs in order to have an excuse to give him money, but Andieta completed them scrupulously and then refused payment. If Todd offered him tobacco, a glass of brandy, or his umbrella on a stormy night, Andieta reacted with icy pride, leaving Todd upset and sometimes insulted. The young man never mentioned his private affairs or his past; he seemed briefly to come to life in order to share a few hours of revolutionary conversation or feverish reading in the bookshop before vanishing like smoke at the end of those evenings. He did not have money to accompany the others to the tavern and would not accept an invitation he couldn't repay.

One night Todd could not bear the uncertainty any longer and followed Andieta through the labyrinth of the port streets, hiding in the shadows of colonnades and around the bends of the absurd alleyways that people told him twisted purposely to keep the devil from entering them. He watched Joaquín Andieta turn up his pants legs, take off his shoes, wrap them in a sheet of newspaper, and carefully put them in his worn satchel, from which he took a pair of peasant sandals to wear. At that late hour there were only a few lost souls about and stray cats pawing through garbage. Feeling like a thief, Todd slunk through the darkness, close upon his friend's heels; he could hear Andieta's agitated breathing and the chafing of skin as he rubbed his hands to combat the needles of icy wind. His steps led to a wretched house on one of those narrow alleys so typical of the city. The stench of urine and excrement struck Todd in the face; the crew that policed the neighborhoods with long hooks to clear the drains rarely came here. He now understood Andieta's precaution in taking off his only pair of shoes: Todd had no idea what he was walking through, only that his feet were sinking into a pestilential broth. In the moonless night a faint light filtered through the battered shutters at the windows, many without windowpanes but closed with boards or pasteboard. Through the cracks he glimpsed a miserable candlelit room. The gentle mist gave the scene an air of unreality. He watched Joaquín Andieta light a match, protecting it from the wind with his body, take out a key, and open a door in the tremulous light of the flame. "Is that you, son?" Todd heard a woman's voice, younger than he had expected. The door immediately closed. He stood a long while in the darkness, staring at the shabby house, fighting a powerful urge to knock at the door, a desire born not of mere curiosity but from an overwhelming affection for his friend. "I'm a bloody idiot," he muttered finally.

He turned and started back to the Club de la Unión to have a drink and read the newspapers, but before he got there he went home, unable to face the contrast between the poverty he had just left and those rooms with their leather furniture and crystal chandeliers. He went back to his lodgings, burning with a fire of compassion not unlike the fever that had so nearly done him in during his first week in Chile.

And that was the state of things at the end of 1845 when the commercial maritime fleet of Great Britain assigned a chaplain in Valparaíso to attend to the spiritual needs of the Protestants. He arrived eager to challenge the Catholics, build a solid Anglican temple, and put new life in his congregation. He announced that his first official act would be to examine the accounts of the missionary project in Tierra del Fuego, the results of which were nowhere in evidence. Jacob Todd had Agustín del Valle invite him to the country, with the idea of giving the new pastor time to cool down, but when he returned two weeks later he found that the chaplain had not forgotten the matter. For a while Todd invented new excuses to forestall the inevitable, but finally he had to face an auditor and then a commission of the Anglican Church. He became entangled in explanations that became more and more fantastic the more clearly the numbers exposed the deficit to the bright light of day. He turned over what money was left in the account but his reputation suffered irreparable damage. The Wednesday musicales in the home of the Sommers were ended for him, and no one in the foreign colony invited him anywhere again; friends avoided him in the street and everyone who had business with him considered it terminated. News of the deception filtered through to his Chilean friends, who discreetly but firmly suggested that he not show his face again in the Club de la Unión if he wanted to avoid the embarrassment of being ejected. He was not welcome at the cricket matches or in the bar of the Hotel Inglés. Soon he was isolated and even his liberal friends turned their backs on him. The del Valle family, as a block, stopped speaking to him, except for Paulina, with whom he maintained a sporadic correspondence.

Still in the north, Paulina had given birth to her first son and revealed in her letters her satisfaction with married life. Feliciano Rodríguez de Santa Cruz, richer by the day if what people said was true, had turned out to be a very unusual husband. He was convinced that the boldness Paulina had shown in running away from the convent and defying her family to marry him should not be diluted in domestic chores but should be used to their mutual benefit. His wife, educated as a lady, scarcely knew how to read or add but she had developed a true passion for business. At first Feliciano was amazed at her interest in learning details about the process of mining and transporting minerals, as well as the ups and downs of the stock exchange, but he had soon learned to respect his wife's uncommon intuition. Following her advice, only seven months after they were married he earned huge profits from speculations in sugar. Grateful, he gave her an ornate tea service of Peruvian silver that weighed nineteen kilos. Paulina, who was nearly immobilized by the bulk of their first child, waved off the gift without looking up from the booties she was knitting.

"I would rather you opened an account in my name in the Bank of London, and from now on deposit twenty percent of the profits I earn for you."

"Why? Don't I give you everything you want, and more?" asked Feliciano, offended.

"Life is long and filled with unpleasant surprises. I do not ever want to be a penniless widow, especially not with children," she explained, rubbing her belly.

Feliciano slammed the door as he left, but his innate sense of fairness was stronger than his aggrieved husband's bad humor. Besides, he decided, that twenty percent would be a powerful incentive for Paulina. He did as she asked even though he had never heard of a married woman with money of her own. If a wife could not travel, sign legal documents, go to court, sell or buy anything without her husband's authorization, certainly it didn't make sense for her to have a bank account to use however she wished. It would be difficult to explain to the bank and to his associates.

"Come back north with us, the future is in the mines and there you can begin all over again," Paulina suggested to Jacob Todd when in one of her brief visits to Valparaíso she learned that he had fallen into disgrace.

"What would I do there, my friend," he murmured.

"Sell your Bibles," Paulina joked, but moved immediately by the other's inconsolable sadness offered him her house, her friendship, and a job in her husband's various enterprises.

Todd, however, was so dejected by his bad luck and public shame that he could not find the strength to begin another adventure in the north. The curiosity and restlessness that had once driven him had been replaced by an obsession to regain the good name he had lost.

"I am ruined, señora, can't you see it? A man without honor is a dead man."

"Times have changed," Paulina consoled him. "Once a stain on a woman's honor could be washed away only with blood. But you see, Mr. Todd, in my case it was cleansed with a pitcher of hot chocolate. And men's honor is much more resilient than ours. Do not despair."

Feliciano Rodríguez de Santa Cruz, who had not forgotten Todd's role in the period of his and Paulina's frustrated love, wanted to lend him enough money to return every last penny for the missions, but Todd decided that between owing money to a friend and owing a Protestant chaplain he preferred the latter, since his reputation was destroyed anyway. Soon thereafter he had to tell the cats and the tarts good-bye because the English widow who ran his boardinghouse asked him to leave, all the while shouting an unending stream of reproaches. The good woman had doubled her efforts in the kitchen to help spread her faith in those regions of immutable winter where spectral winds howled day and night—as Jacob Todd had described them, drunk with eloquence. When she learned the fate of her savings at the hand of the false missionary, she fell into a righteous rage and threw him out of her home. With the help of Joaquín Andieta, who had found other lodgings for him, Todd moved to a room—small but with a view of the sea—in one of the modest neighborhoods of the port. The house belonged to a Chilean family and did not have the European pretensions of his former chambers; it was built according to tradition: whitewashed adobe and red tile roof, entry hall, one large room nearly bare of furniture that served as living room, dining room, and bedroom for the parents, a smaller, windowless room where all the children slept, and the room at the rear that he rented. The owner worked as a schoolmaster, and his wife contributed to their income by making candles in the kitchen. The scent of wax permeated the house. Todd smelled that sweetish aroma in his books, his clothing, his hair, even his soul; it was so deep in his pores that many years later, on the other side of the world, he could still smell candles. He kept to the poor sections of the port where no one cared about the reputation, good *or* bad, of a red-haired Englishman. He ate in taverns that catered to the poor and spent entire days among the fishermen, working on their nets and boats. The physical exercise did him good and for a few hours he could forget his injured pride. Only Joaquín Andieta continued to visit him. They would lock themselves in Todd's room to argue politics and exchange texts of French philosophers while on the other side of the door the schoolmaster's children ran around and the wax of the candles flowed like a thread of molten gold. Joaquín Andieta never referred to the money for the missions, although considering that the scandal was a lively topic of discussion for weeks, he had to have known. When Todd tried to explain that it had never been his intention to steal and that everything was the result of his bad head for figures, his proverbial disarray, and his abominable luck, Joaquín Andieta put a finger to his lips in the universal gesture for silence. In an impulse of shame and affection, Jacob Todd clumsily threw his arms around Andieta and his friend embraced him for an instant but then abruptly dropped his arms, flushed to his ear tips. Both stepped back simultaneously, unable to comprehend how they could have violated the elementary rule of conduct that forbade physical contact between men, except in battle or brutal sports. In the following months the Englishman began to wander off course; he was careless in his appearance and tended to go about unshaven, smelling of candle wax and alcohol. When he overdid the gin, he ranted like a maniac, without pausing or taking a breath, against governments, the English royal family, the military and the police, the system of class privilege, which he compared to the caste system in India, religion in general, and Christianity in particular.

"You need to get out of here, Mr. Todd, you're losing touch," Joaquín Andieta found the courage to tell his friend the day he rescued him just as he was about to be led from the plaza by the civil police.

It was exactly like that, railing like a lunatic on a street corner, that Todd was found by Captain John Sommers, who had debarked from his sailing ship in the port several weeks before. His vessel had taken such a beating in the trip around Cape Horn that it had to be put in dry dock for major repairs. John Sommers had spent an entire month in the home of his brother and sister, Jeremy and Rose. That had decided him; as soon as he returned to England he would look for a place on one of the modern steamships; he was not eager to repeat the experience of being cooped up with his family. He loved Jeremy and Rose, but preferred them at a distance. He had resisted the idea of steam until then because he could not conceive of the adventure of the sea without the challenges of sails and weather, challenges that tested the stuff the captain was made of, but he had to admit finally that the future lay in the new ships, larger, surer, and quicker. When he noticed that he was losing his hair, he naturally blamed it on a sedentary life. Soon boredom began to weigh on him like a suit of armor, and he escaped from the house to walk through the port with the restlessness of a caged animal. When Jacob Todd recognized the captain, he turned down the brim of his hat to save himself the humiliation of another rebuff and pretended not to see him, but the sailor stopped short and greeted him with affectionate claps on the back.

"Let's go drown our sorrows, old friend!" he said, and dragged Todd to a nearby bar.

It happened to be one of those places known among its clients for an honest drink, and they also served a unique dish of well-deserved fame: fried conger eel with potatoes and raw-onion salad. Todd, who tended those days to forget about eating, and was always short of money, thought he might faint when he smelled the delicious aroma of the food. A wave of gratitude and pleasure brought tears to his eyes. Out of courtesy, John Sommers looked away as his friend devoured every last crumb on his plate.

"I never did think that business of missions among the Indians was a good idea," he said, just as Todd was beginning to wonder if the captain had heard about his financial disgrace. "Those poor people don't deserve the misery of being evangelized. What do you plan to do now?"

"I returned what I had left in the account, but I still owe a large sum."

"And no way to pay it, right?"

"Not at the moment, no, but—"

"But nothing, my good fellow. You gave those good Christians an excuse to feel virtuous and now you've given them a scandal to chew on for a while. Entertainment cheap at the price. When I asked you what you plan to do I was referring to the future, not your debts."

"I have no plans."

"Come back to England with me. There's no place here for you. How many foreigners are there in this port? Four derelicts, and they all know each other. Believe me, they will never leave you in peace. In England, on the other hand, you can get lost in the crowd."

Jacob Todd sat staring into the bottom of his glass with such a hopeless expression that the captain ripped loose with one of his hearty laughs.

"Don't tell me you're staying here on account of my sister, Rose!"

It was true. Todd would have found the general rejection a little easier to bear had Miss Rose demonstrated a whit of loyalty or understanding, but she had refused to receive him and had returned unopened the letters he had sent her hoping to clear his name. He never knew that his missives did not reach the hands of the person they were addressed to because Jeremy Sommers, violating the accord of mutual respect between him and his sister, had decided to protect her from her own soft heart and prevent her from committing some new and irreparable foolishness. The captain did not know that either, but he guessed the precautions Jeremy had taken and concluded that he himself would have done the same given the circumstances. The idea of the pathetic Bible salesman as an aspirant for his sister Rose's hand seemed unthinkable: for once he was in total agreement with Jeremy.

"Are my feelings about Miss Rose that obvious?" asked Jacob Todd, perturbed.

"Let us say they're no mystery, my friend."

"I fear that I cannot have the least hope that some day she will accept me . . ."

"I fear the same."

"Would you do me the enormous favor of interceding on my behalf, Captain? If Miss Rose would see me just once, I could explain to her—"

"Don't count on me to act as your go-between, Todd. If Rose returned your affection, you would know it by now. My sister is not at all timid, I assure you. I repeat, dear fellow, that the only thing left is for you to get out of this damned port; you'll be reduced to beggary if you stay here. My ship leaves in three days for Hong Kong, and from there to England. It will be a long trip but you are not in any hurry. Fresh air and hard work are infallible remedies for the stupidity of love. I should know that; I fall in love in every port and am cured as soon as I am back at sea."

"I don't have money for the passage."

"Then you will simply have to work as a sailor and play cards with me every evening. If you haven't forgotten those gambler's tricks you knew when I brought you to Chile three years ago, I expect you will strip me clean on the voyage."

A few days after that conversation, Jacob Todd boarded the ship much poorer than he had arrived. The one person who came to see him off was Joaquín Andieta. The somber youth had asked permission at work to be gone for an hour. He bid Jacob Todd good-bye with a firm handshake.

"We will see each other again, my friend," the Englishman said.

"I don't think so," replied the Chilean, who had a much clearer intuition of destiny.

Suitors

The definitive metamorphosis of Eliza took place two years after Jacob Todd's departure. From the angular little bug she had been in childhood she was transformed into a girl with soft curves and a delicate face. Under the tutelage of Miss Rose, she spent the unpleasant years of her puberty balancing a book on her head and studying piano, at the same time growing native herbs in Mama Fresia's garden and learning age-old recipes for curing known maladies and others yet to be learned, including mustard for an indifference to everyday life, hydrangea leaves for ripening tumors and restoring laughter, violets for enduring loneliness, and verbena, which she put in Miss Rose's soup because this noble plant cures the vagaries of bad humor. Miss Rose was unable to squelch her protégée's interest in cooking and finally resigned herself to watching her waste precious hours amid Mama Fresia's black cooking pots. Miss Rose considered culinary lore as an adornment to a young lady's education in that it prepared her for giving orders to the servants, as she herself did, but that was a far cry from plunging up to one's elbows in pans and skillets. A lady could not smell of garlic and onion, but Eliza preferred practice to theory and went to all their friends looking for recipes she copied in a notebook and then improved in their kitchen. She could spend entire days grinding spices and nuts for tortes or maize for Chilean cakes, dressing turtledoves for pickling and chopping fruit for preserves. By the time she was fourteen, she had surpassed Miss Rose's timid pastry skills and had learned all of Mama Fresia's repertory; at fifteen she was in charge of refreshments for the Wednesday musical evenings, and when local dishes were no longer a challenge she turned to the refined cuisine of the French, which Madame Colbert imparted, and the exotic spices of India, which her uncle John used to bring her and which she identified by smell although she didn't know their names. When the coachman took a message to one of the Sommers' friends, he delivered the envelope along with a treat fresh from the hands of Eliza, who had elevated the local custom of exchanging main dishes and desserts to the category of an art. So great was her dedication that Jeremy Sommers began to imagine her as the owner of her own tearoom, a project which, like all the others her brother had for the girl, Miss Rose discarded without a moment's consideration. A woman who earns her own living, however respectable the enterprise, descends on the social scale, she lectured. Her goal for Eliza was a good husband, and she had set a two-year limit for finding one in Chile; after that she would take Eliza to England, she could not run the risk of having her turn twenty without a fiancé and end up a spinster. The candidate would have to be someone willing to overlook her hazy origins and focus on her virtues. Among the Chileans, not a chance; the aristocracy married their cousins and she wasn't interested in the middle class, she did not want to see Eliza mired in penury. From time to time Rose had contact with impresarios in commerce or the mines who had business with her brother Jeremy, but those men were after the family names and coats of arms of the oligarchy. It was not likely they would be taken with Eliza because there was little in her physical appearance to spark passion: she was small and slender and did not have the milky-white skin or the opulent bust and hips so much in vogue. It was only when you looked at her a second time that you discovered her quiet beauty, her grace, and the intensity in her eyes; she looked like one of the porcelain dolls Captain John Sommers brought from China. Miss Rose was looking for a suitor able to appreciate her protégée's discernment, her strength of character, and her ability to turn situations in her favor, what Mama Fresia called luck and Rose preferred to call intelligence. She was looking for a man with economic solvency and good character who would offer Eliza security and respect, but one her adopted daughter could manage without any fuss. She planned in due time to teach her the subtle discipline of the everyday attentions that nourish the habit of domestic life in a man, the system of daring caresses that reward him and stubborn silences that punish him, secrets for melting his will that she herself had never had occasion to practice, and, of course, the millennial art of physical love. She had never dared speak of that to Eliza but she had several books under double lock and key in her armoire that she would lend her when the moment came. Everything can be said in writing, that was her theory, and in matters of theory no one was wiser than she. Miss Rose, though an old maid, could have taught a graduate course on all the possible and impossible ways to make love.

"You should adopt Eliza legally so that she can claim our name," she told her brother Jeremy.

"She has used it for years, Rose, what more do you want?"

"I want her to be able to marry with her head held high."

"Marry whom?"

Miss Rose did not tell him at that moment but she already had someone in mind. It was Michael Steward, twenty-eight years old, an officer in the English fleet anchored in the port of Valparaíso. She had found out through her brother John that the sailor came from an old family. They would not look fondly on the marriage of their oldest son and only heir to a girl who had no name and no fortune and furthermore lived in some godforsaken country they had never heard of. It was indispensable for Eliza to be provided with an appealing dowry and for Jeremy to adopt her, that way at least the question of her origins would not stand in the way.

Michael Steward had an athletic bearing, an innocent, blue-eyed gaze, blond sideburns and mustache, good teeth, and an aristocratic nose. The weak chin robbed him of perfection and Miss Rose hoped to speak to him in private and suggest that he disguise it by letting his beard grow. According to Captain Sommers, the youth was a model of morality and his impeccable service record guaranteed him a brilliant career in the navy. In Miss Rose's eyes, the fact that he spent so much time at sea would be a great plus for whoever married him. The more she thought about it, the more she was convinced she had found the ideal man, but she knew that given Eliza's nature, she would not accept him for the sake of convenience, she would have to love him. There was hope: the man looked handsome in his uniform, and no one had yet seen him without it.

"Steward is a dunce who happens to have good manners. Eliza would die of boredom married to him," Captain John Sommers protested when Rose told him of her plans.

"All husbands are boring, John. No woman with an ounce of sense gets married to be entertained, she marries to be maintained."

Eliza still looked like a little girl, but her education was complete and soon she would be ready to marry. There was some time left, Miss Rose concluded, but she must act decisively so that a more quick-witted girl did not snatch away the candidate. Once her mind was made up, she concentrated on the task of attracting the officer, using every tactic she could imagine. She scheduled her musical gatherings to coincide with the dates of Michael Steward's shore leaves, with no consideration for her other guests, who for years had saved Wednesday for that sacred engagement. Annoyed, some stopped coming. Which was precisely what Rose had hoped; she was able to transform the placid musicales into lively dancing and replenish the guest list to include young bachelors and marriageable girls from the foreign colony, replacing the tedious Ebelings, Scotts, and Appelgreens who were turning into fossils. The poetry and voice recitals gave way to parlor games, informal balls, contests of wit, and charades. She organized complex picnics and beach outings. They would set off in coaches, preceded at dawn by heavy carts with leather floors and straw canopies and carrying servants charged with setting out countless luncheon baskets beneath tents and parasols. Stretching before them were fertile valleys planted with fruit trees and grapes, wheat and corn fields, the steep coastline where the Pacific Ocean exploded into clouds of foam, and, in the distance, the snowy cordillera profiled starkly against the sky. Somehow Miss Rose would arrange things so Eliza and Steward traveled in the same carriage, sat together, and were partners in the ball games and pantomimes, but in cards and dominos she separated them because Eliza stoutly refused to let anyone beat her.

"You must allow the man to feel superior, child," Miss Rose patiently explained.

"That is very difficult," Eliza, unmoved, responded.

Jeremy Sommers could do nothing to stop his sister's sea swell of expenses. She bought fabrics wholesale and kept two of the maids sewing all day, copying the latest dresses from magazines. She spent far more than was reasonable with the sailors who smuggled contraband, so they would never lack perfumes, Turkish rouge, belladonna and kohl for the mystery of the eyes, and cream made from crushed pearls for blanching the skin. For the first time she could not find time to write, turning all her attention to treats for the English officer, including biscuits and preserves for him to take to sea, everything made in their home and presented in beautiful jars.

"Eliza prepared this for you, but she is too shy to give it to you personally," she would tell Steward, not adding that Eliza cooked anything she was asked to, never questioning whom it was for, and was inevitably surprised when he thanked her.

Michael Steward was not oblivious to the campaign of seduction. Sparing with words, he expressed his thanks in brief, formal letters on navy stationery, and showed up with bouquets when on shore. He had studied the language of flowers, but that refinement fell on barren ground because neither Miss Rose nor anyone in Valparaíso, at that distance from England, had heard of the difference between a rose and a carnation, much less suspected the significance of the color of the ribbon. Steward's efforts to find flowers that gradually grew more intense in color, from pale rose through all shades of pink to the deepest crimson to indicate his growing passion, were entirely wasted. With time, the officer learned to overcome his timidity, and from the painful silence that characterized him in the beginning he passed to a chattiness that made his listeners squirm. Euphorically, he expounded his moral opinions on insignificant topics and often lost himself in pointless comments on the subject of ocean currents and navigation charts. Where he truly shone was in rough sports, which showed off his daring and his muscular build. Miss Rose encouraged him to perform acrobatics, hanging from a tree branch in the garden, and even, after a certain insistence, to delight them with the heel taps, knee bends, and somersaults of a Ukrainian dance he had learned from another sailor. Miss Rose applauded it all with exaggerated enthusiasm, while Eliza watched, silent and serious, without offering her opinion. Weeks went by while Michael Steward weighed and measured the consequences of the step he wanted to take and communicated by letter with his father to discuss his plans. The inevitable delays of the post prolonged his uncertainty for several months. This was, after all, the most serious decision of his life, and it took more courage to face it than fighting any and all potential enemies of the British empire throughout the Pacific. Finally, during one of the musical soirées, after a hundred rehearsals before his mirror, he succeeded in gathering the courage that had been rapidly melting away and steadying a voice that fluted with fear to corner Miss Rose in a corridor.

"I must speak with you in private," he whispered.

Miss Rose led him into her sewing room. She suspected what she was going to hear and was surprised at her own emotions; her cheeks were burning and her heart was racing. She tucked back a strand of hair that had escaped her bun and discreetly wiped the perspiration from her brow. Michael Steward thought he had never seen her so beautiful.

"I believe you have already divined what I want to tell you, Miss Rose."

"Divining is dangerous, Mr. Steward. I am listening . . ."

"It regards my sentiments. I am sure you know what I am referring to. I wish to prove to you that my intentions are of the most honorable and irreproachable seriousness."

"I expect no less from a person like yourself. Do you believe that your feelings are reciprocated?"

"That is s-s-s-something only you can answer," the young officer stuttered.

They stood looking at one another, she with her eyebrows raised expectantly and he fearing the roof would crash down on his head. Determined to act before the magic of the moment turned to ash, the gallant took Miss Rose by the shoulders and bent down to kiss her. Frozen with surprise, Miss Rose could not move. She felt the officer's moist lips and soft mustache on her mouth, unable to imagine how the devil things had gone so wrong, and when finally she could react, she pushed him away violently.

"What are you doing!" she exclaimed, wiping her mouth with the back of her hand. "Can't you see that I am much, much older than you!"

"What does age m-matter?" the officer stammered, confounded, because in truth he had thought that Miss Rose was no more than twenty-seven.

"How dare you! Have you lost your senses?"

"But you . . . you led me to believe . . . I cannot be so mistaken!" the poor man mumbled, stupefied with embarrassment.

"I want you for Eliza, not myself," Miss Rose sputtered with fright, and bolted out the door to run and lock herself in her room, while the hapless suitor asked for his cape and cap and left without a word to anyone, never to return to that house.

From a corner of the hallway, Eliza had heard everything through the half-open door of the sewing room. She, too, had been confused by the attentions to the officer. Miss Rose had always shown such indifference to potential suitors that she was used to thinking of her as an old woman. Only in recent months, as she watched her devote body and soul to games of seduction, had she become aware of her protector's magnificent bearing and luminous skin. She had thought Miss Rose was head over heels in love with Michael Steward and it had never crossed her mind that the bucolic picnics beneath the Japanese parasols and the butter biscuits to ease the discomforts of life at sea had been her protector's stratagem for snagging the officer and delivering him to her on a platter. The idea struck like a dagger to her heart—it took her breath away—because the last thing in this world she wanted was a marriage arranged behind her back. She had just been caught up in the whirlwind of her first love and had sworn, with irrevocable fervor, that she would never marry another.

Eliza Sommers saw Joaquín Andieta for the first time one Friday in the May of 1848 when he came to the house overseeing a cart pulled by several mules and loaded to the top with crates belonging to the British Import and Export Company, Ltd. Packed inside were Persian carpets, crystal chandeliers, and a collection of ivory figurines Feliciano Rodríguez de Santa Cruz had ordered to decorate the mansion he had built in the north, precious cargo that was at risk in the port and safer stored in the Sommers' home until time to forward it to its destination. If the rest of the trip was overland, Jeremy hired men to guard the treasures, but in this case he would route them by way of a Chilean schooner scheduled to sail in a week's time. Andieta was wearing his one suit, out of style, dark, and threadbare, and he had no hat or umbrella. His funereal pallor contrasted with his flashing eyes and his black hair gleamed with moisture from an early autumn mist. Miss Rose went out to meet him, and Mama Fresia, who always carried the keys to the house on a large ring at her waist, led him to the storeroom in the back patio. The youth organized the peons in a long line and they transported the crates from man to man down rugged terrain, up twisting stairs, across superfluous terraces, and through unvisited bowers. As Andieta counted, marked, and recorded in his notebook, Eliza made use of her ability to make herself invisible and watched him at her leisure. Two months before, she had turned sixteen and she was ready for love. As she watched Joaquín Andieta's long ink-stained fingers and heard his voice—deep, but at the same time clear and cool as a flowing brook—issuing brusque orders to the peons, she was shaken to her bones and an overpowering urge to be close enough to smell him forced her from her hiding place behind the potted palms. Mama Fresia, grumbling because the mules had fouled the front entry, and busy with her keys, didn't notice, but out of the corner of her eye Miss Rose caught a glimpse of the girl's flushed face. She didn't think much about it; in her eyes her brother's employee was a cipher, barely a shadow among the many shadows of that cloudy day. Eliza disappeared into the kitchen and after a few minutes returned with glasses and a pitcher of honey-sweetened orange juice. For the first time in her life, this girl who had spent years balancing a book on her head without giving it a thought was conscious of how she walked, the swaying of her hips, the undulation of her body, the angle of her arms, the distance between her shoulders and chin. She wanted to be as beautiful as Miss Rose when she had been the splendid young woman who'd rescued her from her improvised cradle in a Marseilles soap crate; she wanted to sing with the nightingale-sweet voice of Miss Appelgreen when she warbled her Scots ballads; she wanted to dance with the impossible lightness of her dance instructor; and she wanted to die right there, pierced by the sensation, sharp and no more to be denied than a sword, that was filling her mouth with warm blood and, even before she could identify it, crushing her with the terrible weight of idealized love. Many years later, standing before a human head preserved in a jar of gin, Eliza would remember that first meeting with Joaquín Andieta and again experience the same unbearable anguish. She would ask herself a thousand times along the way whether she had had a chance to flee from the devastating passion that would warp her life, whether maybe in those brief instants she could have turned away and saved herself, but every time she formulated the question she concluded that her fate had been determined since the beginning of time. And when the sage Tao Chi'en introduced her to the poetic possibility of reincarnation, she convinced herself that the same drama was repeated in each of her lives; if she had been born a thousand times before and had to be born a thousand times again in the future, she would always come into the world with the mission of loving that same man in the same way. There was no escape for her. But then Tao Chi'en taught her the magical formulas for untangling the knots of karma and freeing herself from forever repeating the same harrowing uncertainty of love in every incarnation.

That day in May, Eliza placed the tray on a bench and offered the cooling drink first to the laborers—in order to gain time while she controlled her shaking knees and won the battle that was mulishly paralyzing her chest and blocking her breathing—and only then to Joaquín Andieta who, absorbed in his task, barely looked up when she handed him the glass. When he did, Eliza moved as close to him as she could, calculating the direction of breeze so it would carry the scent of this man who, she was sure, was hers. With her eyes half closed, she inhaled the aroma of damp clothing, common soap, and fresh sweat. A river of flowing lava swept through her, melting her bones; and in an instant of panic she believed that she was actually dying. Those seconds were so intense that Joaquín Andieta's notebook dropped from his hands, as if some irresistible force had seized it from him, as that same glowing heat washed over him, searing him in its reflection. He looked at Eliza without seeing her; the girl's face was a pale mirror in which he thought he glimpsed his own image. He had only a vague idea of her size and of a dark aureole of hair, but it would not be until their second meeting a few days later that he would sink into the perdition of her black eyes and the watery grace of her gestures. Both stooped down at the same time to pick up the notebook; their shoulders bumped and the contents of the glass splashed onto her dress.

"Watch what you're doing, Eliza!" Miss Rose exclaimed, alarmed, because the force of that instantaneous love had struck her as well.

"Go and change your dress and rinse that one in cold water to see if you can get the stain out," she added sharply.

Eliza, however, did not move, locked to Joaquín Andieta's eyes, trembling, nostrils dilated, unabashedly sniffing, until Miss Rose took her by one arm and led her inside.

"I told you, child; any man, as miserable a man as he may be, can do whatever he wants with you," the Indian reminded her that night.

"I don't know what you're talking about, Mama Fresia," Eliza replied.

That autumn morning when she saw Joaquín Andieta in the patio of her home, Eliza thought she had met her destiny: she would be his slave forever. Although she hadn't lived enough to understand what had happened to her, to express in words the tumult that was drowning her, or to work out a plan, her intuition of the inevitable was fully functional. In some vague but painful way she realized she was trapped, and suffered a physical reaction not unlike the epizootic. For a week, until she saw Andieta again, she tried to fight off convulsive upsets that would not yield to Mama Fresia's miraculous herbs or to the German pharmacist's arsenic powders in cherry liqueur. She lost weight and her bones became as light as a turtledove's, to the terror of Mama Fresia, who went around closing windows to prevent the ocean wind from lifting her up and sweeping her away toward the horizon. The Indian administered various remedies and spells from her vast repertoire, but when she realized that nothing was taking effect she turned to Catholic saintdom. She collected some of her pitiful savings from the bottom of her trunk, bought a dozen candles, and set off to negotiate with the priest. After having the candles blessed during Sunday high mass, she lighted one before each of the saints in the side altars of the church, eight in all, and placed three before the image of Saint Anthony, patron of hopeless, unwed girls, unhappy wives, and other lost causes. The remaining candle she took with her, along with a lock of Eliza's hair and one of her nightdresses, to the most celebrated *machi* in the area, an ancient Mapuche Indian, blind from birth, a white-magic witch famous for her etched-in-stone predictions and her common sense in curing bodily ills and anxieties of the soul. Mama Fresia had spent her adolescent years serving this woman as her apprentice and servant, but she had not, as she had wished, been able to follow in her footsteps because she did not have the gift. Nothing to do for it: you are born with it or you're not. Once she had tried to explain to Eliza what the gift was and the only thing that came to her was that it was the ability to see what lies behind mirrors. Lacking that mysterious talent, Mama Fresia had to renounce her aspiration to be a healer and take a place in the service of the Sommers family.

The *machi* lived alone at the bottom of a ravine in a straw-roofed adobe hovel that looked about to cave in. Around the dwelling was a wasteland of rocks, firewood, plants in chamber pots, skin-and-bones dogs, and huge black birds futilely scratching the dirt for something to eat. Along the path to her hut was a small forest of offerings and amulets left there by satisfied clients to indicate the favors they had received. The *machi* smelled of the sum of all the concoctions she had prepared during her lifetime; her mantle was the color of the dry earth of the landscape; she was barefoot and filthy, but she was laden with a profusion of cheap silver necklaces. Her face was a dark mask of wrinkles; she had only two teeth in her head and her eyes were dead. She received her former disciple without any sign of recognition, accepted the gifts of food and the bottle of anise liquor, signaled Mama Fresia to sit before her, and sat in silence, waiting. A few sticks flickered reluctantly in the center of the hut, the smoke escaping through a hole in the roof. The soot-blackened walls were studded with clay and tin trifles, plants, and a collection of desiccated reptiles.

The heavy fragrance of dried herbs and medicinal barks blended with the stink of dead animals. The two women spoke in Mapudungo, the language of the Mapuches. For a long time, the witch woman listened to the story of Eliza, from the moment of her arrival in the Marseilles soap crate to the recent crisis; then she took the candle, the hair, and the nightdress, and sent her visitor away with instructions to come back after she had completed her spells and rituals of divination.

"Everyone knows there's no cure for this," she pronounced as soon as Mama Fresia stepped across her threshold two days later.

"Is my baby going to die, then?"

"That I cannot say, but she will suffer, oh that I do not doubt."

"What is it she has?

"She has a fixation on love. Strong trouble. That girl left her window open one clear night and it crawled into her body while she was asleep. There's no spell can cure it."

Resigned, Mama Fresia went back home. If the art of that all-wise *machi* could not change Eliza's fate, then the little she knew, and all her saints' candles, were not going to help.

Miss Rose

Miss Rose kept an eye on Eliza with more curiosity than compassion; she knew the symptoms well and, in her experience, time and obstacles extinguish even the most stubborn fires of love. She had been barely sixteen when she'd fallen head over heels in love with a Viennese tenor. She was living in England at that time, and dreamed of being a diva despite the stubborn opposition of her mother and her brother Jeremy, who had been head of the family since their father's death. Neither of them considered the opera to be a desirable occupation for a lady, principally because it was performed in theaters, at night, and wearing low-cut gowns. Nor could she count on the support of her brother John, who had joined the navy and showed up at home barely a couple of times a year, always in a rush. Exuberant and tanned by the sun of far-off lands and exhibiting some new tattoo or scar, he would always manage to disrupt the routines of the small family. He handed out gifts, dazzled them with his exotic tales, and immediately disappeared into the red-light district, where he stayed until the moment to ship out again. The Sommers were country gentry without any great ambitions. They had owned land for several generations, but the father, bored with dumb sheep and poor harvests, had wanted to try his fortunes in London. He loved books so much that he was quite capable of depriving his family of food and going into debt to acquire first editions signed by his favorite authors, but he lacked the greed of dyed-in-the-wool collectors. After fruitless ventures into commerce, he decided to give rein to his true vocation, and ended by opening a shop for antiquarian books and others he published himself. In the back of the bookstore he set up a small press, which he operated with the help of two assistants, and in an upstairs room of the same shop his trade in rare books grew at a snail's pace. Of his three children, only Rose shared his interests; she grew up with a passion for music and reading, and when she was not sitting at the piano or doing her voice exercises they could find her in a corner reading. Her father lamented that Rose was the one who loved books and not Jeremy or John, who could have inherited his business. At his death, the male heirs liquidated the press and bookshop. John went off to sea and Jeremy took over the care of his widowed mother and his sister. He earned a modest salary as an employee of the British Import and Export Company, Ltd., and had a small income from his father, in addition to his brother John's sporadic contributions, which often arrived in the form of contraband instead of negotiable currency. Jeremy, scandalized, would store those accursed boxes in the garret, unopened, until the next visit of his brother, who then took responsibility for selling the contents. The family moved to modest chambers that were expensive for their means but well situated in the heart of London. Jeremy considered it a good investment; they must marry Rose well.

At sixteen, the girl's beauty began to flower and there were suitors to spare, well placed and prepared to die of love, but while her friends busied themselves looking for husbands, Rose was looking for a singing master. Which was how she met Karl Bretzner, a Viennese tenor who had come to London to perform in several Mozart works, which were to culminate one stellar night in *The Marriage of Figaro* with the royal family in attendance. Bretzner's appearance revealed nothing of his enormous talent: he looked like a butcher. His physique—barrel-chested but thin in the pins—lacked elegance, and his ruddy face, topped with a mass of salt-and-pepper curls, added up to a rather vulgar whole, but when he opened his mouth to delight the world with the torrent of his voice he was transformed into a different creature: he grew taller, his potbelly was sucked up into the cavern of his chest, and his Teutonic, apoplectic face was filled with Olympic light. At least that was how he was seen by Rose Sommers, who was able to get tickets for every performance. She would come to the theater long before it opened and, defying the scandalized glances of passersby little accustomed to seeing a girl of her class unaccompanied, wait at the actor's entrance for hours to catch a glimpse of the maestro getting out of his carriage. On Sunday night, the man noticed the beauty stationed in the street, and went over to speak to her. Trembling, she answered his questions and confessed her admiration for him and her wishes to follow in his footsteps in the arduous but divine path of bel canto—to use her words.

"Come to my dressing room after the performance and we shall see what I can do for you," he said in his precious, strongly Austrian-accented voice.

And that she did, walking on air. When the standing ovation faded, an usher sent by Karl Bretzner led Rose behind the wings. She had never seen the inner workings of a theater but she wasted no time admiring the ingenious machines for making storms or the painted landscapes on the drops; her only goal was to meet her idol. She found him enveloped in a gold-trimmed, royal-blue dressing gown, still wearing his makeup and an elaborate wig of white curls. The usher closed the door and left them alone. The room, crammed with mirrors, furniture, and draperies, smelled of tobacco, stage makeup, and mold. In one corner stood a screen painted with scenes of rosy-fleshed women in a Turkish harem and costumes on clothes racks lined the walls. Seeing her idol so near, Rose's enthusiasm flagged for a few moments, but he soon regained the lost ground. He took her hands in his, lifted them to his lips, and kissed them slowly, then from deep in his chest voiced a *do* that rattled the screen of the odalisques. Rose's last hesitations crumbled, like the walls of Jericho, in the cloud of powder that rose from the wig as the artist peeled it from his head with a passionate, virile gesture and tossed it upon a chair where it lay as inert as a dead rabbit. His hair was crushed beneath a tightly knit hair net that, added to the makeup, lent him the air of an aged courtesan.

Upon the same chaise longue where the wig had landed, Rose would offer Bretzner her virginity a couple of days afterward, at exactly three-fifteen in the afternoon. The Viennese tenor had made a date with her, using the pretext of showing her the theater that Tuesday when there was no performance. They met secretly in a tearoom, where he delicately savored five cream éclairs and two cups of chocolate while she stirred her tea, so frightened and excited she couldn't swallow. From there they went straight to the theater. At that hour there was no one around but two women cleaning the foyer and a man readying the oil lamps, torches, and candles for the following day. Karl Bretzner, skilled in the perils of love, produced a bottle of champagne with a magician's dexterity and poured each of them a glass, which they drank down in a toast to Mozart and Rossini. He then installed Rose in the imperial plush box where only the king sat, every inch of which was adorned with chubby cupids and overblown roses, then went down to the stage. Standing on a segment of painted plaster column, lighted by the foot lamps, he sang for her alone an aria from *The Barber of Seville*, displaying all his vocal agility and the soft delirium of his voice with endless embellishments. As the last note of his homage faded he heard the distant sobs of Rose Sommers; with unexpected agility he ran toward her; crossing the hall, he gained the box in two bounds and fell to his knees at her feet. Breathless, he laid his large head upon the girl's skirt, burying his face in folds of moss-colored silk. He wept with her because, without intending it, he, too, had fallen in love; what had begun as yet another fleeting conquest had in a few hours been transformed into incandescent passion.

Rose and Karl got to their feet, supporting one another, stumbling, terrified before the inevitable, and with no idea how, they walked down a long corridor in darkness, climbed a short staircase, and reached the area of the dressing rooms. The cursive letters of the tenor's name marked one of the doors. They went into the room cluttered with furniture and dusty, sweaty costumes where they had been alone for the first time only two days before. The room had no windows and for a moment they sank into the refuge of darkness, recovering breath lost in sobs and sighs while he lighted first a match and then the five candles of a candelabrum. In the trembling yellow light of the flames they admired one another, confused and clumsy, filled with a torrent of emotions but unable to articulate a single word. Rose could not withstand the eyes stripping her bare and hid her face in her hands, but he pulled them away with the same delicacy he had earlier used to demolish the cream pastries. They began with tiny, tear-wet kisses, dove pecks, which developed naturally into serious kisses. Rose had experienced tender, but very hesitant and hasty, encounters with some of her suitors, and one or two of them had managed to brush her cheek with his lips, but she had never imagined it possible to reach such a degree of intimacy that another's tongue could wind around hers like a lewd snake or that she could be slathered with someone else's saliva externally and invaded internally, but her initial repugnance was soon conquered by the stimulus of youth and her enthusiasm for the lyrical. Not only did she return Bretzner's caresses with equal intensity, she took the initiative by removing her hat and the short gray karakul cape around her shoulders. From there to allowing him to unbutton her jacket, and then her blouse, was but a few capitulations. She was able to follow the mating dance step by step, guided by instinct as well as the forbidden books she had furtively pulled from her father's shelves. That was the most memorable day of her life, and she would remember it—adorned and exaggerated—in the most minute detail in the years to come. That was to be her source of experience and knowledge, the fount of inspiration for nourishing her fantasies and, years later, for creating the art that would make her famous in certain very secret circles. That marvelous day she could compare in intensity with only one other, two years later in Valparaíso, in March, when the newborn Eliza fell into her arms as consolation for the children she would never have, for the men she would never love, and for the hearth she would never call hers.

The Viennese tenor turned out to be a very refined lover. He loved and knew women to their marrow, but he was able to erase from his memory the relics of past loves, the frustrations of multiple farewells, the jealousies, disasters, and deceptions of other relationships and give himself with complete innocence to his brief passion for Rose Sommers. His experience had not come from pathetic embraces with squalid whores; Bretzner prided himself on never having had to pay for pleasure because women of varied station, from humble chambermaids to arrogant countesses, gave themselves to him unconditionally after they heard him sing. He learned the arts of love at the same time he learned those of singing. He was ten when he fell in love with the person who was to be his mentor, a Frenchwoman, old enough to be his mother, with the eyes of a tigress and breasts of pure alabaster. She, in turn, had been initiated at the age of thirteen, in France, by Donatien-Alphonse-François de Sade. Daughter of a gaoler in the Bastille, she had met the famous marquis in the filthy cell in which he wrote his perverse stories by the light of a candle. She used to watch him through the bars with a child's simple curiosity, unaware that her father had sold her to the prisoner in exchange for a gold watch, the impoverished noble's last possession. One morning when she was peering through the peephole in the cell door, her father took the large ring of keys from his waist, opened the door, and, as one feeds a lion his prey, with a push thrust the girl into the cell. What happened there she could not remember; it was enough to know that she stayed with de Sade, following him from gaol to the worse poverty of freedom, learning everything he had to teach her. When in 1802 the marquis was locked up in the madhouse of Charenton, she was left on her own without a centime but with a vast storehouse of amatory wisdom that helped her win a husband fifty-two years older than she, and very wealthy. He died not long after, exhausted by the excesses of his young wife, and she finally was free and with money to do whatever she wished. She was thirty-four years old; she had survived her brutal apprenticeship at the side of the marquis, the poverty of bread crusts in her childhood, the turmoil of the French Revolution, the terror of the Napoleonic wars, and now she had to put up with the dictatorial repression of the empire. She had had enough, her spirit yearned for a truce. She decided to look for a safe place to spend the rest of her days in peace, and chose Vienna. It was during this period in her life that she met Karl Bretzner, her neighbors' son; he was barely ten, but even by then he was singing like a nightingale in the cathedral choir. Thanks to her, now the friend and confidante of the Bretzners, the boy was not, as the choir director had recommended, castrated that year to preserve his cherubic voice.

"Do not touch him, and before you know it he will be the best-paid tenor in Europe," she predicted. She was not mistaken.

Despite the enormous discrepancy in age, an unusual relationship developed between the woman and the young Karl. She admired the boy's purity of sentiment and his dedication to music; in her he found the muse who not only saved his manhood but also taught him to use it. By the time his voice had changed and he had begun to shave, he had mastered the eunuch's proverbial talent in pleasing a woman in ways not foreseen by nature and custom, but with Rose Sommers he took no risks. No fierce assault in a flurry of overly daring caresses, for this was not a time to shock with tricks of the seraglio, he decided, never suspecting that in less than three practical lessons his student would surpass him in inventiveness. He was a man who was careful about details and he knew the hallucinatory power of *le mot juste* in the hour of love. With his left hand he undid one by one the small mother-of-pearl buttons down Rose's back while with the right he took the pins from her hair, never losing the rhythm of kisses interspersed with a stream of compliments. He spoke of the smallness of her waist, the pristine whiteness of her skin, the classic roundness of her throat and shoulders, all of which, he said, kindled a fire in him, an uncontrollable madness.

"I am deranged. I do not know what is happening to me, never have I, never shall I, love anyone as I do you. This is the miraculous meeting of two souls destined never to part," he murmured again and again.

He recited his entire repertoire, but without hypocrisy, deeply convinced of his own honesty and dazzled by Rose. He untied the strings of her corset and removed petticoats until she was wearing only her long batiste underdrawers and a sheer camisole that revealed the strawberries of her nipples. He did not remove her high-laced kid shoes with the curved heels or the white stockings fastened at her knees with embroidered garters. At that point he stopped, panting, with a planetary clamor in his breast, convinced that Rose Sommers was the most beautiful woman in the universe, an angel, and that his heart was going to explode and scatter him in pieces if he did not calm himself. He picked her up effortlessly, crossed the room, and stood her before a large mirror with a golden frame. The winking light of the candles and the theatrical wardrobe on the walls, a confusion of brocades, feathers, velvets, and faded laces, gave the scene an air of unreality.

Disarmed, drunk with emotion, Rose looked at herself in the mirror and did not recognize that woman in her undergarments, her hair wild and cheeks aflame, whom some man, also unrecognizable, was kissing on the neck as he greedily fondled her breasts. That avid interlude gave the tenor time to catch his breath and some of the lucidity he had lost during their preliminary skirmishes. He began taking off his clothes, facing the mirror, uninhibited, and—it must be said—looking much better out of his clothes than in them. He needs a good tailor, Rose thought. She had never seen a naked man, not even her brothers as children, and her information was based on overblown descriptions in the racy books and Japanese postcards she had discovered in her uncle John's luggage, in which the male organs were depicted in frankly optimistic proportions. The rosy, perky gherkin revealed before her eyes did not frighten her, as Karl Bretzner had feared, but instead provoked irrepressible and joyful giggles. And that set the tone for what followed. Instead of the solemn, rather doleful ceremony a deflowering can be, they pleasured themselves in playful caperings, chasing one another around the room, hopping over furniture like children; they drank the rest of the champagne and opened another bottle to spray one another with bubbling foam; risqué phrases rolled out with laughter, whispers brought oaths of love, as they bit and licked and frolicked in the bottomless tidal pool of newly discovered love, all through the afternoon and well into the night, without a thought for the time or for the rest of the universe.

Only they existed. The Viennese tenor led Rose to epic heights, and she, a diligent student, followed without hesitation and, once at the summit, took wing on her own with surprising natural talent, guided by signs and asking what she could not guess, dazzling her maestro and finally besting him with her improvised skills and the annihilating gift of her love. When they could bear to pull themselves apart and return to reality, the clock showed ten o'clock. The theater was empty, darkness ruled outside, and, to top everything off, a fog thick as meringue had settled in.

A frenetic exchange began between the lovers—notes, flowers, bonbons, copied verses, and small sentimental trinkets—that lasted as long as the season in London. They met where they could; passion caused them to lose all prudence. To gain time they looked for hotel rooms near the theater, indifferent to the possibility of being recognized. Rose escaped the house with ridiculous excuses, but her terrified mother said nothing to Jeremy of her suspicions, praying that her daughter's madness was temporary and would disappear without leaving a mark. Karl Bretzner came late to rehearsals, and from whipping off his clothes at any hour he caught a cold and missed two performances. Far from being sorry, he used the time for lovemaking enhanced by feverish chills. He would come to the rented room with flowers for Rose, champagne to drink and to bathe in, cream pastries, poems written on the fly to read in bed, aromatic oils to rub into places until then sealed, erotic books they paged through seeking the most inspiring scenes, ostrich feathers for tickling, and countless other props for their games. The girl felt that she was opening like a carnivorous flower, emitting demonic perfumes to attract her man like a Venus's-flytrap, crushing him, swallowing him, digesting him, and finally spitting out the splinters of his bones. She was suffused with unbearable energy, she was drowning, she could not sit quiet an instant, devoured with impatience. In the meantime, Karl Bretzner was floundering in confusion, at times uplifted to the point of frenzy, at others drained, trying to meet his musical obligations, but he was deteriorating in full view and the critics, implacable, said that Mozart whirled in his grave when he heard the Viennese tenor execute—literally—his compositions.

With panic the lovers watched the moment of parting draw near, and entered the phase of love obstructed. They discussed running away to Brazil or committing suicide together, but the possibility of marriage was never mentioned. In the end, the appetite for life was stronger than the temptation of tragedy, and after Bretzner's last performance they hired a carriage and traveled to a seaside hotel in the north of England. They had decided to enjoy a few days in anonymity before Karl Bretzner went ahead to Italy to honor his contracts. Rose would meet him in Vienna once he found appropriate lodgings, got settled, and sent money for the journey.

They were breakfasting beneath an awning on the terrace of their small hotel, legs covered with a wool blanket because of the sharp, cold air of the coast, when they were interrupted by Jeremy Sommers, indignant and solemn as a prophet. Rose had left such a clear trail that it had been easy for her older brother to follow and find her in this out-of-the-way resort. When she saw him, her cry was more one of surprise than fear, emboldened as she was by the tumult of her love. At that instant, she felt for the first time a sense of what she had done, and the weight of the consequences was revealed in all its magnitude. She rose to her feet, resolved to defend her right to live her life however she pleased, but her brother cut her off before she could speak, directing his remarks to the tenor.

"You owe my sister an explanation. I suppose you have not told her that you are married and that you have two children," he sputtered to the seducer.

That was the one thing Karl Bretzner had failed to tell Rose. They had talked themselves out; he had confessed even the most intimate details of previous love affairs, not overlooking the excesses of the Marquis de Sade that his mentor, the French woman with the eyes of a tiger, had described to him, because Rose had demonstrated a morbid curiosity to know when, with whom, and especially how he had made love, from the time he was ten until the day before he met her. And once he learned how much she liked listening to him and how she incorporated the information into her own theory and practice, he told her everything, without reservation. But of his wife and children he had said nothing, out of compassion for this beautiful virgin who had given herself to him unconditionally. He hadn't wanted to destroy the magic of that coming together: Rose Sommers deserved to enjoy her first love to the fullest.

"You owe me satisfaction," Jeremy Sommers challenged, slapping Bretzner across the face with his glove.

Karl Bretzner was a man of the world, and he had no intention of doing anything as barbaric as fight a duel. He understood that the moment had come for him to retreat, and he regretted not having a few moments in private to try to explain things to Rose. He did not want to leave her with a broken heart or with the idea that he had seduced her in bad conscience only to abandon her. He needed to tell her once more how much he truly loved her and that he was sorry he was not free to live out their dreams, but he saw on Jeremy Sommers' face that he would not allow that. Jeremy took the arm of his sister, who seemed stupefied, and led her firmly to the carriage, denying her the opportunity to say good-bye to her lover or to collect her few belongings. He drove her to the home of an aunt in Scotland, where she was to stay until her condition could be determined. If the worst happened, which was how Jeremy referred to a possible pregnancy, her life and the honor of the family would be forever besmirched.

"Not a word of this to anyone, not even to Mama or John, you understand?" were the only words he spoke during the journey.

Rose lived a few weeks of uncertainty, until she knew she was not pregnant. That brought a sigh of enormous relief, as if the heavens had absolved her. As atonement, she spent three months knitting for the poor, reading, and writing on the sly without shedding a single tear. During that time, she reflected on her fate and something shifted inside, because when she left her aunt's home she was a different person. Only Rose was aware of the change. She reappeared in London exactly as she had left, smiling, tranquil, interested in opera and literature, without a word of bitterness to Jeremy for having dragged her from the arms of her lover or of nostalgia for the man who had deceived her, Olympian in her posture of ignoring gossip and the mournful faces of her family. On the surface she seemed the same girl she had always been; not even her mother could find the chink in her perfect composure that would allow her a reproach or counsel. On the other hand, the widow was not in a situation to help or protect her daughter, a cancer was rapidly devouring her. The one modification in Rose's behavior was her fancy for spending hours closed in her room, writing. In her tiny hand she filled dozens of notebooks, which she kept under lock and key. As she never tried to post a letter, Jeremy Sommers, who feared nothing so much as ridicule, stopped worrying about the vice of writing and assumed that his sister had had the good judgment to forget the ill-omened Viennese tenor. Not only had she not forgotten him, however, she remembered with noonday clarity every detail of what had happened and each word he had spoken or whispered. The only thing she erased from her mind was the disenchantment of having been deceived. Karl Bretzner's wife and children simply disappeared, because they had never been given a place in the vast fresco of her memories of love.

Rose's retreat to her aunt's home in Scotland had not eliminated gossip, but as the rumors could not be confirmed, no one dared openly snub the family. One by one, the many suitors who had besieged Rose returned, but she sent them away, using the excuse of her mother's illness. Things kept quiet simply never happened, Jeremy Sommers maintained, eager to snuff out every vestige of that episode with silence. Rose's shameful escapade lived on in the limbo of things not given words, although at times the brother and sister made oblique references that kept their rancor alive but also united them in the shared secret. Years later, when it no longer mattered to anyone, Rose dared tell her brother John, with whom she had always played the role of the spoiled and innocent little girl. Shortly after the death of their mother, Jeremy Sommers was offered the directorship of the British Import and Export Company, Ltd. in Chile. He left with his sister, Rose, carrying the secret with them, intact, to the other side of the world.

They arrived in Valparaíso at the end of the winter of 1830, when that city was still a hamlet even though there were already European companies and families there. For Rose their destination was a punishment, and she assumed it stoically, resigned to pay for her misstep with that inescapable exile, though not allowing anyone, most of all her brother Jeremy, to suspect her desperation. Her discipline in not complaining and not talking, even in dreams, about her lost lover sustained her when she was beset with difficulties. They moved into the best available hotel, wanting to guard against winds and humidity because of an epidemic of diphtheria, which the local barbers combated with cruel and futile surgical interventions they performed with their razors. Spring, and then summer, somewhat improved Rose's bad impression of Chile. She determined to forget about London and make the best of her new surroundings, despite the provincial atmosphere and the sea winds that pierced one's bones on even the sunniest days. She convinced her brother, and he his office, of the need to acquire a decent house in the firm's name and to ship furniture from England. She presented it as a matter of authority and prestige: it was unthinkable that the representative of such an important office should be lodging in a rundown hotel. Eighteen months later, when baby Eliza came into their lives, brother and sister were living in a large house on Cerro Alegre. Miss Rose had relegated her former lover to a sealed compartment of her memory and was wholly dedicated to winning a prominent position in local society. In the following years, Valparaíso grew in size and was modernized at the same pace that Rose left her past behind to become the exuberant, happy-appearing woman who eleven years later would enslave Jacob Todd. The false missionary was not the first to be rejected, but Miss Rose had no interest in marrying. She had discovered an extraordinary formula for never emerging from her idyllic romance with Karl Bretzner, reliving each and every moment of their incendiary passion, along with fantasies she invented in the silence of her spinster nights.

Love

No one better than Miss Rose could know what was happening in Eliza's lovesick soul. She immediately guessed the man's identity, because only a blind man could have missed the connection between the girl's bizarre behavior and the delivery by her brother's employee of the crates of treasures for Feliciano Rodríguez de Santa Cruz. Her first impulse had been to write off the young man as a nonentity, too poor to be significant, but she quickly realized that she herself had sensed his dangerous attraction and had not stopped thinking about him. Naturally, she had first focused on his mended clothing and mournful pallor, but a second look had been enough to appreciate his aura: the tragic, damned poet. Furiously embroidering in her sewing room, she kept mulling over the reversal of fate that was affecting her plans to find Eliza a congenial and wealthy husband. In her thoughts she wove a web of plots to nip that love in the bud before it began, from sending Eliza to a boarding school for girls in England or to her own ancient aunt in Scotland to pouring out the truth to her brother so he would fire his employee. In the depths of her heart, however, quite despite herself, was germinating the secret hope that Eliza could live out her passion to the end, to compensate for the fathomless void the tenor had left in her own life eighteen years before.

In the meantime, for Eliza the hours passed with paralyzing slowness in a whirl of confused emotions. She didn't know whether it was day or night, Tuesday or Friday, whether it had been a few hours or several years since she'd met that young man. She felt that her blood had turned to froth, and she broke out in hives that faded as suddenly and inexplicably as they had appeared. She saw her beloved everywhere: in the shadows of the corners, in the shapes of the clouds, in her teacup, and most of all in her dreams. She did not know his name but did not dare ask Jeremy Sommers because that would unleash a wave of suspicions, but she entertained herself for hours imagining an appropriate name for him. She needed desperately to talk with someone about her love, to analyze every detail of his brief visit, to speculate on what they should have said to each other and what they had communicated with glances, blushes, and designs, but she had no one in whom to confide. She longed for a visit from Captain John Sommers, that uncle with the heart of a buccaneer who had been the most fascinating character in her childhood, the only one capable of understanding and helping in such a difficult time. She had no doubt at all that if Jeremy Sommers got wind of her feelings he would declare all-out war on his firm's humble employee, and she could not predict Miss Rose's reaction. She decided that the less that was known in her home the more she and her future sweetheart would be free to act. She never imagined a scenario in which her love was not returned with the same depth of feeling, for to her it was impossible to believe that a love of such magnitude could have stunned only her. The most elementary logic and justice indicated that somewhere in the city he was suffering the same delicious torment.

Eliza hid to touch her body in secret places she had never explored before. She closed her eyes, and then it was his hand that caressed her with the delicacy of a bird, his lips she kissed in the mirror, his waist she embraced around the pillow, his the murmurs of love carried to her on the wind. Not even her dreams escaped the power of Joaquín Andieta. She would see him appear like a huge shadow looming over her and devouring her in a thousand outlandish and disturbing ways. Moon-calf, devil, archangel—she didn't know. She did not want to wake, and with fanatic determination she practiced the skill learned from Mama Fresia for entering and leaving dreams at will. She came to have such mastery of this art that her illusory lover appeared in bodily form; she could touch him, smell him, and hear his voice, perfectly clear and close by. If only she could always be asleep she would need nothing more, she thought: she could go on loving him from her bed through eternity. She would have perished in the delirium of that passion if Joaquín Andieta hadn't come to the house a week later to pick up the boxes of treasures being sent to their client in the north.

She learned the night before that he was coming, not through instinct or premonition, as she would imply years later when she told Tao Chi'en the story, but because at dinner she heard Jeremy Sommers giving instructions to his sister and Mama Fresia.

"The same employee who brought the load will come to get it," he added in passing, never suspecting the hurricane of emotions his words—for different reasons—unleashed among the three women.

The girl spent the morning on the terrace, her eyes glued to the road rising up the hill toward the house. About midday she saw the cart pulled by six mules and followed by armed peons on horseback. She felt an icy peace, as if she had died, unaware that Miss Rose and Mama Fresia were watching her from the house.

"All that I have invested in educating her and she falls in love with the first good-for-nothing who crosses her path," muttered Miss Rose.

She had decided to do whatever she could to forestall disaster, but without much conviction, because she knew too well the obstinate temper of first love.

"I will take him to the cargo. Tell Eliza to go in the house and don't let her come out for any reason," she ordered.

"And how do you want me to do that?" Mama Fresia asked, grumbling.

"Lock her up if you have to."

"*You* lock her up, if you can. Don't get me into it," she replied, and left, bedroom slippers slapping.

There was no way to keep the girl from going up to Joaquín Andieta and handing him a letter. She did it openly, looking him in the eye, and with such fierce determination that Miss Rose did not have the gall to intercept her or Mama Fresia to stand in her way. Then the women understood that the sorcery was much stronger than they had imagined and that no locked door or blessed candles were enough to break the spell. The young man also had spent that week obsessed with the memory of the girl who he believed was the daughter of his employer, Jeremy Sommers, and therefore far beyond his reach. He had no inkling of the impression he had made, and it never crossed his mind that by offering him that memorable glass of juice on his first visit she was declaring her love; as a result, he was wildly surprised when she handed him a sealed envelope. Disconcerted, he slipped the envelope into his pocket and continued to supervise the task of loading the boxes into the cart, as his ears burned, his clothes grew damp with sweat, and a fever of shivers ran down his spine. Motionless and silent, Eliza watched closely from a few steps away, ignoring Miss Rose's furious and Mama Fresia's remorseful expressions. When the last crate was tied onto the cart and the mules turned to head down the hill, Joaquín apologized to Miss Rose for the nuisance, greeted Eliza with a brief nod of his head, and left as quickly as he could.

Eliza's note contained only two lines, telling him where and how to meet her. The strategy was of such simplicity and boldness that she might have been taken as an expert in duplicity: Joaquín was to present himself three days thence on Cerro Alegre at 9:00 P.M. in the shrine of the Virgen del Perpetuo Succor, a chapel built a short distance from the Sommers' home as a haven for travelers on foot. Eliza had chosen that place because it was nearby and the date because it was Wednesday. Miss Rose, Mama Fresia, and the servants would be busy with dinner and no one would notice if she slipped out for a while. After the departure of the crestfallen Michael Steward there had been no reason for dances and the premature winter was not conducive to them, but Miss Rose maintained the custom in order to deflate the gossip circulating about her and the navy officer. To have suspended the musical evenings in Steward's absence would have been equivalent to confessing that he was the only reason for holding them.

By seven, Joaquín Andieta was already waiting impatiently. In the distance he saw the glow of bright lights from the house, the parade of carriages bringing guests, and the torches of the coachmen waiting along the road. Once or twice he had to hide as watchmen came by to check the lamps on top of the shrine, which the wind kept blowing out. The building was a small adobe rectangle only slightly larger than a confessional, topped with a painted wood cross and housing a plaster image of the Virgin. A tray held rows of burned-down votive candles and a vase containing withered flowers. There was a full moon, but the sky was striped with clouds that from time to time completely blacked out the moonlight. At nine exactly he felt the girl's presence and saw her silhouette, cloaked from head to foot in a dark mantle.

"I have been waiting for you, señorita," was all he could think to stammer, feeling like an idiot.

"I have been waiting for you forever," she replied without the least hesitation.

She threw back her mantle and Joaquín saw she was dressed for a party, though her skirt was tucked up and she was wearing rough sandals. She was carrying her white stockings and chamois dancing slippers to keep from muddying them on the road. Her black hair, parted in the center, was caught back on both sides of her head into braids decorated with satin ribbons. They sat at the back of the shrine on the mantle that she lay on the floor, hidden behind the statue, unspeaking, very close but not touching. For a long time, they lacked the courage to look at one another in the soft shadows, stupefied by their closeness, breathing the same air and aflame despite the cold wind that threatened to leave them in blackness.

"My name is Eliza Sommers," she said finally.

"And I am Joaquín Andieta," he replied.

"I thought maybe your name was Sebastián."

"Why?"

"Because you look like Saint Sebastián the martyr. I don't go to the Papist church, I am a Protestant, but Mama Fresia has sometimes taken me when she goes to make promises to her saints."

The conversation ended there because they didn't know what else to say; they stole glances out of the corners of their eyes and then blushed in unison. Eliza could smell his scent of soap and sweat but didn't dare move closer to sniff him, as she wanted to. The only sounds in the shrine were the whispering wind and their agitated breathing. After a few minutes, Eliza announced that she had to go back to the house before she was missed, and they said good-bye, brushing hands. They met the next few Wednesdays, always at a different time and for only brief intervals. In each of those tumultuous meetings they moved forward with giant steps through the delirium and torment of love. Hurriedly, they told each other what was indispensable to tell, because words seemed a waste of time; soon they held hands and kept on talking, their bodies closer and closer as their souls moved toward each other, until on the night of the fifth Wednesday they kissed on the lips, first tentatively, then exploring, and finally, losing themselves in pleasure until the fever consuming them was totally unleashed. By then they had exchanged abbreviated summaries of Eliza's sixteen years and Joaquín's twenty-one. They discussed the improbable basket with batiste sheets and mink coverlet in contrast to the Marseilles soap crate, and it came as a relief to Andieta that Eliza was not the daughter of either Sommers but was, like him, born of obscure origins, although they were still separated by a social and economic abyss. Eliza learned that Joaquín was the fruit of a passing ravishment; his father had vanished as quickly as he had sown his seed, and the boy had grown up not knowing his father's name, carrying his mother's, and, marked as a bastard, limited at every turn of the road. The family drove their dishonored daughter from their bosom and disregarded her illegitimate son. His grandparents and his uncles, merchants and minor civil servants in a middle class mired in prejudice, lived in the same city, only a few blocks away, but their paths never crossed. On Sundays they went to the same church, but at different hours, because the poor never went to noon mass. Branded by the stigma, Joaquín never played in the same parks or went to the schools his cousins attended, although he wore their old clothes and played with their discarded toys, which a kindhearted aunt sent to her banished sister through convoluted means. Joaquín Andieta's mother had been less fortunate than Miss Rose, and had paid more dearly for her weakness. The women were about the same age, but while the English lady looked young, the other was worn down by poverty, consumption, and the dismal task of embroidering bridal gowns by candlelight. Bad luck had not diminished her dignity and she had brought up her son with inviolable principles of honor. Joaquín had learned at a very early age to hold his head high, defying any glimmer of mockery or pity.

"One day I will take my mother out of that shack she lives in," Joaquín vowed during their whispered conversations in the shrine. "I will give her a decent life, like the one she had before she lost everything."

"She didn't lose everything. She has a son," Eliza replied.

"I was her misfortune."

"Her misfortune was to fall in love with a bad man. You are her redemption," she declared.

The meetings between the two young people were very brief and never at the same hour, and Miss Rose could not watch Eliza day and night. She knew something was happening behind her back, but she could not go so far as to lock Eliza in her room or send her to the country, as duty prescribed, and she refrained from mentioning her suspicions to her brother Jeremy. She was sure that Eliza and her beloved were exchanging letters but was never able to intercept one, though she alerted all the servants. The letters did exist and were of such intensity that had Miss Rose seen them she would have been appalled. Joaquín never sent them, he handed them to Eliza at each of their meetings. In the most feverish language he told her what he did not dare in person, out of pride and propriety. She hid the letters in a box buried thirty centimeters deep in the small kitchen garden by the house, where every day she pretended to be diligently weeding Mama Fresia's vegetables and medicinal herbs. Those pages, reread a thousand times in stolen moments, were the principal sustenance of her passion, because they revealed an aspect of Joaquín Andieta that did not emerge when they were together. They seemed written by a different person. That haughty young man, always on the defensive, somber and tormented, who embraced her madly and then pushed her away as if burned by the contact, in writing opened the floodgates of his soul and described his emotions like a poet. Later, when for years Eliza would follow Joaquín Andieta's faint trail, those letters would be her only grasp on the truth, irrefutable proof that their delirious love was not an invention of her adolescent imagination but that it was real, a brief blessing and an extended torment.

After the first Wednesday in the shrine, Eliza's attacks of indigestion vanished without a trace, and nothing in her behavior or her appearance revealed her secret except the demented gleam in her eyes and a more frequent use of her talent for making herself invisible. At times she gave the impression of being in several places at once, confusing everyone, or it might be that no one could remember where or when they had last seen her and just as they started to call her she would materialize with the air of someone who doesn't know anyone was looking for her. She spent time with Miss Rose in her sewing room or cooking with Mama Fresia, but she had become so quiet and transparent that neither woman felt she was seeing her. Her presence was subtle, nearly imperceptible, and when she went away no one realized it until hours later.

"You're like a ghost! I'm tired of looking for you. I don't want you to leave the house, not even leave my sight," Miss Rose ordered again and again.

"I've been here all afternoon," Eliza would reply, undaunted, quietly appearing in a corner with a book or embroidery in her hand.

"Make some noise, child, *por Dios*! How can I see you when you're quieter than a rabbit?" Mama Fresia would ask in turn.

Eliza said all right, and then did just as she wanted, but she took pains to seem obedient and stay in good favor. After a few days she had acquired an astonishing skill for clouding reality, as if she had practiced the magician's art all her life. Faced with the impossibility of catching her in a lie she could prove, Miss Rose chose to worm her way into Eliza's confidence by constantly bringing up the subject of love. There were more than enough excuses: gossip about her friends, romantic books they had shared or librettos of new Italian operas, which they learned by memory, but Eliza never said a word to betray her feelings. Miss Rose watched—vainly—for telltale signs: she went through the girl's clothes and searched her room, she turned her doll and music box collections, her books, her notebooks upside down, but could not find Eliza's diary. Had she found it she would have been disappointed, because there was no mention of Joaquín Andieta in those pages. Eliza wrote only to remember. She put down everything in her diary, from recurring dreams to an ever growing list of recipes and domestic lore, such as the way to fatten a hen or remove a grease stain. There were also speculations about her birth, the expensive basket and Marseilles soap crate, but not a word about Joaquín Andieta. She did not need a diary to remember him. It would be several years before she began to record her Wednesday rendezvous in those pages.

Finally came the night the lovers did not meet at the shrine but in the Sommers' home. To reach that moment, Eliza had suffered the torments of an infinity of doubts; she realized this was a decisive step. Just for meeting in secret, unchaperoned, a girl sacrificed her honor, her most precious treasure, without which she had no future. "A woman without virtue is nothing, she can never become a wife and mother, better she tie a stone around her neck and jump into the sea," had been drummed into her time and time again. She believed there was no extenuating excuse for the sin she was about to commit; she did it with premeditation and conscious intent. At two in the morning, when no one was awake in the city and only nightwatchmen were making their rounds, peering into darkness, Joaquín Andieta managed to sneak like a thief onto the terrace of the library, where Eliza was waiting for him in her nightgown, barefoot, shivering with cold and anxiety. She took his hand and led him blindly through the house to a back room where the family's clothing was kept in huge armoires, along with boxes of trimmings for dresses and hats that Miss Rose used and reused through the years. Flat on the floor, wrapped in lengths of linen, were the drawing room and dining room drapes, awaiting the turn of seasons. It had seemed the safest place to Eliza, far from the other rooms. At any rate, as a precaution she had put valerian in the small glass of anisette Miss Rose drank before going to bed, and into the brandy Jeremy sipped as he smoked his Cuban cigarette after dinner. Eliza knew every centimeter of the house; and since she knew exactly where the floor creaked and how to open doors so they wouldn't squeak, she could guide Joaquín in the darkness with no light but her memory, and he followed, docile and pale with fear, shutting out the voice of his own conscience blending with that of his mother relentlessly reminding him of a decent man's code of honor. I will never do to Eliza what my father did to my mother, he vowed as he groped his way along, holding the girl's hand, knowing that any such pledge was pointless, for he had already lost the battle with the pulsing desire that had bedeviled him since the first time he'd seen her. In the meantime, Eliza was torn between the warning voices echoing through her head and the force of instinct, with all its awesome devices. She had no clear idea of what was going to happen in the room with the armoires, but she had already given in.

The Sommers' home, suspended in the air like a spiderweb at the mercy of the wind, was impossible to keep warm despite the charcoal braziers the servants kept burning during seven months of the year. The sheets were always damp from the persistent breath of the sea and one slept with a hot-water bottle at one's feet. The only place that was always warm was the kitchen, where the woodstove, an enormous affair with many uses, was never allowed to go out. During the winter, wood creaked, boards popped loose, and the framework of the house threatened to launch itself like an ancient frigate. Miss Rose never grew accustomed to the Pacific storms, just as she never got used to the temblors. True earthquakes, the ones that flattened everything, happened more or less every six years, and in each of those she showed surprising self-composure, but the daily vibrations that shook their lives left her in a foul mood. She did not like to put her china and glassware on shelves at ground level, as Chileans did, and when the dining room furniture shook and plates shattered, she cursed the country at the top of her lungs.

The storeroom where Eliza and Joaquín made love on the huge bundle of flowered cretonne draperies that in summer replaced the green velvet parlor drapes was on the ground floor. They loved one another surrounded by solemn armoires, hatboxes, and Miss Rose's cloth-wrapped spring dresses. Neither the cold nor the smell of mothballs bothered them, because they were beyond practical concerns, beyond fear of the consequences, and beyond their own puppylike clumsiness. They did not know what to do, but they made it up as they went, befuddled and confounded, in total silence, guiding one another with little skill. At twenty-one, he was as much a virgin as she. At fourteen he had decided to become a priest to please his mother, but at sixteen he had fallen into reading liberal books and declared himself an enemy of the clergy, though not of religion, and had decided to remain chaste until he accomplished his plan to move his mother from her wretched home. It seemed a small repayment for her countless sacrifices. Despite their virginity and their terrible fear of being surprised, they were able to find in the darkness what they sought. They unfastened buttons and ties, shed their modesty and found themselves naked, sucking in each other's breath and saliva. They inhaled feral scents, feverishly put this here and that there with an honest desire to decipher enigmas, plumb the other's depths, and lose themselves in the same soul. They left summer drapes stained with warm sweat, virginal blood, and semen, but neither of them noticed those signs of love. In the darkness they could barely make out each other's outlines and gauge how much room they had to keep from knocking down stacks of boxes and clothes racks in the furor of their embraces. They blessed the wind and the rain on the roof tiles because those sounds masked the creaking of the floor, but the thundering of their hearts and the rage of their panting and sighs of love were so deafening that they couldn't understand why they didn't wake the whole house.

Before dawn, Joaquín Andieta left by the same library window and Eliza went back to bed, drained. While she slept, wrapped in several blankets, he had a two hours' walk downhill through the storm. Silently he slipped through the town without attracting the attention of the watchman, and reached his house just as the church bells were ringing for early mass. He had planned to go in quietly, wash, change the collar of his shirt, and go off to work in his wet suit, since he had no other, but his mother was awake, waiting for him with toasted stale bread and hot water for maté, as she did every morning.

"Where have you been, son?" she asked, so sadly that he could not deceive her.

"Discovering love, Mama," he answered, throwing his arms around her, his face radiant.

Joaquín Andieta lived the torment of a political romanticism that had no echo in that country of practical and prudent people. He had become a fan of the theories of Lamennais, which he read in mediocre and confusing translations from the French in the same way he read the Encyclopedists. Like his mentor, he professed a Catholic liberalism in politics and the separation of church and state. He declared himself a fundamental Christian, like the apostles and martyrs, but an enemy of priests, who, he said, had betrayed Jesus and his true doctrine, comparing them to bloodsuckers feeding on the credulity of the faithful. He was very careful, nonetheless, not to expound such ideas before his mother, who would have died of mortification. He also considered himself an enemy of the useless and decadent oligarchy, and of the government because it did not represent the interests of the people, only the rich, as his colleagues proved with many examples in their meetings at the Santos Tornero bookshop and as he patiently explained to Eliza, although she seemed scarcely to hear him, more interested in smelling him than in listening to his speeches. He was prepared to give his life for the pointless glory of a burst of heroism, but he had a visceral fear of looking Eliza in the eyes and talking of his sentiments. They established the routine of making love at least once a week in that same room with the armoires, now their nest. They had counted on so few precious moments together that it seemed senseless to her to waste them philosophizing; if they were going to talk, she would rather hear about his tastes, his past, his mother, and his plans to marry her someday. She would have given anything to have him say in person the magnificent phrases he wrote to her in his letters. To tell her, for example, that it would be easier to measure the intentions of the wind or the patience of the waves on the shore than the intensity of his love; that there was no winter night cold enough to damp the ever burning fires of his passion; that he spent the days dreaming and nights awake, assailed by the madness of memories and counting, with the anguish of a condemned man, the hours until he would hold her again. "You are my angel and my damnation; in your presence I reach divine ecstasy and in your absence I descend to hell. What is this hold you have over me, Eliza? Do not speak to me of tomorrow or yesterday, I live only for the instant, for the *today*, when I can again sink into the infinite night of your dark eyes." Nourished by Miss Rose's novels and the romantic poets, whose verses she knew by heart, the girl lost herself in the intoxicating delight of feeling adored like a goddess, failing to see the discrepancy between those inflamed declarations and the real person of Joaquín Andieta. In his letters he was transformed into the perfect lover, able to describe his passion with such angelic spirit that guilt and fear disappeared to give rise to the absolute exaltation of his emotions. No one had loved like that before; they had been chosen among mortals for a passion like no other, Joaquín told her in his letters, and she believed him. Nevertheless, he made love hurriedly, like a starving man, without savoring it, like someone succumbing to a vice, tormented by guilt. He did not take the time to know her body or reveal his to her; he was overcome by the urgency of desire, and their secret. He always felt as if they never had enough time, though Eliza calmed him, explaining that no one came to that room at night, that the Sommers were both drugged, that Mama Fresia was asleep in her hut at the back of the patio, and that the rest of the servants' rooms were in the attic. Instinct provoked the girl's boldness, driving her to discover the multiple possibilities of pleasure, but soon she learned to hold back. Her initiatives in the game of love put Joaquín on the defensive; he felt criticized, wounded, his virility threatened. He was tormented by the worst suspicions, because he could not imagine such natural sensuality in a sixteen-year-old girl whose horizons were the walls of her home. Fear of pregnancy made things worse, because neither of them knew how to avoid it. Joaquín vaguely understood the mechanics of fertilization and assumed that if he withdrew in time they were safe, but he did not always achieve that. He was aware of Eliza's frustration, but did not know how to comfort her, and instead of trying, he took immediate refuge in his role as her intellectual mentor, where he felt secure. When she longed to be stroked, or at least to rest her head on her lover's shoulder, he pulled away, quickly dressed, and wasted the precious time they had left laying out new arguments for the same political theories he had repeated a hundred times. Eliza felt restless after those embraces, but she did not dare admit it, not even in the deepest part of her being, because that would be questioning the quality of their love. Then she fell into the trap of feeling sorry for her lover, making excuses for him, thinking that if they had more time, a safe place, everything would be fine. Much better than their rolling about were the hours afterward inventing things that hadn't happened and the nights dreaming of what might happen the next time in the room with the armoires.

With the same gravity she invested in all her acts, Eliza gave herself to the task of idealizing her lover until he became an obsession. All she wanted was to serve him wholeheartedly for the rest of her life, to sacrifice herself and suffer to prove her selflessness, to die for him if necessary. She was so befogged by the witchery of that first passion that she did not see that her love was not returned with equal intensity. Her lover was never completely present. Even in the most rousing embraces on the pile of drapes, his mind was somewhere else, ready to leave or already absent. He revealed himself only partly, fleetingly, in an exasperating game of Chinese shadow plays, but when he left, when she was so starved for love that she was at the point of bursting into tears, he would hand her another of his marvelous letters. Then the entire universe would turn into a prism whose one purpose was to reflect her emotions. Captive to the demanding task of besotted love, she never doubted her capacity to give without reserve, and therefore did not recognize Joaquín's ambiguity. She had invented a perfect lover, and she obstinately nurtured that illusion. Her imagination compensated for the unrewarding embraces with her lover that left her in the dark limbo of unsatisfied desire.

PART TWO

1848–1849

The News

September twenty-first, the first day of spring according to Miss Rose's calendar, they aired the rooms, hung the feather beds and bedding in the sun, waxed the wood furniture, and changed the curtains in the drawing room. Mama Fresia washed the flowered cretonne without comment, convinced that the dried stains were mouse urine. In the patio, she prepared great pots of hot, strained, *quillay* bark, soaked the curtains one whole day, starched them with rice water, and dried them in the sun; then two women ironed them, and when they were good as new she hung them at the windows of the drawing room to welcome the new season. In the meantime, Eliza and Joaquín, indifferent to Miss Rose's springtime pandemonium, indulged their love on the green velvet drapes, more cushiony than the cretonne. It wasn't cold anymore, and the nights were bright. They had been lovers for three months, and Joaquín Andieta's letters, sprinkled with poetic figures and torrid declarations, were noticeably fewer and farther between. Eliza sensed that her lover was somewhere else, that at times she embraced a ghost. Despite the anguish of unsatisfied love and the heavy load of so many secrets, the girl had regained a superficial calm. She spent the hours of the day in her usual occupations, absorbed in her books and her piano exercises, or busy about the kitchen and sewing room, not showing the slightest interest in leaving the house, although if Miss Rose asked her to, she went along with the willingness of someone who has nothing better to do. She got up early and went to bed early, as always; she had a good appetite and looked healthy, although these symptoms of perfect normality raised terrifying suspicions in the minds of Miss Rose and Mama Fresia. They never let her out of their sight. They doubted that the intoxication of love had dissipated so suddenly, but as the weeks went by and Eliza showed no signs of distress they slowly relaxed their vigilance. Maybe the candles to Saint Anthony did help, the Indian speculated; maybe it wasn't love after all, Miss Rose thought without much conviction.

The news of the gold discovered in California reached Chile in August. First it was a wild rumor from the mouths of drunken sailors in the brothels of El Almendral, but a few days later the captain of the schooner *Adelaida* announced that half his crew had deserted in San Francisco.

"There's gold everywhere, you can shovel it up, they say there are nuggets the size of oranges! Anyone with a lick of gumption can be a millionaire!" he reported, choked with excitement.

In January of that year, near the mill of a Swiss farmer on the banks of the American River, a man by the name of Marshall had found a scale of gold in the water. The yellow pellet that unleashed the madness was found nine days after the war between Mexico and the United States had ended with the signing of the Treaty of Guadalupe Hidalgo. By the time the news spread, California no longer belonged to Mexico. That territory had been largely ignored before it was known that it was sitting on a never-ending treasure. North Americans had thought of it as Indian hunting grounds, and the pioneers had preferred Oregon, which they'd found better suited for agriculture. Mexico had considered it a wasteland bristling with thieves and hadn't bothered to send troops to defend it during the war. But a little later, Sam Brannan, a newspaper editor and Mormon preacher sent to spread the faith, went up and down the streets of San Francisco broadcasting the news. He might not have been believed, considering he had a slightly murky reputation—it was rumored that he had misappropriated God's money and when the Mormon church asked him to return it he had said he would . . . if he got a receipt signed by God—but he backed up his words with a small pouch filled with gold dust, which passed from hand to hand inflaming his audience. At the cry of "Gold! Gold!" three out of four men dropped everything and set out for the placers. They had to close the only school because there weren't any children left. In Chile the news had the same impact. The average salary was twenty cents per day, and the newspapers wrote that the long-lost El Dorado had been found, the city the conquistadors had dreamed of, where the streets were paved with pure gold. "The riches of the mines recall the stories of Sinbad and Aladdin's lamp; without fear of exaggeration, the day's take averages an ounce of pure gold," proclaimed the newspapers, and they added that there was enough to make thousands rich for decades. The wildfire of greed flared immediately among Chileans, who had the souls of miners, and the rush to California began the next month. They were already halfway there compared to any adventurer crossing the Atlantic. The trip from Europe to Valparaíso took three months, and then two more to reach California. The distance between Valparaíso and San Francisco was less than seven thousand miles, while from the east coast of North America, passing around Cape Horn, it was nearly twenty thousand. That, as Joaquín Andieta calculated, represented a considerable head start for the Chileans, and the first to get there would stake the best claims.

Feliciano Rodríguez de Santa Cruz came to the same conclusion, and he decided to leave immediately with five of his best and most loyal miners, promising them a reward as incentive to get them to leave their families and jump into such a risky enterprise. He spent three weeks organizing supplies for a stay of several months in that land to the north, which he imagined as desolate and savage. He was miles ahead of most of the reckless who set out blindly, destitute, spurred by the temptation of an easy fortune but with no hint of the dangers and exertion involved. He was not about to break his back slaving like a common laborer, which was why he was going to be well supplied and take workmen he trusted, he explained to his wife, who was expecting their second child but insisted she wanted to go with him. Paulina planned to make the voyage with two nursemaids, their cook, and a cow and several chickens to provide milk and eggs for the babies during the trip, but for once her husband stood firm in his refusal. The idea of setting off on such an odyssey with a family on his back was clearly on the level of idiocy. His wife had lost her mind.

"What was that captain's name? Mr. Todd's friend?" Paulina interrupted in the middle of his harangue, balancing a cup of chocolate on her enormous belly as she nibbled a cream-filled flaky pastry, a recipe of the Clarisa nuns.

"You mean John Sommers?"

"I mean that man who was fed up with navigating under sail and was talking about steamships."

"That's the one."

Paulina sat thinking awhile, stuffing her mouth with pastries and totally ignoring the list of dangers her husband was invoking. By now she was Rubenesque, and little remained of the slender girl with the shaved head who had run off from the convent.

"How much do I have in my account in London?" she asked finally.

"Fifty thousand pounds. You are a very wealthy woman."

"Not enough. Can you lend me twice that amount with ten percent interest payable in three years?"

"Where do you get such harebrained ideas, woman? For

God's sake! What the devil do you want with that much money?"

"I want to buy a steamship. The real money isn't in gold, Feliciano; when all's said and done, it's just yellow crap. The real money is in the miners. They are going to need everything when they get to California, and they will have ready cash. They say that the steamships plow right ahead; they are not at the mercy of the wind, and are bigger and faster. Sailing ships are a thing of the past."

Feliciano went ahead with his plans, but experience had taught him not to disdain his wife's financial premonitions. For several nights he couldn't sleep. Wide-eyed, he paced through the ostentatious rooms of his mansion, stepping carefully among sacks of provisions, boxes of tools, barrels of gunpowder, and piles of weapons for the voyage, measuring and pondering Paulina's words. The longer he thought about it, the sounder it seemed to invest in transport, but before making a decision he consulted his brother, who was his partner in all his business negotiations. His brother listened open-mouthed, and when Feliciano had set out the plan, he clapped his hand to his head.

"Caramba, brother! Why didn't we think of that?"

In the meantime, Joaquín Andieta was, like thousands of other Chileans his age, no matter their situation, dreaming of bags of gold dust and nuggets scattered across the ground. Several of his acquaintances had already left, including one of his comrades at the Santos Tornero bookshop, a young liberal who ranted against the rich and was the first to denounce the evils of money, but who could not resist the siren call of gold and had taken off without a good-bye to anyone. For Joaquín, California represented his one way out of poverty, his only chance to take his mother out of the slums and seek a cure for her lungs, to stand before Jeremy Sommers with his head high and his pockets filled to ask for Eliza's hand. Gold . . . gold within his reach. . . . He could see pouches bulging with gold dust, baskets of huge nuggets, greenbacks in his pockets, the palace he would build, more solid and with more marble than the Club de la Unión, to shut the mouths of the relatives who had humiliated his mother. He also saw himself leaving the Iglesia de La Matriz with Eliza Sommers on his arm, the happiest bride and groom on the planet. It was just a question of daring. What future did Chile offer? In the best of cases, growing old counting the products that passed over the desk of the British Import and Export Company, Ltd. What could he lose, since he had nothing to his name to begin with? He was ill with gold fever; he lost his appetite and couldn't sleep, he went around in a high heat, staring at the sea with the eyes of a madman. His bookseller friend lent him maps and books about California, and a pamphlet on how to pan for treasure, which he read avidly as he thought up desperate schemes to finance the adventure. Reports in the newspapers could not be more tempting: "In one kind of mine called dry diggings, the only tool needed to pry gold from the rocks is a common pocketknife. In other places the gold is already loose and to wash it up one uses a simple machine called a sluice, or rocker, an ordinary round-bottomed trough some ten feet long and two wide across the top. No capital is necessary, so the competition is fierce, but men who were barely able to make ends meet for a month now have thousands of dollars of precious metal."

When Andieta mentioned the possibility of sailing north, his mother protested as loudly as Eliza had. Without ever having seen each other, the two women said exactly the same thing: If you go, Joaquín, I will die. Both tried to make him see the countless dangers of such an endeavor, and swore to him that they would a thousand times rather live with him in inescapable poverty than have him pursue an illusory fortune and risk losing him forever. His mother told him that she wouldn't leave the hovel where she lived even if she were very wealthy, because all her friends were there and she had nowhere else in this world to go. And as for her lungs, nothing could be done for them, she said, except wait for them to give out. Eliza, for her part, offered to run away with him if her family wouldn't let them marry. Joaquín didn't listen, however, rapt in his nightmare of gold, convinced he would never have another chance like this and that if he let it go by it would be unpardonable cowardice. He put into his new mania the same intensity he had once devoted to espousing liberal ideals, but he lacked the means to realize his plans. He couldn't live out his destiny unless he could raise the sum for the passage and outfit himself with the bare necessities. He went to the bank to ask for a small loan, but he had no collateral and with one look they saw he was as poor as a church mouse; he was icily rejected. For the first time he considered going to his mother's family, whom he had never spoken to in his life, but he was too proud. He was haunted by the vision of a dazzling future; it was all he could do to go on with his work; the long hours at his desk became a martyrdom. He would sit holding his pen in the air, staring blindly at the blank page as he repeated by heart the names of the ships that could take him north. Nights drained away in tumultuous dreams and nervous insomnia; he awakened exhausted, his imagination boiling over. He made childish errors, while all around him the exaltation of gold reached the level of hysteria. Everyone wanted to go, and those who couldn't go in person set up corporations, invested in hastily formed companies, or sent a trusted representative in their stead with an agreement to share the profits. Bachelors were the first to set sail; soon married men were leaving their children and starting off without a backward look, despite harrowing stories of obscure illnesses, disastrous accidents, and brutal crimes. The most peaceful men were ready to confront the dangers of pistols and knives, the most prudent abandoned the security won with years of daily struggle and threw themselves into the adventure with their carpetbags of illusions. Some spent their life's savings on a passage, others paid for the voyage by hiring on as sailors or signing indentures, but there were so many candidates that Joaquín Andieta could not find a berth on a single ship, even after days of haunting the docks.

By December he couldn't take any more. As he was copying the particulars of a cargo that had arrived in the port, as he did meticulously every day, he altered the figures in the registry, then destroyed the original documents of off-loading. Through the art of bookkeeping sleight of hand, he caused several boxes of revolvers and bullets originating in New York to disappear. For the next three nights he avoided the night watch, jimmied the locks, and sneaked into the warehouse of the British Import and Export Company, Ltd. to steal the contents of those boxes. He had to make several trips because the booty was heavy. First he filled his pockets with guns, and strapped others to his arms and legs beneath his clothing; then he carried out sacks of bullets. Several times he was nearly caught by the night guards, but luck was with him and each time he slipped away in time. He knew he had a couple of weeks before anyone would claim the boxes and discover the theft; he supposed, too, that it would be all too easy to follow the trail of the missing documents and altered figures to the guilty person, but by then he would be on the high seas. And when he had made his own fortune he would return every last cent, with interest, since the only reason for committing such a deed, he repeated a thousand times, was his desperation. This was a matter of life and death. Life as he understood it lay in California; to stay trapped in Chile was to condemn himself to a slow death. He sold part of his loot at a ridiculous price in dives in the port and the rest among his friends in the Santos Tornero bookshop after making them swear they would guard his secret. Those hotheaded idealists had never held a weapon in their hands but they had spent years preparing verbally for a Utopian revolt against the conservative government. It would have been a betrayal of their propositions not to buy the black-market revolvers, especially at such bargain prices. Joaquín Andieta kept two revolvers for himself, determined to use them to shoot his way out if he had to, but he said nothing to his closest friends about his plans to leave. That night in the back room of the bookshop, he, too, placed his right hand over his heart and swore, in the name of the republic, that he would give his life for democracy and justice. The next morning he bought a third-class passage on the first schooner scheduled to sail north, along with a few sacks of toasted flour, beans, rice, sugar, jerked horse meat, and bacon, which if doled out with parsimony could get him through the journey. He bound his few remaining *reales* around his waist with a tight sash.

On the night of December twenty-second, he kissed Eliza and his mother good-bye, and the next morning set off for California.

Mama Fresia discovered the love letters by chance when she was digging onions in her narrow garden in the patio and the pitchfork hit a tin box. She didn't know how to read, but she only had to glance at them to know what she had found. She was tempted to take them to Miss Rose, because just holding them in her hand she could sense the threat; she would have sworn that the red ribbon-tied packet throbbed like a living heart, but her affection for Eliza was stronger than prudence and instead of going to her *patrona* she put the letters back in the biscuit tin, hid it beneath her full black skirts, and with a heavy sigh went to the girl's room. She found Eliza sitting in a chair, her back straight and her hands clasped in her lap as if she were at mass, staring out her window at the sea, so filled with anguish that the air around her felt dense and heavy with premonitions. Mama Fresia set the box on Eliza's knees and stood waiting for an explanation—in vain.

"The man is a devil. He will bring you nothing but trouble," she said finally.

"It has already begun. He left six weeks ago for California, and I haven't had my period."

Mama Fresia slumped down on the floor with her legs crossed, as she did when her bones could not carry her another step, and began to rock back and forth, moaning softly.

"Quiet, Mamacita, Miss Rose can hear us," Eliza plead.

"A child of the gutter! A *huacho*! what are we going to do, child? What are we going to do?" Mama Fresia could not stop lamenting.

"I am going to marry him."

"How, if he's gone?"

"I will have to find him."

"Ay! Sweet blessed Jesus! Have you lost all your senses? I will give you something and in a few days you will be like new."

So Mama Fresia brewed borage tea and made up a potion of chicken shit dissolved in black beer, which she made Eliza drink three times a day; she also made her soak in sulfur baths and applied mustard compresses to her stomach. The result was that Eliza turned yellow and went around bathed in a sticky sweat that smelled like rotted gardenias, but after a week there were still no signs of a miscarriage. Mama Fresia concluded that the creature was male and obviously had a curse on it, and that was why it clung so tightly to its mother's insides. This state of affairs was beyond her, it was the work of the devil and only the woman who had taught her, the *machi,* could deal with a problem of this magnitude. That same evening she asked her *patrona*'s permission to be gone for a while, and once again she walked the steep path to the ravine to stand dejected before the ancient blind witch woman. As a gift, she took her two jars of quince preserves and a stuffed duck flavored with rosemary.

The *machi* listened to the latest developments, nodding wearily, as if she already knew what had happened.

"I told you before that a fixation is very stubborn: it burrows into the brain and breaks the heart. There are many fixations, but love is the worst."

"Can you do something so my little girl can cast out the *huacho*?"

"*That* I can do. But that won't cure her. She will have to follow the man."

"He went far away to look for gold."

"After love, the worst fixation is gold," the *machi* intoned.

Mama Fresia understood that it would be impossible to get Eliza out of the house and take her to the *machi*'s ravine, let her do her work, and get the girl back home without Miss Rose finding out. The *machi* was a hundred years old and hadn't left her wretched hut in fifty of them, so neither was she going to come to the Sommers'. There was no other way, she would do it herself. The *machi* gave her a slender coligüe twig and a dark, stinking pomade, then explained in detail how to dab the sprig in the salve and insert it in Eliza. Then she taught her the words of the incantation that would free the creature from the devil and at the same time protect the mother's life. Mama Fresia would have to perform this ceremony on a Friday night, the one day in the week that was authorized for doing it, she warned. Mama Fresia went home very late and very tired, with the coligüe and pomade under her mantle.

"Pray, child, because in two nights' time I will do the cure," she told Eliza when she took in her breakfast chocolate.

Captain John Sommers disembarked in Valparaíso on the day set by the *machi*. It was the second Friday in the full summer of February.

The bay was seething with activity, with fifty ships at anchor and others waiting their turn outside the port to come in. As always, Jeremy, Rose, and Eliza were at the dock to welcome this admirable Sommers, who as usual was loaded down with trinkets, stories, and gifts. Average citizens, who had appointments to visit the ships and buy contraband, blended in with seamen, travelers, stevedores, and customs employees, while a group of prostitutes, stationed at a certain distance, was studying the lay of the land. In recent months, ever since news of gold had stirred the greed of men on every shore of the world, ships had entered and left at a crazed pace, and the brothels couldn't keep up. The most intrepid women, however, were not satisfied with the steady stream of business in Valparaíso and had calculated how much more they could earn in California, where, if what you heard was true, there were two hundred men for every woman. In the port, people jockeyed around carts, draft animals, and bundles; the air was filled with a babel of tongues, ships' horns, and guards' whistles, and the smell of fish baking in great baskets in the sun mixed with the stench of animal excrement and human sweat. Miss Rose, holding a vanilla-perfumed handkerchief to her nose, scrutinized the passengers in the dinghies, looking for her favorite brother as Eliza sniffed the air in quick gulps, trying to separate and identify the odors. She was the first to sight Captain Sommers. She was so relieved that she almost burst out crying. She had been waiting for him for several months, sure that he alone would understand the anguish of her frustrated love. She hadn't said a word about Joaquín Andieta to Miss Rose, much less Jeremy Sommers, but she was sure that her seafaring uncle, whom nothing could surprise or frighten, would help her.

The moment the captain stepped onto dry land, an exhilarated Eliza and Miss Rose threw themselves on him; he clasped them both in his formidable arms, lifted them off the ground, and whirled like a top to the gleeful shouts of Miss Rose and the protests of Eliza, who was about to throw up. Jeremy Sommers greeted his brother with a handshake, asking himself how it was possible that he hadn't changed a hair in the last twenty years and was as rollicking as ever.

"What's this, my little pumpkin? You look a little peaky," the captain said, examining Eliza.

"I ate some green fruit, Uncle," she said, dizzy and leaning against him to keep from falling.

"I know you two didn't come down here to welcome me. What you want is to buy some perfumes, I'll wager? I'll tell you who has the best, straight from the heart of Paris."

At that moment, a foreigner walking by bumped the captain with his suitcase, which he was carrying on his back. John Sommers swung around, incensed, but when he recognized the culprit jokingly shouted one of his characteristic curses, and grabbed his arm.

"Come meet my family, Chino," he called cordially.

Eliza stared openly at the man because she had never seen an Asian close up and at last she had before her a citizen of China, the fabulous country that figured in so many of her uncle's tales. This was a man of uncertain age, rather tall compared to Chileans, although beside the hearty English captain he looked like a boy.

He walked without grace, had the smooth face and slender body of a youth, and an ancient expression in his obliquely set eyes. His doctoral restraint contrasted with a childlike laugh that burst from the bottom of his chest when Sommers spoke to him. He was wearing trousers cut off at the shin, a loose muslin smock, a sash about his waist in which had tucked a large knife, cloth slippers and a beat-up straw hat, and a long braid trailed down his back. He greeted them with several nodding bows, without setting down his suitcase or meeting anyone's eyes. Miss Rose and Jeremy Sommers, uncomfortable at the familiarity with which their brother was treating a person of obviously inferior rank, did not know what to do, and responded with a brief nod. To Miss Rose's horror, Eliza held out her hand, but the man pretended not to see it.

"This is Tao Chi'en, the worst cook I've ever had, but he knows how to cure almost any ailment—that's the only reason I didn't make him walk the plank," the captain joked.

Tao Chi'en made a new series of little bows, laughed for no apparent reason, and then backed away. Eliza wondered if he understood English. Behind the backs of the two women, John Sommers whispered to his brother that this Chinaman could sell him the best-quality opium and powdered rhinoceros horn for impotence, in case one day he decided to break the bad habit of celibacy. Hiding behind her fan, Eliza listened, intrigued.

That afternoon in the house, at tea time, the captain handed out the gifts he had brought: English shaving soap, a set of Toledo steel scissors, and Havana cigars for his brother, tortoiseshell combs and a Manila shawl for Rose, and, as always, a jewel for Eliza's trousseau. This time it was a pearl necklace, which she thanked him for profusely and put in her jewel box along with the others he had given her. Thanks to Miss Rose's obstinacy and her uncle's generosity, her dowry chest was filling up with treasures.

"This business of a trousseau seems a bit foolish, especially when there's no bridegroom in hand," the captain joked. "Or maybe there is one on the horizon?"

Eliza exchanged a terrified glance with Mama Fresia, who had just at that moment brought in the tea tray. The captain said nothing, but asked himself whether his sister Rose had noticed the changes in Eliza. So what was feminine intuition good for, anyway?

They spent the rest of the evening listening to the captain's wondrous stories about California, even though he hadn't been there since the discovery of gold and the only thing he could say about San Francisco was that it wasn't much of a town but that it did sit on the most beautiful bay in the world. The brouhaha about gold was all that anyone was talking about in Europe and the United States, and the news had reached even the distant shores of Asia. His ship was crammed with passengers on their way to California, men of all ages and conditions, ignorant of the most elementary notion of mining; many had never seen a fleck of gold in their lives. There was no comfortable or quick way to get to San Francisco; a sailing ship took months, under the most precarious conditions, the captain explained, but traveling across the American continent, defying the immensity of the land and the Indian raids, took longer, and there was even less chance of getting there alive. Those who came by ship via Panama crossed the isthmus first in long boats along rivers roiling with predators and then on muleback through deep jungle. When they reached the Pacific Coast they took another ship north, having endured devilish heat, poisonous reptiles, mosquitoes, and plagues of cholera and yellow fever, to say nothing of unspeakable human wickedness. Travelers who had been spared falling off cliffs on their mounts and had survived the dangers of the swamps to reach the other ocean found themselves victims of bandits who robbed them of their belongings or mercenaries who charged a fortune to take them to San Francisco, piling them like cattle onto ships coming apart at the seams.

"Is California very big?" Eliza asked, trying not to let her voice reveal her heart's anxiety.

"Bring me a map and I'll show you. It's much larger than Chile."

"And how do you get to where the gold is?"

"They say there's gold everywhere."

"But say, for example, you wanted to find someone in California. . . ."

"That would be very difficult," the captain answered, studying Eliza's expression with curiosity.

"Are you going there on your next trip, Uncle?"

"I have a tempting offer that I think I will accept. Some Chilean investors want to establish a regular cargo and passenger service to California. They need a captain for their steamship."

"Then we shall see you more often, John!" Rose exclaimed.

"You do not have any experience on steamships," Jeremy noted.

"Maybe not, but I know the sea better than anyone."

On the night of the appointed Friday, Eliza waited for the house to quiet down before going to the little shed in the farthest patio to meet Mama Fresia. She got out of bed and went downstairs barefoot, wearing only a cotton nightgown. She had no idea what nostrum she was going to be given, but she was sure it would be far from delightful. In her experience all medicines were unpleasant, but her mamacita's were foul. "Don't you worry, *niña,* I'm going to give you enough liquor that when you wake up you won't remember any pain. One thing, though," she had told her. "We will need a lot of rags to catch the blood." Eliza had often made that same trip through the dark house to meet her lover, so she did not have to feel her way, but that night she went very slowly, dragging her feet, hoping for one of those Chilean earthquakes capable of flattening everything to give her a good excuse not to meet Mama Fresia. Her feet were icy and a shiver ran down her back. She didn't know if it was cold, fear of what was going to happen, or the last nudge of her conscience. From her first suspicion that she was pregnant she had heard a voice calling her. It was the voice of the baby in her womb, crying out for its right to live, she was sure. She tried not to hear it, and not to think; she was trapped and as soon as she began to show there would be no hope or forgiveness for her. No one would be able to understand her fall; there was no way to recover her lost honor. Neither prayers nor Mama Fresia's candles could prevent her disgrace. Her lover wasn't going to turn around in midtrip and hurry back to marry her before you could see she was pregnant. It was already too late for that. She was terrified at the thought of ending up like Joaquín's mother, branded with a shameful stigma, shunned by her family and living in poverty and loneliness with an illegitimate child; she couldn't bear rejection, she would rather die once and for all. And she might die that very night at the hands of the good woman who had brought her up and loved her more than anyone in this world.

The family started to go to bed early, but the captain and Miss Rose stayed locked up in her little sewing room, whispering for hours. Every voyage John Sommers brought books to his sister and as he left carried mysterious packets that Eliza suspected contained things Miss Rose had written. She had seen her carefully wrapping up the notebooks, the ones she spent leisurely afternoons filling with cramped writing. Out of respect, or some strange reluctance, no one mentioned them, just as no one said anything about the muted watercolors she painted. Writing and painting were treated like minor aberrations, nothing to be truly ashamed of, but nothing to boast about, either. Eliza's culinary skills were received with the same indifference by the Sommers, who tasted the dishes in silence and changed the subject if visitors commented on them. On the other hand, they offered undeserved applause when it came to her valiant efforts at the piano, even if barely good enough to stumble along accompanying a singer. All her life Eliza had seen Miss Rose writing and had never asked about it, just as she had never heard whether Jeremy and John themselves did. She was curious to know why her uncle was so furtive when he carried Miss Rose's notebooks away, but without anyone's stating it she knew that this was one of the fundamental secrets upon which the family's equilibrium depended, and to violate it would be to bring down with one puff the house of cards they lived in. For a long while now Jeremy and Rose had been asleep in their rooms, and her uncle John had gone out on horseback after his long talk with his sister. Knowing the captain's habits, the girl could imagine him carousing with some of his flighty women friends, the ones who said hello in the street when Miss Rose wasn't with them. She supposed that he danced and drank, but as she had barely heard whispers about prostitutes, the idea of anything more sordid never occurred to her. The possibility of doing for money or sport what she had done with Joaquín Andieta for love never entered her mind. According to her calculations, her uncle would not be home until early the next morning, which is why she nearly jumped out of her skin when, as she reached the ground floor, someone grabbed her arm in the dark. She felt the warmth of a large body against hers, a breath of liquor and tobacco in her face, and immediately identified her uncle. She tried to slip loose as she struggled to slap together some story about why she was there in her nightgown at that hour, but the captain marched her to the library dimly lit by moonbeams falling through the window. He sat her down in Jeremy's English leather armchair while he looked for matches to light the lamp.

"All right, Eliza, now you're going to tell me what the hell's going on," he ordered in a tone he had never used with her.

In a flash of lucidity, Eliza knew that the captain would not be her ally, as she had hoped. The tolerance he liked to boast of would not be forthcoming in this instance; if the good name of the family was in question, his loyalty would be with his brother and sister. Mute, the girl held his eyes, defying him.

"Rose tells me that you've fallen in love with some fellow or other who is clearly on his uppers, is that right?"

"I saw him twice, Uncle John. And that was months ago. I don't even know his name."

"But you haven't forgotten him, have you? First love is like smallpox, it leaves its scars. Were you alone with him?"

"No."

"I don't believe you. You think I'm a fool? Anyone can see how you've changed, Eliza."

"I don't feel well, Uncle. I ate some green fruit and my stomach's upset, that's all. I was just on my way to the privy."

"You have the eyes of a bitch in heat!"

"What a terrible thing to say, Uncle."

"I'm sorry, child. Don't you see that I love you very much and I'm worried about you? I can't allow you to ruin your life. Rose and I have worked out an excellent plan. Would you like to go to England? I can arrange for the two of you to sail within the month; that will give you time to buy what you need for the voyage."

"England?"

"You will travel in first class, like queens, and once in London you will stay in a charming hotel a few blocks from Buckingham Palace."

Eliza understood that her uncle and aunt had arranged her future. The last thing she wanted was to go off in the opposite direction from Joaquín, putting two oceans between them.

"Thank you, Uncle. I would love to know England," she said with all the sweetness she could muster.

The captain poured himself one brandy after another, lighted his pipe, and spent two solid hours telling Eliza about the advantages of life in London, where a young lady like her could mix in the best society, go to balls, attend the theater and concerts, buy beautiful dresses, and make a good marriage. She was at an age to do that. And wouldn't she like to go to Paris and Italy, too? No one should die without seeing Venice and Florence. He would personally see that she got everything she wanted, hadn't he always done that? The world is filled with handsome, interesting men of good standing; she would find that out for herself as soon as she got out of the godforsaken port she was buried in. Valparaíso was no place for a girl as pretty and well educated as she. It wasn't her fault that she fell in love with the first male to cross her path; she had been locked up all her life. And about that boy, what was his name? Someone who worked for Jeremy, wasn't he? She would soon forget him. Love, he assured her, inexorably burns itself out, or with distance is pulled up by the roots. No one could give her better advice than he could; whatever else, he was an expert on distance and love turned to ash.

"I do not know what you are talking about, Uncle. Based on one glass of orange juice, Miss Rose has invented a novel about my being in love. This person came to deliver some crates, I offered him some juice, he took it, and then he left. That's all. Nothing happened, and I have never seen him again."

"If it is as you say, you are fortunate. That's one fantasy you won't have to eradicate."

John Sommers continued drinking and talking till early dawn, while Eliza, curled up in the English leather chair, fell asleep thinking that her prayers had been heard in heaven after all. It wasn't a timely earthquake that had saved her from Mama Fresia's terrible ministrations but her uncle. In the hut in the patio, the Indian waited the whole night long.

The Farewell

Saturday afternoon John Sommers invited his sister Rose to visit the ship owned by the Rodríguez de Santa Cruz brothers. If everything worked out in the current negotiations, he would be captaining it, at last fulfilling his dream of sailing with steam. Later Paulina received them in the salon of the Hotel Inglés, where she was staying. She had traveled from the north to set the ball rolling on her project, seeing that her husband had been in California for several months. They took advantage of the constant stream of ships coming and going to communicate via a vigorous correspondence in which declarations of love were interwoven with business plans. Paulina had incorporated John Sommers into their enterprise solely on intuition. She remembered vaguely that he was the brother of Jeremy and Rose Sommers, some people from the English colony her father had invited to the hacienda once or twice, but she had seen him only once and hadn't exchanged more than a few courteous words with him. Their one connection was their shared friendship with Jacob Todd, but in recent weeks she had made inquiries and was very satisfied with what she had heard. The captain had a solid reputation among seafaring men and in commercial accounting offices. He was a man whose experience and word could be trusted, which was more than you could say for many in these mad times when anyone could rent a ship, form a company of adventurers, and set sail. In general they were flim-flam men and their ships were lucky to stay afloat, but that mattered little or not at all since as soon as they reached California the associations evaporated, the ships were abandoned, and everyone shot off in search of gold. Paulina, however, had a long-term vision. To begin with, she was not obliged to respect the whims of strangers, because her only partners were her husband and her brother-in-law, and besides, the major part of the capital was hers, so she was free to make her own decisions. Her ship—which she christened the *Fortuna*—even though rather small and a veteran of seven years at sea, was in impeccable condition. Paulina was prepared to pay the crew well to keep them from deserting to the gold frenzy, but she also assumed that without the iron hand of a good captain no salary was big enough to maintain discipline on board. It was her husband and brother-in-law's plan to export mining tools, lumber, work clothing, domestic utensils, dried beef, grains, beans, and other nonperishable produce, but as soon as she set foot in Valparaíso she realized that this plan had occurred to a number of others and the competition would be ferocious. She took a good look around and saw the riot of vegetables and fruits of that generous summer. There was more than could be sold. Vegetables were growing in every patio and trees were bowed beneath the weight of their fruit; few people were inclined to pay for what they could have for free. She thought about her father's estate, where summer's bounty rotted on the ground because no one had enough interest to pick it up. If they could get it to California it would be more valuable than gold itself, she thought. Fresh produce, Chilean wine, medicines, eggs, good clothing, musical instruments, and—why not—theater extravaganzas, operettas, music hall performances. Hundreds of immigrants were streaming into San Francisco every day. For the moment they were mainly adventurers and outlaws, but soon settlers would be coming from the other side of the United States: honest farmers, lawyers, doctors, teachers, all kinds of decent people ready to build a life with their families. Where there are women, there is civilization, and when that time comes in San Francisco my ship will be there with all the necessities, she decided.

Paulina received Captain John Sommers and his sister, Rose, at tea time, when the heat of midday was waning and a fresh breeze was blowing from the sea. She was overdressed in comparison with the sober port society, head to toe butter-colored mousseline and lace, with a cluster of curls over each ear and more jewelry than was acceptable at that hour of the day. Her two-year-old son was kicking in the arms of a uniformed nursemaid and a woolly little dog at her feet gobbled the bits of cake she placed in its mouth. The first half hour was taken up with introductions, drinking tea, and remembering Jacob Todd.

"What has become of our good friend?" inquired Paulina, who would never forget the eccentric Englishman's intervention in her love affair with Feliciano.

"I haven't heard anything from him in some time," the captain informed her. "He went to England with me a couple of years ago. He was terribly depressed, but the sea air did him good and by the time he got off the ship he had recovered his good humor. The last I knew, he was thinking of forming a Utopian colony."

"A what?" Paulina and Miss Rose exclaimed in unison.

"A group to live outside society, with their own laws and government guided by principles of equality, free love, and communal labor, as I remember. At least that was how he explained it a thousand times during the voyage."

"He is even madder than we thought," Miss Rose concluded, feeling a touch of sadness for her loyal suitor.

"People with original ideas always end up being considered mad," Paulina noted. "Now, to come to the point. I have an idea I would like to discuss with you, Captain Sommers. You know the *Fortuna*. How long would it take to steam between Valparaíso and the Golfo de Penas?"

"Golfo de Penas? But that's to the south! And it's not called the Gulf of Sorrows for nothing."

"Yes, it's farther south than Puerto Aysén."

"And what will I do there? There's nothing but islands, forest, and rain, señora."

"Do you know those waters?"

"Yes, but I thought we were talking about going to San Francisco."

"Try these little pastries, they are delicious," she offered, petting the dog.

While John and Rose Sommers were talking with Paulina in the salon of the Hotel Inglés, Eliza was roaming through El Almendral with Mama Fresia. It was near the time when students and guests were beginning to gather for the Academy dancing class, and, most untypically, Miss Rose had let Eliza go for a couple of hours with her nana as chaperone. Usually she did not let her protégée go near the Academy without her, but the dancing master did not serve alcoholic beverages until after sunset, which kept the more troublesome youths away during the early evening. Eliza decided to seize the unique opportunity of getting out of the house without Miss Rose, and convinced Mama Fresia to help her in her plans.

"Give me your blessing, Mamita," she asked. "I have to go to California to look for Joaquín."

"How can you do that, alone and pregnant!" Mama Fresia exclaimed with horror.

"If you don't help me, I'll do it alone."

"I am going to tell Miss Rose everything!"

"If you do, I'll kill myself. And then I will come and haunt you for the rest of your days. I swear I will," the girl returned with fierce determination.

The day before, she had seen a group of women in the port negotiating for a ticket. Because they looked so different from the women she normally saw in the street, heads covered winter or summer beneath their black mantles, she assumed these were the girls her Uncle John partied with. "They are worse than dogs, *niña*; they go to bed for money and have their big toes in hell," Mama Fresia had told her once. Eliza had overheard some things the captain told Jeremy Sommers about the Chilean and Peruvian women on their way to California with plans to relieve the miners of their gold, but she couldn't imagine how they were going to do that. If those women could make the voyage alone, and survive without help, she could do it, too, she resolved. She walked quickly, her heart thudding and her face half hidden behind her fan, sweating in the December heat. She had brought her little velvet bag with the jewels of her trousseau. Her new ankle boots were acute torture and her corset squeezed her waist; the stench of the open sewers that drained all the city's waste increased her nausea, but she walked erect as she had learned in years of balancing a book on her head and of playing the piano with a metal rod strapped to her back. Mama Fresia, moaning and muttering prayers in her tongue and slowed by varicose veins, and her pounds, could barely keep up with her. Where are we going, child? *Por Dios*. . . . But Eliza couldn't answer because she didn't know. She was sure of one thing: there was no question of pawning her jewels and buying a ticket to California, because there was no way to do it without her uncle John learning. Even though dozens of ships came and went every day, Valparaíso was a small city, and everyone in the port knew Captain John Sommers. She had no identification papers, and no chance at all of obtaining a passport, because the United States legation in Chile had been closed due to a frustrated love affair between some North American diplomat and a Chilean lady. Eliza concluded that the only way she could follow Joaquín Andieta to California would be to stow away. Her uncle John had told her that sometimes voyagers were sneaked onto a ship with the help of a crew member. Sometimes they managed to stay hidden the whole trip, other times they died and their bodies went into the sea without anyone's ever knowing, but if they were discovered both the stowaway and the ones who had helped him were punished. That was one of the times, he said, when he exercised his unquestionable authority as captain with the greatest rigor: on the high seas there was no law or justice but his.

Most of the illegal transactions in the port, according to her uncle, were carried out in the bars. Eliza had never been inside such a place, but when she saw a female figure heading for a nearby doorway she recognized her as one of the women who had been on the dock the day before looking for a way to get on one of the ships. She looked very young; she was short, broad-hipped, full-busted, had two black braids down her back, and was wearing a cotton skirt, embroidered blouse, and a shawl around her shoulders. Without a second thought, Eliza followed her, while Mama Fresia stood in the street voicing her warnings. "No one goes in there but bad women, *niña*, it's a mortal sin!" Eliza pushed the door open and took several seconds to adjust to the darkness and the blast of tobacco and rancid beer that struck her in the face. The place was crowded with men, and all eyes turned to look at the two women. For an instant, there was an expectant silence, followed immediately by a chorus of whistles and vulgarities. The other woman, a veteran of these scenes, marched toward a table at the rear of the room, slapping away right and left at hands trying to touch her, but Eliza stepped back blindly, horrified, not really understanding what was happening or why those men were shouting at her. As she backed toward the door she crashed into a customer coming in. This individual grunted something in another language and caught her when she slipped. He was shocked when he saw who it was. Eliza, all virginal dress and fan, was completely out of place. She in turn immediately recognized the Chinese cook her uncle had spoken to the day before.

"Tao Chi'en?" she asked, grateful for her good memory.

The man greeted her by joining his hands before his face and bowing over and over as the whistling continued from the bar. Two sailors got to their feet and stumbled toward them. Tao Chi'en pointed toward the door and they both left.

"Miss Sommers?" he asked once they were outside.

She nodded, but had no opportunity to say more because they were interrupted by the two sailors from the bar, who loomed in the doorway, pretty clearly drunk and looking for trouble.

"You dare to bother this pretty little lady, you stinking Chink?" they threatened.

Tao Chi'en ducked his head, half-turned, and made a move to leave, but one of the men stopped him short by grabbing his braid and tugging on it while his buddy exhaled his winey breath in Eliza's face, mumbling propositions. Tao Chi'en turned with the reflexes of a cat and faced the aggressor. His outsized knife was in his hand, the blade gleaming like a mirror in the summer sun. Mama Fresia grunted and without even thinking shouldered the nearer sailor like a plow horse, grabbed Eliza's arm, and raced off down the street with an agility unsuspected in anyone of her pounds. The two women ran several blocks, putting distance between them and the red-light district, not stopping until they reached San Agustín plaza, where Mama Fresia collapsed, trembling, onto the first bench in sight.

"Ay, *niña*! If my *patrona* ever finds out, she will kill me. Let's go straight home."

"I haven't done what I came to do, Mamita. I have to go back to that bar."

Mama Fresia crossed her arms, stoutly refusing to budge, while Eliza strode back and forth trying to organize a plan in the midst of her confusion. There wasn't much time. Miss Rose's instructions had been very clear: at exactly six o'clock the coach would be in front of the dance academy to take them back home. She had to act quickly, she knew she would not have a second chance. This was their standoff when Eliza saw Tao Chi'en walking serenely in their direction with his hesitant step and imperturbable smile. He repeated the usual ritual of his greeting and then spoke to Eliza in good English to ask whether the honorable daughter of Captain John Sommers needed assistance. Eliza clarified that she was Sommers' niece, not his daughter, and with a rush of sudden confidence, or desperation, confessed that in fact she did need his help, but that it was an extremely private matter.

"Something the captain cannot know?"

"No one can know."

Tao Chi'en begged her pardon. The captain was a good man, he said; it was true that his employer had been underhanded when he shanghaied him for his crew, but he had treated him well and Tao could not think of betraying him. Crushed, Eliza sank down on the bench with her face in her hands, while Mama Fresia watched them, not understanding a word of their English but guessing the drift. Finally, she leaned over to Eliza and tugged a few times on the velvet pouch that held the jewels.

"Do you think that anyone does anything for free in this world, *niña*?" she asked.

Eliza got the point. She dried her tears and, indicating a place beside her on the bench, invited the man to sit down. She dug into the pouch and pulled out the pearl necklace her uncle John had given her the day before and laid it on Tao Chi'en's knees.

"Can you hide me in a ship? I have to go to California," she explained.

"Why? That's no place for women, only bandits."

"I'm looking for something."

"Gold?"

"Something more valuable than gold."

The man stared, openmouthed, because he had never seen a woman capable of such extremes in real life, only in classic novels in which the heroines always died at the end.

"With this necklace you can buy your passage. You don't have to hide," said Tao Chi'en, who was not inclined to complicate his life by breaking the law.

"No captain will take me without notifying my family."

Tao Chi'en's initial surprise turned into frank amazement. This woman was actually planning to dishonor her family and was expecting him to help her! A devil had gotten into her body, no doubt of it. Again Eliza reached into the pouch; she took out a gold brooch set with turquoises and set it beside the necklace.

"Have you ever loved anyone more than life itself, señor?" she asked.

Tao Chi'en looked into the girl's eyes for the first time since they had met, and he must have seen something in them because he picked up the necklace and hid it beneath his shirt, then handed the brooch back to Eliza. He stood up, adjusted his cotton pants and the butcher knife in his sash, and again bowed ceremoniously.

"I no longer work for Captain Sommers. Tomorrow the brigantine *Emilia* sails for California. Come tonight at ten and I will get you on board."

"How?"

"I do not know. We shall see."

Tao Chi'en proffered another courteous farewell and walked away so silently and quickly that he seemed to have vanished like smoke. Eliza and Mama Fresia arrived at the dance academy just in time to meet the coachman, who had killed a half-hour wait while drinking from his flask.

The *Emilia* was a ship of French registry, once svelte and swift, but she had plowed through many seas, and centuries before had lost the impetus of youth. She was crisscrossed with ancient marine scars, she carried a crust of mollusks on her matronly hips, her exhausted joints moaned in the pounding seas, and her stained and repatched sail looked like a petticoat ready for the ragbag. She sailed from Valparaíso on the radiant morning of February 18, 1849, carrying eighty-seven passengers of the male sex, five women, six cows, eight hogs, three cats, eighteen sailors, a Dutch captain, a Chilean pilot, and a Chinese cook. Eliza was also aboard, but the only person who knew of her existence was Tao Chi'en.

The first-class passengers were crowded into staterooms on the forward deck, without much privacy but considerably more comfortable than those in tiny cabins with four bunks each, or out on the open deck after casting lots to see where to stow their bundles. One cabin below the waterline was assigned to the five Chilean women who were off to test their luck in California. In the port of Callao, two Peruvians came aboard and were unceremoniously shoved in with them, two to a bunk. Captain Vincent Katz instructed his crew, as well as the passengers, that they were not to have the least social contact with the females, for he was not about to allow indecent congress on his ship, and in his eyes it was obvious that those women were not the most virtuous—although, inevitably, his orders were violated over and over during the voyage. The men greatly missed female companionship, and the humble bawds off on an adventure hadn't a peso in their pockets. The cows and hogs, well secured in small pens on the second deck, were to provide fresh milk and meat for the passengers, whose diet would consist primarily of beans, hardtack, salted meat, and whatever fish they could catch. To compensate for such monotony, the more affluent passengers brought some of their own provisions, especially wine and cigars, but most on board endured their hunger. Two of the cats were set loose to hold down the rats, which otherwise would have reproduced uncontrollably during the two months of the voyage. The third traveled with Eliza.

The belly of the *Emilia* held the assorted luggage of the passengers and cargo destined for the California trade, organized in such a way as to obtain maximum usage of the limited space. Nothing would be touched until the final destination, and no one went there except the cook, the one person with authorized access to the strictly rationed dried staples. Tao Chi'en kept the keys at his waist, and personally answered to the captain for the contents of the storerooms. There, in the darkest, deepest pit of the ship, in a two-by-two-meter hole, went Eliza. The walls and ceiling of her cavern were trunks and cases of merchandise; her bed was a sack, and the only light came from a candle stub. She had a soup bowl for food, a jug for water, and a bucket for her physical needs. She could take a couple of steps and stretch among the bales and crates, and could cry and scream as much as she wished, because the sloshing of the waves against the ship swallowed her voice. Her one contact with the outside world was Tao Chi'en, who invented a variety of pretexts to come down to feed her and empty her bucket. Her only company was the cat, closed in the hold to control the rats, but during the terrible weeks of the sailing the unfortunate animal slowly went crazy, and finally, sadly, Tao Chi'en cut its throat with his knife.

Eliza was taken aboard in a sack over the back of a stevedore, one of many loading cargo and luggage in Valparaíso. She never learned how Tao Chi'en had managed to win the man's complicity and evade the vigilance of the captain and the pilot, who entered in a log everything that came onto the ship. She had escaped a few hours earlier thanks to a complicated scheme that involved a fake written invitation from the del Valle family to come visit for a few days at their hacienda. It was not an outlandish subterfuge. On previous occasions the daughters of Agustín del Valle had invited her to the country and Miss Rose had allowed her to go, always accompanied by Mama Fresia. She said good-bye to Jeremy, Miss Rose, and her uncle John with false lightheartedness, feeling a weight like a stone in her chest. She saw them sitting at the breakfast table reading English newspapers, completely innocent of her plans, and an overwhelming indecision nearly caused her to stay. They represented security and well-being; they were her only family, but she had crossed the line of decency; there was no turning back. The Sommers had brought her up within the strict norms of good behavior and such a serious slip sullied their good name. If she fled, the family reputation would be stained but at least they would have the benefit of the doubt: they could always say she had died. Whatever story the Sommers offered the world, she wouldn't have to watch them suffer the shame. The odyssey of going to find her lover seemed to be her one possible course, but in that moment of silent farewell she was assaulted by such sadness that she came close to bursting into tears and confessing everything. Then the last image of Joaquín Andieta the night he had left materialized with startling precision to remind her of her debt to their love. She caught up some loose strands of hair, set her Italian straw bonnet on her head, and left waving good-bye.

She took with her the suitcase Miss Rose had packed with her best summer dresses, a little money she had taken from Jeremy Sommers' room, and the jewels of her trousseau. She had been tempted to take Miss Rose's as well, but at the last moment was stayed by her respect for the woman who had been a mother to her. In her own room, in the empty coffer, she left a brief letter thanking them for all they had done for her and reiterating how much she loved them. She added a confession about the things she had taken, to protect the servants from being accused. Mama Fresia had put her stoutest boots in the suitcase, along with her notebooks and the bundle of Joaquín Andieta's love letters. She also took a heavy Castile woolen mantle, a gift from her uncle John. They left without arousing the least suspicion. The coachman left them in the street of the del Valle home and drove out of view without waiting for the gate to be opened. Mama Fresia and Eliza set off toward the port to meet Tao Chi'en at the place and the time they had agreed upon.

He was waiting for them. He took the suitcase from Mama Fresia's hands, and motioned to Eliza to follow him. The girl and her nana embraced for a long time. They knew they would never see each other again, but neither shed tears.

"What are you going to tell Miss Rose, Mamacita?"

"Nothing. I am leaving right now to go to my people in the south; no one will ever find me."

"Thank you, Mamita. I will never forget you."

"And I am going to pray that everything goes well with you, *niña*," were the last words Eliza heard from Mama Fresia's lips before she followed the Chinese cook into a fisherman's hut.

In the dark, windowless wood shack reeking of fish, its only ventilation the door, Tao Chi'en handed Eliza a pair of baggy trousers and a worn smock, indicating that she should put them on. He made no move to go outside or discreetly turn away. Eliza hesitated; she had never removed her clothes before a man, except Joaquín Andieta, but Tao Chi'en, who lacked a sense of privacy, failed to perceive her confusion; the body and its functions were natural to him, and he considered modesty more inconvenient than virtuous. Eliza realized that this was not the time for scruples; the ship was leaving that morning and the last dinghies were loading on the stragglers' luggage. She removed her straw bonnet, undid the buttons on her kidskin boots and her dress, untied the ribbons of her petticoats and, nearly swooning with shame, gestured to Tao Chi'en to help her undo her corset. As the articles of a young English lady's clothing piled up on the floor one by one, she was losing contact with known reality and irreversibly entering the strange illusion that would be her life in the months to come. She had the clear sensation of beginning a new story in which she was both protagonist and narrator.

Fourth Son

Tao Chi'en had not always had that name. In fact, he had no name until he was eleven; his parents were too poor to worry about details, he was simply called Fourth Son. He was born nine years before Eliza in a village in the province of Kwangtung, a day and a half's walk from the city of Canton. He came from a family of healers. For countless generations the men of his blood had passed from father to son their knowledge of medicinal plants, the art of drawing off bad humors, magic for frightening away demons, and skills for regulating energy: *qi*. The year Fourth Son was born, the family found itself in worse poverty than ever, and for some time they had been losing their land to moneylenders and gamblers. The officials of the empire collected taxes, kept the money, then imposed new tributes to cover up what they had stolen, and for good measure demanded illegal commissions and bribes. Fourth Son's family, like most of the peasants, could not pay. If they managed to save a few coins of their meager income from the mandarins, they immediately lost them gambling, one of the few diversions available to the poor. They could bet on frog and grasshopper races, cockroach fights, or fan-tan, along with many other popular games.

Fourth Son was a happy child who laughed over nothing, but he also had an unusual ability to concentrate and a keen curiosity for learning. By the time he was seven he knew that the talent of a good healer consists of maintaining the balance between yin and yang. At nine he knew the properties of the regional plants and could help his father and older brothers in the tiresome preparation of the plasters, salves, tonics, balms, syrups, powders, and pills of the peasant pharmacopoeia. First Son and his father traveled by foot from village to village offering treatments and remedies while Second Son and Third Son cultivated the wretched piece of land that was the family's only capital. Fourth Son had the mission of collecting plants, and he liked doing that because it allowed him to wander outside the village unsupervised, inventing games and imitating the songbirds. Sometimes, if she had enough strength after her endless household chores, his mother went with him. Because she was a woman, she could not work the land without drawing the derision of the neighbors. The family scratched to make ends meet, falling deeper and deeper into debt, until the fateful year of 1834 when their worst demons descended with full fury. First a pot of boiling water overturned on the youngest sister, barely two, scalding her from head to foot. They applied egg white to the burns and treated her with the herbs indicated in such injuries, but in less than three days the child died, exhausted from suffering. The mother never recovered. She had lost other sons and daughters in infancy; each had left a bleeding wound, and the little girl's accident was like the grain of rice that makes the bowl overflow. She began to decline before their eyes, thinner every day, her skin greenish, her bones brittle, and all her husband's brews could not stay the implacable advance of her mysterious illness until the morning they found her rigid, a smile of relief on her lips and her eyes at peace because at last she was going to meet the children she had lost. The funeral rites were very simple, because she was a woman and because they could not pay a monk. Neither did they have rice to offer relatives and neighbors during the ceremony; but at least they made sure that her spirit did not take refuge in the roof, the well, or the rats' nests, and later come out to haunt them. Without the one whose strength and patience had kept the family together through every trial, it was impossible to fend off calamity. It was a year of typhoons, bad harvests, and famine; the vast land of China was overrun with beggars and bandits. The one girl child left in the family, who was seven, was sold to an agent and never heard from again. First Son, destined to take his father's place in the calling of itinerant healer, was bitten by a rabid dog and died soon after, foaming at the mouth, his back arched like a bow. Second Son and Third Son were of an age to work, and to them fell the task of looking after their father in life, along with the future responsibilities of carrying out the funeral rites at his death and honoring his memory and that of their male ancestors for five generations. Fourth Son was of no particular value and was another mouth to feed, so his father sold him into ten years of servitude to merchants whose caravan passed near the village. The boy was eleven years old.

Thanks to one of those happy events that often changes the course of a life, that period of slavery, which could have been a hell for the boy, would turn out to be much better than the years he had spent under the paternal roof. Two mules pulled the cart loaded with the heavy goods of the caravan. A nerve-racking squeal accompanied every turn of the wheels, purposely left unoiled in order to frighten away demons. Fourth Son was tied with a rope to one of the animals to keep him from running away. Barefoot and thirsty, with his meager bundle of belongings on his back, he saw the roofs of his village and all the familiar landscape fade away behind him. He wept bitterly from the moment he left his father and brothers. Life in their little hut was the only life he had known, and it had not been unhappy; his parents had treated him gently, his mother had told him stories, and any excuse was cause to laugh and celebrate, even in times of the worst poverty. He trotted along behind the mule, convinced that every step was taking him deeper and deeper into the territory of evil spirits, and fearing that the squealing of the wheels, and the little bells hanging from the cart, would not be enough to protect him. He could barely understand the merchants' dialect, but the few words he could capture struck fear into his bones. They were talking about the many unhappy spirits roaming the region, lost souls of the dead who had not received a proper funeral. Famine, typhus, and cholera had strewn the landscape with corpses and there were not enough living left to honor so many dead. Fortunately, ghosts and demons had a reputation for being a little slow; they didn't know how to turn a corner and were easily distracted with offerings of food or paper gifts. Sometimes, however, nothing could keep them away and they might suddenly reappear, eager to earn their freedom by murdering strangers and inhabiting their bodies to make them carry out unthinkable deeds. The caravan had traveled for hours; the summer heat and the thirst were intense; the little boy tripped every two steps, and his impatient new masters urged him on by flicking his legs with a willow switch, though with no real malice. As the sun set, they decided to stop and make camp. They relieved the animals of their load, built a fire, brewed tea, and split into small groups to play fan-tan and mah-jongg. Finally they remembered Fourth Son and handed him a bowl of rice and a glass of tea, which he attacked with the voraciousness of months of hunger. As they were eating, they were surprised by deafening yells and found themselves engulfed in a cloud of dust. The travelers' howls were added to those of the attackers, and the terrorized boy dragged himself beneath the cart as far as the rope he was tied by would allow. This was no legion from hell, he quickly realized, but a band of robbers, one of many that, flaunting defiance of bumbling imperial soldiers, afflicted the highways and byways in those hopeless times. As soon as the merchants recovered from their first shock, they seized their weapons and confronted the attackers amid a tumult of yells, threats, and shots that lasted but a few minutes. When the dust settled, one of the bandits had escaped and two others were lying on the ground, gravely wounded. The merchants tore the cloth masks from their faces and revealed two ragged adolescents armed with clubs and crude spears. The brigands were decapitated with dispatch so that they would suffer the humiliation of leaving this world in pieces, not whole as they had come into it, and their heads were impaled on stakes on either side of the road. As the merchants were catching their breath, they found one member of the caravan writhing on the ground with a serious spear wound in the thigh. Fourth Son, who had been paralyzed with fear beneath the cart, came wriggling out of his hiding place and respectfully asked the honorable merchants if he could attend the wounded man; since there was no alternative, they gave Fourth Son permission to proceed. He asked for tea to wash away the blood, then opened his pack and pulled out a bottle containing *bai yao*. He rubbed the white salve on the wound, wrapped the leg tightly, and proclaimed without hesitation that in fewer than three days the wound would have healed. And so it did. That incident saved Tao Chi'en from spending the next ten years working like a slave and being treated worse than a dog: the merchants took notice of his skills and sold him in Canton to a famous traditional physician and acupuncture master—a *zhong yi*—who needed an apprentice. With that wise man, Fourth Son acquired knowledge he would never have obtained from his rustic father.

His aged master was a placid man, slow to speak, with a face as round as the moon, and bony, sensitive hands, his best instruments. The first thing he did with his servant was give him a name. He consulted astrological and seers' books to find the name that corresponded to the boy: Tao. The word had several meanings, among them "way," "direction," "sense," and "harmony," but especially it represented the journey of life. The master gave Tao his own family name.

"You will be called Tao Chi'en. That name will start you on the road of medicine. Your destiny will be to ease pain and achieve wisdom. You will be a *zhong yi*, like me."

Tao Chi'en. . . . The young apprentice received his name gratefully. He kissed his master's hands and smiled for the first time since he had left his home. The impulse of joy that once made him dance with happiness for no reason at all beat again in his chest, and his smile did not fade for weeks. He skipped around the house, savoring his name like a sweet in his mouth, repeating it aloud and dreaming of it, until he was fully identified with it. His master, a follower of Confucius in practical matters and of Buddha in ideology, taught him with a firm hand but with great gentleness the discipline that led to making him a good physician.

"If I succeed in teaching you everything I mean to, someday you will be an enlightened man," he told him.

He maintained that rites and ceremonies were as necessary as the norms of good behavior and respect for hierarchies. He said that knowledge was of little use without wisdom, and that there was no wisdom without spirituality, and that true spirituality always included service to others. As he explained many times, the essence of a good physician consisted of a capacity for compassion and a sense of the ethical, without which qualities the sacred art of healing degenerated into simple charlatanism. He liked the ready smile of his apprentice.

"You have already traveled a good distance along the path of wisdom, Tao. The wise man is always joyful," he maintained.

Throughout the year, Tao Chi'en got out of bed at dawn, like any student, to do his hour of meditation, chants, and prayers. He had one day of rest on which to celebrate the New Year; working and studying were his only occupations. Before anything else, he had to learn

Chinese script to perfection, it was the official medium of communication in that enormous land of hundreds of peoples and languages. His master was inflexible in regard to the beauty and precision of calligraphy, which distinguishes the refined man from the scoundrel. He also insisted on developing in Tao Chi'en the artistic sensitivity which, according to him, characterized the superior being. Like all civilized Chinese, he had an immeasurable aversion to war and was, in contrast, inclined toward the arts of music, painting, and literature. By his side, Tao Chi'en learned to appreciate the delicate lace of a spiderweb pearled with dewdrops in the light of dawn and to express his pleasure in inspired poems written in elegant calligraphy. In the opinion of the master, the only thing worse than not writing poetry was writing it badly. In his master's house the boy attended the frequent reunions in which the guests admired the garden and created verses in the impulse of the instant, while he served tea and listened, enthralled. One could win immortality by writing a book, especially a book of poems, said the master, who had written several. To the homespun practical knowledge he had acquired by watching his father at work Tao Chi'en added the impressive theoretical volume of ancestral Chinese medicine. The youth learned that the human body is composed of five elements: wood, fire, earth, metal, and water, and that those elements are associated with five planets, five atmospheric conditions, five colors, and five notes. Through the proper use of medicinal plants, acupuncture, and cupping glasses, a good physician could prevent and cure various maladies and control masculine energy—active and light—and feminine energy—passive and dark: yin and yang. The goal of this art, however, was not so much to eliminate illness as to maintain harmony. "You must choose your food, orient your bed, and conduct your meditation according to the season of the year and the direction of the wind. In that way you will always resonate with the universe," the master counseled.

The *zhong yi* was content with his fate, although the lack of descendants weighed like a shadow over his serenity of spirit. He had never had sons, despite the miraculous herbs regularly ingested during an entire lifetime to cleanse his blood and fortify his member, and the remedies and spells applied to two wives, both dead in their youth, as well as the many concubines who followed. He had to accept with humility that it had not been the fault of those self-denying women but the apathy of his virile liquors. None of the remedies for fertility he had used to help others aided him, and finally he became resigned to the irrefutable fact that his loins were barren. He stopped punishing his wives with fruitless demands and enjoyed them to the full, in accord with the precepts of the beautiful pillow books in his collection. However, the aged physician, far more interested in acquiring new knowledge and exploring the narrow path of wisdom, had long ago, one by one, shed the concubines whose presence distracted him from his intellectual pursuits. He did not have to have a young woman before his eyes in order to describe her in elegant poems; memory was sufficient. He had also surrendered hope for sons of his own, but he needed to prepare for the future. Who would help him in the last stage of his life and at the hour of his death? Who would clean his tomb and venerate his memory? He had trained apprentices before, and with each had nourished the secret ambition of adopting him, but none was worthy of the honor. Tao Chi'en was no more intelligent or intuitive than the others, but he carried within him an obsession for learning that the master immediately recognized because it was identical to his own. He was, besides, a sweet and entertaining lad; it was easy to become fond of him. In the years they lived together, he gained such an appreciation of Tao that often he asked himself how it was possible that he was not a child of his blood. Nevertheless, esteem for his apprentice did not blind him; in his experience the changes of adolescence may be very profound, and he could not predict what kind of man Tao would make. As the Chinese proverb says, "Brilliance in youth does not guarantee worth in maturity." He feared he would be mistaken, as he had been before, and he preferred to wait patiently for the true nature of the boy to be revealed. In the meanwhile, he guided him, as he did the young trees in his garden, to help him grow straight. At least this one learns quickly, the aged physician thought, calculating how many years he had left to live; according to the astral signs and careful observation of his body, he would not have time to train a new apprentice.

Soon Tao Chi'en learned to select their supplies in the market and herb shops. Watching the physician as he worked, he came to know the intricate mechanisms of the human body, procedures for cooling fevers and fiery temperaments, for giving warmth to those who suffered the cold of approaching death, for stirring the juices in sterile men, and for stopping the flux of watery bowels. He made long trips through the fields to look for the best plants at the precise point of maximum efficacy, then wrapped them in damp rags to keep them fresh on his way back to the city. When he turned fourteen, his master considered him ready to practice and regularly sent him to attend prostitutes, with the stringent order to abstain from any commerce with them because, as he himself would see when he examined them, death rode on their shoulders.

"Diseases of the brothels kill more people than opium and typhus. But if you carry out your obligations and learn at a good pace, in due time I will buy you a young virgin," his master promised.

Tao Chi'en had suffered hunger as a boy, but his body stretched until he became taller than any other member of his family. At fourteen, he felt no attraction toward those girls for hire, merely scientific curiosity. They were too different from him; they lived in a world that was so remote and secret that he could not consider them truly human. Later, when the sudden onslaught of nature unhinged him and he was staggering around like a drunk tripping over his shadow, his teacher regretted having let his concubines go. Nothing so distracted a good student from his responsibilities as the explosion of virility. A woman would calm him, and in passing be useful in giving him practical knowledge, but the idea of buying one was bothersome—the master was comfortable in his solely masculine universe—and he gave Tao herbal teas to calm his ardor. The *zhong yi* did not remember the hurricane of carnal passions, and with the best intention gave his student the pillow books from his library to read as part of his education, not thinking to measure the debilitating effect they would have on his wretched pupil. He made Tao memorize each of the two hundred twenty-two positions of love, along with their poetic names, until he could identify them unhesitatingly in the exquisite illustrations of the books, all of which added immeasurably to the young man's distraction.

Tao Chi'en became as familiar with Canton as once he had been with his small village. He liked that ancient, chaotic, walled city of twisting streets and canals, where palaces and huts were jumbled together indiscriminately and there were people who lived and died on boats on the river without ever stepping onto dry land. He grew used to the humid, hot climate of a long summer lashed with typhoons but pleasant in the winter months of October to March. Canton was sealed to foreigners, although from time to time pirates flying flags of other nations made a surprise raid. There were a few locations where from November to May foreigners could trade their merchandise, but there were so many taxes, regulations, and obstacles that most international merchants chose to set up business in Macao. Early in the morning, when Tao Chi'en was on his way to the market, it was not unusual to find newborn baby girls thrown like garbage into the street or floating in the canals, often chewed on by dogs or rats. No one wanted them, they were disposable. Why feed a daughter who had no value and was going to end up as a servant in the home of her future husband? "Better a deformed son than a dozen girls as wise as Buddha," was the popular saying. There were too many children anyway. Brothels and opium dens proliferated on all sides. Canton was a populous city, rich and lighthearted, filled with temples, restaurants, and gaming houses, where all the festivals of the calendar were noisily observed. Even punishments and executions became a cause for a celebration. Great crowds gathered to cheer on the executioners with their bloody aprons and collections of sharp knives that could lop off a head with a single sure-handed blow. Justice was meted out promptly and simply, with no appeal or unnecessary cruelty except in the case of betrayal of the emperor, the worst possible crime, which was paid for with slow death and the banishment of all relatives, thereby reduced to slavery. Minor crimes were punished by lashing or by placing the guilty party's head in a wood stock for several days so that he could not rest or reach his head with his hands to eat or scratch. Squares and markets were home to the popular storytellers who, like mendicant monks, traveled about the country preserving a centuries-old oral tradition. Jugglers, acrobats, snake charmers, transvestites, traveling musicians, magicians, and contortionists performed in the streets, while all around them seethed a commerce in silk, tea, jade, spices, gold, tortoiseshell, porcelain, ivory, and precious stones. Vegetables, fruits, and meats were offered in colorful profusion: cabbages and tender bamboo shoots were displayed beside cages of the cats, dogs, and raccoons that at a client's request the butcher killed and skinned in one maneuver. There were long alleys where only birds were sold—for no one was ever without birds—and their cages, from the simplest to those made of the finest woods inlaid with silver and mother-of-pearl. Other passageways in the market were devoted to exotic fish, which were known to attract good fortune. Tao Chi'en, always curious, would entertain himself looking at everything and making friends, and then he would run to complete his errands in the sector where the supplies for his vocation were sold. He could identify it blindfolded from the penetrating scent of spices, plants, and medicinal barks. Dried serpents were rolled up and set in heaps like dusty coils of rope; toads, salamanders, and strange marine creatures were strung on cords like beads; crickets and large beetles with hard phosphorescent shells languished in boxes; monkeys of all kinds awaited their turn to die; bear and orangutan paws, antelope and rhinoceros horns, tiger eyes, shark fins, and claws of mysterious nocturnal birds were sold by weight.

Tao Chi'en's first years in Canton were spent in study, work, and service to his aged mentor, whom he came to respect like a grandfather. Those were happy years. The memory of his own family faded and he forgot the faces of his father and his brothers, but not his mother's, because she appeared to him frequently. Study soon ceased to be a task and became a passion. Every time he learned something new, he flew to his master to blurt it out to him. "The more you learn, the sooner you will know how little you know," the ancient would say, laughing. On his own initiative, Tao Chi'en decided to learn Mandarin and Cantonese, because the dialect of his village seemed very limited. He absorbed the knowledge of his master so swiftly that the old man jokingly accused him of stealing even his dreams, but his passion for teaching made him generous. He shared with the boy everything he wanted to investigate, not only in matters of medicine but other aspects of his vast reserve of knowledge and refined culture. Magnanimous by nature, he was nonetheless severe in his criticism and demanding of effort, because, as he said, "I do not have much time left and I cannot take all I know to the other world, someone must use it upon my death." However, he also warned his pupil against greed for learning, for that could fetter a man as surely as gluttony or lust. "The wise man desires nothing; he does not judge, he makes no plans, he keeps his mind open and his heart at peace," he maintained. He reprimanded Tao Chi'en with such sadness when the youth failed that he would have preferred a lashing, but that practice went against the nature of the *zhong yi*, who never allowed anger to determine his actions. The only occasions on which he ceremoniously punished Tao Chi'en with a willow switch, without anger but with firm didactic purpose, was when he could prove beyond a shadow of a doubt that his apprentice had yielded to the temptation of gambling or had paid for a woman. Tao Chi'en used to juggle the market bills in order to make bets in the gaming houses, whose attraction he could not resist, or for a brief, student-rate consolation in the arms of one of his patients in the brothels. It never took the master long to discover these offenses, because if Tao lost in gambling he could not explain what had happened to the change, and if he won he was incapable of hiding his euphoria. As for women, his master could smell them on his skin.

"Take off your shirt, I will have to apply the bamboo and see if finally you understand, my son. How many times have I told you that the worst evils in China are gambling and brothels? In the former, men lose the product of their labors, and in the latter they lose their health and life. You will never be a good physician or a good poet if you have those vices."

In 1839, when the Opium War between China and Great Britain broke out, Tao Chi'en was sixteen years old. At that point the country was overrun with beggars. Masses of humanity poured from the countryside and appeared with their tatters and pustules in the cities, where they were driven back, forced to wander the highways of the empire like packs of starving dogs. Bands of robbers and rebels fought an endless war of ambushes against the government troops. It was a period of destruction and pillage. The weakened imperial armies, under the command of corrupt officers receiving contradictory orders from Peking, could do nothing against the powerful and well-disciplined English fleet. They could not draw upon popular support because the peasants were so weary of seeing their paddies destroyed, their villages in flames, and their daughters raped by soldiers. At the end of almost four years of struggle, China had to accept a humiliating defeat and pay the equivalent of twenty-one million dollars to their British conquerors, yield Hong Kong to them, and grant them the right to establish "concessions," residential enclaves protected by extraterritorial laws. There the foreigners lived with their own police, services, and government and laws, guarded by their own troops. The "concessions" were true foreign nations inside Chinese territory, from which the Europeans controlled trade, principally opium. They did not enter Canton until five years later, but after the acupuncture master witnessed the degrading defeat of his venerated emperor and saw the economy and morale of his nation sag, he decided there was no reason to go on living.

During the war years the aged *zhong yi*'s spirit visibly deteriorated and he lost the serenity so arduously won over the course of his lifetime. His withdrawal and inattention to material matters reached such a point that after his master had eaten nothing for days, Tao Chi'en had to spoon food into his mouth. The accounts became hopelessly entangled and creditors began to beat at the door, but his master dismissed them, for anything having to do with money seemed a repugnant burden from which sages were naturally immune. In the senile confusion of his last years, Tao's teacher forgot his good intentions in regard to adopting his apprentice and providing him with a wife; in truth, his mind was so cloudy that he often sat staring at Tao Chi'en with a perplexed expression, unable to remember his name or to place him in the labyrinth of faces and events that assailed him without order or harmony. But he had enough spirit still to direct the details of his burial, because for enlightened Chinese the most important event in life was one's funeral. The idea of putting an end to his depressing life by means of an elegant death had been with him for some time, but he awaited the outcome of the war with the secret and irrational hope of seeing the triumph of the armies of the celestial empire. The foreigners' arrogance was intolerable; he felt a great scorn for those brutal *fan wey*, white ghosts who seldom washed, who drank milk and alcohol, and who were ignorant of the elementary norms of good behavior and incapable of honoring their ancestors as custom demanded. To him, the commercial accords seemed a favor the emperor had granted the ingrate barbarians who, instead of bowing before him with praise and gratitude, kept demanding more. When the treaty of Nanking was signed, it was the final blow for the *zhong yi*. The emperor, and every citizen of China down to the most humble, was dishonored. How could one recover his dignity following such an affront?

The ancient sage poisoned himself by swallowing gold. When his disciple returned from one of his excursions into the country to gather plants, he found the *zhong yi* in the garden, lying on silk cushions and dressed in white as a sign of mourning for himself. By his side, his tea was still warm and the ink from his brush still fresh. On his small desk was an unfinished poem, and a dragonfly cast a shadow upon the smooth parchment. Tao Chi'en kissed the hands of this man who had given him so much, then paused in the crepuscular light for an instant to appreciate the tracery of the dragonfly's transparent wings, just as his master would have wished him to do.

An enormous crowd attended the sage's funeral, because during his long life he had helped thousands of persons live in good health and die without agony. Government officials and dignitaries filed by with the greatest solemnity, literati recited their best poems, and courtesans showed up in their finest silks. A seer determined the most favorable day for the burial and an artist who crafted funeral offerings visited the house of the deceased to copy his possessions. He went around the property slowly, without taking measurements or notes, although beneath his voluminous sleeves he was making marks in a wax tablet with his fingernail. Later he constructed paper miniatures of the rooms and furnishings of the house, including the dead man's favorite objects, to be burned with bundles of paper money. He must not in the other world be deprived of the things he had enjoyed in this one. The coffin, which was huge and decorated like an imperial carriage, passed through the streets of the city between two rows of soldiers in dress uniform preceded by horsemen attired in brilliant colors and a band of musicians playing cymbals, drums, flutes, bells, triangles, and a variety of stringed instruments. The noise was unbearable, befitting the importance of the deceased. Flowers, clothing, and food were heaped upon his grave; candles and incense were lighted; and, finally, the money and quantities of paper objects were burned. The ancestral gold-sheathed tablet engraved with the master's name was placed upon the grave to receive his spirit, while the body returned to the earth. It was the role of the eldest son to accept the tablet and install it in a place of honor in his home beside those of other male ancestors, but the physician had no one to carry out that duty. Tao Chi'en was only a servant and it would have been an unforgivable breach of etiquette for him to offer. He was genuinely moved; among the throng he was surely the only one whose tears and wailing represented true grief, but the ancestral tablet ended up in the hands of a distant nephew whose moral obligation it would be to bring offerings and pray before it every two weeks and on each anniversary.

Once these solemn funeral rites were realized, the creditors fell like jackals upon the master's possessions. They ravaged the sacred texts and the laboratory, pawed through the herbs, spoiled the medicinal preparations, destroyed his carefully crafted poems, carried off his furniture and art objects, trampled the beautiful garden, and auctioned off the ancient mansion. Only shortly before, Tao Chi'en had safely hidden the gold acupuncture needles, a case containing medical instruments and a few essential remedies, and a small amount of money he had been filching for the last three years, ever since his master had begun to lose his way in the barren landscape of senile dementia. It was not his intention to steal from the venerable *zhong yi*, whom he revered like a grandfather, but to use the money to feed him, because he saw the debts piling up and feared the future. The suicide had precipitated events, however, and Tao Chi'en found himself in possession of an unexpected bonanza. Taking those funds could cost him his head, for his would be a crime of inferior against superior, but he was sure that no one would know except the spirit of the deceased, who undoubtedly would have approved his action. Would he not prefer rewarding his faithful servant and disciple to paying one of the many debts he owed to ravenous creditors? With this modest treasure and a change of clean clothing, Tao Chi'en fled the city. It occurred to him, fleetingly, to return to the village of his birth, but he immediately discarded that plan. To his family, he would always be Fourth Son, he would owe submission and obedience to his older brothers. He would have to work for them, accept the wife they chose for him, and resign himself to lifelong poverty. Nothing called him in that direction, not even filial obligations to his father and his ancestors, which fell to his older brothers anyway. What he needed was to go somewhere far away, somewhere the long arm of Chinese justice could not reach. He was twenty years old, and he had one year left before he would have fulfilled the ten years of his servitude, and any one of the creditors could claim the right to use him as a slave for that time.

Tao Chi'en

Tao Chi'en took a sampan to Hong Kong with the intention of beginning a new life. Now he was a *zhong yi*, trained in traditional Chinese medicine by the finest master in Canton. He owed eternal gratitude to the spirits of his venerable ancestors, who had worked out his karma in such a glorious manner. The first thing he must do, he decided, was take a wife, for he was of an age, and more, to marry, and celibacy was too heavy a load. The absence of a wife was a sign of poverty that could not be hidden. He cherished the prospect of acquiring a delicate young woman with beautiful feet. Her "golden lilies" should not be more than three or four inches long, and should be plump and soft to the touch, like the feet of an infant of a few months. He was fascinated by the way a young girl walked on those minuscule feet, with short, very hesitant steps, as if she were always about to fall, hips thrown back and swaying like the reeds at the edge of the pond in his master's garden. He detested large, muscular, and cold feet like those of a peasant woman. In his village, from afar, he had seen girls with bound feet, the pride of their families, who undoubtedly would marry them well, but only when he visited the prostitutes in Canton had he held two of those golden lilies in his hands and swooned in ecstasy over the tiny embroidered slippers that always covered them—necessarily, because for years and years the destroyed bones seeped a foul-smelling substance. After he touched such feet, he realized that their elegance was the fruit of constant pain, and that made them even more valuable.

Then he properly appreciated the books in his master's collection that were devoted to women's feet, describing the five classes and eighteen different styles of golden lilies. His wife must also be very young, for beauty lasted but a brief time: it began sometime around the twelfth year and ended shortly after the woman reached twenty. These things his master had explained to him. It was not for nothing that the most celebrated heroines of Chinese literature always died at the precise moment of their greatest charm. Fortunate were those who departed this world before they were ruined by age and could still be remembered in the fullness of their fresh beauty. There were also practical reasons to prefer a nubile girl: she would give him male children and it would be easy to tame her nature and make her truly submissive. Nothing as disagreeable as a shrieking woman; he had seen some who spit at their husbands and children and slapped them about, even in the street in front of the neighbors. Such humiliation at the hands of a woman was the worst shame for a man. In the sampan that slowly carried him the ninety miles between Canton and Hong Kong, leaving his past life farther behind by the minute, Tao Chi'en dreamed of that girl, of the pleasure and the sons she would give him. Again and again he counted the money in his pocket, as if with abstract calculations he could make it grow, but it was clear that it would not stretch far enough for a wife of the quality he desired. Nevertheless, he was not content, however great his urgency, to settle for less and live the rest of his days with a wife who had large feet and a strong character.

The island of Hong Kong appeared suddenly before his eyes, with its profile of mountains and green vegetation, emerging like a siren from the indigo waters of the China Sea. As soon as his light boat docked in the port, Tao Chi'en noted the presence of the despised foreigners. He had seen a few of them before, but at a distance; now he saw them so near that had he dared he could have touched them to test whether those huge, graceless creatures were truly human.

With amazement, he discovered that many of the *fan wey* had red or yellow hair, pale eyes, and skin the color of boiled lobsters. He thought the women very ugly; they were wearing hats bedecked with feathers and flowers, perhaps trying to cover that diabolical hair. They were dressed in an extraordinary fashion, in stiff clothing that bound their bodies tightly. He supposed that was why they moved like automatons and did not greet each other with friendly bows; they passed by stiff as poles, not looking at anyone, suffering the summer heat in their uncomfortable clothing. There were a dozen European ships in the port, surrounded by thousands of Asian boats of all sizes and colors. In the streets he saw a few carriages driven by uniformed men, lost among the many vehicles propelled by humans: litters, palanquins, handbarrows, and porters simply carrying their fare on their backs. The smell of fish came like a slap, reminding him that he was hungry. First he must locate a place to eat, which he would know by its long strips of yellow silk.

Tao Chi'en ate like a prince in a restaurant crowded with people talking and laughing at the tops of their voices, an unmistakable sign of contentment and good digestion, where he savored the delicate dishes that had long been forgotten in the house of his master. The *zhong yi* had been a great gourmet during his lifetime and had prided himself on having had the best cooks in Canton in his service, but during his latter years he had lived on green tea and rice with a few shreds of vegetables. At the time Tao Chi'en had escaped his servitude, he was as thin as any of the countless people in Hong Kong who suffered from tuberculosis. This was his first decent meal in a very long time, and the onslaught of tastes, aromas, and textures was ecstasy. He ended the feast with the pleasure of a pipe. He went outside floating and laughing aloud, like a madman: he had never felt so filled with enthusiasm and good luck. He breathed in the air about him, so reminiscent of Canton, and decided that it would be easy to conquer that city just as nine years earlier he had conquered the other one. First he would look for the market and the district of the healers and herbalists, where he would find a place to live and offer his professional services. Then he would consider the matter of the woman with the tiny feet.

That very afternoon, Tao Chi'en found lodging in the attic of a large house divided into compartments that housed one family per room, a veritable anthill. His room, a dark tunnel a meter wide by three meters long, windowless, dark, and hot, trapped the fumes from the cooking and chamber pots of the other renters, mixed with the unmistakable stench of general filth. Compared to his master's refined home it was like living in a rat hole, but he remembered that his parents' home had been even poorer. As an unmarried man he did not need more space or luxury, he decided, only a corner where he could put his pallet and few belongings. Later, when he married, he would look for an appropriate dwelling where he could prepare his medicines, attend his patients, and be served by his wife as was fitting. For the moment, while he established contacts indispensable to his work, this space at least gave him a roof and a bit of privacy. He left his things and went to bathe, shave the front of his skull, and rebraid his queue. As soon as he was presentable, he left to look for a gaming house, determined to double his capital in the least possible time and get started along the path of success.

In less than two hours at fan-tan, Tao Chi'en lost all his money; he did not lose his medical instruments only because he had not thought to bring them. The shouting in the gaming hall was so thunderous that bets were made by signaling through the dense tobacco smoke. Fan-tan was a simple game: it consisted of a handful of counters underneath a cup. Bets were taken, the chips counted out four at a time, and the person who guessed how many were left—one, two, three, or none—won. Tao Chi'en could scarcely follow the hands of the man who threw the chips and counted them. It seemed to him that he had been cheated, but to accuse the banker in public would have been an offense so grave that were he in error he would have paid with his life. Every day in Canton, the bodies of insolent losers were picked up in the area of the gaming houses; it would be no different in Hong Kong. Tao returned to his tunnel in the attic and threw himself down on his mat and wept like a baby, thinking of the switchings he had received at the hands of his former acupuncture master. His despair lasted until the following morning, when he recognized his impatience and his arrogance with abysmal clarity. Then he burst out laughing, grateful for the lesson, convinced that the mischievous spirit of his master had presented it to teach him something more. He had been awakened in total darkness by the noise of the house and the street. It was late morning, but no natural light reached his hole. Groping in the dark, he put on his only change of clean clothing. He was still laughing as he took his medical kit and set out for the market. In the tattoo artists' shops, covered from top to bottom with pieces of cloth and paper exhibiting their patterns, one could choose from among thousands of designs, from discreet flowers in indigo-blue ink to fantastic five-color dragons whose unfolded wings and fiery breath could decorate the entire back of a husky man. He spent half an hour bargaining and finally made a deal with an artist willing to trade a modest tattoo for a tonic to flush the liver. In less than ten minutes, he had tattooed on the back of his right hand, the hand he used for making bets, the word "No" in simple and elegant characters.

"If you like the tonic, recommend my services to your friends," Tao Chi'en requested.

"If you like my tattoo, do the same," the artist replied.

Tao Chi'en always claimed that that tattoo brought him luck. He went from the shop into the hurly-burly of the market, pushing and elbowing his way through the narrow alleyways seething with humanity. He did not see a single foreigner, and the market looked exactly like the one in Canton. The noise was like a roaring waterfall: vendors crying the merits of their merchandise and clients bargaining at the top of their lungs in the midst of a deafening riot of caged birds and whimpering animals awaiting their turn for the blade. The pestilence of sweat, live and dead animals, excrement and garbage, spices, opium, street kitchens—all the products and creatures of earth, air, and sea—was so thick you could rub it between your fingers. He saw a woman selling crabs. She took them live from a sack, boiled them a few minutes in a pot of water the murky consistency of the bottom of the sea, dipped them out with a slotted spoon, doused them with soy sauce, and served them to passing customers on a piece of paper. The woman's hands were covered with warts. Tao Chi'en negotiated a month's lunches in exchange for treating her skin.

"Ah. I see you like crabs very much," she said.

"I detest them, but I will eat them as a penitence so I never forget a lesson I must remember forever."

"And if at the end of a month I am not cured, who will give me back the crabs you have eaten?"

"If at the end of the month you have your warts, my reputation is ruined. Who will buy my medicines then?" Tao smiled.

"Very well."

And so began Tao's new life in Hong Kong as a free man. In two or three days the inflammation faded and the tattoo appeared as a clean design of blue veins. All that month, as he went from stand to stand in the market offering his professional services, he ate only once a day, always boiled crabs, and lost so much weight he could stick a coin between his ribs. Every creature he put into his mouth, conquering his revulsion, made him smile, thinking of his master, who liked crabs as little as he. The woman's warts disappeared in twenty-six days and she gratefully spread the good news around the neighborhood. She offered Tao a second month of crabs if he would cure her cataracts, but he believed he had suffered enough punishment and could grant himself the luxury of never tasting a crab again for the rest of his life. At night he dragged back to his hole, exhausted, counted his money by candlelight, hid it under a floorboard, and then warmed water on the charcoal brazier to endure his hunger with tea. From time to time, if he began to feel weak in the knees or in his resolve, he bought a scoop of rice, a bit of sugar, or a pipe of opium, which he savored slowly, grateful that there were gifts in the world as dazzling as the consolation of rice, the sweetness of sugar, and the perfect dreams of opium. He spent money on nothing but rent, English classes, shaving his foreskull, and having his change of clothes laundered because he did not want to go about like a beggar. His teacher had always dressed like a mandarin. "Good appearance is a sign of civility, a *zhong yi* is not the same as a country healer. The poorer the patient, the richer your clothing should be, out of respect," he had taught his pupil. Gradually Tao's reputation spread, first among the people in the market and their families, then through the port, where he treated sailors for injuries from brawls, scurvy, venereal chancres, and delirium tremens.

After six months, Tao Chi'en had a faithful clientele and had begun to prosper. He moved to a room with a window, furnished it with a large bed, which he would use when he married, a chair, and an English desk. He also bought a few items of clothing; for years he had wanted to dress well. He had made up his mind to learn English because it hadn't taken long to learn where the power lay. A handful of British controlled Hong Kong, made the laws and administered them, and commanded the course of commerce and politics. The *fan wey* lived in exclusive neighborhoods and had dealings with wealthy Chinese only to do business, always in English. The remaining masses shared the same space and time, but it was as if they did not exist. China's most refined products flowed through Hong Kong directly to the drawing rooms of a Europe fascinated with that centuries-old, remote culture. Chinoiserie was the rage. Silk caused a furor in the fashion world; one could not be without graceful bridges with little lanterns and weeping willows imitating the marvelous secret gardens of Peking; pagoda rooftops ornamented summer houses; and dragon and cherry blossom motifs were repeated ad nauseum in decor. There was no English mansion without an Oriental drawing room with its Coromandel screen, its collection of porcelains and ivories, its fans embroidered by childish hands in the forbidden stitch, its imperial canaries in carved cages. The ships that carried those treasures to Europe did not return empty; they brought opium from India to sell as contraband, and trinkets that devastated small local industries. The Chinese had to compete with the English, Dutch, French, and North Americans to do business in their own country. But the greatest disaster was opium. It had been used in China for centuries as a diversion and for medicinal purposes, but when the English flooded the market it became an uncontrollable evil. It attacked all sectors of the society, weakening it, causing it to crumble like stale bread.

At first the Chinese looked on the foreigners with scorn and disgust, with the great superiority of those who feel they are the only truly civilized beings in the universe, but in the space of a few years they learned to respect and fear them. As for the Europeans, they were imbued with the same concept of racial superiority, sure of their role as heralds of civilization in a land of dirty, ugly, weak, noisy, corrupt, and savage people who ate cats and snakes and killed their own children at birth. Few were aware that the Chinese had known writing a thousand years before they had. While businessmen were imposing a culture of drugs and violence, missionaries were evangelizing. Christianity must be propagated at any cost; it was the one true faith, and the fact that Confucius had lived fifteen hundred years before Christ was insignificant. The British considered the Chinese barely human, but they intended to save their souls and rewarded conversions with rice. The new Christians would consume their ration of divine bribery and move on to the next church to be converted all over again, amused by the mania of the *fan wey* for preaching their beliefs as if they were unique. For the practical and tolerant Chinese, spirituality was closer to philosophy than to religion; it was a question of ethics, never dogma.

Tao Chi'en took lessons from a compatriot who spoke a soupy English devoid of consonants but wrote it with absolute correctness. Compared to Chinese characters, the European alphabet had an enchanting simplicity, and after five weeks Tao Chi'en could read the British newspapers without stumbling over the letters, although every fifth word he had to look up in the dictionary. He spent hours every night studying. He missed his venerable master, who had marked him forever with a thirst for knowledge as persistent as the drunk's thirst for alcohol or the ambitious man's thirst for power. He no longer had his mentor's library or his inexhaustible fount of experience; he could not run to him to ask for advice or to discuss a patient's symptoms; he lacked a guide, he felt like an orphan. Since his mentor's death he had not written or read poetry, had not taken the time to admire nature, to meditate, or to observe the daily rites and ceremonies that had previously enriched his life. He felt filled with noise inside; he longed for the void of silence and solitude his master had taught him to cultivate as life's most precious gift. In the practice of his office he was learning about the complex nature of humankind, the emotional differences between men and women, the illnesses treatable with remedies and those that also required the magic of the right words, but he had no one to share those experiences with. The dream of buying a wife and having a family was always in his mind, but misty and tenuous, like a beautiful landscape painted on silk; in contrast, his wish to acquire books, to study and find other masters willing to help him along the road of knowledge was turning into an obsession.

This was the state of affairs when Tao Chi'en met Dr. Ebanizer Hobbs, an English aristocrat who had none of their usual arrogance and who, unlike other Europeans, was interested in the local color of the city. Tao Chi'en saw him first in the market picking through the herbs and potions in a healer's shop. Hobbs knew only ten words of Mandarin, but he spoke them in such a booming voice and with such conviction that a small crowd—half mocking, half frightened—had gathered around him. He was easy to see from a distance because his head rose far above the Chinese. Tao Chi'en had never seen a foreigner in this part of the city, so far from the sectors they normally frequented, and he moved closer to observe him better. Hobbs was a young man still, tall and slender, with noble features and large blue eyes. Tao Chi'en found to his delight that he could translate the *fan wey's* ten words, that he knew at least that many more in English, and that it might be possible to communicate. He greeted the Englishman with a cordial bow and the foreigner answered by clumsily imitating his gesture. Both smiled, and then broke out laughing, chorused by the friendly chortles of the spectators. They began an eager dialogue of twenty words badly pronounced on both sides and a comic pantomime performed to the growing hilarity of the curious. Soon there was a group sizable enough to block traffic, all weak with laughter, which attracted a British mounted policeman who ordered the throng to disperse immediately. That was the birth of a solid alliance between the two men.

Ebanizer Hobbs was as aware of the limitations of his calling as Tao Chi'en was of his. The former wanted to learn the secrets of the Eastern medicine he had seen flashes of during his travels through Asia, especially the control of pain through needles inserted at nerve terminals and the use of combinations of plants and herbs to treat a number of illnesses that in Europe were considered fatal. Tao Chi'en was fascinated by Western medicine and its aggressive methods of treatment; his was a subtle art of balance and harmony, a slow process of rerouting misdirected energy, preventing illness, and seeking the causes of symptoms. Tao Chi'en had never practiced surgery, and his knowledge of anatomy, extremely precise in regard to the different pulses and acupuncture points, was limited to what he could see and touch. He knew from memory the anatomical drawings in the library of his former master, but it had never occurred to him to dissect a cadaver. That custom was not accepted in Chinese medicine: his wise master, who had practiced the art of healing for a lifetime, had rarely seen an internal organ and was incapable of a diagnosis if he encountered symptoms that did not fit within the repertory of known ills. Ebanizer Hobbs, on the other hand, dissected cadavers and looked for the cause; that was how one learned. Tao Chi'en did that for the first time in the basement of the English hospital, on a night of typhoons, as assistant to Dr. Hobbs, who that same morning had placed his first acupuncture needles to relieve a migraine in the consulting office where Tao Chi'en attended his patients. In Hong Kong there were a few missionaries interested in curing the body as well as converting the souls of their congregation, with whom Dr. Hobbs maintained excellent relations. These evangelists were much closer to the local population than the British physicians of the colony, and they admired the methods of Eastern medicine. They opened the doors of their small hospitals to the *zhong yi*. The enthusiasm of Tao Chi'en and Ebanizer Hobbs for study and experimentation inevitably led to friendship. They met almost in secret, because had their mutual respect and admiration been common knowledge, they would have risked their reputations. Neither European nor Chinese patients admitted that the other race had anything to teach them.

As Tao Chi'en became more comfortable financially, the wish to buy a wife began to occupy his dreams again. On his twenty-second birthday, he once again added up his savings, as he often did, and was elated to find that he had enough for a woman with tiny feet and a sweet nature. As he did not have parents to assist him in making his choice, as custom demanded, he had to consult an agent; there he was shown portraits of various candidates, but they all looked alike; he found it impossible to deduce a girl's looks—much less her personality—from those modest ink sketches. It was forbidden for him to see the prospective wife with his own eyes, or hear her voice, as he would have liked; neither did he have a female family member to do it for him. One thing was allowed: he could view a girl's feet as she stood behind a curtain, but he had been told that not even that was reliable because the agents often cheated and substituted the golden lilies of a different woman. He had to trust in fate. He came close to leaving the decision to the dice but the tattoo on his right hand reminded him of past misadventures in games of chance, and he chose to commend the task to the spirits of his mother and his acupuncture master. After going to five temples to make offerings, he cast the I Ching sticks, where he read that it was the propitious moment, and so chose his bride. The method did not fail him. When he lifted the red silk kerchief from the face of his new wife—following minimal ceremonies, since he did not have money for a more splendid wedding—he saw a harmonious face with eyes cast obstinately to the ground. He repeated her name three times before she dared look at him with tear-filled eyes, trembling with fright.

"I will be good to you," he promised, as emotional as she.

From the moment he lifted that red cloth, Tao adored the girl fate had bequeathed him. That love took him by surprise; he had not imagined that such feelings could exist between a man and a woman. He had never heard anyone discuss that kind of love, he had only read vague references in classical literature in which maidens, like landscapes or the moon, were the obligatory subjects of poetic inspiration. Even so, he had believed that in the real world women were either creatures for working and reproducing, like the peasant women he had grown up among, or else were expensive ornaments. Lin did not fit into either of those categories, she was a mysterious and complex person capable of disarming him with her irony and challenging him with her questions. She made him laugh like no one else could, invented impossible stories, provoked him with word games. In Lin's presence, everything seemed to be lighted with an irresistible glow. That miraculous discovery of intimacy with another person was the most profound experience of his life. He had had his share of hurried, cock-of-the-walk encounters with prostitutes, but had never had the time and love to know anyone deeply. To open his eyes in the morning and see Lin sleeping beside him made him laugh with happiness, and an instant later tremble with anguish. What if one morning she didn't wake up? The sweet fragrance of her perspiration in their nights of love, the fine line of her eyebrows lifted in an expression of perpetual surprise, the impossible slenderness of her waist, everything about her choked him with tenderness. Oh, and the two of them laughing! That was best of all, the natural joy of that love. His old master's pillow books, which had caused such empty excitement in his adolescence, proved to be a great benefit at the hour of their pleasure. As befitted a young, well-bred virgin, Lin was modest in her everyday behavior, but almost as soon as she lost her fear of her husband, her spontaneous and passionate femininity emerged. In a short time, that eager student learned the two hundred twenty-two manners of making love and, always willing to follow in that headlong race, suggested to her husband that he invent new ones. Fortunately for Tao Chi'en, the refined knowledge learned in theory in his mentor's library included countless ways of pleasing a woman, and he knew that vigor counted for much less than patience. His fingers were trained to perceive the body's pulses and to locate its most sensitive points blindfolded. His warm, strong hands, expert in soothing his patients' pain, became instruments of infinite pleasure for Lin. Furthermore, he had discovered something the honorable *zhong yi* had forgotten to teach him: that the best aphrodisiac is love. In bed they could be so happy that by night life's problems were erased. But those problems were many, which was evident all too soon.

The spirits Tao Chi'en had invoked to help in his matrimonial choice had done their work to perfection: Lin had bound feet and was as sweet and timid as a squirrel. But Tao Chi'en had not thought to ask that his wife also be strong and healthy. The same woman who seemed inexhaustible at night was during the day transformed into an invalid. She could walk no farther than a block or two on her tiny, mutilated feet. It is true that when she walked, she moved with the soft delicacy of a reed in the breeze, as the ancient acupuncture master had written in one of his poems, but it was no less true that a short trip to the market to buy a cabbage for dinner was true torment to her golden lilies. She never complained aloud, but he had only to see her perspire and bite her lips to guess the effort of every step. She also had weak lungs.

She breathed with the sharp whistle of the goldfinch, lived through the rainy season with a runny nose and in the dry season choked because the warm air seemed to pass no farther than her lips. Neither her husband's herbs nor the tonics of his friend the English doctor could help her. When she became pregnant she grew worse, for her fragile build could barely support the weight of the child. In the fourth month, she stopped going out altogether, and sat listlessly before the window watching life passing in the street. Tao Chi'en hired two servant girls to take over the domestic chores and stay with her, because he feared that Lin would die in his absence. He doubled his working hours and for the first time harassed his patients to pay, which filled him with shame. He could feel the critical gaze of his master reminding him of the duty to serve without expecting a return, for "he who knows most has the greatest obligation toward humanity." He could not, nevertheless, work for free or in exchange of favors as he had before; he needed every cent to keep Lin comfortable. By then he had rented the second floor of an old house, where he installed his wife with refinements that neither of them had known before, but he wasn't satisfied. It was in his mind to get her a house with a garden; that way she would have beauty and pure air. His friend Ebanizer Hobbs told him—since Tao himself refused to see the evidence—that Lin's tuberculosis was very advanced and that there was no garden capable of curing her.

"Instead of working from dawn to midnight to buy her silk dresses and beautiful furniture, stay with her as much as possible, Dr. Chi'en. You must enjoy her while you have her," Hobbs counseled.

The two physicians agreed, each from the perspective of his own experience, that the birth would be a test of fire for Lin. Neither was expert on this subject, for in Europe as well as China births were in the hands of midwives, but the men decided to study in that area.

Neither Hobbs nor Tao Chi'en had any confidence in the expertise of some low, coarse woman—which was how they regarded all the women who practiced midwivery. They had watched them work, with their revolting hands, their witchery, and their brutal methods for separating the baby from the mother, and were determined to spare Lin that miserable experience. She, however, did not want to give birth in the presence of the two men, especially when one of them was a *fan wey* with pale eyes, someone who could not even speak the language of civilized beings. She begged her husband to go to the neighborhood midwife, because the most elementary decency prohibited her from spreading her legs before a foreign devil, but this time Tao Chi'en, always ready to please her, was inflexible. Finally, they agreed that he personally would attend her while Ebanizer Hobbs stayed in the next room to lend verbal support, should it be needed.

The first indication of the coming birth was an asthma attack that nearly cost Lin her life. Her efforts to breathe were enmeshed with those of her womb to expel the infant, and both Tao Chi'en, with all his love and science, and Ebanizer Hobbs, with his medical texts, were helpless to know what to do. Ten hours later, when the moans of the mother had been reduced to the harsh gurgling of someone drowning and the baby gave no signs of being born, Tao Chi'en raced out to look for the midwife and despite his revulsion practically dragged her home. As Chi'en and Hobbs had feared, the woman was a foul-smelling old drab with whom it was impossible to exchange the least medical information because her knowledge came not from science but from long experience and ancient instinct. She began by shoving the two men aside, forbidding them even to put their heads through the curtains that separated the two rooms. Tao Chi'en never learned what happened behind that barrier but he felt better when he heard Lin breathing without choking and screaming. In the following hours, while Ebanizar Hobbs slept exhausted in a chair and Tao Chi'en desperately consulted the spirit of his master, Lin brought a lifeless girl child into the world. As the baby was female, neither the midwife nor the father made any effort to revive her, though both gave themselves to the task of saving the mother, who was losing what little strength she had at the rate the blood flowed from between her legs.

Lin scarcely mourned the death of the baby girl, as if she knew she would not live long enough to have raised her. Slowly she recovered from the difficult delivery and for a while tried to be the happy companion of their nighttime game. With the same discipline she had used to mask the pain of her feet, she pretended enthusiasm for her husband's passionate embraces. "Sex is a voyage, a sacred voyage," she had often said to him, but now she lacked the spirit to accompany him. Tao Chi'en so longed for that love that one by one he ignored the telltale signs and kept believing to the end that Lin was the same as she had been. For years he had dreamed of sons, but now all he wanted was to protect his wife from another pregnancy. His feelings for Lin had become a veneration that he could confess only to her; he thought that no one could understand such consuming love for a woman, that no one knew Lin as he did, that no one knew the light she brought to his life. I am happy, I am happy, he kept repeating to drive away the dark premonitions that assaulted him when he dropped his guard. But he was not happy. He didn't laugh now with the same lightheartedness, and when he was with Lin he took little pleasure from it, except in some perfect moments of carnal intimacy, because he was watching her every minute, worried, always thinking of her health, aware of her fragility, measuring the rhythm of her breathing. He came to despise her golden lilies, which in the early days of their marriage he had kissed with sublime passion. Ebanizer

Hobbs wanted Lin to take long outings in the open air to strengthen her lungs and pique her appetite, but she could barely take ten steps without faltering. Tao could not stay beside his wife every minute, as Hobbs suggested, because he had to provide for them. Each instant he was away from her seemed life wasted in unhappiness, time stolen from love. He placed all his experience with herbs at the service of his beloved, all the knowledge he had acquired over years of practicing medicine, but one year after the birth Lin had become a shadow of the happy girl she had once been. Her husband kept trying to make her laugh, but their laughter rang false to them both.

One day Lin could not get out of bed. She lay choking, her strength draining away, coughing blood and trying to breathe. She refused to eat anything except spoonfuls of a clear soup, because the effort exhausted her. She slept in spurts during the few moments she wasn't coughing. Tao Chi'en calculated that for six weeks her breathing had been a liquid rasping, as if she were underwater. When he picked her up in his arms, he could tell how much weight she was losing, and his heart shrank with terror. He had watched her suffer so much that her death should have come as a relief, but the fateful morning when he awakened embracing Lin's icy body, he thought he, too, would die. A long and terrible scream born from the depths of the earth, like the roar of a volcano, shook the house and waked everyone in the vicinity. The neighbors came and kicked down the door to find him naked in the middle of the room, holding his wife in his arms and howling. They had to pry her body from his arms and hold him down until Ebanizer Hobbs arrived and made him drink a dose of laudanum capable of felling a lion.

Tao Chi'en sank into widowerhood with total despair. He made an altar with the portrait of Lin and some of her belongings, and spent hours staring at it in desolation. He stopped seeing his patients or sharing studies and research with Ebanizer Hobbs, activities on which their friendship was based. He was repelled by the advice of the Englishman, who maintained that what he needed was a bit of the hair of the dog, and that the best way to get over his grief was to visit the brothels in the port, where he could choose all the women he wanted with deformed feet—Hobbs's term for golden lilies. How could his friend suggest such an abhorrent idea? The woman didn't live who could replace Lin; he would never love another, of that Tao Chi'en was sure. All he accepted from Hobbs during that period were his generous bottles of whiskey. For weeks he lived in a haze of alcohol; gradually his money ran out and he had to sell or pawn his possessions, until the day came that he couldn't pay his rent and had to move to a cheap hotel. Then he remembered that he was a *zhong yi* and began to work again, although he barely managed, unshaven, dirty, the hair in his queue flying. Since he had a good reputation, his patients put up with his unkempt appearance and drunken errors with resignation, but gradually they stopped coming to see him. And Ebanizer Hobbs stopped calling on him to treat difficult cases because he had lost confidence in Tao's judgment. Until that time they had complemented each other well: the Englishman was for the first time able to perform surgery boldly, thanks to the powerful drugs and golden needles that soothed pain, reduced hemorrhaging, and shortened the time of healing, and the Chinese physician had learned to use the scalpel and other techniques of European science. But with his trembling hands and eyes clouded by intoxication and tears, Tao Chi'en represented a danger more than he did support and assistance.

In the spring of 1847, Tao Chi'en's destiny took a sudden turn, as it had once or twice before in his life. As he lost his regular patients and the rumor spread of his downhill course as a physician, he had to concentrate more in the poorest sections of the port, where no one asked for references. The cases were routine: contusions and knife and bullet wounds. One night Tao Chi'en was called to an emergency in a tavern to stitch a sailor's injuries following a royal free-for-all. They led him to the back of the room where a man was lying unconscious, his head split open like a watermelon. His opponent, a gigantic Norwegian, had picked up a heavy wood table and used it as a club to defend himself against his attackers, a gang of Chinese intending to beat him to a pulp. They had rushed the Norwegian and would have made mincemeat out of him had not several Scandinavian sailors drinking at the same bar come to his rescue, and what had begun as an argument among drunken gamblers turned into a racial brawl. By the time Tao Chi'en arrived, anyone who could walk had long since disappeared. The Norwegian, uninjured, was escorted to his ship by two English policemen, and the only ones left in sight were the tavern keeper, the dying victim, and the ship's pilot, who had worked out an arrangement to send the police on their way. Had the victim been European he would have been taken to the British hospital, but since he was Asian the port authorities were not putting themselves out too much.

Tao Chi'en took one look and could see that nothing could be done for that poor devil whose skull was cracked wide open and his brains spilling out. This he explained to the pilot, a bearded, heavyset Englishman.

"Damned chink! Can't you stop the blood and sew him up?" he demanded.

"With his head like that? Why sew him up? He has a right to die in peace."

"He can't die! My ship sails at dawn and I need this man onboard. He's my cook!"

"Very regrettable," Tao Chi'en replied with a courteous bow of his head, trying to hide his disgust at the *fan wey*'s insensitivity.

The pilot ordered a bottle of gin and invited Tao Chi'en to have a drink with him. If the cook was beyond consolation they might as well lift a glass in his name, he said, so his fucking ghost, a pox on him, didn't come and pull their toes at night. They sat down a few feet from the dying man to take their time getting drunk. Occasionally Tao Chi'en bent down to take the man's pulse, calculating that he couldn't have more than a couple of minutes longer to live, but the man was slower to die than he'd thought. The *zhong yi* was oblivious to how the Englishman was pouring him drink after drink while barely downing his. Soon Tao felt so dizzy he couldn't remember what he was doing in that place anyway. And an hour later, when his patient twice shuddered violently and actually died, Tao Chi'en missed it because he had rolled to the floor, unconscious.

He waked to the blinding light of midday, opened his eyes, squinting, and as soon as he could raise his head saw nothing but sky and water all around him. It took him quite a while to realize that he was lying faceup on a large coil of rope on the deck of a ship. The pounding of the waves against the hull beat in his head like a clanging bell. He thought he heard voices and shouting, but he wasn't sure of anything; he could just as easily have been in hell. He struggled to his knees and crawled forward a couple of meters, but was overcome by nausea and collapsed back onto the deck. A few minutes later he felt the shock of a pail of cold water splash over his head and heard a voice speaking to him in Cantonese. He looked up and saw a beardless, sympathetic face greeting him with a wide smile from which half the teeth were missing. A second pail of seawater shook him from his stupor. The young Chinese man who had so solicitously dumped water on him squatted down beside him, laughing loudly and slapping his thighs as if Tao's pathetic condition were irresistibly funny.

"Where am I?" Tao Chi'en managed to stammer.

"Welcome aboard the *Liberty*! We're sailing west, I think."

"But I don't want to go anywhere. I have to get off. Immediately."

New guffaws met this statement. When finally the man could control his hilarity, he explained to Tao that he had been "shanghaied," just as he himself had been a couple of months earlier. Tao Chi'en felt he was going to faint. He knew what that meant. If there weren't enough men to fill out a crew, the captain or pilot fell back on stopgap measures: getting some unwary bar patron drunk, even knocking him out and "signing him on" against his will. Life at sea was rough, and paid badly; accidents, malnutrition, and illness cut into the ranks; on each voyage one or more sailors died and their bodies ended up on the ocean floor with no one to give them another thought. Added to that, the captains tended to be despots who did not have to give an accounting to anyone and who punished the slightest offense with a lashing. In Shanghai it was so bad they'd had to reach a gentleman's agreement among captains to put an end to kidnapping free men and stealing one another's crew. Before the accord, every time a sailor came into port to have a few drinks he ran the risk of waking up on a different ship. The pilot of the *Liberty* had decided to replace his dead cook with Tao Chi'en—in his eyes all the "yellow" race were alike, one was as good as the next—so after getting Tao drunk he had him hauled aboard. Before Tao came to, the pilot had stamped his thumbprint on a contract that signed him up for two years. Slowly, the magnitude of what had happened sank into Tao Chi'en's soggy brain. The idea of rebelling was never a consideration, that would be suicide, but he intended to desert the minute they touched land, wherever on the planet that might be.

The young Asian helped Tao get to his feet and wash his face, then led him belowdecks to where the berths and hammocks were lined up. He assigned Tao a bunk and a box to store his gear in. Tao Chi'en feared he had lost everything, but found the case containing his medical instruments on the wood planks that would be his bed. The pilot had had the good sense to save it. Lin's portrait, however, was left behind on its altar. He realized with horror that the spirit of his wife might not be able to locate him in the middle of the ocean. The first few days at sea were torture; at times he was tempted by the thought of jumping overboard and ending his suffering once and for all. Almost as soon as he could stay on his feet he was assigned to the rudimentary galley, where the pots hung from hooks, clanging together with every toss of the waves, making a deafening racket. The fresh provisions brought aboard in Hong Kong were rapidly depleted and soon there was nothing but fish, salted meat, beans, sugar, lard, wormy flour, and biscuits so stale that sometimes they had to be hacked into pieces. Every bite of food was smothered in soy sauce. Each sailor had a pint of liquor per day to drown his sorrows and rinse out his mouth, because inflamed gums were one of the problems of life at sea. For the captain's table, Tao Chi'en had eggs and English marmalade, which he had been directed to protect with his life. Rations were calculated to last the trip if no unusual difficulties arose—such as storms that blew them off course, or lying becalmed—complemented with fresh fish netted along the way. Great culinary skill was not expected of Tao Chi'en; his role was to dole out the food, liquor, and fresh water assigned to each man and to do battle against spoilage and rats. He also had a normal share of swabbing and sailing chores, like any other sailor.

After a week he began to enjoy the fresh air, the hard work, and the company of those men who came from the four corners of the earth, each with his stories, his nostalgia, and his skills. During breaks from work they would play instruments and tell tales of the phantoms of the waves and the exotic women in distant ports. The crew came from many places, from many tongues and customs, but they were united by something that resembled friendship. Isolation, and the knowledge that they needed one another, made comrades of men who on dry land would not have given one another a second look. Tao Chi'en began to laugh again, as he hadn't laughed since Lin's illness. One morning the pilot called him to introduce him to Captain John Sommers, whom Tao had seen only from a distance, on the bridge. He found himself facing a tall, darkly bearded, steely-eyed man tanned by the winds of many latitudes. He spoke to Tao through the pilot, who knew a little Cantonese, but Tao replied in his book English, with the affected, aristocratic accent he had learned from Ebanizer Hobbs.

"Mr. Oglesby tells me that you are some kind of healer?"

"I am a *zhong yi*, a physician."

"Physician? What do you mean, physician?"

"Chinese medicine is several centuries older than the English, Captain." Tao Chi'en laughed gently, using his friend Ebanizer Hobbs's exact words.

Captain Sommers raised his eyebrows, angered by the lowly crew member's insolence, but was disarmed by the truth of the statement. He laughed with good nature.

"Well, we'll see. Mr. Oglesby, pour us three glasses of brandy. We're going to drink a toast to our doctor, here. This is a rare luxury. For the first time we're carrying our own physician onboard!"

Tao Chi'en did not effect his plan to desert in the first port reached by the *Liberty,* because he didn't know where to go. To return to his life as a miserable widower in Hong Kong made as little sense as to go on sailing. Here or there, it was all the same, and at least as a seaman he would travel and learn the ways medicine was practiced in other parts of the world. The one thing that really tormented him was that in all that wandering across the waves Lin might not be able to find him, however much he screamed her name to the winds.

In the first port, he went ashore, like the others, with a six-hour pass, but instead of spending that time in taverns, following the captain's orders he dove into the market in search of spices and medicinal plants. Now that we have a doctor, we'll need remedies, he'd said. He gave Tao a pouch with a specified sum of coins, and warned him that if he gave a thought to escaping or tricking him, he would hunt him down and slit his throat with his own hands, for the man hadn't been born who could cheat him and get away with it.

"Is that clear, Chinaman?"

"It is clear, Englishman."

"You address me as sir!"

"Yes, sir," Tao Chi'en replied, looking down, because he was learning not to look white men in the face.

His first surprise had been to discover that China was not the absolute center of the universe. There were other cultures—more barbaric, that was true, but much more powerful. He had not suspected that the British controlled a large part of the globe, just as he had never suspected that other *fan wey* were masters of far-reaching colonies in distant lands spread across four continents, as Captain John Sommers went to the trouble of explaining to him the day that Tao pulled his infected tooth as they were sailing off the coast of Africa. He accomplished that operation cleanly and almost painlessly, thanks to a combination of his gold needles in the captain's temples and a paste of cloves and eucalyptus applied to his gums. When it was over, and the relieved and grateful patient was polishing off his bottle of liquor, Tao Chi'en dared ask where they were going. It was upsetting to him to travel blindly, the blurred horizon between sea and an infinite sky the only reference.

"We're sailing in the direction of Europe, but for us nothing changes. We are seafarers, always on water. Do you want to go back home?"

"No, sir."

"Do you have a family somewhere?"

"No, sir."

"Then it's the same to you whether we're going north or south, east or west, isn't that true?"

"Yes, but I like to know where I am."

"Why is that?"

"Because if I fall overboard, or the ship sinks, my spirit will need to know where it is in order to find its way back to China; if not it will wander around aimlessly. The gates to heaven are in China."

"Where did you get that daft idea?" the captain said, laughing. "So, in order to get to paradise you have to die in China? Take a look at the map, man. Your country is the largest, that's true, but there's a lot of the world outside China. Here is England, it is only a small island, but if you add our colonies you will see that we are masters of more than half the globe."

"How did you do that?"

"The same way we did it in Hong Kong: with war and deceit. Let's say that it's a blend of naval power, greed, and discipline. We are not superior, we're crueler, and greedier. I am not particularly proud of being English, and after you've traveled as much as I have, you won't be proud of being Chinese, either."

During the next two years, Tao Chi'en stepped on terra firma only three times, one of which was in England. He lost himself among the huge throngs in the port, and walked through the streets of London looking at new things with the eyes of an enchanted child. The *fan wey* were filled with surprises; on the one hand, they lacked any touch of refinement and behaved like savages, but on the other, they were capable of amazing inventiveness. He confirmed that in their own country the English suffered the same arrogance and bad manners they exhibited in Hong Kong: they had no respect for him, and knew nothing of courtesy or etiquette. He tried to buy an ale, but they pushed him out of the inn: No yellow dogs allowed in here, they told him. Soon he joined some other Asian sailors and they found a place run by an elderly Chinese man where they could eat, drink, and smoke in peace. Listening to the stories the other men told, Tao calculated how much he still had to learn, and decided that first would be how to use his fists and his knife. Knowledge is not of much use if you can't defend yourself: the wise acupuncture master had also forgotten to teach him that fundamental principle.

In February of 1849 the *Liberty* moored in Valparaíso. The next day, Captain John Sommers called Tao to his cabin and handed him a letter.

"This was given to me in the port. It's for you and it's from England."

Tao Chi'en took the envelope, blushed, and a huge smile illuminated his face.

"Don't tell me it's a love letter," the captain joked.

"Better than that," Tao answered, slipping it between his shirt and his skin. The letter could only be from his friend Ebanizer Hobbs, the first he had received in the two years he had been at sea.

"You have done a good job, Chi'en."

"I thought, sir, you did not like my cooking." Tao Chi'en said, and smiled.

"As a cook, you're a disaster, but you know your medicine. In two years' time I've not lost a single man, and none of the crew has scurvy. Do you know what that means?"

"Good fortune."

"Your contract is up today. I suppose I could get you drunk and make you sign an extension. I might do that to another man, but I owe you some favors and I pay my debts. Do you want to go on with me? I will raise your wages."

"Where are you going?"

"To California. But I'm going to leave this ship; I have been offered a steamship, an opportunity I've been waiting a long time for. I would like you to come with me."

Tao Chi'en had heard of steamships, and had a horror of them. The idea of enormous boilers filled with red-hot water to produce steam and power infernal machinery could have occurred only to people always in a hurry. Wasn't it far better to travel to the rhythm of the winds and currents? Why challenge nature? He had heard rumors of boilers that exploded at sea, cooking the crew alive. Bits of human flesh, parboiled like shrimp, shooting off in all directions to become fish food while the souls of those wretches, fragmented in the force of the explosion and swirling steam, could never rejoin their ancestors. Tao Chi'en clearly remembered how his young sister had looked after the pot of hot water emptied over her, as clearly as he remembered her horrible moans of pain, and her convulsions as she died. He was not prepared to run that kind of risk. Neither was he overly tempted by the gold in California, although he had heard it lay about on the ground like rocks. He did not owe John Sommers anything. The captain was a little more tolerant than most of the *fan wey*, and he treated his crew with a certain evenhandedness, but he was not his friend, and never would be.

"No, thank you, sir."

"Don't you want to see California? You can get rich in a thrice, and go back to China a man of parts."

"Yes, but on a sailing ship."

"Why is that? Steamships are more modern, and much faster."

Tao Chi'en did not try to explain his reasons. He stood silent, staring at the deck, cap in hand, while the captain finished drinking his whiskey.

"I can't force you," Sommers said finally. "I will give you a letter of recommendation to my friend Vincent Katz who captains the brigantine *Emilia*; she is also sailing to California in the next few days. Katz is a rather strange Dutchman, very strict and very religious, but he is a good man and a good sailor. Your trip will be slower than mine, but perhaps we will see each other in San Francisco, and if you regret your decision you can always come back to work with me."

Captain John Sommers and Tao Chi'en shook hands for the first time.

The Voyage

Curled in her burrow in the storeroom, Eliza began to die. To the darkness and the sensation of being walled up in life was added the odor, a foul blend of the contents of bales and boxes, barrels of salted fish, and deposits of ocean extracts crusted on the old planks of the ship. Her acute sense of smell, so useful for getting through the world with closed eyes, had become an instrument of torture. Her only company was a strange tricolored cat buried, like her, in the hold and there to keep it free of rats. Tao Chi'en assured her that she would get used to the stench and to being closed up because in times of necessity the body adapts to nearly everything; he added that the voyage would be a long one and that she could not come out in the fresh air, so she would be better off not to think if she didn't want to go mad. She would have water and food, he promised, he would take care of that when he could come down to the hold without arousing suspicion. The ship was small, but it was crowded and it would be easy to find reasons to slip down there.

"Thank you. When we reach California I will give you the turquoise brooch."

"Keep it, you already paid me. You will need it. Why are you going to California?"

"To be married. My sweetheart's name is Joaquín. He was infected by gold fever and went off to make his fortune. He said he would be back, but I can't wait for that."

Almost as soon as the ship left the bay of Valparaíso and was in open water Eliza began to rave. For hours she lay in darkness in her own filth, like an animal, so ill that she didn't remember where she was, or why; finally the door of the wooden hatch opened and Tao Chi'en appeared, lighted by the flame of a candle stub and carrying a plate of food. He needed only one look to realize that the girl would not be able to get anything down. He gave the meal to the cat and went back to look for a pail of water so he could clean her up. He began by giving her strong ginger tea to drink and inserting a dozen of his golden needles until her stomach was settled. Eliza paid little attention when he removed all her clothing, washed her delicately with seawater, rinsed her with a cup of freshwater, and massaged her from head to foot with the balm recommended for malarial fevers. Minutes later she was asleep, wrapped in her Castile mantle with the cat at her feet, while Tao Chi'en was up on deck washing her clothes in the sea, trying not to call attention, although the sailors were resting at that hour. The new passengers were as seasick as Eliza, to the indifference of those from Europe who had been traveling for three months and had passed that test.

In the following days, while the new passengers on the *Emilia* grew accustomed to the battering of the waves and established the routines they would follow for the rest of the journey, Eliza was growing steadily sicker in the depths of the ship. Tao Chi'en went down as often as he could to take her water and try to calm her nausea, surprised that, instead of diminishing, her discomfort was increasing by the hour. He tried to give her relief with the known treatments for such cases and with others he improvised, but Eliza could keep almost nothing in her stomach and was getting dehydrated. He prepared water with salt and sugar, and with infinite patience gave it to her by spoonfuls, but two weeks went by without any apparent improvement and the moment came when the girl's skin hung as loose as strips of parchment and she could no longer get up to do the exercises Tao insisted on. "If you don't move, your body will swell and your mind will grow dark," he kept telling her. The ship called briefly in the ports of Coquimbo, Caldera, Antofagasta, Iquique, and Arica, and in each he tried to convince Eliza to get off and find a way to go back home, because he could see her growing weaker and weaker and he was afraid.

They had left the port of Callao behind them when Eliza's condition took a lethal turn. In the market Tao Chi'en had found a supply of coca leaves, whose medicinal properties he knew well, and three live hens he intended to hide and kill one by one, for the sick girl needed something more appetizing than their meager ship's rations. He cooked the first hen in a broth rich with fresh ginger and went below ready to feed Eliza the soup if he had to force it down her throat. He lighted a whale-oil lamp, picked his way through the cargo, and approached the rat hole of his patient, who was lying with her eyes closed and did not seem to know he was there. Beneath her spread a large pool of blood. The *zhong yi* grunted and bent over her, fearing that the pitiful creature had found a way to commit suicide. He couldn't blame her, in similar circumstances he would have done the same he thought. He lifted her nightdress, but saw no visible wound, and when he touched her he realized she was still alive. He shook her until her eyes opened.

"I am pregnant," she admitted finally in a thread of a voice.

Tao Chi'en clapped his hands to his head, lost in a litany of laments in the dialect of his native village, a tongue he had not spoken in fifteen years: had he known, he would never have helped her, what was she thinking to leave for California pregnant?, she was crazy, just what he needed, a miscarriage, if she died he was lost, what kind of mess had he gotten himself into?, was he stupid?, why hadn't he guessed the reason for her haste in leaving Chile?

He added a few oaths and curses in English, but she was again unconscious and far beyond any reproach. He held her in his arms, rocking her as he would a child as his rage melted into overwhelming compassion. For an instant it occurred to him to go to Captain Katz and confess the whole matter, but he could not predict his reaction. That Dutch Lutheran, who treated the women on board as if they were carriers of the plague, would undoubtedly be furious when he learned that he had another woman aboard, this one a stowaway, and pregnant, and half dead in the bargain. And what punishment would he save for Tao Chi'en? No, he couldn't say a word to anyone. His only salvation would be to wait until Eliza passed on, if that was her karma, and then throw her body overboard along with the bags of garbage from the kitchen. The most he could do for her, if he saw her suffering too much, would be to help her die with dignity.

He was just leaving when he sensed a strange presence on his skin. Frightened, he lifted the lamp and with absolute clarity saw in the circle of the trembling flame his adored Lin watching him from a short distance away, and, on her translucid face that teasing expression that was her greatest charm. She was wearing her green silk dress with the gold embroidery, the one she saved for great occasions, and her hair was pulled back into a simple bun secured with ivory picks and with a fresh peony over each ear. That was how he had seen her for the last time, when the neighbor women had dressed her for the funeral ceremony. So real was the apparition of his wife there in the hold that he was thrown into a panic: spirits, however good in life, tended to treat mortals very cruelly. He rushed toward the ladder, but Lin blocked the way. Tao Chi'en fell to his knees, trembling, clutching the lamp, his one tie with reality. He attempted a prayer to exorcise devils, in case they had taken Lin's form to confuse him, but he could not remember the words and only a long moan of love for her and nostalgia for the past came from his lips. Then Lin bent down to him with her unforgettable delicacy, so close that had he dared he could have kissed her, and whispered that she had not come so far to frighten him but to remind him of the duties of an honorable physician. She herself had nearly bled to death after the birth of her daughter, and he had been able to save her. Why did he not do the same for this young woman? What had happened to her beloved Tao? Had he perhaps lost his kind heart and turned into a cockroach? A premature death was not Eliza's karma, she assured him. If a woman is prepared to travel the world buried in a nightmarish hole in order to find her man, it is because she has much *qi*.

"You must help her, Tao, if she dies without seeing her lover she will never be at peace and her ghost will pursue you forever," Lin warned him before she faded away.

"Wait!" Tao begged, reaching out to stop her, but his fingers closed on air.

Tao Chi'en lay prostrate on the floor for a long time, struggling to recapture his reason, until his crazed heart stopped galloping and the faint scent of Lin had evaporated from the hold. "Don't go, don't go," he repeated a thousand times, sick with love. Finally he was able to get to his feet, open the hatch, and go out to the fresh air.

It was a warm night. The Pacific Ocean was gleaming like silver in the moonlight and a light breeze bellied the worn sails of the *Emilia*. Many passengers had already gone to bed or were playing cards in their cabins; others had hung their hammocks to pass the night amid the chaos of machines, harnesses, and boxes that covered the decks, and some were amusing themselves at the stern, watching the playful dolphins in the foam of the wake. Tao Chi'en looked up toward the enormous dome of the sky with gratitude. For the first time since her death, Lin had visited him openly. Before beginning his life as a sailor he had seen her nearby from time to time, especially when he was deep in meditation, but then it had been easy to confuse the tentative presence of her spirit with his widower's longing. Lin tended to touch him lightly with her fine fingers as she passed, but he would be left with the doubt of whether it was really she or just a figment of his tormented soul. Moments earlier in the hold, however, he had had no doubts: Lin's face had been as radiant and clear as the moon over that sea. He felt her with him, and was content, as in those long ago nights when she nestled in his arms after they made love.

Tao Chi'en went to the crew's quarters where he had a narrow wood bunk far from what little ventilation filtered through the hatch. It was impossible to sleep there in the thick air and funk from the sleeping men, but he hadn't had to do that since leaving Valparaíso because the summer weather allowed him to stretch out on the deck. He looked for his trunk, nailed to the floor to secure it in the tossing of the ship, removed the key from around his neck, opened the padlock, and took out a vial of laudanum. Then he quietly drew a double ration of freshwater and went to get rags from the kitchen, which would do for lack of something better.

He was on his way back to the hold when he was stopped by a hand on his arm. He turned in surprise and saw one of the Chilean women who, defying the captain's explicit order to stay out of sight after sunset, had come out to entice clients. He recognized her immediately. Of all the women on board, Azucena Placeres was the most sympathetic and most outgoing. During the first days she was the only one willing to help seasick passengers and had also dutifully nursed a young sailor who had fallen from the mast and broken his arm. She had won the respect even of the stern Captain Katz, who, from that time, had looked the other way when she broke the rules. Azucena offered her services as a nurse for free, but if anyone made so bold as to lay a hand on her firm flesh he had to pay in coin of the realm, because, as she said, there was no reason to confuse a good heart with stupidity. This is my only capital, she would say, jauntily slapping herself on the buttocks, and if I'm not careful with it, I'll screw up for real. Azucena Placeres spoke to Tao in four words that can be understood in any language: chocolate, coffee, tobacco, and brandy. As always when she met him, she expressed in graphic sign language her wish to exchange any of those luxuries for her favors, but the *zhong yi* pushed her aside and kept on his way.

For a good part of the night Tao Chi'en sat beside the feverish Eliza. He worked over her weakened body with the limited resources of his bag, his long experience, and a wavering tenderness until she expelled a bloody little mollusk. Tao Chi'en examined it in the lamplight and determined that without the slightest doubt it was a five- or six-week fetus, and was whole. To clean out her womb, he inserted his needles in the girl's arms and legs, provoking strong contractions. When he was sure of the results, he sighed with relief: all that remained was to ask Lin to do her part to prevent infection. Until that night he had thought of Eliza as a business arrangement, and he had the pearl necklace in the bottom of his trunk to prove it. She was just a stranger, a girl for whom he had no particular feelings, a *fan wey* with big feet and an aggressive temperament who hadn't had any luck in getting a husband since, it was easy to see, she had no inclination to please or serve a man. Now, with the misfortune of this miscarriage, she would never marry. Not even her lover, who had already abandoned her once anyway, would want her for a wife—in the unlikely event that she ever found him. He had to admit that for a foreigner Eliza was not all that ugly, at least there was a slightly Oriental air about her almond eyes and her hair, as long, black, and shiny as the proud tail of an imperial horse. If she had had that diabolical yellow or red hair, like so many women he had seen since leaving China, he might never have gone near her; however, neither her looks nor her strong character would help her now; her bad luck was cast, there was no hope for her: she would end up walking the streets in California. He had been with many such women in Canton and Hong Kong. He owed a large part of his medical knowledge to the years he had practiced on the bodies of those luckless girls abused by beatings, sickness, and drugs. Several times during that long night he asked himself whether it wouldn't be more noble to let her die, despite Lin's instructions, and save her from a horrible fate, but she had paid him in advance and he should carry out his part of the deal, he told himself. No, that wasn't the only reason, he concluded, since from the beginning he had questioned his own motives for helping this girl stow away. The risk was enormous, he wasn't sure he had committed such a foolish act merely for the value of the pearls. Something in Eliza's valiant determination had moved him, something about the fragility of her body and the bold love she professed for her lover reminded him of Lin.

Finally, near dawn, Eliza stopped bleeding. She was delirious with fever and shivering despite the unbearable heat of the hold, but her pulse was steadier and she was breathing calmly in her sleep. She was not, however, out of danger. Tao Chi'en wanted to stay with her and watch her, but he calculated that soon the bell would sound to summon him to his watch. He dragged himself up the companionway, fell facedown on the planks of the deck, and slept like a baby until a friendly shove from the foot of another sailor woke him to his duties. He plunged his head into a pail of seawater to wash the sleep from his eyes and, still in a stupor, went to the kitchen to boil the oatmeal that constituted breakfast. Everyone ate it without comment, even the sober Captain Katz—except for the Chileans, who chorused a protest despite being better provided for than anyone, having been the latest to come aboard. Other passengers had polished off their provisions of tobacco, alcohol, and sweets in insufferable months at sea before reaching Valparaíso. Word had spread that some of the Chileans were aristocrats and that was why they didn't know how to wash their own underdrawers or boil water for tea. The ones traveling in first class had brought servants who would work for them in the gold mines, because the concept of dirtying their hands personally had never crossed their minds. Others paid the sailors to wait on them, since the women, in a block, refused: they could earn ten times the price by welcoming their countrymen for ten minutes in the privacy of the women's room, so there was no reason to spend two hours washing dirty laundry. The crew and the rest of the passengers mocked those spoiled sissies but never to their faces. The Chileans had good manners, they seemed timid enough and made a great show of courtesy and gentlemanliness, but it took only the tiniest spark to inflame their arrogance. Tao Chi'en tried to avoid them. They did not mask their scorn for him or for the two Negro passengers who boarded the ship in Brazil; they had paid for their passage but they were the only ones who were not given a cabin or allowed to eat at table with the others. Tao preferred the five humble Chilean women, with their solid practical sense, their unflagging good humor, and the maternal feelings that flowered in times of emergency.

He finished his watch like a sleepwalker, his thoughts on Eliza, but couldn't find a free minute to see her until that night. At midmorning the sailors had caught an enormous shark, which died on deck, thrashing wickedly in its death throes while no one dared go near enough to club it. It fell to Tao Chi'en, in his role as cook, to supervise the task of skinning it, chopping it into pieces, cooking part of the meat and salting the rest, while the sailors washed the blood from the deck and the passengers celebrated the horrific spectacle with the last remaining bottles of champagne, anticipating a feast at dinner. Tao kept the heart for Eliza's soup and the fins to dry: they would be worth a fortune in the aphrodisiac market. As the hours went by in the chores involving the shark, Tao Chi'en imagined Eliza dead in the heart of the ship. He felt a surge of happiness when at last he went down and found that she was still alive and looking better. The hemorrhaging had stopped, the jug of water was empty, and everything indicated that there had been moments of lucidity during that long day. Briefly, he thanked Lin for her help. The girl struggled to open her eyes; her lips were dry and her face flushed with fever. He helped her to her feet and fed her a strong broth of *tangkuei* to build up her blood. When he was sure she would keep it in her stomach, he gave her a few sips of fresh milk, which she drank avidly. Invigorated, she announced that she was hungry and asked for more. The cows they were carrying onboard, unused to the sea, were producing very little; nothing but bones, there was already talk of slaughtering them. Tao Chi'en found the idea of drinking milk repulsive but his friend Ebanizer Hobbs had advised him of its properties for replenishing lost blood. If Hobbs recommended it in the diet of someone gravely wounded, it should have the same effect in this instance, Tao decided.

"Am I going to die, Tao?"

"Not yet." He smiled and patted Eliza's head.

"How long before we reach California?"

"A long time. Don't think about that. Now you must urinate."

"No, please!" she protested.

"Why not? You must!"

"In front of you?"

"I am a *zhong yi*. You cannot feel embarrassed with me. I have seen everything there is to see of your body."

"I can't move, I can't survive this voyage, Tao, I would rather die," Eliza sobbed, steadying herself on him as she sat on the pot.

"Be brave, girl. Lin says you have much *qi* and you have not come this far to die in midjourney."

"Who says that?"

"Not important."

That night Tao Chi'en realized that he could not care for Eliza alone, he needed help. The next morning, as soon as the women came out of their cabin and went to the stern, as they always did to wash their clothes and braid their hair, and to mend the feathers and bugle beads of their professional attire, he beckoned Azucena Placeres to come talk to him. During the voyage none of the women had worn their whoring clothes but dressed in heavy, dark skirts, plain blouses, and house slippers; they wrapped themselves in their mantles, combed their hair into two braids down their backs, and skipped their makeup. They looked like a group of simple housewives busy at domestic chores. Azucena gave a happy wink to her partners in crime and followed Tao into the kitchen. There he handed her a large piece of chocolate that he had stolen from the stores for the captain's table and tried to explain his problem, but she didn't understand a word of English and he began to lose patience. Azucena Placeres smelled the chocolate and a childlike smile illuminated her round Indian face. She took the cook's hand and placed it on her breast, pointing toward the women's cabin, empty at that hour, but he pulled away his hand, took hers, and led her to the hatchway to the hold. Azucena, half surprised, half curious, held back a little but he did not give her a chance to refuse, he opened the hatch and pushed her down the ladder, constantly smiling to calm her. For a few instants they were in darkness, until he found the lamp hanging from a beam and lighted it. Azucena giggled; finally this strange Chinese man had understood the terms of the bargain. She had never done it with an Asian and she was very curious to know if their equipment was like other men's, but the cook showed no sign of profiting from their privacy; instead he pulled on her arm, dragging her through the labyrinths of the cargo. She was afraid he was a little unhinged and began to tug and try to get loose, but he held on, forcing her to follow him until the lamplight fell onto the hole where Eliza lay.

"*Jesús, María, y José*!" Azucena yelled, crossing herself in terror when she saw Eliza.

"Ask her to help us," Tao Chi'en told Eliza in English, shaking her awake.

It took Eliza a good quarter of an hour to stammer out the simple instructions from Tao Chi'en, who had taken the turquoise brooch from Eliza's bag of jewels and was brandishing it before the eyes of the trembling Azucena. The deal, he told her, as Eliza translated, was to come down twice a day to bathe and feed Eliza, without anyone's knowing. If she did that, he would give her the brooch in San Francisco, but if she said a single word to anyone, he would slit her throat. He had taken the knife from his sash and was waving it under her nose; in the other hand he held the brooch so the message would be very clear.

"You understand?"

"Tell this crazy Chinaman I understand and to put that knife away, because he could kill me, mean to or not."

For a time that seemed endless, Eliza fought her way through delirium, tended by Tao Chi'en at night and Azucena Placeres by day. Early in the morning and at siesta time, when most of the passengers were drowsing, Azucena would slip down to the kitchen and get the key from Tao Chi'en. At first she was shaking with fear when she went down to the hold, but soon her natural good nature, and the brooch, overcame her fright. She would begin by rubbing

Eliza with a soapy rag until she had removed the sweat of her agony, then force her to eat some oatmeal and chicken broth fortified with the *tangkuei* Tao Chi'en prepared. She gave Eliza herbs, according to his directions, and on her own initiative brewed her a daily cup of borage tea. She blindly trusted in that remedy to flush a pregnancy from a womb: borage and an image of the Virgin of Carmen were the first things she and her companions-in-adventure had tucked into their travel trunks, because without those protections the roads of California could be very hard to travel. Eliza was lost in the land of death until the morning they anchored in the port of Guayaquil, not much more than a small community overrun by exuberant Ecuadorian vegetation; few ships anchored there except to negotiate for tropical fruit or coffee, but Captain Katz had promised to deliver some letters to a family of Dutch missionaries. He had had that correspondence with him for six months and he was not a man to fail on a promise. The previous night, in heat like a bonfire, Eliza had sweated out the last drop of temperature and dreamt that she was climbing barefoot up the side of an erupting volcano; she awakened sopping wet but lucid and with a clear brow. All the passengers, including the women and a good part of the crew, disembarked for a few hours to stretch their legs, bathe in the river, and stuff themselves with fresh fruit, but Tao Chi'en stayed onboard to teach Eliza to light and smoke the pipe he had in his trunk. He had doubts about the girl's treatment; that was one time he would have given anything to have the counsel of his wise master. He understood the need to keep her calm and help pass the time in the prison of the hold, but she had lost a lot of blood and he was afraid the drug would thin what little she had left. He made his decision hesitantly, after entreating Lin to watch over Eliza's sleep.

"Opium. It will put you to sleep, and so time will pass quickly."

"Opium! That brings madness!"

"You're mad anyway, so you have little to lose," Tao said, smiling.

"You want to kill me, don't you?"

"Of course. I wasn't able to kill you when you were bleeding to death so I will now with opium."

"Tao, I am afraid of it."

"Much opium is bad. A little is comfort and I will give you only a little."

Eliza didn't know how much "little" or "much" *was*. Tao Chi'en had her drink his potions—dragon bone and oyster shell—and rationed the opium to give her a few hours of merciful half sleep but not allow her to lose herself forever in a paradise of no return. She spent the next weeks flying through other galaxies, far from the unhealthy burrow where she lay prostrate and awakened only when Tao or Azucena came to feed her, bathe her, and make her walk a little in the narrow labyrinths of the hold. She did not feel the torment of fleas and lice or smell the nauseating stench she had at first been unable to bear, because the drugs deadened her prodigious sense of smell. She floated in and out of her dreams without control, nor could she remember them, but Tao Chi'en was right: time passed quickly. Azucena Placeres did not understand why Eliza was traveling under such conditions. None of her group had paid for a passage, they had a contract with the captain, who would get his pay when they reached San Francisco.

"If the stories are true, in a single day you can make hundreds of dollars. The miners pay with pure gold. They go for months without seeing a woman, they're desperate. Talk with the captain and pay him when you get there," she would insist to Eliza in the brief times she was up.

"I am not one of you," Eliza replied, groggy in the sweet fog of the drugs.

Finally, in a moment of lucidity, Azucena Placeres got Eliza to confess part of her story. Immediately, the idea of helping a fugitive of love captured the woman's imagination, and from then on she cared for the invalid with even greater attention. Now she not only fed her and bathed her, she stayed with her for the pleasure of watching her sleep. If Eliza was awake, Azucena told her about her own life and taught her to pray the rosary that, according to her, was the best way to pass hours without thinking and at the same time get to heaven without too much effort. Nothing better for a person in her profession, she explained. She saved part of the money she took in to buy indulgences from the Church, thus reducing the days she would have to spend in purgatory in the next life, although, according to her calculations, she would never have enough to cover all her sins. Weeks went by when Eliza didn't know whether it was night or day. She had a vague sensation of sometimes relying on a female presence at her side, but then she would sleep and wake confused, not knowing if she had dreamed Azucena Placeres or whether in fact a small woman existed who had black hair, a flat nose, and high cheekbones, and looked like a young version of Mama Fresia.

The climate grew a little cooler as they left Panama behind, where the captain had forbidden anyone to go ashore because of fear of yellow fever; he sent two sailors in a dinghy to scout for freshwater, since what little they had left was like swamp water. They sailed past Mexico, and once the *Emilia* was plowing the waters of northern California they encountered winter. The suffocating heat of the first part of the voyage was replaced with cold and wet; out of suitcases came fur hats, boots, gloves, and woolen petticoats. From time to time the brigantine met other ships and saluted from a distance, without slowing. At each religious service the captain gave thanks for their progress, because he knew of ships that had sailed as far as the shores of Hawaii or beyond before finding favorable winds. Besides playful dolphins, large, solemn whales accompanied them for long stretches. At dusk, when the water turned red with reflections from the setting sun, the enormous cetaceans made love in a froth of golden foam, calling to one another with deep, submarine bawling. And sometimes, in the silence of the night, they came so close to the ship that the heavy, mysterious whisper of their presence was easily heard. All fresh provisions had been exhausted and rations were spare; except for playing cards and fishing there was no entertainment of any kind. The voyagers spent hours discussing the details of the associations created for the adventure, some with strictly military rules, even uniforms, others more informal. All of them, basically, had been formed to finance travel and equipment, work the mines, transport the gold, and then share the profits. No one knew anything about the terrain, or the distances. One of the associations stipulated that the members would return every night to the ship, where they were intended to live for several months, and deposit the day's gold in a strongbox. Captain Katz explained to them that the *Emilia* could not be rented like a hotel because he planned to return to Europe as soon as possible, and that the mines were hundreds of miles from the port, but he was ignored. They had been sailing fifty-two days. The monotony of the infinite waves was affecting nerves and quarrels erupted over the least pretext. When a Chilean passenger was just at the point of firing his blunderbuss at a Yankee sailor with whom Azucena Placeres was flirting too openly, Captain Vincent Katz confiscated all weapons, including straight razors, with the promise that he would return them as soon as they sighted San Francisco. The one person authorized to handle knives was the cook, who had the thankless task of slaughtering the domestic animals one by one. Once the last cow ended up in the stewpots, Tao Chi'en improvised an elaborate ceremony to obtain the pardon of the sacrificed animals and cleanse himself of their spilled blood, then disinfected his knife by passing it several times through the flame of a torch.

As soon as the ship had sailed into California waters, Tao Chi'en began gradually cutting back on Eliza's tranquilizing herbs and opium. He gave his attention to feeding her, and made her exercise so she would be able to walk out of her confinement on her own two feet. Azucena Placeres patiently washed Eliza with a soapy cloth and even improvised a way to wash her hair in a few cupfuls of water as she told Eliza sad tales about her life as a whore and of her fantasy of getting rich in California and returning to Chile as a lady, with six trunks of clothes fit for a queen and one gold tooth. Tao Chi'en was wondering how he was going to get Eliza off the ship, but he had brought her aboard in a seabag and surely he could use the same method to smuggle her ashore. And once on land, the girl was no longer his responsibility. The idea of a definitive parting produced a mixture of tremendous relief and inexplicable anxiety.

The *Emilia* was now only a few leagues from its destination, hugging the coast of northern California. According to Azucena Placeres, it looked so much like Chile that she was sure they had been traveling in circles, like a crab, and were back in Valparaíso. Thousands of sea lions and seals scrambled from the rocks and fell heavily into the water, setting off the loud screeching of gulls and pelicans. There was no sign of a human being along the coast, not a trace of a town or a shadow of the Indians who for centuries, they'd been told, had inhabited those enchanted lands. Finally they were approaching the rocky islands that announced the proximity of the famous Golden Gate, the threshold of the bay of San Francisco. A thick fog enveloped the ship like a blanket, and visibility was reduced to half a meter; the captain ordered a halt and dropped anchor, fearing a collision. They were so close now that the passengers' impatience was turning to a near riot.

Everyone was talking at once, eager to get onto dry land and race off to the placers in search of treasure. Most of the companies formed to explore the mines had broken up in the last days; the tedium of the sailing had made enemies of former partners and each man was thinking only of himself, sunk in reveries of enormous wealth. Some had declared their love for the prostitutes, wanting the captain to marry them before debarking because they had heard that the scarcest commodity in those barbarous lands was women. One of the Peruvian whores accepted the proposal of a Frenchman who had been onboard so long he no longer remembered his own name, but Captain Vincent Katz refused to celebrate the marriage when he learned the man already had a wife and four children in Avignon. The other women rejected their suitors outright, because, they said, they had made this tedious voyage in order to be free and rich, not to become an unpaid servant to the first beggar who asked them to marry.

Trapped in the milky unreality of the fog in forced immobility, the men's enthusiasm dimmed with every hour. Finally, on the second day, the skies abruptly cleared. They weighed anchor and set off under full canvas on the last stage of the long voyage. Passengers and crew came out on deck to admire the narrow opening of the Golden Gate, then sailed six more miles under a diaphanous sky, pushed by the April winds. On either side rose densely wooded hills gashed with wounds inflicted by restless waves. The Pacific lay behind them, and before them, like a lake of silver, stretched the splendid bay. A salvo of hurrahs greeted the end of the arduous journey and the beginning of the gold adventure for those men and women—and the twenty crewmen as well, who had at that very instant decided to abandon the ship to its fate and test their luck with the others in the mines. The only persons left unfazed were the Dutch captain, Vincent Katz, who stood at his post beside the wheel without a trace of emotion—he was not moved by the gold, his only desire was to return to Amsterdam in time for

Christmas with his family—and Eliza Sommers who, in the belly of the ship, did not know until many hours later that they had arrived at their destination.

The first thing to strike Tao Chi'en when they entered the bay was the forest of masts to his right. It was impossible to count them, but he estimated more than a hundred ships abandoned as if in the heat of battle. On shore, any peon earned more in a day than a sailor in a month of sailing; men deserted not only for gold, but also for the enticement of making money as porters, bakers, and blacksmiths. Some of the empty ships had been rented as storehouses or temporary hotels; others had been left to rot, covered with algae and gulls' nests. The second thing Tao Chi'en saw was a community opening like a fan on the hillsides, a jumble of campaign tents, wood and cardboard shacks, and a few simple, but well constructed, buildings, the first in that mushrooming town. As soon as they dropped anchor a boat came alongside, not the harbormaster's, as they had expected, but one belonging to a Chilean eager to welcome his compatriots and pick up the mail. He was Feliciano Rodríguez de Santa Cruz, who had changed his sonorous name to Felix Cross so the Yanquis could pronounce it. Even though several of the passengers were his personal friends, no one recognized him: every trace of the affected fop in a frock coat and waxed mustache they had last seen in Valparaíso had vanished. Before them stood a hirsute caveman with the weathered skin of an Indian clad in a mountain man's gear: boots to midthigh, and two pistols at his waist. He was accompanied by a black with an equally savage look, he, too, armed like a highwayman. He was a fugitive slave who, as he stepped onto California soil, had become a free man, but as he was unwilling to suffer the misery of the mines he had chosen to earn his living as a hired gun. When Feliciano identified himself, he was greeted with cries of enthusiasm and practically carried on his friends' shoulders to the nearest stateroom, where he was bombarded with questions about the latest news. Of prime interest was whether gold was as abundant as everyone said, to which Cross replied, "More," and produced from his pouch a yellow substance that looked like squashed shit; he explained that this was a half-kilo nugget and that he was prepared to trade it for whatever liquor they had onboard; no deal was made, however, because there were only three bottles left, the rest having been consumed on the voyage. The nugget had been found, Feliciano told them, by valiant miners from Chile now working for him along the banks of the American River. Once they had drunk a toast with the last of the liquor and the Chilean had picked up the letters from his wife, he left them with a few words on how to survive in that land.

"Until a few months ago we had a code of honor, and even the worst ruffians behaved with decency. You could leave your gold in a tent with no guard and no one would touch it, but now all that has changed. The law of the jungle rules, the only ideology is greed. Don't let yourself be parted from your weapons, and always travel in pairs or groups, because this is a land of thieves."

Several dinghies had by then surrounded the ship, crewed by men shouting out all kinds of deals, eager to buy anything the passengers had because it could be sold on shore for five times its value. Unwary travelers quickly discovered the art of speculation. The harbormaster showed up in the afternoon, accompanied by a customs agent and trailing two boats filled with several Mexicans and two Chinese who offered to ferry the ship's cargo to the dock. They charged a fortune, but there was no alternative. The harbormaster showed no inclination to check passports or verify the passengers' identities.

"Documents? None of that! You have come to the paradise of freedom. There are no stamped papers here," he cried.

He was, on the other hand, intensely interested in the women. He prided himself on being the first to try out each and every female who got off a ship in San Francisco, although there weren't as many as he would have wished. He told them how the first women to appear in the city, several months ago, were welcomed by a throng of euphoric males who stood in line for hours to take their turn, paying in gold dust, nuggets, coins, even bars. Those first two had been brave Yankee girls who had made the trip from Boston, crossing to the Pacific by way of the isthmus of Panama. They auctioned their services to the highest bidders, earning in one day their normal income for a year. Since then, more than five hundred whores had arrived, nearly all of them Mexicans, Chileans, and Peruvians, except for a few North American and French women, although their total number was insignificant compared to the growing invasion of young single men.

Azucena Placeres did not hear the Yankees' news because Tao Chi'en took her down to the hold as soon as he learned of the presence of the customs agent. They weren't going to be able to sneak Eliza ashore in a sack over a stevedore's shoulder, as she had come aboard, because it appeared that all goods were going to be checked. Eliza was surprised when she saw them; both were unrecognizable. Tao was wearing a freshly laundered smock and trousers; his tightly braided hair gleamed as if it had been oiled, and he had carefully shaved the last hair from his foreskull and face, while Azucena Placeres had changed from country garb into full battle dress and was wearing a blue gown with feathers trimming the décolletage; her upswept hair was crowned by a hat, and her cheeks and lips were rouged.

"The journey's over and you're still alive, girl," she trumpeted gaily.

Her plan was to lend Eliza one of her most splendid outfits and smuggle her off the ship as just another of their band—not far off the mark, she told Eliza, since that was going to be her only choice of career once on land.

"I have come to marry my sweetheart," Eliza replied, for the hundredth time.

"No sweetheart is going to do you any good. If in order to eat you have to hustle your ass, you'll hustle your ass. You can't be choosy at this point, girl."

Tao Chi'en interrupted them. If for two months there had been seven women on the ship, they couldn't take eight off, he reasoned. He had noticed the band of Mexicans and Chinese who had come aboard to unload the ship and who were waiting on deck to hear the captain's and the custom agent's orders. Tao instructed Azucena to braid Eliza's long hair in a queue like his own while he went to look for a set of his clothes. They dressed the girl in cut-off pants, a smock tied at the waist with a cord, and a straw hat like a Japanese parasol. In those two months of slogging through the desert sands of hell, Eliza had lost weight and looked as thin and pale as rice paper. In Tao Chien's too large clothes she looked like a sad, undernourished, little Chinese boy. Azucena Placeres wrapped her in her robust laundress's arms and planted an emotional kiss on her forehead. She had grown fond of Eliza, and in the depths of her heart was happy that she had a sweetheart waiting for her, because she could not imagine Eliza subjected to the brutalities of the life she herself led.

"You look like a lizard." Azucena Placeres laughed aloud.

"What if they discover me?"

"What's the worst that can happen? That Katz will make you pay for your passage? You can pay for it with your jewels, isn't that what they're for?"

"No one must know you are here," said Tao Chi'en. "That way, Captain Sommers won't be looking for you in California."

"If he finds me, he will take me back to Chile with him."

"Why would he do that?" Azucena interjected. "Your reputation is already ruined, and that is something rich people cannot tolerate. Your family must be very happy that you disappeared, it saves them having to throw you out."

"Only throw you out? In China they would kill you for what you have done."

"Well, Chino, we are not in your country. Don't frighten the little thing. You can go with an easy heart, Eliza. No one will notice you. All eyes will be on me," Azucena Placeres assured her, making her exit in a whirlwind of blue feathers, the turquoise brooch pinned to her bosom.

And so it went. The five Chileans and two Peruvians, in their most exuberant sporting attire, were the spectacle of the day. They climbed down to the boats by way of a rope ladder—preceded by seven fortunate sailors who had drawn straws for the privilege of bearing the weight of those buttocks on their heads—in the midst of a chorus of whistles and applause from the hundreds of spectators crowded into the port to welcome them. No one paid the least attention to the Mexicans and Chinese who, like a line of ants, were passing bundles from hand to hand. Eliza went on one of the last boats, beside Tao Chi'en, who told his compatriots that the boy was a deaf mute and a little slow, so there was no point in trying to communicate with him.

The Argonauts

Tao Chi'en's and Eliza Sommers' feet first touched the soil of San Francisco on a Tuesday in April of 1849, at two o'clock in the afternoon. By then thousands of adventurers had briefly passed through on their way to the placers. A persistent wind made walking difficult, but the day was clear and they could appreciate the panorama of the bay in all its splendid beauty. Tao Chi'en cut a bizarre figure with his doctor's case, which he was never without, his seabag, his straw hat, and a multicolored wool serape he had bought from one of the Mexican stevedores. It didn't matter, really; looks weren't what counted in that town. Eliza's legs were trembling; she hadn't used them in two months, and she felt as landsick as she had before at sea, but the man's clothing gave her an unfamiliar freedom; she had never felt so invisible. Once she got over the feeling that she was naked, she could enjoy the breeze blowing up her sleeves and pants legs. Accustomed to the prison of her petticoats, she could now breathe deeply. She was struggling to carry her small suitcase filled with the exquisite dresses Miss Rose had packed with the best intentions, and when he noticed her difficulty Tao Chi'en took it from her and slung it over his shoulder. The Castile wool blanket rolled up beneath her arm weighed as much as the suitcase, but she realized she couldn't leave it, it would be her most precious possession at night. Eyes to the ground, hidden beneath her straw hat, she stumbled along through the awesome anarchy of the port. The village of Yerba Buena, founded in 1769 by a Spanish expedition, had fewer than fifteen hundred inhabitants, but the adventurers had begun to flock in with the first news of gold. Within a few months, that innocent little village awakened with the name San Francisco and a fame that had reached the farthest points of the globe. More than a true city, it was an enormous camp for men on the move.

Gold fever left no one unaffected: smiths, carpenters, teachers, doctors, soldiers, fugitives from the law, preachers, bakers, revolutionaries, and harmless madmen of various stripes who had left family and possessions behind to traverse half the world in search of adventure. "They look for gold, and along the way lose their souls," Captain Katz had repeated tirelessly in the brief religious services he imposed every Sunday on the passengers and crew of the *Emilia*, but no one paid any attention, blinded by dreams of the sudden riches that would change their lives. For the first time in history, gold lay scattered on the ground, unclaimed, free, and plentiful, within the reach of anyone with the will to go after it. Argonauts came from distant shores: Europeans fleeing wars, plagues, and tyrannies; Americans, ambitious and short-tempered; blacks pursuing freedom; Oregonians and Russians dressed in deerskin, like Indians; Mexicans, Chileans, and Peruvians; Australian bandits; starving Chinese peasants who were risking their necks by violating the imperial order against leaving their country. All races flowed together in the muddy alleyways of San Francisco.

The main streets, laid out as broad semicircles touching the beach at both ends, were intersected by other, straight, streets descending from the steep hills to end at the dock, some so abrupt and deep in mud that not even mules could climb them. Suddenly a storm would blow in, raising whirlwinds of sand along the shore, but soon the air would be calm again and the sky blue. There were already several solid buildings and dozens under construction, including some announcing themselves as future luxury hotels, but everything else was a shambles of temporary dwellings, barracks, shacks of sheet metal, wood, or cardboard, canvas tents, and straw roofs. The recent rains of winter had turned the dock into a swamp; any vehicle that had ventured there sank hub-deep in mire, and planks were laid across ditches deep in garbage, thousands of broken bottles, and other refuse. There were no drains or sewers, and the wells were contaminated; cholera and dysentery reaped scores of lives—except among the Chinese, who by custom drank tea, and the Chileans, who had been raised on polluted water and were therefore immune to lesser bacteria. The heterogeneous throng pulsed with frenzied activity, pushing, bumping into building materials, barrels, boxes, burros, and carts. Chinese porters balanced their loads on each end of a long pole, indifferent to whom they struck as they went by; strong and patient Mexicans swung bundles equal to their own weight onto their backs and trotted off up the hills; Malaysians and Hawaiians seized any pretext to start a fight; Americans charged into temporary businesses on horseback, bowling over anyone in their way; native-born Californians strutted around in handsome embroidered jackets, silver spurs, and slit pants legs trimmed with a double row of gold buttons from belt to boot tops. Shouts from fights and accidents added to the din of hammers, saws, and picks. Shots rang out with terrifying frequency, but no one was affected by one more dead man; on the other hand, the theft of a box of nails immediately drew a crowd of indignant citizens ready to mete out justice with their own hands. Property was much more valuable than life; any robbery over a hundred dollars was paid for on the gallows. There were scores of gaming houses, bars, and saloons decorated with images of naked women in lieu of the real article. Everything imaginable—especially liquor and weapons—was sold at exorbitant prices because no one had time to bargain. Customers nearly always paid in gold, not even stopping to wipe up the dust clinging to the scales. Tao Chi'en decided that the famous Gum San, the Golden

Mountain he had heard so much about, was a hell, and calculated that at these prices his savings would not go very far. Eliza's little bag of jewels would be worthless, because the only acceptable tender was pure gold.

Eliza made her way through the crowd as best she could, close behind Tao Chi'en and grateful to be wearing men's clothing because she saw no sign of a woman anywhere. The *Emilia*'s seven female passengers had been carried off to one of the many saloons, where undoubtedly they had already begun earning the two hundred seventy dollars they owed Captain Vincent Katz for their passage. Tao Chi'en had found out from the stevedores that the town was divided into sectors and that every nationality had its neighborhood. He was warned not to go near the Australian roughnecks, who might waylay a passerby for pure fun, and then was pointed the way to a cluster of tents and shacks where the Chinese lived. And that was the direction in which they started walking.

"How am I going to find Joaquín in all this uproar?" Eliza asked, feeling lost and helpless.

"If there is a Chinese barrio, there must be a Chilean one. Look for it."

"I'm not planning to leave you, Tao."

"Tonight," he warned, "I'm going back to the ship."

"Why? Aren't you interested in gold?"

Tao Chi'en walked faster, and she adjusted her pace to his in order not to lose sight of him. Soon they came to the Chinese sector—Little Canton, it was called—a couple of unwholesome streets where Tao immediately felt at home because not a single *fan wey* was to be seen; on the air floated delicious odors of the food of his country and he heard several Chinese dialects, mainly Cantonese. To Eliza, in contrast, it was like being transported to another planet; she did not understand a single word, and it seemed to her that everyone was furious because they were all yelling and waving their arms. Again she did not see any women, but Tao pointed to a couple of barred windows at which she saw despondent faces. Tao had been two months without a woman and those at the window called to him but he knew the ravages of venereal diseases too well to run that risk. These were peasant girls bought for a few coins and brought here from the most remote provinces of China. He thought of his sister, sold by his father, and was bent double by a wave of nausea.

"What's the matter, Tao?"

"Bad memories. Those girls are slaves."

"I thought there weren't any slaves in California."

They went into a restaurant, identified by the traditional yellow streamers. There was a large table crowded with men sitting elbow to elbow and wolfing down food. The sound of lively conversation and chopsticks clattering against tin plates was music to Tao Chi'en's ears. They stood in a double line until they could sit down. It wasn't a matter of choosing what to eat but of grabbing anything that came within arm's reach. It took skill to catch a plate on the fly before someone more enterprising intercepted it, but Tao Chi'en got one for Eliza and another for himself. She eyed with suspicion a dubious green liquid in which pale threads and gelatinous mollusks were floating. She prided herself on knowing any ingredient by its smell, but what sat before her did not look edible, it reminded her of swamp water swarming with polliwogs; it did, however, have the advantage of not requiring chopsticks, she could drink it directly from the bowl. Hunger overcame skepticism and she dared take a taste, while behind her a line of impatient customers yelled at her to hurry. The dish was delicious and she would happily have eaten more, but she was denied the opportunity by Tao Chi'en, who took her by one arm and led her outside. She followed him, first, from shop to shop to replace the medicinal supplies for his kit and to talk with the two Chinese herbalists in the town, and then to a gambling den, one of the many on every corner. This was a wooden building with a pretense of luxury and decorated with paintings of voluptuous, half-clad women. Gold dust was weighed to exchange for coins at the rate of sixteen dollars per ounce, or sometimes the whole pouch was laid on the table. Americans, French, and Mexicans made up the majority of the customers but there were also adventurers from Hawaii, Chile, Australia, and Russia. The most popular games were the monte that had originated in Mexico, *lasquenet*, and twenty-one. Since the Chinese preferred fan-tan, and wagered only a few cents, they were not welcome at the high-rolling tables. There were no blacks gambling, although some were providing music or waiting tables; Eliza and Tao later learned that if they went into a bar or gambling hall they would be given one free drink but would then have to leave or be thrown out. There were three women in the saloon, two young Mexican girls with large sparkling eyes, dressed in white and smoking cigarette after cigarette, and a pretty, rather mature Frenchwoman wearing a tight corset and heavy makeup. They made the rounds of the tables, urging the men to bet and drink, and often disappeared with some customer behind a heavy drapery of red brocade. Tao Chi'en was told that they charged an ounce of gold for an hour of their company in the bar and several hundred dollars to spend the night with a lonely man, although the Frenchwoman was more costly, and she had no truck with Chinese or blacks.

Eliza, overlooked in her disguise as an Asian boy, sat in a corner, exhausted, while Tao talked with various people, inquiring about gold and life in California. For Tao Chi'en, protected by the memory of Lin, it was easier to resist the temptation of the women than of gambling. The sound of the fan-tan chips and the dice on the tabletops called to him with the voice of a siren. The sight of the decks of cards in the players' hands made him break out in a sweat, but he forbore, fortified by the conviction that good luck would abandon him forever if he broke his promise. Years later, after many adventures, Eliza asked him what good luck he was referring to, and he, without a moment's hesitation, answered, The luck of being alive and of having met her. That evening he learned that the placers were located along the Sacramento, American, and San Joaquín rivers and their hundreds of tributaries, but the maps were untrustworthy, and distances immense. The easy surface gold was growing scarce. True, there were still plenty of lucky miners who came across a nugget the size of a shoe, but most had to be content with a handful of dust won with considerable effort. There was a lot of talk about gold, they told Tao, but little about the sacrifice needed to get it. It took an ounce a day to make any profit, and that was only if you were willing to live like a dog, because the prices of things were outrageous, and the gold melted away in the blink of an eye. Merchants and moneylenders, on the other hand, were getting rich, like one of Tao's countrymen who had taken in laundry and after a few months was able to build a solid house and was thinking of going back to China to buy several wives and devote himself to producing male offspring, or another who lent money to gamblers at 10 percent interest per hour, that is, more than 87,000 percent per year. Tao's informants told fantastic tales of enormous nuggets, of beds of dust mixed in with sand, of veins in quartz rock, and of mules' hooves shearing off rock face to reveal a treasure, but getting rich demanded hard work as well as luck. The Americans were short on patience; they didn't know how to work as a team, and were defeated by greed and a lack of discipline. Mexicans and Chileans knew about mining, but they squandered their earnings; Oregonians and Russians wasted time fighting and drinking. The

Chinese, on the other hand, got ahead however poor their beginnings because they were frugal; they did not get drunk and worked like ants eighteen hours a day without rest or complaint. The *fan wey* were indignant about the success of the Chinese; Tao was warned to play a part, act stupid, not provoke them or they would get the same treatment given arrogant Mexicans. Yes, they told him, there was a settlement of Chileans; it was some distance from town on the hill over to the right; they called the place Chilecito, Little Chile, but it was pretty late to be going there with no company but his simpleminded brother.

"I am going back to the ship," Tao Chi'en announced to Eliza when finally they left the hall.

"I feel dizzy, I think I'm going to fall."

"You have been very sick, you need to eat well and rest."

"I can't do that alone, Tao. Please, don't leave me yet . . . "

"I have a contract, the captain will send someone to look for me."

"And who will do that? All the ships are deserted. There is no one left onboard. Your captain can yell himself hoarse and none of his sailors will come."

"What am I going to do with her," Tao Chi'en asked himself aloud in Cantonese. His responsibility ended in San Francisco, but he didn't feel able to abandon Eliza to her fate in this place. He was trapped, at least until she was stronger and could meet other Chileans, or find where her slippery lover had gotten to. That shouldn't be difficult, he supposed. However chaotic San Francisco might seem, there were no secrets anywhere for the Chinese; he could afford to wait until the next day and take her to Little Chile. Darkness had turned everything into a dream world. Nearly all the shelters were canvas, and with lamps lighted inside they were as transparent and glowing as diamonds. The torches and bonfires in the streets, and the music from the gaming halls, contributed to the impression of unreality. Tao Chi'en looked for somewhere they could spend the night; he found a kind of large shed some twenty-five meters long and eight wide built of boards and tin salvaged from grounded ships and topped by the sign "Hotel." Inside were two floors of cots, simple wooden planks where a man could curl up and sleep, along with a counter at the rear where liquor was sold. There were no windows, and the only fresh air filtered through cracks in the board walls. For a dollar you bought the right to a night's rest, and you provided your own bedding. The first to get there claimed the cots and latecomers had to hit the floor, and although there were empty beds, they weren't given one because they were Chinese. They stretched out on the dirt floor using a bundle of clothing for a pillow and the serape and Castile blanket for their only cover. Soon the place was filled with men of assorted races and types lying elbow to elbow in tight rows, clothed, weapons in hand. The stench of filth, tobacco, and human exhalations, plus the snoring and strange cries of those lost in nightmares, made it hard to sleep, but Eliza was so tired she blacked out the passing hours. She woke at dawn shivering with cold, huddled close to Tao Chi'en's back, and that was when she noticed that he smelled of the sea. On the ship his scent had been indistinguishable from the immensity of the ocean around them, but that night she learned that this was the specific aroma of Tao's body. She closed her eyes, pressed closer to him, and soon fell back asleep.

The next morning they both set off to look for Little Chile, which she recognized immediately both by the Chilean flag fluttering boldly atop a pole and because most of the men were wearing *maulinos*, the typical cone-shaped hats. The settlement consisted of some eight or ten densely populated blocks, including a few women and children who had traveled with their men, all busy at some task or activity. People were living in tents or board shacks and huts set in the middle of a junkyard of tools and garbage. There were also restaurants, makeshift hotels, and brothels. Eliza and Tao estimated that there were a couple of thousand Chileans in that barrio, but no one had counted them, and, in fact, it was nothing more than a place for new arrivals to pause a while. Eliza was happy to hear the language of her country and to see a sign on a ragged tent advertising *pequenes* and *chunchules*. She went right to it and, disguising her Chilean accent, asked for a helping of the latter. Tao Chi'en stood staring at that strange food served on a piece of newspaper instead of a plate, unable to guess what the devil it was. Eliza explained that it was deep-fried hog tripe.

"I ate your Chinese soup yesterday. Today you eat my Chilean *chunchules,"* she ordered.

"How is it you two Chinese speak Spanish?" the vendor asked amiably.

"My friend doesn't, and I do only because I spent time in Peru," Eliza replied.

"And what are you looking for around here?"

"A Chilean named Joaquín Andieta."

"What do you want him for?"

"We have a message for him. Do you know him?"

"A lot of people have passed through here in recent months. No one stays more than a few days, they're soon off to the placers. Some come back, some don't."

"And Joaquín Andieta?"

"I don't remember, but I'll ask."

Eliza and Tao Chi'en sat down in the shade of a pine to eat. Twenty minutes later the vendor returned with a short-legged, wide-shouldered man who looked like an Indian from the north of Chile, who said that Joaquín Andieta had started off in the direction of the placers of Sacramento at least a couple of months ago, although no one kept time by calendars or kept track of other folks' whereabouts.

"Then we're going to Sacramento, Tao," Eliza decided as soon as they left Little Chile.

"You can't travel yet. You need to rest awhile."

"I will rest there, when we find him."

"I would rather go back to Captain Katz. California is not the place for me."

"What is the matter with you? Has your blood turned to water? There's no one left on the ship, only that captain with his Bible. Everyone has gone off looking for gold and you plan to go back and work as a cook for a miserable salary?"

"I don't believe in easy fortune. I want a peaceful life."

"Well, if not gold, there must be something else that interests you."

"Learning."

"Learning what? You already know so much."

"I have everything to learn!"

"Then you have come to the perfect place. You know nothing about this country. They need doctors here. How many men do you think there are in the mines? Thousands! And they all need a doctor. This is the land of opportunity, Tao. Come to Sacramento with me. Besides, if you don't come with me, I won't get far."

For a bargain price, given the lamentable condition of the vessel, Tao Chi'en and Eliza started north, sailing the entire length of San Francisco Bay. The ship was crammed with passengers with elaborate mining equipment; no one could move in that space crowded with boxes, tools, baskets, sacks of provisions, gunpowder, and weapons. The captain and his second mate were a pair of Yankee seamen sinister in appearance but good sailors and generous with the limited rations, even their bottles of liquor. Tao Chi'en negotiated the cost of Eliza's ticket and he was given his passage in exchange for working as crew. The passengers, all with pistols in their waistbands, in addition to knives or straight razors, scarcely spoke to one another the first day except to curse some jab from an elbow or foot, inevitable in that tight space. At dawn on the second day, after a long, cold, damp night anchored close to the shore because of the impossibility of navigating in the dark, everyone felt as if he were surrounded by enemies. The scruffy beards, filth, unappetizing food, mosquitoes, opposing winds and currents all contributed to the general irritation. Tao Chi'en, the only one without plans or goals, appeared to be the only serene person aboard, and when he was not fighting the sail he was admiring the extraordinary panorama of the bay. Eliza, in contrast, was miserable in her disguise as a slow-witted deaf-mute boy. Tao Chi'en presented her as his younger brother and quickly found her a place in a corner more or less protected from the wind, where she sat, so quiet and still that after a bit no one remembered her existence. Her Castile blanket dripped water, she was shivering with cold, and her legs had fallen asleep, but she was fortified by the thought that every minute she was getting closer to Joaquín. She touched her bosom, where she was carrying his love letters, and silently recited them by memory. By the third day the passengers had lost much of their aggression and were lying sprawled in their soaking-wet clothes, half drunk and very dispirited.

The bay was much longer than they had imagined; the distances marked on their pathetic maps had no bearing on actual miles, and just when they thought they were approaching their destination it turned out they still had to sail through a second bay, one called San Pablo. Along the shores they glimpsed a few camps and boats overflowing with people and goods, and beyond them thick woods. Even then their voyage wasn't over; they had to maneuver a canal with swift water and sail into Suisun Bay, the third, where navigating became even slower and more difficult, and then up the deep, narrow river that led to Sacramento. At last they were near the place where the first gold had been found. That insignificant little flake the size of a woman's fingernail had provoked this uncontrollable invasion, changing the face of California and the soul of the North American nation, as Jacob Todd, transformed into a journalist, would write a few years later. "The United States was founded by pilgrims, pioneers, and humble immigrants with an ethic of hard work and courage in the face of adversity. Gold has brought out the worst of the American character: greed and violence."

The captain of their ship told them that the city of Sacramento had sprung up overnight, within the last year. The port was bustling with ships; it boasted of well-laid-out streets, wood houses and buildings, commerce, a church, and a good number of gaming houses, bars, and brothels; even so, it resembled the scene of a shipwreck, because the ground was littered with bags, harnesses, tools, and all manner of refuse left behind by miners in a hurry to get to the placers. Huge black birds swooped over garbage crawling with flies. Eliza estimated that in a couple of days she could cover the town house by house; it would not be difficult to find Joaquín Andieta. Their fellow passengers, made animated and friendly by the proximity of the port, shared the last swallows of liquor, clapped one another on the back, and sang chorus after chorus about a girl named Susanna to the confoundment of Tao Chi'en, who could not understand such a sudden transformation. He debarked with Eliza before the others because they had so little baggage, and made a beeline for the Chinese district where they found something to eat and a place to sleep in a tent of waxed canvas. Eliza could not follow the conversations in Cantonese, and all she had on her mind was finding out something about her lover, but Tao Chi'en reminded her that she was not to speak and asked her to be calm and patient. That same night the *zhong yi* was called on to treat a countryman's dislocated shoulder, snapping the joint back into place and earning the immediate respect of the camp.

The next morning Tao and Eliza went in search of Joaquín Andieta. They saw passengers from the ship already starting for the placers; some had obtained mules to carry their equipment but most were going on foot, leaving a good part of their possessions behind. Tao and his "brother" asked around the entire town without finding a trace of the person they were seeking, although some Chileans thought they remembered someone by that name who had passed through a month or two earlier. They suggested the pair head on upriver, where they might find him: it was all a matter of luck. A month was an eternity. No one kept account of who had been there the day before, and names, or where anyone else was going, meant nothing. The sole obsession was gold.

"What shall we do now, Tao?"

"Work. We can't get along without money," he replied, picking up a few pieces of canvas he found among the abandoned supplies.

"I can't wait. I must find Joaquín. I have a little money."

"Chilean *reales*. They won't do you much good."

"And the jewels I have left? They must be worth something."

"Keep them. They have little value here. We'll have to work and buy a mule. My father went from town to town as a healer. My grandfather, too. I can do the same, but here the distances are much greater. I need a mule."

"A mule? We already have one. You! How stubborn you are!"

"Not as stubborn as you!"

They collected a few poles and some odd boards, borrowed some tools, and built a shelter using the canvas pieces as a roof. It was a miserable hovel ready to collapse with the first wind, but at least it protected them from the night dew and spring rains. Word had spread of Tao Chi'en's skills and he was soon visited by Chinese patients who gave witness to the extraordinary talent of the *zhong yi*, then Mexicans and Chileans, and finally a few Americans and Europeans. When they learned that Tao Chi'en was as competent as any of the three white doctors, and charged less, many people conquered their repugnance of the "celestials" and decided to test Asian science. Some days Tao Chi'en was so busy that Eliza had to help him. It fascinated her to watch his delicate, skillful hands finding pulses on arms and legs, stroking the bodies of the ill as if caressing them, inserting his needles in mysterious points that only he seemed to know. How old was he? She had asked him once, and he replied that counting all his reincarnations he had to be between seven and eight thousand years old. Looking at him, Eliza guessed about thirty, although at some moments, when he laughed, he seemed much younger than she. When he leaned over a sick patient with total concentration, however, he seemed as ancient as a turtle; it was easy then to believe that he had lived many centuries. She would watch with awe as he examined a glass of urine and by the odor and color was able to determine hidden ills, or as he studied a patient's pupils with a magnifying glass to deduce what was lacking or overly abundant in his organism. Sometimes all he did was place his hand on the stomach or head of an ill person, close his eyes, and give the impression of being lost in a long daydream.

"What were you doing?" Eliza once asked.

"I was feeling his pain and passing him energy. Negative energy produces suffering and illness; positive energy can heal."

"And what is it like, that positive energy?"

"Like love: warm and luminous."

Extracting bullets and treating knife wounds were routine procedures, and Eliza lost her horror of blood and learned to stitch human flesh as calmly as formerly she had embroidered sheets for her trousseau. Having practiced surgery beside the Englishman Ebanizer Hobbs turned out to be extremely useful to Tao Chi'en. In that land infested with venomous snakes there were more than a few snakebite victims, who arrived swollen and blue on the backs of their comrades.

Polluted water democratically distributed cholera, for which no one knew a remedy, as well as other illnesses of spectacular but not always fatal symptoms. Tao Chi'en charged very little, but always in advance, because in his experience a frightened man pays without argument, while one who is cured wants to bargain. Every time he asked for money his former mentor materialized wearing an expression of reproach, but Tao refused to budge. "I cannot afford the luxury of being generous in these circumstances, master," he mumbled. His fees did not include anesthesia; whoever wanted the comfort of drugs or the gold needles had to pay extra. He made an exception with thieves, who after a quick trial were lashed or had their ears cut off; the miners were proud of their speedy justice and no one was willing to pay for or guard a jail.

"Why don't you charge criminals?" Eliza asked him.

"Because I would rather they owe me a favor," he replied.

Tao Chi'en seemed ready to settle in. He did not tell his friend, but he wanted to stay in one place long enough for Lin to find him. His wife had not communicated with him for several weeks. Eliza, in contrast, was counting the hours, eager to get on her way, and as the days went by she was filled with conflicting sentiments about her companion in adventure. She was grateful for his protection and the way he looked after her, dependent on him for food and shelter at night, for his herbs and needles—to strengthen her *qi*—he said, but she was irritated by his calm, which she mistook for a lack of action. Tao Chi'en's serene expression and easy smile captivated her at times but at others grated on her nerves. She did not understand his absolute indifference to trying his luck in the mines while everyone around him, especially his Chinese compatriots, thought of nothing else.

"But you are not interested in gold, either," he replied, unruffled, when she nagged him.

"I came for a different reason! Why did you come?"

"Because I was a sailor. Until you asked me, I didn't plan to stay."

"But you are not a sailor, you're a physician."

"Here I can be a physician again, at least for a while. You were right, there is a lot to be learned in this place."

And that was what he was doing, learning. To find out about the medicines of the shamans he hunted out Indians, who by now had lost everything in the stampede for gold and were reduced to filthy bands of nomads in mangy coyote skins and European rags. They wandered from pillar to post, dragging their weary women and hungry children, using their finely woven wicker baskets to try to pan gold from the rivers, but they no sooner found a promising spot than they were chased away. When left in peace, they set up small villages of huts or tents and stayed for a while, until once more they were forced to leave. They came to know the Chinese physician, to welcome him with a show of respect because they considered him a medicine man, and were pleased to share what they knew. Eliza and Tao Chi'en would sit with them in a circle around a pit filled with hot stones where they cooked a pap of boiled acorns or roasted seeds and grasshoppers that Eliza found delicious. Then they smoked, speaking in a mixture of English, signs, and the few words of their native Indian tongue the outsiders had learned.

During that period some Yanqui miners mysteriously disappeared, and although their bodies had not been found their buddies accused the Indians of having murdered them; in retaliation the miners had attacked an Indian village, taken forty prisoners, including women and children, and as a lesson had executed seven of the men.

"If that's how they treat the Indians who own this land, Tao, you can be sure they will treat anyone Chinese much worse. You need to make yourself invisible, like me," Eliza said, terrified when she learned what had happened.

But Tao Chi'en had no time to learn tricks of invisibility, he was busy studying plants. He made long outings, collecting samples to compare with plants he had used in China. He would hire a team of horses, or walk miles beneath a burning sun, taking Eliza along as interpreter, to the *ranchos* of the Mexicans who had lived in that region for generations and knew its natural world. They had only recently lost California in the war against the United States, and their huge ranches, which once had sustained hundreds of peons in a communal system, were beginning to break up. The treaties between the countries were still only paper and ink. At first the Mexicans, who were skilled miners, taught the newcomers the processes for obtaining gold, but every day more foreigners came to invade territory they felt was theirs. In practice, the Yanquis scorned them, as they scorned anyone of a different race. A relentless persecution was waged against the Hispanics; they were denied the right to work the mines because they were not Americans, although Australian convicts and European adventurers were accepted. Thousands of unemployed peons tried their luck in the mines, but when the harassment became intolerable, they moved south or turned to crime. In the rustic dwellings of the few remaining families, Eliza was able to spend time in the company of women, a rare luxury that for a brief while recalled the tranquil, happy days in Mama Fresia's kitchen. Those were the only occasions she emerged from her enforced muteness and spoke in her own language. Those strong and generous maternal women who worked elbow to elbow with their men in the most demanding chores, hardened by work and by demands upon them, were fond of that fragile Chinese lad, awed that he spoke Spanish like one of them. They gladly shared secrets of nature that had been used for centuries to ease many ills and, in passing, delicious recipes that Eliza wrote in her notebooks, sure that sooner or later they would be valuable to her. In the meantime, the *zhong yi* ordered from San Francisco the Western medicines his friend Ebanizer Hobbs had taught him to use in Hong Kong. He also cleared a piece of land by their shack, fenced it to protect it from deer, and planted the basic herbs of his calling.

"Heavens, Tao! Do you plan to be here until those scrawny little things grow?" Eliza complained, exasperated by the sight of wilted stems and yellow leaves, and getting no answer but a vague shrug.

She felt that with every day that went by she was farther from her goal, and that Joaquín Andieta was plunging deeper and deeper into unknown territory, maybe toward the mountains, while she was wasting time in Sacramento passing herself off as the slow-witted brother of a Chinese healer. She often berated Tao, calling him terrible names, but she had the good sense to do it in Spanish—as he must have been doing when he spoke to her in Cantonese. They had perfected a sign language for communicating in front of others, and from being together constantly they came to look so much alike that no one doubted they were related. When they were not busy with some patient, they would wander through the port and shops, making friends and asking about Joaquín Andieta. Eliza did the cooking, and Tao Chi'en soon got used to her cuisine, although from time to time he went off to the Chinese eating halls where he could eat his fill for a dollar or two. They used signs in public, but in private spoke only in English. Despite the occasional insults in two languages, they spent most of their time working side by side as good comrades, and found many excuses to laugh. Tao was surprised that he could share a sense of humor with Eliza, even with the obstacles of language and cultural differences. It was, in fact, those very differences that were the greatest source of amusement;

he couldn't believe that a woman would do and say such outlandish things. He would watch her with inexpressible curiosity and tenderness; he was tongue-tied with admiration for her, and in his mind granted her the courage of a warrior, but if he saw her at a vulnerable moment she seemed a child and he was overcome with a desire to protect her. Although she had gained a little weight, and her color was improved, it was obvious that she was still weak. As soon as the sun set she would begin to nod, unroll her blanket, and go to sleep, and he would lie down beside her. They became so accustomed to those hours of intimacy, of breathing in unison, that their bodies adjusted in their sleep and if one turned the other would follow, so they were always touching. Sometimes they awoke entwined, tangled in their covers. If Tao woke first, he savored those instants that brought memories of happy hours with Lin, lying motionless so Eliza would not perceive his desire. He never suspected that Eliza did the same, grateful for that male presence that allowed her to imagine what her life with Joaquín Andieta might have been had she been more fortunate. Neither of the two ever mentioned what happened at night, as if that were a parallel existence they were not aware of. As soon as they dressed, the secret spell of those embraces disappeared entirely and they were again brother and sister. On rare occasions Tao Chi'en left alone on mysterious nocturnal sallies from which he returned with great stealth. Eliza did not need to ask where he went because she could smell him: he had been with a woman; she could even identify the cloying perfumes of the Mexican whore. She would burrow deep in her blanket, trembling in the darkness, alert to the least sound around her, knife in hand, frightened, calling Tao with her thoughts. She could not rationalize the longing to cry that swept over her, the feeling that she had been betrayed. She understood vaguely that men must be different from women; she herself felt absolutely no need for sex. Their chaste nocturnal embraces were enough to fill her need for companionship and tenderness, and not even when thinking of her long-lost lover did she feel the need for times like those in the room of the armoires. She was unsure, but thought that in her case love and desire might be one and the same, and so without the former the latter did not arise, or that her long illness on the ship might have destroyed something basic in her body. Once, because she hadn't menstruated for several months, she dared ask Tao Chi'en whether she could have children, and he assured her that as soon as she regained her strength and health she would be back to normal, and that that was the purpose of the acupuncture needles. When her friend slipped quietly in beside her after one of his absences she pretended to be sleeping soundly even though she lay awake for hours, offended by the scent of another woman between them. As soon as they got off the ship in San Francisco she had gone back to the modest ways Miss Rose had taught her. Tao Chi'en had seen her naked all through the weeks at sea, and knew her inside and out, but he divined her reasons and asked no questions except to inquire about her health. Even when he inserted his needles he was careful not to offend her modesty. They did not undress in front of each other and had reached a tacit accord for respecting the privacy of the pit that served as a latrine behind their shack, but everything else they shared, from money to clothing.

Many years later, going over the notes in her diary for that period, Eliza asked herself with amazement why neither of them had recognized the undeniable attraction they felt, why they had used the pretext of sleep to touch each other but feigned coolness during the day. She concluded that at the time loving someone of another race seemed impossible; they believed there was no place for a couple like them anywhere in the world.

"You were thinking only of your lover," amended Tao Chi'en, who by then had gray hair.

"And you of Lin."

"In China it is possible to have several wives, and Lin was always tolerant."

"You were also put off by my big feet," she teased him.

"That is true," he answered with complete seriousness.

In June a merciless summer set in, mosquitoes multiplied, snakes slithered from their holes to parade at will, and Tao Chi'en's plants budded as robustly as they had in China. The hordes of argonauts kept arriving, ever faster and in greater numbers. As Sacramento was the port of access, it did not suffer the fate of dozens of other towns, which had sprung up like mushrooms at the site of gold beds, briskly prospered, then vanished as the easy pickings dried up. This town grew by the minute; new shops opened and land was no longer given away, as it had been at first, but was sold at prices as high as those in San Francisco. There was a skeletal government, and frequent meetings to determine administrative details. Speculators appeared—pettifoggers, evangelists, professional gamblers, bandits, madams with their gay-life girls—along with other heralds of progress and civilization. Hundreds of men passed through, aflame with hope and ambition, headed for the placers as others, drained and sick, returned after months of backbreaking work, wild to squander their earnings. The numbers of Chinese rose daily, and soon there were a couple of rival gangs. These tongs were closed clans; their members helped each other like brothers with problems of everyday life and work, but they also spread corruption and crime. Among the new arrivals was another *zhong yi* with whom Tao Chi'en spent hours of total happiness comparing treatments and quoting Confucius. He reminded Tao of Ebanizer Hobbs, because he was not content to repeat traditional treatments; he, too, sought new alternatives.

"We must study the medicine of the *fan wey*, ours is not sufficient," he argued, and Tao agreed fully, because the more he learned the greater was his impression that he knew nothing and that a lifetime would not be enough to study all he had yet to learn.

Eliza organized a business in empanadas, delicious meat pies, which she sold at the price of gold, first to Chileans and then to North Americans, who quickly became addicted to them. She had begun making them with beef, when she was able to buy it from the Mexican ranchers who drove cattle from Sonora, but since that meat was often scarce she experimented with venison, hare, wild geese, turtle, salmon, and even bear. Her faithful customers gratefully ate them all, because the alternatives were canned beans and salt pork, the unvarying diet of the miners. No one had time to hunt, fish, or cook; there were no greens or fruits to be had and milk was a luxury rarer than champagne. There was no shortage, however, of flour and fat, and sugar; nuts, chocolate, some spices, dried peaches and plums were also available. Eliza's pastries and cookies enjoyed the same success as the empanadas, and, remembering Mama Fresia's, she added bread baked in a clay oven she improvised. When she could get eggs and bacon, she put out a sign offering breakfast, and men would stand in line to sit in the sunshine and eat at a broken-down table. That delicious meal, cooked by a deaf-mute Chinese boy, reminded them of family Sundays at home, far, far away. A large helping of fried eggs and bacon, freshly baked bread, a fruit tart, and plenty of coffee cost three dollars. Some customers, from sentiment, and grateful because they hadn't tasted anything like that for months, left another dollar in the jar for tips. One day in midsummer, Eliza came to Tao Chi'en with her savings in her hand.

"With this we can buy horses and go," she announced.

"Go where?"

"To look for Joaquín."

"I have no interest in finding him. I'm staying."

"Don't you want to know this country? There is so much to see and learn, Tao. While I am looking for Joaquín, you can acquire your famous knowledge."

"My plants are growing and I don't like to be moving all the time."

"Very well. I will go."

"You won't get far on your own."

"We shall see."

That night they slept in opposite corners of the shack, without a word. The next morning Eliza left early to buy what she needed for her quest, not an easy task in her guise as a deaf mute, but she returned at four in the afternoon leading a Mexican horse, ugly and covered with bald spots but sturdy. She had also bought boots, two shirts, heavy pants, leather gloves, a wide-brimmed hat, a couple of sacks of staples, a tin plate, a cup and spoon, a good steel knife, a water canteen, a pistol, and a rifle she didn't know how to load, much less shoot. She spent the rest of the afternoon organizing her gear and sewing her jewels and remaining money into the cotton sash—the one she used to flatten her breasts—in which she always carried the little bundle of love letters. She resigned herself to leaving behind her suitcase with the dresses, petticoats, and high-button shoes she had never given away. With her Castile blanket she improvised a kind of saddle like the ones she had often seen in Chile. She took off Tao Chi'en's clothes, which she had worn for months, and put on her new ones. Then she honed her knife on a leather strop and cut her hair to chin length. Her long black braid lay on the ground like a dead snake. She studied herself in a piece of broken mirror and was satisfied with what she saw: with a dirty face and eyebrows thickened with a bit of charcoal, the deceit would be perfect. That was the moment Tao Chi'en returned from one of his sessions with the other *zhong yi,* and for a minute he failed to recognize the armed cowboy who had invaded his property.

"I am leaving tomorrow, Tao. Thank you for everything; you are more than a friend, you are my brother. I will miss you. . . ."

Tao Chi'en said nothing. As night fell, Eliza lay down, fully dressed, in one corner and he went outside to sit in the summer breeze and count the stars.

The Secret

The same afternoon that Eliza had left Valparaíso hidden in the belly of the *Emilia*, the three Sommers had dined in the Hotel Inglés at the invitation of Paulina, the wife of Feliciano Rodríguez de Santa Cruz, then returned late to their home on Cerro Alegre. They had not learned of the girl's disappearance until a week later because they believed she was at the hacienda of Agustín del Valle, accompanied by Mama Fresia.

The next day John Sommers signed his contract as captain of the *Fortuna*, Paulina's brand-new steamship. A simple document containing the terms of their agreement sealed the pact. It took only one meeting for them to feel confident about each other; they had no time to waste in legal minutia, the craze to get to California was all that interested them. All of Chile was obsessed with the topic, despite the calls for cool heads published in newspapers and repeated in apocalyptic homilies from church pulpits. It took the captain only a few hours to sign on his crew because the long lines of applicants bitten with gold fever snaked all the way along the docks. Many spent the night sleeping on the ground in order to not lose their places. To the amazement of other seamen, who could not imagine his reasons, John Sommers would not take any passengers, so his ship was practically empty. He offered no explanations. He had a piratical plan to prevent his sailors from deserting ship once they reached San Francisco, but he kept that to himself because had he divulged it, he would never have signed on a soul. Nor did he inform the crew that before heading north they would make an unscheduled detour to the south. He would wait until they were on the high seas to do that.

"So you believe you are capable of captaining my ship and keeping a tight rein on the crew, eh, Captain?" Paulina asked once more as she handed him the contract to sign.

"Yes, señora, have no fear about that. I can sail in three days' time."

"Very well. Do you know what they need most in California, Captain? Fresh produce: fruit, vegetables, eggs, good cheeses, sausages. And that is what we are going to provide."

"How? It would all spoil before we get there."

"We are going to pack it in ice," she said without batting an eye.

"In what!"

"Ice. First you will sail south and pick up ice. Do you know where San Rafael Bay is?"

"Near Puerto Aysén."

"I am happy you know that area. I have been told that there is a beautiful blue glacier there. I want you to fill the *Fortuna* with blocks of ice. What do you think of my idea?"

"Forgive me, señora, it seems mad to me."

"Precisely. That is why no one has thought of it. Carry tons of rock salt, a good store of sacks, and use them to wrap large blocks. Ah! I expect you will need to provide warm clothing for your men so they won't freeze. And by the way, Captain, please do not discuss this with anyone, I do not want to be beaten to the punch."

John Sommers was more than a little dubious as he said good-bye. At first he thought the woman was unhinged, but the more he thought about it, the more he liked the adventure. After all, he had nothing to lose. She was taking the chances; he, on the other hand, would earn his salary even if all the ice melted on the way. And if her madcap scheme bore fruit, his contract stated that he would receive a healthy bonus. At week's end, when the news of Eliza's disappearance broke, he was on his way to the glacier with boilers throbbing and did not learn about it until he was back in Valparaíso to load on the produce Paulina had ready to be transported in a bed of prehistoric ice to California, where her husband and her brother-in-law would sell it at many times its value. If everything worked out as planned, in three or four voyages of the *Fortuna*—and she wisely had calculated about how long it would take other companies to copy her initiative and plague her with competition—Paulina would have made more money than she had ever dreamed of. As for the captain, he, too, had a product he planned to auction to the highest bidders: books.

When Eliza and her nana had not returned home on the expected day, Miss Rose sent the coachman with a note to see if the del Valle family was still at the hacienda and if Eliza was all right. An hour later Agustín del Valle's wife appeared at their door, highly alarmed. She knew nothing at all about Eliza, she said. The family had not left Valparaíso because her husband was laid low with the gout. She had not seen Eliza in months. Miss Rose had sufficient savoir faire to gloss things over. Her error. She was so sorry. Eliza was with a different friend. Such a silly mix-up. She was so grateful that Señora del Valle had taken the trouble to come personally. . . . Not surprisingly, Señora del Valle did not believe a word, and before Miss Rose could contact her brother Jeremy at his office, the flight of Eliza Sommers was the talk of Valparaíso.

Miss Rose spent the remainder of the day in tears, and Jeremy Sommers in speculation. When they searched Eliza's room, they found her farewell note and read it several times, vainly searching for some clue. Neither could they locate Mama Fresia to question her, and only then did they realize that the woman had worked for them for eighteen years and they did not know her last name. They had never asked where she came from or whether she had a family. Mama Fresia, like the other servants, belonged to that vague limbo of useful wraiths.

"Valparaíso is not London, Jeremy. They cannot have gone very far. We must look for them."

"Do you realize what a hornet's nest we will stir up when we begin to make inquiries among our friends?"

"What do I care what people say! The only thing that matters is to find Eliza quickly, before she gets into difficulty."

"Frankly, Rose, if she has left us in this manner, after all we have done for her, she already *is* in difficulty."

"What do you mean? What kind of difficulty?" Miss Rose asked, terrified.

"A man, Rose. That is the only reason that a girl commits an indiscretion of this magnitude. You know that better than anyone. Who can Eliza possibly be with?"

"I cannot imagine."

Miss Rose could imagine perfectly. She knew the party responsible for this calamitous state of affairs: that gloomy-looking fellow who had brought cargo to the house several months ago, Jeremy's employee. She did not know his name, but she was going to find out. She did not, however, tell her brother anything because she believed there might still be time to rescue the girl from the pitfalls of forbidden love. She remembered with the precision of a notary every detail of her own experience with the Viennese tenor: the anguish of those days was etched in her mind. She did not love him now, that was true, she had purged him from her soul centuries before, but the mere sound of his name was enough to start a bell clanging in her breast. Karl Bretzner was the key to her past and her personality; their fleeting affair had shaped her destiny and the woman she had become. If she should ever love again as she had then, she thought, she would do the same all over again, even knowing how that passion had twisted her life. Maybe Eliza would have better luck and her love would work out; maybe in her case her lover was free and did not have children or a deceived wife. She had to find the girl, confront the accursed seducer, force them to marry, and then present the fait accompli to Jeremy, who, with time, would accept them. It would be difficult, given her brother's rigidity in questions of honor, but if he had forgiven her, he would forgive Eliza as well. Persuading him would be her task. She had not played the role of mother for all those years just to cross her arms when her only daughter made a misstep.

While Jeremy Sommers locked himself in a stubborn, dignified silence that did nothing, incidentally, to protect him from loose tongues, Miss Rose swung into action. Within a few days she had discovered the identity of Joaquín Andieta and to her horror learned that, in addition to everything else, he was a fugitive from justice. He was accused of juggling the books of the British Import and Export Company, Ltd., and of having stolen merchandise from them. She knew then that the situation was far more serious than she had imagined: Jeremy would never accept such an individual into the bosom of their family. Worse yet, the minute he caught up with his former employee he would send him off to jail, even if he were Eliza's husband. Unless, Miss Rose muttered with rage, she could find some way to get her brother to withdraw charges against that little worm and clear his name for the good of all. First she would have to find the lovers, then see how she could work the rest out. She was very careful not to reveal what she had learned, and the remainder of the week she kept making inquiries here and there until in the Santos Tornero bookshop someone mentioned the name of Joaquín Andieta's mother. She obtained her address by asking in all the churches; as she suspected, the Catholic priests kept close tabs on their parishioners.

Friday, at midday, she went to call on Andieta's mother. She went there filled with purpose, animated by righteous indignation and ready to speak her mind, but she felt her resolve weakening the farther she advanced through the twisting alleyways of that district where she had never before set foot. She regretted the dress she had chosen, lamented her overly ornate hat and white high-button shoes; she felt ridiculous. She knocked at the door, slowed by a feeling of shame that turned into honest humility when she saw Andieta's mother. She had never imagined such devastation. Before her stood an ordinary little woman with feverish eyes and a sad expression. She seemed ancient, but when Rose looked more closely she could see that the woman was still young and had once been beautiful; there was no doubt that she was very ill. Señora Andieta was not surprised to find Rose at her door; she was accustomed to having wealthy women bring sewing and embroidery for her to do. Her customers passed her name to friends; it wasn't unusual for a lady she didn't know to knock at her door. This one was a foreigner, though, she could tell by that butterfly-bright dress; no Chilean woman would dare wear anything like that. She said hello without smiling, and invited Rose in.

"Please sit down, señora. What may I do for you?"

Miss Rose sat on the edge of the chair that had been offered to her, but she could not speak a word. Everything she had planned to say vanished from her mind in the flash of deep compassion she felt for that woman, for Eliza, and for herself, and tears poured like a river, flooding her face and her heart. Upset, Joaquín Andieta's mother took Rose's hand in her own.

"What is it, señora? Can I help?"

And then between sobs, in her Anglicized Spanish, Miss Rose disclosed that her only daughter had disappeared more than a week ago, that she was in love with Joaquín, that they had met several months before, that the girl hadn't been the same ever since, that she was burning with love—anyone could see that, except for herself, Miss Rose, who was so self-absorbed and distracted that she had not concerned herself in time and now it was too late because they had both run away. Eliza had ruined her life just as she, Miss Rose, had ruined hers. And she kept spinning out more and more words, unable to stop, until she had told that stranger what she had never told anyone. She told her about Karl Bretzner and her orphaned love, and the twenty years that had slipped by uncounted in her slumbering heart and barren womb. With streaming tears she poured out the losses she had kept silent all her life, the rage hidden beneath good breeding, the secrets carried like invisible shackles to save appearances, and the exuberant, youthful years wasted by the simple bad fortune of having been born a woman. And when finally she was out of breath from sobbing, she sat there unable to understand what had come over her or the source of the heady relief beginning to enfold her.

"Have a little tea," said Joaquin Andieta's mother after a long silence, placing a chipped teacup in her hand.

"Please, I beg you, tell me whether Eliza and your son are lovers. I am not mad, am I?" Miss Rose whispered.

"You may be right, señora. Joaquín was not in his right senses, either, but he never told me the girl's name."

"Help me. I must find Eliza."

"I can tell you that she is not with Joaquín."

"How do you know that?"

"Didn't you tell me that the girl disappeared only a week ago? My son left in December."

"Left, you say? Where did he go?"

"I do not know."

"I understand, señora. In your place, like you, I would try to protect my son. I know that he has problems with the law. I give you my word of honor that I will help him; my brother is the manager of the British Company and he will do what I ask. I will not tell anyone where your son is; all I want is to talk with Eliza."

"You daughter and Joaquín are not together, believe me."

"I know that Eliza followed him."

"She cannot have followed him, señora. My son went to California."

The day that Captain John Sommers returned to Valparaíso with the *Fortuna* loaded with blue ice, he found his brother and sister waiting for him on the dock, as usual, but one look at their faces and he knew that something very serious had happened. Rose was pale and wan, and as soon as he hugged her she started crying uncontrollably.

"Eliza has disappeared," Jeremy informed him, so angry he could barely mouth the words.

As soon as they were alone, Rose told John what she had learned from Joaquín Andieta's mother. In those endless days of waiting for her favorite brother, and of trying to tie up loose ends, she had convinced herself that the girl had followed her lover to California, because that was what she would have done herself. John Sommers spent the next few days asking questions around the port. He found that Eliza had not bought a passage on any ship and that her name was not on any passenger list; on the other hand, authorities listed the departure of a Joaquín Andieta in December. Given the possibility that the girl could have changed her name to throw them off the trail, the captain made the same rounds again, this time with a detailed description—but no one remembered seeing her. A young girl, nearly a child, traveling alone or with an Indian servant, would immediately have attracted attention, he was assured; besides, very few women were going to San Francisco, and all of them of light morals, with the exception of an occasional captain's or businessman's wife.

"She can't have taken a ship without leaving a trace, Rose," the captain concluded after a careful accounting of his inquiries.

"And Andieta?"

"His mother told you the truth. His name is listed."

"He took some things from the British Company. I am sure he did it only because he had no other way to pay for his journey. Jeremy has no idea that the thief he is looking for is Eliza's lover. I just hope he never finds out!"

"Aren't you tired of carrying so many secrets, Rose?"

"What do you want me to do? My life is built on appearances, not truths. Jeremy is like stone, you know him as well as I. What can we do about the girl?"

"I am leaving tomorrow for California, the ship is loaded. If there are as few women as they say, it will be easy to find her."

"That is not enough, John!"

"Can you think of anything better?"

That night at dinner Miss Rose insisted once again on the need to mobilize all available resources to find the girl. Jeremy, who had stayed at the margin of his sister's frenzied activity without offering any advice or expressing any emotion other than dismay at being involved in a social scandal, offered the opinion that Eliza was not deserving of all the fuss.

"This atmosphere of hysteria is extremely unpleasant. I suggest you exert some self-control. Why look for her? Even if you find her, she will never enter this house again," he proclaimed.

"Does Eliza mean nothing to you?" Miss Rose rebuked him.

"That is not the point. Eliza committed an unpardonable offense against society, and she must pay the piper."

"As I have paid for nearly twenty years?"

A frozen silence fell over the dining room. The family had never spoken openly about Rose's past, and Jeremy was not even certain that John knew what had happened between his sister and the Viennese tenor, because he himself had been careful not to reveal it.

"Paid what, Rose? You were forgiven, and protected. You have no reason to reproach me."

"Why were you so generous with me but cannot be with Eliza?"

"Because you are my sister and it is my duty to protect you."

"Eliza is like my own daughter, Jeremy!"

"But she is not. We have no obligation to her; she does not belong to this family."

"Oh, but she does!" Miss Rose cried.

"Enough!" the captain interrupted, banging the table with his fist as plates and cups danced.

"Yes, Jeremy, she belongs! Eliza is one of us," Miss Rose repeated, sobbing and burying her face in her hands. "She is John's daughter."

Jeremy listened, aghast, as his brother and sister recounted the secret they had kept for sixteen years. That man of few words, so self-controlled that he seemed invulnerable to human emotion, exploded for the first time, and everything held back for forty-six years of perfect British self-possession boiled up, choking him with a torrent of reproaches, rage, and humiliation.

"How could I have been so stupid! Dear God, living beneath the same roof, in a nest of lies, and never suspecting, confident that my brother and sister were the right sort and that we trusted one another, when, in fact, it was all a fiction, a web of lies; who knows how many things you have systematically hidden from me? But this is the crowning blow. Why the devil did you not tell me? What have I done to cause you to treat me like a monster? To deserve to be manipulated in this way? To have you take advantage of my generosity all the while you are scorning me? Because there is no other face to put on the way you have surrounded me with deceit, and excluded me. You have used me, happy to have me pay the bills. It has been the same all my life, ever since we were children you have made sport of me behind my back. . . ."

Mute, finding no way to justify their behavior, Rose and John accepted the tongue-lashing, and when Jeremy's tirade was exhausted the room filled with silence. All three were drained. For the first time in their lives they were seeing one another with the mask of good manners and courtesy torn away. Something fundamental, something that had sustained the fragile equilibrium of their three-legged family table, seemed irrevocably broken. Nevertheless, as Jeremy began to catch his breath, his features again assumed their usual impenetrable arrogance, and he brushed back a lock of hair from his forehead and straightened his tie. Only then did Miss Rose stand, walk to the back of his chair, and place one hand on his shoulder, the only gesture of intimacy she dared; her heart ached with tenderness for that solitary brother, that silent, melancholy man who had been like a father to her, whose eyes she had never made the effort to meet. She realized that, in fact, she knew nothing about him and that she had never in her entire life touched him.

Sixteen years before, on the morning of March 15, 1832, Mama Fresia had gone out into the garden and seen an ordinary box of Marseilles soap covered with newspaper. Curious, she had looked to see what it was and when she lifted the paper discovered a newborn baby. She had run into the house yelling, and an instant later her *patrona* was bending over the infant. Miss Rose was twenty at the time, fresh and beautiful as a peach; she was wearing a topaz-colored dress and the wind was playing with her hair, just as Eliza remembered or imagined it. Between them, the women lifted the box and carried it to the sewing room, where they removed the papers and picked up the baby girl clumsily wrapped in a wool sweater. She had not been outside long, they deduced, because despite the cold morning wind the baby's body was warm and she was sleeping peacefully. Miss Rose ordered the Indian woman to look for a clean blanket, sheets, and scissors to cut diapers. When Mama Fresia returned, the sweater had disappeared and the naked baby was yelling in Miss Rose's arms.

"I recognized the sweater immediately. I had knitted it for John the year before. I hid it because you would have recognized it, too," she explained to Jeremy.

"Who is Eliza's mother, John?"

"I don't remember her name—"

"You do not know her name! How many bastards have you strewn across the world?" Jeremy exclaimed.

"She was a girl from the port, a young Chilean. I remember her as being very pretty. I never saw her again, and I didn't know she was pregnant. When Rose showed me the sweater a couple of years later, I remembered that because it was cold, I had given it to the girl when we were on the beach but forgotten to ask for it back. You have to understand, Jeremy, that is how a sailor's life is. I am not a beast—"

"You were drunk."

"That's possible. When I learned that Eliza was my daughter, I tried to find the mother, but she had disappeared. She may have died. I don't know."

"For some reason, that woman decided that we should bring up the girl, Jeremy, and I have never been sorry that we did. We gave her affection, a good life, an education," Miss Rose added. "Possibly the mother couldn't give her anything and that is why she wrapped Eliza in the sweater and brought her here, so we would know who the father was."

"And that is all? A filthy sweater? That proves absolutely nothing! Anyone could be the father. The woman very cleverly pawned her daughter off on us."

"I was afraid that would be your reaction, Jeremy," his sister replied. "And that is precisely why I didn't tell you then."

Three weeks after telling Tao Chi'en good-bye, Eliza was with five miners panning for gold on the banks of the American River. She had not traveled alone. The day she left Sacramento she had joined a group of Chileans leaving for the placers. They had bought mounts and pack animals, but no one had any experience with livestock and the Mexican ranchers had skillfully disguised the age and defects of the horses and mules they bought. These were pathetic beasts, doped, their bald spots painted over with dye, and within a few hours after starting they had come up lame. Everyone in the party was carrying a full load of tools, weapons, and tin utensils, so that the dreary caravan crept along amid a clanging of metal. Along the way, they began shedding equipment, which lay scattered among the crosses that dotted the landscape to indicate the dead. Eliza had introduced herself as Elías Andieta, only recently arrived from Chile with instructions from his mother to look for his brother Joaquín, and prepared to travel California from top to bottom to carry out his duty.

"How old are you, kid?" the miners had asked Eliza.

"Eighteen."

"You look more like fourteen. Aren't you kind of young to be looking for gold?"

"I am eighteen, and I am not looking for gold, only my brother Joaquín," she repeated.

The Chileans were young, cheerful, and had not yet lost the enthusiasm that had motivated them to leave their country and travel so far, although they were beginning to realize that the streets were not paved with treasure, as they had been told. At first Eliza did not show them her face and kept her hat pulled down over her eyes, but soon she noticed that the men paid little attention to one another. They took for granted that she was still a boy and were not surprised by her size, her voice, or her behavior. Each of them was self-absorbed and didn't notice that she went off from them to relieve herself or that when they came to a pool of water where they could take a dip, while they were taking off their clothes Eliza jumped in with hers on, even her hat, claiming that that way she could do her laundry at the same time. Besides, cleanliness was the least of their worries, and after a few days Eliza was as filthy and sweaty as her companions. She discovered that their grime made them all equally sordid: her bloodhound-sharp nose could scarcely distinguish her own body odor from theirs. The heavy cloth of her trousers chafed her legs; she was not used to riding long distances, and the second day her buttocks were so raw she could scarcely take a step, but the others were tenderfoots, too, and in as much pain as she. The dry, hot climate, the thirst, fatigue, and constant assault of mosquitoes, quickly killed any banter. They rode forward in silence, metal clanking, sorry before they began. For weeks they looked for a good place to set up and look for gold, time that Eliza used to ask around about Joaquín Andieta. Neither the information they had gathered nor their badly drawn maps were of much use, and when they did reach a good site for panning they found hundreds of miners ahead of them. Every prospector had the right to claim a hundred square feet; they marked their site, working it every day and leaving their tools there when they were away, but if they were gone for more than ten days, someone else could claim the spot and register it in his name. The worst crimes, claim-jumping and stealing, were punished with the gallows or with a horsewhipping, after a quick trial in which the miners played the roles of judge, jury, and executioner. Eliza's party met bands of Chileans everywhere. Recognizing them by their clothing and accent, they would embrace enthusiastically, share their *mate*, liquor, and the jerked meat they called *charqui*; they would exchange colorful tales of misadventures and sing nostalgic songs beneath the stars, but the next day they would say good-bye: there was no time for excessive cordiality. From their speech and conversation, Eliza deduced that some of her countrymen were privileged young men from Santiago, upper-class dandies who a few months before had been wearing frock coats, patent leather boots, kid gloves, and slicked-back hair, but in the placers it was nearly impossible to tell them from the rough peasants with whom they were working side by side. Class affectations and prejudices went up in smoke when they met the brutal reality of the mines, but not racial hatred, which exploded in deadly fights on the least pretext. The Chileans, more numerous and more enterprising than other Hispanics, had drawn the Yanquis' hatred. Eliza heard that back in San Francisco, a group of drunken Australians had attacked Little Chile, setting off a pitched battle. Several Chilean companies had peons from their fields working at the placers, hands who for generations had worked for a pittance under a feudal system and so were not surprised that whatever gold they found wasn't theirs but the *patrón*'s. In the eyes of the North Americans, that was simple slavery. American laws favored the individual: each piece of land was reduced to the area a man could work by himself. The Chilean associations scoffed at the law, registering claims in the names of each of their peons in order to work more sites.

California was swarming with white men of various nationalities in flannel shirts, pants tucked into their boats, revolvers in their belts; Chinese in quilted jackets and full trousers; Indians in ruined military jackets and bare behinds; Mexicans in white cotton and enormous sombreros; South Americans in short ponchos and broad leather belts in which they carried knife, tobacco, gunpowder, and money; travelers from the Sandwich Islands, barefoot and wearing brilliant silk sashes—all in a hodgepodge of colors, cultures, religions, and tongues, but with a single obsession. Eliza asked each of them about Joaquín Andieta and urged them to spread the word that his brother Elías was looking for him. As she moved deeper and deeper into that territory, she realized how enormous it was and how difficult it would be to find her lover in the middle of fifty thousand foreigners constantly on the move.

Eliza's party of bone-weary Chileans finally decided to stop and set up camp. They had come to the valley of the American River in a time of baking heat, with only two mules and Eliza's horse left: the rest of the animals had fallen along the way. The land was dry and cracked, with no vegetation but pines and oaks, although a swift-running, clear river rushed down from the mountains, leaping over large boulders and cutting through the valley like a knife. On both banks were rows and rows of men, digging and filling pails with sandy dirt they washed through a sluice, a contrivance that looked like a child's cradle. They worked bareheaded in the sun, legs in icy water, clothes soaking wet; they slept stretched out on the ground, weapons in hand; they ate hard tack and salted meat, drank water polluted by the hundreds of excavations upriver and liquor so adulterated that many ended up with cirrhosis or the D.T.'s. Eliza watched two men die within a few days, writhing with pain and bathed in the foamy sweat of cholera, and was thankful for the wisdom of Tao Chi'en, who had taught her not to drink water that hadn't been boiled. No matter how thirsty she was, she waited until evening when they camped to brew tea or *mate*. From time to time they would hear shouts of jubilation, which meant someone had found a gold nugget, but most were content with extracting a few precious grains from tons of useless dirt. Months earlier, it had still been possible to see gold particles gleaming beneath the clear water, but now nature was turned upside down by human greed, the landscape altered by heaps of dirt and rocks, great pits, rivers and streams diverted from their beds and the water caught in countless pockets, thousands of tree stumps where once there had been forests. Getting at the gold sometimes called for the determination of titans.

Eliza did not mean to stay, but she was worn out and knew that she could not keep aimlessly riding on alone. Her companions had staked a claim at the last of a line of miners, some distance from the nearest burgeoning town with its tavern and general store where miners could buy basic supplies. Their neighbors were three Oregonians who worked and drank with uncommon endurance and wasted no time greeting new arrivals; on the contrary, they let Eliza and her companions know immediately that they did not honor the right of greasers to exploit American soil. One of the Chileans countered with the argument that the Oregonians had no claim, either, since the land belonged to the Indians, and the two would have drawn their weapons if the others hadn't intervened and cooled things down. The air was filled with a constant uproar of shovels, picks, rolling rock, running water, and curses, but the sky was limpid and the air scented with bay. Every evening the Chileans would drop with fatigue while the counterfeit Elías Andieta started a small campfire to brew coffee and water his horse. Out of pity, Eliza also watered the wretched mules, even though they weren't hers, and unbuckled their loads to give them a rest. Fatigue clouded her vision and she could barely control the trembling of her knees; she realized that Tao Chi'en had been right when he warned her that she needed to build up her strength before setting out on this adventure. She thought about the little board and canvas shack in Sacramento, where at that hour Tao would be meditating or writing with pen and China ink in his beautiful calligraphy. She smiled, amazed that her nostalgia did not evoke Miss Rose's peaceful sewing room or Mama Fresia's warm kitchen. How I have changed, she sighed, looking at hands blistered and burned by the harsh sun.

In the morning, Eliza's partners sent her to the store to buy the supplies they would need to survive, and one of those cradlelike things for processing the dirt, because they saw how much more efficient that contrivance was than their simple pans. The one street in the town—if that was what the cluster of buildings could be called—was a mud pit littered with garbage. The store, built of logs and boards, was the center of social life in that community of solitary men. Anything bought in the area was sold there, and liquor was served in large quantities, along with a little food. At night, when the miners came to drink, a violinist livened things up with his melodies. A few men would tuck a kerchief into their belts, a sign that they were playing the part of women, and the others took turns asking them to dance. There wasn't a single woman for miles around, but occasionally a mule-drawn wagon would pass through filled with prostitutes. They were avidly awaited and generously compensated. The store owner was a talkative, good-natured Mormon with three wives in Utah, who offered credit to anyone who would convert to his faith. He never took a drink, and while he sold liquor, he preached against the vice of drinking it. He had heard about a man named Joaquín and he thought the last name might be Andieta, he told Eliza when she questioned him, but that man had come through quite some time ago and the proprietor couldn't say what direction he had taken. He remembered him because he had gotten into a fight between some Americans and Hispanics over a piece of land. Chileans? Maybe. All he was sure of was that he spoke Spanish; he could have been a Mexican, he said, to him all greasers looked alike.

"And how did it turn out?"

"The Americans ended up with the land and the others had to move on. How else would it be? This Joaquín and another man stayed here at the store for two or three days. They laid out some blankets there in a corner, and I let them take it easy until they mended a little because they were pretty well beat up. They weren't a bad sort. I remember your brother, he was a young fellow with black hair and big eyes, pretty good-looking."

"That's the one," said Eliza, her heart galloping.

PART THREE

1850–1853

El Dorado

Four men, two on each side tugging at heavy ropes, led the bear into a ring where a fired-up crowd sat waiting. They dragged him to the center of the arena and tied one hind leg to a post by a twenty-foot chain and then spent fifteen minutes undoing the ropes while he clawed and snarled with world-stopping rage. He weighed more than thirteen hundred pounds, his coat was dark brown, one eye was blind, he carried the rakes and scars of old fights on his back, but he was still young. Foaming slobber dripped from jaws filled with yellow teeth. Standing erect, slashing futilely with his prehistoric claws, he looked over the crowd with his one good eye, jerking desperately at his chain.

This town had sprung up from nothing in a few months' time, built in a sigh by transients who never intended it to last. In place of a bullring, such as those in California's Mexican settlements, it had a large cleared space that was used for breaking horses and corralling mules; the fence was reinforced with boards and wood bleachers had been added to accommodate spectators. The late November steel-colored sky threatened rain, but it wasn't cold and the ground was dry. From behind the barrier, hundreds of spectators answered the animal's every roar with a chorus of jeers. The only women, a half dozen young Mexicans wearing embroidered white dresses and smoking their eternal cigarettes, were as conspicuous as the bear, and the men greeted them with shouts of "*Olé*!" while bottles of liquor and bettors' bags of gold dust passed from hand to hand. The gamblers, in their city clothes, fancy vests, wide neckties, and top hats, stood out among the rowdy, unkempt rabble. Three musicians were playing favorite tunes on crudely made violins, and as soon as they spiritedly attacked "Oh! Susanna," the miners' hymn, a pair of bearded clowns dressed like women leaped into the ring and athletically danced a jig amidst obscenities and thunderous clapping, lifting their skirts to show hairy legs and ruffled drawers. They were rewarded with a generous shower of coins, cheers, and raucous laughter. When they left, a solemn bugle call and drumroll announced the beginning of the contest, followed by the guttural roar of an electrified crowd.

Lost in the throng, Eliza watched the spectacle with fascination and horror. She had bet the little money she had left, hoping to multiply it in the next minutes. At the third blast of the trumpet a wooden gate was raised and a young, gleaming, black bull trotted into the ring, snorting. For an instant the gallery was silenced with awe and then a full-throated "*Olé*!" engulfed the animal. He stopped, dazed, uplifted head crowned by long, unblunted horns, his intelligent eyes measuring distances, his rear hooves pawing the sand, until a growl from the bear caught his attention. His opponent had seen him and was scratching out a hole a few steps from his post, in which he lay flat, hugging the ground. At the cries from the crowd, the bull put his head down, tensed his flanks, and, raising a cloud of sand, charged, blind with rage, snuffling, steam issuing from his nostrils and slobber streaming from his lips. The bear was waiting. He took the first hook of the horn in the back; it tore a bloody furrow in his thick fur but he did not budge an inch. The bull trotted completely around the ring, confused, while the crowd egged him on with catcalls; he charged again, trying to lift the bear with his horns, but the bear took its punishment without moving, until he saw his chance and with one sure slash tore open the bull's nose. Pouring blood, crazed with pain and disoriented, the attacker made a series of blind thrusts, wounding his enemy again and again but unable to rout him from the hole. Suddenly the bear rose up and grasped the bull's neck in a terrible embrace, clamping his teeth in its flesh. For long moments they danced together around the circle described by the chain while the sand grew red with blood and the galleries echoed with the yells of the men. Finally the bull broke free, staggered a few steps, his legs wobbly and his gleaming obsidian hide stained crimson, until he collapsed onto his knees and sank to the ground. A great clamor celebrated the bear's victory. Two horsemen rode into the ring, shot the loser squarely between the eyes, roped him by the hind legs, and dragged him from the ring. Eliza pushed her way to the exit, nauseated. She had lost her last forty dollars.

During the summer and autumn months of 1849, Eliza rode the length of the mother lode from south to north, from Mariposa to Downieville and back again, following the ever fainter trail of Joaquín Andieta from the rivers to the foothills of the Sierra Nevada. At first when she asked about him very few remembered anyone with that name or description, but toward the end of the year his figure began to take on real proportions, and that gave the girl strength to continue her search. The rumor had circulated that Joaquín's brother was looking for him, and several times during that month the echo returned her own voice. More than once when she inquired about Joaquín she was identified as his brother even before she could introduce herself. In that broad region, mail from San Francisco arrived after months of delay, and newspapers took weeks, but there was no shortage of news that spread by word of mouth. How could Joaquín not have heard that she was looking for him? Since he had no brothers, he must be wondering who this Elías was, and if he had an iota of intuition, she thought, he would associate that name with hers. Even if he didn't catch on, at least he must be curious to know who was posing as his relative. At night Eliza could scarcely sleep, fretting over various theories and haunted by the persistent doubt that her lover's silence could be explained only because he was dead—or didn't want to be found. And what if, in fact, he was running away from her, as Tao Chi'en had hinted? She spent her days on horseback and slept at night on the ground, anywhere, in her clothes, with her Castile blanket as a cover and her boots as a pillow. Dirt and sweat no longer bothered her; she ate when she could, her only precaution not to drink water before she boiled it and not to look Anglos in the eye.

By that time there were more than a hundred thousand argonauts in California, and more kept arriving, scattered all through the mother lode, turning the world upside down, moving mountains, diverting rivers, destroying forests, pulverizing rock, displacing tons of sand, and digging monumental pits. At the places where gold was found, the idyllic land, which had remained untouched since the beginning of time, was turned into a lunar nightmare. Eliza was constantly exhausted, but she had gotten her strength back and lost her fear. She started menstruating again when it was least convenient, difficult to disguise in the company of men, but she welcomed it as a sign that her body was finally healed. "Your acupuncture needles served me well, Tao. I hope to have children some day," she wrote her friend, sure that he would understand without further explanations. She was never without her weapons, although she didn't know how to use them and hoped she would never find herself in a spot where she had to. Once only she had shot into the air to frighten off some young Indians who came too close and looked threatening to her, but if she'd had to fight she would have come off badly because she couldn't hit a burro at five paces. She had not refined her marksmanship but had improved her talent for making herself invisible. She could ride into a town without attracting attention, blending into groups of Hispanics where a boy of her looks would go unnoticed. She learned to imitate Peruvian and Mexican accents to perfection and so pass for one of them when she was looking for company. She also changed her British English for American and adopted certain indispensable swearwords in order to be accepted among them. She learned that if she talked their lingo they respected her; the rules were to not offer any explanations, to say as little as possible, to not ask for anything, to work for her food, to stand up to provocation, and to hold tight to the small Bible she had bought in Sonora. Even the crudest among them felt a superstitious reverence for that book. They were amazed by the beardless youth with a woman's voice who read the Holy Scripture every evening, but did not make fun of him openly; just the opposite, some became his protectors, ready to beat up anyone who did. Among those solitary and brutal men who had sallied forth in search of fortune like the mythic heroes of ancient Greece only to find themselves reduced to an elemental existence, often sick, prone to violence and alcohol, there was an unconfessed tenderness and longing for order. Sentimental songs brought tears to their eyes; they would pay any price for a piece of the apple pie that gave them a moment's respite from homesickness, and they rode miles out of their way to pass a place where children lived, and then sit watching them in silence, as if they were some kind of miracle.

"Don't worry, Tao, I don't travel alone, that would be insane," Eliza wrote her friend. "It's best to go in large groups, well armed and on guard, because the gangs of outlaws have multiplied in recent months. The Indians are fairly peaceful, although they look frightening, but when they see an unprotected rider they may take his most prized possessions: his horse, weapons, and boots. I join up with other travelers: salesmen going from town to town with their merchandise, miners looking for new veins, families of farmers, hunters, the speculators and land agents who are beginning to overrun California, gamblers, gunmen, lawyers, and other scoundrels who tend to be the most entertaining and generous travel companions. There are preachers about; they are always young and look like holy madmen. Imagine how much faith it takes to travel three thousand miles across virgin prairies for the purpose of battling others' sins. They leave their towns filled with strength and passion, determined to carry the word of Christ to distant California, with no worry for obstacles or dangers along the road because God is marching at their side. They call the miners 'worshipers of the golden calf.' You have to read the Bible, Tao, or you will never understand Christians. Those pastors are defeated by broken spirits, not material reverses; they feel impotent before the overpowering force of greed. It is comforting to see them when they have just arrived, still innocent, but sad to meet them when they have been deserted by God, dragging from one camp to the next under a burning sun, thirsty, preaching in squares and taverns to an indifferent audience that listens with hats on and five minutes later is getting drunk with the whores. I met a troupe of itinerant actors, Tao, poor devils who stop in every town to entertain with pantomimes, off-color songs, and crude comedy. I traveled with them for several weeks, and they worked me into the show. If we could find a piano, I played, but if not, I was the ingenue of the company and everyone was amazed by how well I played the part of a woman. I couldn't stay with them, though, because the confusion was driving me crazy; I didn't know whether I was a woman dressed as a man, a man dressed as a woman, or an aberration of nature."

Eliza made friends with the mailman, and whenever possible rode with him, because he kept on the move and had contacts; if anyone could find Joaquín Andieta it would be him, she thought. He delivered mail to the miners and carried back bags of gold for safekeeping in banks. He was one of the many visionaries made rich by gold fever without ever having held a pick or a shovel in his hands. He charged two and a half dollars to take a letter to San Francisco and, profiting from the miners' hunger for news from home, he asked an ounce of gold for every letter he brought them. He made a fortune with that business; he had customers to spare and no one complained about the prices since there was no alternative; they couldn't abandon the mines to go get their mail or deposit their earnings from a hundred miles away. Eliza also sought the company of Charley, a little man who always had some story to tell, who was in competition with the Mexican drovers who transported goods on mule back. Although he wasn't afraid of anything, including the devil, he always welcomed company because he needed ears for his stories. The longer she watched him, the surer Eliza was that, like her, this was a woman dressed as a man. Charley's hair was bleached by the sun, he chewed tobacco, swore like a stage robber, and was never without his gloves or his pistols, but once Eliza got a glimpse of his hands and they were small and white like a young girl's.

She fell in love with freedom. In the Sommers' home she had lived shut up within four walls, in a stagnant atmosphere where time moved in circles and where she could barely glimpse the horizon through distorted windowpanes. She had grown up clad in the impenetrable armor of good manners and conventions, trained from girlhood to please and serve, bound by corset, routines, social norms, and fear. Fear had been her companion: fear of God and his unpredictable justice, of authority, of her adoptive parents, of illness and evil tongues, of anything unknown or different; fear of leaving the protection of her home and facing the dangers outside; fear of her own fragility as a woman, of dishonor and truth. Hers had been a sugar-coated reality built on the unspoken, on courteous silences, well-guarded secrets, order, and discipline. She had aspired to virtue but now she questioned the meaning of the word. When she had given herself to Joaquín Andieta in the room of the armoires she had committed an unpardonable sin in the eyes of the world, but in hers love justified everything. She did not know what she had lost or gained with that passion. She had left Chile with the purpose of finding her lover and becoming his slave forever, believing that was the way to extinguish her thirst to submit and her hidden wish for possession, but now she doubted that she could give up those new wings beginning to sprout on her shoulders. She regretted nothing she had shared with her lover, nor was she ashamed of the fires that had changed her life; just the opposite, she felt that they had tempered her, made her strong, given her pride in making decisions and paying the consequences for them. She owed no one an explanation; if she had made mistakes she had been duly punished by giving up her family, suffering in the hold of the ship, losing her baby, and facing a future of total uncertainty. When she found she was pregnant, trapped, she had written in her diary that she had lost her right to happiness. However, in those last months of riding across the golden landscape of California she felt she was flying free, like a condor. She was awakened one morning by the whinnying of her horse with the full light of dawn in her face, surrounded by tall sequoias that, like centenary guards, had watched over her sleep, by gentle hills, and, far in the distance, purple mountaintops; at that moment she was filled with an atavistic happiness that was entirely new. She realized that she had lost the feeling of panic that had lain curled in the pit of her stomach like a rat, threatening to gnaw her entrails. Her fears had dissipated in the awesome grandeur of this landscape. To the measure that she confronted danger, she was becoming bolder: she had lost her fear of fear. "I am finding new strength in myself; I may always have had it and just didn't know because I'd never had to call on it. I don't know at what turn in the road I shed the person I used to be, Tao. Now I am only one of thousands of adventurers scattered along the banks of these crystal-clear rivers and among the foothills of these eternal mountains. Here men are proud, with no one above them but the sky overhead; they bow to no one because they are inventing equality. And I want to be one of them. Some are winners with sacks of gold slung over their backs; some, defeated, carry nothing but disillusion and debts, but they all believe they are masters of their destiny, of the ground they walk on, of the future, of their own undeniable dignity. After knowing them I can never again be the lady Miss Rose intended me to be. Finally I understand Joaquín, why he stole precious hours from our love to talk to me about freedom. So, this was what he meant. . . . It was this euphoria, this light, this happiness as intense as the few moments of shared love I can remember. I miss you, Tao. There's no one I can talk to about what I see, what I feel. I don't have a friend in all this lonely country, and in my role as a man I have to watch everything I say. I go about with a scowl so people will think I'm tough. It is tedious to be a man, but being a woman is worse still."

Wandering here and there, Eliza got to know that rugged land as if she had been born there; she could find her way and estimate distances; she knew poisonous snakes from harmless ones and hostile bands of Indians from friendly ones; she read the weather from the shape of the clouds and time by the angle of her shadow; she knew what to do if she came across a bear and how to approach an isolated cabin and not get shot. Sometimes she met newcomers hauling complicated mining equipment up the slopes, which eventually they would abandon as useless, or met groups of feverish men coming down from the hills after months of futile labor. She would never forget the bird-pecked corpse swinging from an oak and wearing a placard of warning. In her pilgrimage she saw Americans, Europeans, Kanakas, Mexicans, Chileans, Peruvians, and long lines of silent Chinese under the command of a overseer who, although of their race, treated them like servants and paid them with crumbs. They carried bundles on their backs and boots in their hand because they had always worn slippers and could not bear that weight on their feet. They were frugal people; they lived on nothing and spent as little as possible. They bought their boots too large because they thought the big ones were worth more, and were stunned when they learned that the price was the same for the small sizes. Eliza sharpened her instinct for side-stepping danger. She learned to live for the day, without making plans, as Tao Chi'en had counseled her. She thought of him often and wrote frequently, but she could send letters only when she came to a town with mail service to Sacramento. It was like throwing bottles with messages into the sea because she didn't know if Tao was still living there, and the one reliable address she had was for the Chinese restaurant. If her letters ever got there, they would surely give them to him.

She wrote him about the magnificent scenery, the heat and the thirst, the voluptuous curves of the hills, the thick oaks and slim pines, the icy rivers with water so clear you could see the gold glittering in the beds, the wild geese honking in the sky, the deer and the huge bears, the miners' rough life and the mirage of easy fortunes. She told him what both of them already knew: that it wasn't worth wasting one's life to chase after yellow dust. And she guessed Tao's response—that neither did it make sense to waste it following an illusory love—but she kept on going because she couldn't stop. Joaquín Andieta was beginning to fade away; her excellent memory could not limn her lover's features clearly; she had to reread his love letters to be sure that in truth he had existed, that they had loved one another and that the nights in the room of the armoires were not her invention. So she renewed the sweet torment of solitary love. To Tao Chi'en she described the people she met along her way, the masses of Mexican immigrants in Sonora, the only town where there were children to run through the streets, the humble women who would invite her into their adobe houses, never knowing she was one of them, the thousands of young Americans who came to the placers that autumn after crossing the continent from the Atlantic Coast to the Pacific. It was estimated that the number of recent arrivals was forty thousand, each of them expecting to get rich in the blink of an eye and return home in triumph. They called themselves the forty-niners, a name that became popular and was soon adopted by all those who had come to California, either earlier or later. Back East, whole towns were left without men, peopled only by women, children, and prisoners.

"I see very few women in the mines, but there are some with enough pluck to accompany their husbands in this dog's life. Their children die in epidemics or accidents, they bury them, weep over them, and go on working from sunup to sundown to keep this barbaric life from stealing every vestige of decency. They roll up their sleeves and wade into the water to look for gold, but some find out that washing other peoples' clothes or baking biscuits and selling them is more productive; they can earn more in a week than their men do in a month's back-breaking work in the placers. A man on his own happily pays ten times its value for a loaf of bread baked by a woman's hands; if I try to sell the same thing, dressed as Elías Andieta, they give me only a few cents, Tao. Men are willing to walk miles just to see a woman up close. A girl sitting in the sun outside a tavern will within minutes have a collection of pouches of gold on her knees, gifts from besotted men grateful for the provocative sight of skirts. And prices keep going up; the miners get poorer and poorer and the merchants richer and richer. In a moment of desperation, I paid a dollar for an egg and ate it raw with salt and pepper and a splash of brandy, as Mama Fresia taught me: an infallible remedy for despair. I met a boy from Georgia, a poor crazy thing, but they tell me he wasn't always like that. At the first of the year he hit a vein of ore and scraped nine thousand dollars from the rocks with a knife, but then lost it all in one afternoon playing monte. Oh, Tao, you cannot imagine how much I long to take a bath, brew some tea, and sit down and talk with you. I would like to put on a clean dress and the earrings Miss Rose gave me, so you would see me looking pretty and not as a mannish woman. I'm writing everything that happens to me in my diary so I can tell you all the details when we see each other, because of this much I am sure: one day we will be together again. I think about Miss Rose and how angry she must be with me but I can't write her until I find Joaquín, because until then no one must know where I am. If Miss Rose ever suspected the things I have seen and heard, she would die. Mr. Sommers would say that this is an uncultivated land: no morality, no laws; the vices of gambling, liquor, and brothels rule, but for me this land is a blank page; here I can start life anew and become the person I want. No one knows me but you; no one knows my past, I can be born again. There are no lords and servants here, only working people. I have seen former slaves who have put together enough gold to establish newspapers, schools, and churches for their race; they fight slavery from here in California. I met a black man who bought his mother's freedom. The poor woman arrived here sick and old, but now she earns whatever she wants selling meals; she bought a ranch and goes to church on Sundays dressed in silk and riding in a four-horse carriage. Did you know that many black sailors deserted their ships, not just for the gold but because here they find their only chance at freedom? I remember the Chinese slave girls behind the iron bars you pointed out to me in San Francisco; I can't forget them, they haunt me like souls in pain. In this part of the world a prostitute's life is brutal, too; some kill themselves. Men wait hours to greet the new teacher with respect but they are brutal to the saloon girls. You know what they call them? 'Soiled doves.' And the Indians commit suicide, too, Tao. They run them out of everywhere; they drift around, hungry and desperate. No one will hire them, then they charge them with loitering and put them in chains to perform forced labor. Mayors pay five dollars for a dead Indian; they are killed for sport and sometimes they scalp them. There is no shortage of white men who collect such trophies and tie them to their saddles. You would be pleased to know that there are Chinese who have gone to live with the Indians. They go far off to the woods in the north where there is still hunting. They say there aren't many buffalo left on the prairies."

Eliza left the bear fight penniless and hungry; she hadn't eaten since the previous day, and she swore she would never again bet her grubstake on an empty stomach. When she had nothing left to sell, she spent a couple of days wondering how on earth to survive, until she looked for work and found that earning a living was easier than she had suspected, and in any case preferable to the task of finding someone else to pay the bills. Without a man to protect her and support her, a woman is lost, Miss Rose had drummed into her, but Eliza discovered that was not always so. In her role as Elías Andieta she found work she could have done dressed as a woman. Working as a laborer or a cowboy was not in the cards; she didn't know how to use a tool or a lasso, and she wasn't strong enough to wield a shovel or bulldog a steer, but there were other jobs available. That day she turned to her pen, as she had done so many times before. The idea of writing letters had come from the good advice of her friend the mailman. If she couldn't set up shop in a tavern, she would spread her Castile mantle in the middle of a square, line up inkwell and paper, then hawk her skills in a loud voice. Many miners could barely read or sign their names; they had never written a letter in their lives but they waited for mail with heartrending anxiety: it was their only contact with faraway families. The steamships of the Pacific Mail arrived in San Francisco every two weeks with bags of mail, and as soon as one topped the horizon, people ran to stand in line at the post office. It took postal workers ten or twelve hours to sort the contents of the sacks, but no one objected to waiting all day. From there to the mines the mail took several weeks more. Eliza offered her services in English and Spanish; she read the letters and answered them. If it was all her customer could do to dream up two laconic sentences saying he was still alive and to say hello to everyone, Eliza would patiently question him and add a more flowery account until she filled at least a page. She charged two dollars per letter, regardless of length, but when she incorporated sentimental phrases the man would never have thought of, she usually got a good tip. Some men brought letters for her to read, and she doctored them a little, too, so the pitiful fellow would have the consolation of a few words of kindness. The men's wives, weary of waiting on the other side of the continent, often wrote nothing but complaints, reproaches, or a string of Christian cautions, forgetting that their men were sick with loneliness. One sad Monday a sheriff came to get Eliza to write down the last words of a prisoner condemned to die, a young man from Wisconsin accused that same morning of stealing a horse. Imperturbable, despite being only nineteen, he dictated to Eliza: "Dear Mama, I hope you are well when you get this news and tell Bob and James that they're going to hang me today. Greetings, Theodore." Eliza tried to soften the message a little, to save the poor mother a heart attack, but the sheriff said there wasn't time to pretty things up. Minutes later, a group of honest citizens led the criminal to the center of town, sat him on a horse after placing a rope around his neck, threw the other end over the branch of an oak, then slapped the horse on the rump and Theodore was hanged without further ado. That wasn't the first hanging Eliza saw. At least this punishment was quick, but if the accused was of another race he was usually horsewhipped before he was executed and, even though she tried to get out of earshot, the screams of the condemned and the howls of the spectators pursued her for weeks.

That day she was about to ask in the tavern if she could set up her scribe's table when she was distracted by a commotion in the distance. Just as the crowd was pouring out of a bear fight, a caravan of mule-driven wagons was approaching down the one street in town, preceded by an Indian boy beating a drum. These were not ordinary wagons; the canvas tops were gaudily painted, and fringe and pompons and Chinese lanterns hung from their roofs; the mules were bedecked like circus animals and plodded forward amid a deafening clanging of copper bells. Sitting on the driver's seat of the first carriage was a large woman with hyperbolic breasts; she was dressed in men's clothes and clenching a piratical pipe between her teeth. The second wagon was driven by an enormous character dressed in ratty wolf skins; his head was shaved, he had hoops in his ears, and he was armed for war. Each of the wagons was towing a second in which the rest of the carnival rode: four young women done up in threadbare velvets and faded brocades and throwing kisses to the open-mouthed throng. The stupor lasted but an instant; as soon as the covered wagons were recognized, an explosion of yells and "Hurrahs!" shook the afternoon air. In the early days the soiled doves had reigned without competition, but that situation had changed when the first families and preachers settled in the new towns, jolting consciences with threats of eternal damnation. Lacking churches, the preachers held religious services in the very saloons where vices flourished. For an hour the sale of liquor would be suspended, the cards put away, and lascivious paintings turned to the wall while the men endured the pastors' warnings regarding their heresy and license. Gathered on the second-floor balcony, the "painted ladies" would philosophically listen to the chastisement, consoled by the knowledge that an hour later everything would be back to normal. As long as business didn't suffer, they didn't much care if the ones who paid them to fornicate turned around and blamed them for doing so and taking their money, as if the men weren't guilty, only the women who tempted them. There were clear lines drawn between decent women and those in the easy life. Fed up with bribing authorities and suffering humiliations, some of the hookers would pack up their trunks and go elsewhere, where sooner or later the cycle would be repeated. The concept of a traveling bawdy house offered the advantage of avoiding unpleasantness with wives and churchgoers and, in addition, opened horizons to the most remote areas, where they were paid double. The enterprise prospered in good weather, but it was nearly winter; soon snow would be falling and the roads would be impassable. This was one of the last rounds of the caravan.

The wagons rolled down the street and stopped at the edge of town, followed by a parade of men titillated by alcohol and the recent contest between the bull and the bear. Eliza followed along to have a close look at this novelty. She realized she would not have many customers for her letter writing and would have to find another way to earn her supper. Taking advantage of the clear day, several volunteers offered to unhitch the mules and help unload a battered piano that they set on the grass, following the orders of the madam, whom they all knew by the delicate name of Joe Bonecrusher. In a thrice, a strip of land had been cleared; tables were set up and as if by magic bottles of rum and postcards of naked women appeared. There were also two boxes of pornographic books, advertised as "bedroom novels with the hottest scenes in France." They sold for ten dollars apiece, a bargain price, because with them you could get excited as many times as you wanted and lend them to your friends as well; the books were a much better investment than a real woman, Joe Bonecrusher explained, and to prove it, she read a paragraph while her public listened in sepulchral silence, as if to a prophetic revelation. A chorus of "Hot damns!"

greeted the end of the reading, and within minutes there wasn't a book left. In the meantime, it had grown dark and the party had to be lighted with torches. The madam announced the exorbitant price of the bottles of rum, but you could dance with the girls for only a fourth of that. Did anyone here know how to play the fucking piano? she asked. That was when Eliza, whose stomach was growling, stepped forward without a moment's hesitation and sat down at the out-of-tune instrument, invoking Miss Rose. She hadn't played in ten months, and did not have a good ear, but the years of training with the metal rod and the knuckle-rapping of her Belgian professor came to her aid. She attacked one of the naughty songs Miss Rose and her brother, the captain, used to sing together in the innocent days of the musical gatherings, before fate lashed its tail and Eliza's world was turned upside down. To her surprise, her clumsy playing was well received. In less than two minutes, a rustic violin materialized to accompany her, the dancing heated up, and men grabbed the four women to prance around the improvised dance floor. The ogre in the wolf skins whipped off Eliza's hat and plunked it down on the piano with a gesture so determined that no one dared ignore it, and soon it was filling up with tips.

One of the wagons was used as headquarters and dormitory for the madam and her adopted son, the little boy with the drum; the rest of the women traveled jammed together in the second, and the two towed vehicles were converted into bedrooms. Each was fitted out with colorful scarves; a four-poster bed with canopy; a gold-framed mirror; a porcelain pitcher and washbasin; faded, slightly moth-eaten, but still exotic oriental rugs; and candlesticks with fat candles for light. This theatrical decor incited the customers and disguised the dust of the roads and the wear and tear of use. While two of the women danced to the music, the other two hastily performed their business in the covered wagons. The madam, whose fingers had a magical touch with the cards, never left the gaming tables or her duty of collecting in advance for her doves' services, selling rum and encouraging the revelry, her eternal pipe clamped between her teeth. Eliza played all the songs she knew by heart, and when she exhausted her repertoire began with the first again, without anyone's noticing the repetition, over and over, until she was giddy with fatigue. When the colossus saw Eliza was flagging, he called a break, scooped the money out of the hat and stuck it in the piano player's pockets, then took her by the arm and practically carried her to the first wagon where he placed a glass of rum in her hand. Eliza pushed it away weakly; to drink that on an empty stomach would be like being hit on the head with a hammer. The man then dug through a clutter of boxes and baskets and produced bread and some sliced onion that Eliza attacked trembling with anticipation. When she had devoured that, she looked up and saw the giant in the wolf skins studying her from his tremendous height. His face lighted up with an innocent smile filled with the whitest, most even teeth in this world.

"You have the face of a woman," he said, and Eliza started.

"My name is Elías Andieta," she answered, putting her hand to her pistol as if ready to defend her name with gunshots.

"Mine is Babalú the Bad."

"Is there a good Babalú?"

"There was."

"What happened to him?"

"He met up with me. Where are you from, boy?"

"Chile. I'm looking for my brother. Haven't you heard talk of Joaquín Andieta?"

"I haven't heard about anyone with that name. But if your brother has his balls set right, sooner or later he'll come visit us. Everyone knows Joe Bonecrusher's girls."

Business Dealings

Captain John Sommers anchored the *Fortuna* in San Francisco Bay, far enough from land that no hothead would be bold enough to jump overboard and swim to shore. He had warned the crew that the cold water and the currents would do in a swimmer in less than twenty minutes, in case the sharks didn't get there first. This was his second venture with ice, and he felt more confident. Before sailing into the narrow channel of the Golden Gate he had opened several casks of rum and generously distributed the contents among the sailors; once they were drunk he drew a pair of large pistols and ordered the men to lie facedown on the deck. The mate fastened shackles around their feet, to the shock of the passengers who had come aboard in Valparaíso and who when they witnessed the scene from the upper deck did not know what the devil was happening. In the meantime, the Rodríguez de Santa Cruz brothers had sent a flotilla of boats to ferry the passengers and precious cargo to the dock. When it was time to ready the ship for the return trip the crew would be freed, after being given more rum and a bonus of double their salaries in good gold and silver coins. While that didn't compensate for not being able to strike off inland to look for the mines, as nearly all had planned to do, at least it was some consolation. The captain had used the same method on his first voyage, with excellent results: he prided himself on having one of the few merchant ships that had not been abandoned in the gold madness.

No one dared defy that English pirate—son of a whorish mother and Francis Drake, as they described him—because they had no doubt that he was capable of emptying his blunderbusses into the chest of anyone who rebelled.

The produce Paulina had shipped from Valparaíso was stacked on the docks of San Francisco: eggs and fresh cheeses, the vegetables and fruit of a Chilean summer, butter, cider, fish and shellfish, superior sausages, beef, and a variety of poultry, stuffed and ready for the oven. Paulina had commissioned nuns to make their colonial sweets—custards and flaky pastries—as well as the favorite dishes of the Chilean kitchen, all of which had been transported in chambers of blue ice. The first shipment had been snapped up in fewer than three days at such an astonishing profit that the brothers neglected their other dealings to concentrate on the miracle of the ice. The blocks of iceberg melted slowly during the sailing, but there was enough left that the captain intended to sell it at a usurer's price in Panama. It was impossible to keep the phenomenal success of the first trip quiet, and the news that some Chileans were sailing with blocks of a glacier onboard spread like wildfire. Soon companies were formed to attempt the same with Alaskan icebergs, but it was impossible to enlist a crew and obtain fresh produce that could compete with those from Chile, and Paulina was able to steam ahead with her business, sans rivals, during the time she obtained a second steamship to expand her empire.

Captain Sommers' erotic books also sold in the blink of an eye, but under a mantle of discretion and without passing through the hands of the Rodríguez de Santa Cruz brothers. Whatever else, the captain wanted to avoid rousing virtuous voices, as had happened in other cities where censors had confiscated the books for being immoral and burned them in public bonfires. In Europe, they circulated secretly in deluxe editions among wealthy gentlemen and collectors, but the greatest profits came from editions for popular consumption. The books were printed in England, where they were clandestinely sold for a few pennies, but in California the captain earned fifty times that price. In view of the enthusiasm for this type of literature, it had occurred to him to add illustrations since most of the miners could scarcely read newspaper headlines. New editions were already in print in London with bawdy drawings, in the long run, all that appealed to the buyers.

That same evening, John Sommers, seated in the dining room of the best hotel in San Francisco, supped with the Rodríguez de Santa Cruz brothers, who in a few months' time had recovered their gentlemanly appearance. There was no trace of the hairy Neanderthals who only months before had been prospecting for gold. The real fortune was right there, in clean transactions they could carry out in plump hotel easy chairs with whiskey in hand, like civilized folk and not ruffians, they said. Added to the five Chilean miners they had brought with them at the end of 1848 were eighty peasants, humble and submissive people who knew nothing about mining but who learned quickly, followed orders, and were not rebellious. The brothers kept them working on the banks of the American River under the command of loyal overseers while they themselves looked after the ships and the business. They bought two vessels to ply the route from San Francisco to Sacramento, and two hundred mules to transport merchandise to the placers, merchandise they sold directly without involving middlemen. The fugitive slave who had worked as a bodyguard turned out to be a wizard with numbers and he now did the bookkeeping, looking, like his employers, the grand lord with top hat and cigar despite the grumbles of whites who had no tolerance for his color but had no choice but to negotiate with him.

"Your wife asked me to tell you that she is coming on the next voyage of the *Fortuna* and bringing the children, the maidservants, and the dog. She said for you to be thinking about a place to live, because she doesn't plan to stay in a hotel," the captain communicated to Feliciano Rodríguez de Santa Cruz.

"What a ridiculous idea! This gold rush will come to a dead stop and the city will go back to being the sleepy town it was two years ago. There are already signs that the gold is about mined out; they're not finding those boulder-size nuggets anymore. And who will care anything about California when that happens?"

"When I first came here it looked like a refugee camp, but it's become the kind of city God had in mind. Frankly, I don't think it will dry up and blow away: it's the gateway to the Pacific."

"That's what Paulina says in her letter."

"Follow your wife's advice, Feliciano; she has a sharp nose for business," his brother interposed.

"Besides, there's no way to stop her. She's coming with me on the next voyage. Let us not forget that she owns the *Fortuna.*" The captain smiled.

They were served fresh Pacific oysters, one of the few gastronomic treats of San Francisco, and doves stuffed with almonds and pear preserves from Paulina's shipment, which the hotel had immediately bought up. The red wine also came from Chile and the champagne from France. Word had spread about the arrival of the Chileans with the ice, and all the restaurants and hotels in the city were filled with customers eager to indulge in fresh delicacies before they were depleted. The men were lighting cigars to accompany their coffee and brandy when John Sommers felt a clap on the back that nearly knocked the glass from his hand. He turned and found himself staring at Jacob Todd, whom he had not seen for more than three years, when he had delivered him to England, poor and humiliated. Todd was the last person he expected to see, and it took a moment to recognize him because the former fraudulent missionary was now the caricature of a Yankee. He had lost weight and hair; two long sideburns framed his face; he was wearing a checked suit, snakeskin boots, and a jarring Virginia planter's hat; pencils, notebooks, and sheets of newspaper protruded from the four pockets of his jacket. They embraced like old comrades. Jacob Todd had been in San Francisco for five months writing articles on the gold fever that were regularly published in England as well as in Boston and New York. He had come to California thanks to the generous intervention of Feliciano Rodríguez de Santa Cruz, who had not tossed the old debt he owed the Englishman out the window. Like a good Chilean, he never forgot a favor—or an insult!—and when he learned of the Englishman's straits he had sent money, a ticket, and a note explaining that California was as far as his friend could go without beginning to start back the other way. In 1845 Jacob Todd had gotten off Captain John Sommers' ship with renewed health and energy, eager to put behind him the shameful incident in Valparaíso and devote himself body and soul to establishing in England the Utopian community he had so long dreamed of. He carried a thick notebook, yellowed by use and sea air, filled with ideas. Every detail of the community had been studied and planned down to the smallest detail; he was certain that many young people—the old would not be interested—would abandon their dreary lives to become part of an idealistic brotherhood of free men and women under a system of absolute equality, without authorities, police, or religion. Potential candidates for the experiment were not as quick to respond as he had expected, but after a few months he had two or three willing to give it a try. All he needed was a Maecenas to finance the costly undertaking, which would require a sizable piece of land because the community was to live apart from the aberrations of the world and yet must satisfy all its wants. Todd had initiated conversations with a crackpot lord who had a large estate in Ireland, when rumors about the scandal in Valparaíso caught up with him in London and dogged him till he had no breathing room left. Again doors closed to him and he lost his friends and disciples; his nobleman disclaimed him and his dream of Utopia went down the drain. As once before, Jacob Todd sought consolation in alcohol, and he sank into a swamp of devastating memories. He was living like a rat in a third-rate boardinghouse when the lifeline thrown by his friend reached him. He did not think twice. He changed his name and set sail for the United States, hoping to find a bright new destiny. His one goal was to bury his shame and live in anonymity until the time he could revive his idyllic project. First and foremost he must get a job; his income had been reduced and the glorious days of idleness had come to a halt. When he reached New York he had introduced himself to a couple of newspapermen, offering his services as a correspondent in California, and then had made the trip west across the isthmus of Panama because he didn't have the heart to go by way of the Straits of Magellan and find himself back in Valparaíso where his shame awaited, undiminished, and the beautiful Miss Rose would hear his name besmirched once more. In California his friend Feliciano Rodríguez de Santa Cruz helped him find a place to live and employment on the oldest newspaper in San Francisco. Jacob Todd, now Jacob Freemont, started working for the first time in his life, discovering to his amazement that he enjoyed it. He wandered the region writing about anything that caught his eye, including Indian massacres, immigrants flooding in from every corner of the planet, uncontrolled price gouging by merchants, the miners' quick justice, and vice in general. One of his articles nearly cost him his life. He described, not naming names but with perfect clarity, the way some gaming houses operated with marked dice, oiled cards, watered liquor, drugs, prostitution, and the practice of getting women dead drunk and then for a dollar selling them to as many men who wanted the right to make sport with them. "All of this protected by the same authorities who should be combating such vices," he wrote in conclusion. He was threatened by gangsters, the chief of police, and politicians, and sometimes had to lie low until tempers cooled. Despite that misstep, his articles appeared regularly and his was becoming a pen people respected. As he told his friend John Sommers, in seeking anonymity he was finding celebrity.

At the end of the meal, Jacob Freemont invited his friends to see the sensation of the day: a Chinese girl whom one could watch but not touch. Her name was Ah Toy and she had sailed on a clipper with her husband, an elderly merchant who had the good taste to die at sea and leave her free. She lost no time in a widow's laments and to enliven the rest of the journey she became the lover of the captain, who turned out to be a generous man. When she debarked in San Francisco, showily gowned and with a heavy purse, she noticed the lustful gazes that followed her and was struck with the brilliant idea of charging for those looks. She rented two rooms, cut holes in the dividing wall, and then charged an ounce of gold for the privilege of looking at her. Jacob Freemont's friends followed him in good humor, and with the bribe of a few dollars they were able to jump the line and be among the first to enter. They were led into a narrow room thick with tobacco smoke where a dozen men stood elbow to elbow with noses pressed to the wall. They peered through the uncomfortable peepholes, feeling like ridiculous schoolboys, and saw in the next room a beautiful young woman dressed in a silk kimono slit on both sides from waist to toes. Underneath it, she was naked. The voyeurs groaned at each of the languid movements that revealed part of her delicate body. John Sommers and the Rodríguez de Santa Cruz brothers doubled over laughing, unable to believe that hunger for women could be so consuming. Afterward they went their separate ways, and the captain and the newspaperman left to have a last drink. After listening to the account of Jacob's voyages and adventures, the captain decided to confide in him.

"Do you remember Eliza, the girl who lived with my brother and sister in Valparaíso?"

"Perfectly."

"She ran away from home nearly a year ago and I have good reason to believe that she is in California. I have tried to find her but no one knows anything about her or anyone of her description."

"The only women who have come here alone are prostitutes."

"I don't know how she came—if she did. The one fact we have is that she left in search of her lover, a young Chilean by the name of Joaquín Andieta."

"Joaquín Andieta! I know him, he was my friend in Chile."

"He is a fugitive from justice. Accused of theft."

"I can't believe it. Andieta was an upstanding young man. In truth, he had such a strong sense of pride and honor that it made it difficult to get close to him. And you are telling me that he and Eliza are in love?"

"I know only that he embarked for California in December of 1848. Two months later, the girl disappeared. My sister believes she came here, following Andieta, although I can't imagine how she did that without leaving a trail. Since you move around through the camps and towns in the north, I thought you might find out something . . ."

"I will do what I can, Captain."

"My brother and sister would be eternally grateful, Jacob."

Eliza Sommers stayed with the caravan of Joe Bonecrusher, where she played the piano and shared her tips fifty-fifty with the madam. She bought books of songs in both English and Spanish to liven up the long nights of entertainment, and for idle hours, which were many. She taught the Indian lad to read, and helped with the daily chores and the cooking. Everyone in the carnival said that they had never eaten better. With the same eternal dried beef, beans, and bacon, she prepared savory dishes created in the inspiration of the moment; she bought Mexican condiments and added them to Mama Fresia's Chilean recipes, with delicious results: she had only lard, flour, and preserved fruits, but she made pies, and when she could get eggs and milk her creations rose to celestial gastronomic heights. Babalú the Bad was not a believer in men cooks, but he was the first to wolf down the young pianist's banquets and so had to stifle his sarcastic comments. In the habit of being on guard during the night, the giant slept like a log most of the day, but as soon as a whiff from the cook pots wafted to his dragon nostrils his eyes flew open and he sat down near the kitchen to wait. He had an insatiable appetite and there was no way to fill his gigantic belly. Before the arrival of Chile Boy, as they called the supposed Elías Andieta, his basic diet had been whatever game he caught, split down the middle, seasoned with a handful of salt, and laid on the coals till it was black. Following that method, he would eat a whole deer in a couple of days. Exposed to the cuisine of the pianist, he refined his palate, hunted every day, selected the most delicate prize, and delivered it skinned and dressed.

On the road, Eliza led the caravan on her sturdy nag, which despite its sorry appearance was as princely as the finest purebred, with her useless rifle strapped onto her saddle and the young Indian drummer riding on the horse's croup. She felt so comfortable in men's clothes that she wondered whether she would ever be able to dress like a woman again. Of one thing she was sure: she would never wear a corset, not even on the day of her marriage to Joaquín Andieta. If they came to a river the women seized the opportunity to collect water in barrels, wash clothes, and bathe. Those were Eliza's most difficult moments; she had to invent more and more contrived excuses for cleaning up out of sight of observers.

Joe Bonecrusher was a corpulent Pennsylvania Dutch woman

who had found her destiny in the wide-open spaces of the West. She had a prestidigitator's skill with cards and dice, and she was passionate about cheating. She had earned a living betting, until she got the idea to organize a crew of girls and travel the mother lode "prospecting for gold," which was what she called her method of mining. She was sure that the young pianist was homosexual and that was why she made room for him in her heart beside the young Indian. She did not allow her girls to tease him or Babalú to call him names: it wasn't the kid's fault that he was born without a beard and with that baby face, just as it wasn't hers that she had been born a man in a woman's body. These were just jokes God invented to screw things up. She had bought the Indian boy for thirty dollars from some vigilantes who had killed the rest of his tribe. He was four or five at the time, nothing but a skeleton with a worm-filled belly, but within a few months of forcibly feeding him and taming his rage so he didn't destroy everything within reach or beat his head against the wagon wheels, he had grown a hand's width and his true warrior's nature had emerged: he was stoic, hermetic, and patient. She named him Tom No-Tribe so he would never forget the debt of revenge. "The name is the person," Indians said, and Joe believed it; that was why she had invented her own name.

The soiled doves of the caravan consisted of two sisters from Missouri who had made the long trip overland and lost the rest of their family on the way; Esther, a girl of eighteen who had run away from her father, a religious fanatic who beat her; and a beautiful Mexican, the daughter of a white father and an Indian mother, who passed for white and had learned four phrases in French to bamboozle men who had only one thing in mind, because according to popular myth French girls were the best. In that society of adventurers and ruffians, there was also a racial hierarchy: whites accepted cinnamon-skinned girls but scorned any mixture with black. All four women were grateful for having run across Joe Bonecrusher. Esther was the only one without previous experience; the others had practiced their trade in San Francisco and knew the bad life. They hadn't worked in the "best" houses; they knew about beatings, sickness, drugs, and the evil of pimps; they had had countless infections, suffered brutal remedies, and had had so many abortions that they were sterile, which they considered a blessing, not a tragedy. Joe had rescued them from that vile world and taken them out of the city. Then she had supported them during their long martyrdom of withdrawal to rid them of addiction to opium and alcohol. The women repaid her with the loyalty of daughters, and besides, she treated them fair and square. The intimidating presence of Babalú discouraged violent customers and hateful drunks; they ate well and the rambling wagons seemed a favorable atmosphere for good health and spirits. In those far-reaching spaces of hills and forests they felt free. There was nothing easy or romantic about their lives; they had saved a little money and could leave, if they wanted, yet they didn't because that small band of humans was the closest thing to a family they had.

Joe Bonecrusher's girls, too, were convinced that young Elías Andieta, with his effeminate manners and high voice, was homosexual. That gave them leave to undress, wash, and talk about any subject when he was around, as if he were one of them. They accepted him so naturally that Eliza tended to forget she was supposed to be male, although Babalú made it his job to remind her. He had taken on the task of making a man out of this lily-livered weakling, and he watched Elías closely, quick to correct him when he sat with his legs crossed or shook back his short mane with a very unmanly gesture. He taught him to clean and oil his weapons, but gave up trying to teach him to shoot because every time his student pressed the trigger, he closed his eyes. He was not impressed by Elías Andieta's Bible; on the contrary, he suspected he used it to justify his childish ways and complained that if the boy did not want to become a damned preacher, why the hell did he read all that foolishness, anyway?; he'd be better off reading dirty books to see if that gave him any ideas about acting like a man. Babalú was barely able to sign his name and read with great difficulty, but he would die before admitting it. He said that his sight was failing and he couldn't see the letters well, although he could shoot a terrified hare between the eyes at three hundred yards. He used to ask Chile Boy to read out-of-date newspapers and the Bonecrusher's erotic books aloud, not so much for the sexy parts as the romantic, which always brought him near to tears. The plot invariably had to do with burning love between a member of the European nobility and a common peasant girl, or sometimes the reverse, an aristocratic lady who lost her mind over a rustic but honest and proud man. In these tales the women were always beautiful and the gallants tireless in their ardor. The backdrop was a series of bacchanals, but unlike pornographic dime novels these had a plot. Eliza would read aloud, masking her shock, as if she had always been exposed to the worst vices, while Babalú and three of the doves listened, mesmerized. Esther did not participate in those sessions because to her it seemed a worse sin to describe the acts than to perform them. Eliza's ears burned but she could not help but recognize the unexpected elegance with which these lusty tales were written; some of the sentences even reminded her of the impeccable style of Miss Rose. Joe Bonecrusher, who was not the least interested in carnal passion of any sort and so was bored by the reading, personally saw that not a word wounded the innocent ears of Tom No-Tribe. "I am raising him to be an Indian chief, not a pimp for whores," she said, and in her wish to make him strong she also refused to let the boy call her Grandmother.

"Hell's fire, I'm not anyone's grandmother. I'm the Bonecrusher, do you hear what I'm saying, you damn brat?"

"Yes, Grandma."

Babalú the Bad, an ex-convict from Chicago, had crossed the continent on foot long before the gold rush. He spoke Indian tongues and had done a little of everything to earn a living, from strongman in a traveling circus, where he might lift a horse over his head or pull a wagonload of sand by his teeth, to stevedore on the docks of San Francisco. That was where he had been discovered by Joe Bonecrusher and had taken a job in the caravan. He could do the work of several men, and with him they needed no further protection. Together he and his employer could scare off any number of attackers, as they had demonstrated on more than one occasion.

"You have to be strong or they grind you down, Chile Boy," Babalú counseled Eliza. "Don't think I've always been the way you see me. Once I was like you, weak and soft, but I began lifting weights and now look at my muscles. No one tries anything with me."

"Babalú, you're more than six feet tall and weigh as much as a cow. I'll never be like you!"

"Size has nothing to do with it, man. It's balls that count. I may have been big but they laughed at me just the same."

"Who laughed at you?"

"Everyone, even my mother, may she rest in peace. I'm going to tell you something nobody knows."

"Yes?"

"You remember Babalú the Good? That was me before. But ever since I was twenty I've been Babalú the Bad, and things have gone much better for me."

Soiled Doves

In December, overnight, winter descended upon the foothills and thousands of miners had to abandon their claims and move to town to wait for spring. A merciful blanket of snow covered that vast terrain tunneled by greedy ants, and what gold was left again lay quietly in nature's silence. Joe Bonecrusher directed her caravan to one of the new little towns in the mother lode, where she rented a dilapidated barn in which to hibernate. She sold the mules, bought a great wood trough for a bathtub, one cookstove and two for heat, and a few lengths of cheap cloth and boots for everyone because in the rain and the cold you couldn't do without them. She set them all to scrubbing out the barn and making curtains to mark off rooms; she installed the canopy beds, the golden mirrors, and the piano. Then she went off to pay a courtesy call to the taverns, the general store, and the blacksmith shop, the centers of social activity. In the way of a newspaper, the town had a one-sheet bulletin printed on an aged hand press that had been hauled across the continent, in which Joe placed a discreet announcement of her business. Besides the girls, she offered bottles of what she called "The Finest Cuban and Jamaican Rum"—although, in truth, it was a savage brew that would curl a man's soul—"torrid" books, and a couple of gambling tables. Customers showed up promptly. There was another brothel, but novelty was welcomed. The madam of the other establishment launched a campaign of slander against her rivals but refrained from openly confronting the formidable duo of Joe Bonecrusher and Babalú the Bad. In their new quarters there was frolicking behind the improvised curtains, dancing to the tune of the piano, and betting of considerable sums under the watchful eye of the boss lady, who did not permit any fighting or cheating under her roof—unless her own. Eliza watched men lose in a couple of nights what they'd won with months of titanic effort, then weep on the bosom of the girls who had helped clean them out.

In a short time the miners became very fond of Joe. Despite her piratical mien the woman had a motherly heart, and that winter fate put it to the test. The area was visited by an epidemic of dysentery that felled half the town, killing several of its victims. As soon as Joe heard about someone near death in some distant cabin, she borrowed a couple of horses from the blacksmith and rode with Babalú to help the poor devil. They were often accompanied by the smith, a formidable Quaker who disapproved of the mammoth woman's livelihood but was always ready to help a neighbor. Joe would cook for the stricken miner, clean him up, wash his clothes, and console him by reading letters from his far-off family for the hundredth time, while Babalú and the blacksmith shoveled snow, hauled water, cut wood and stacked it by the stove. If the man was really bad off, Joe would wrap him in blankets, throw him over her horse like a sack of flour, and take him back home, where the girls would look after him with the dedication of nurses, happy to have the chance to feel virtuous. There wasn't much they could do besides make the patients drink liters of sugary tea so they wouldn't get dehydrated, keep them clean, warm, and in bed, with the hope that the trots would not drain their souls or fever cook their bones. Some died, and the rest took weeks to come back to the world. Joe was the only person who had the pluck to defy the winter and ride out to the most isolated cabins; sometimes she found bodies turned to ice statues. They weren't all victims of disease; more than once the fellow had shot himself in the mouth because he couldn't take any more growling guts, loneliness, and delirium. Once or twice Joe had to close her business, because the floor of the barn was crowded with mats and her doves had all they could do to take care of the patients. The town sheriff trembled when Joe appeared with her Dutch pipe and booming prophet's voice to demand help. No one could refuse her. The same men who gave a bad name to the town tamely submitted to helping her. There was nothing resembling a hospital; the only doctor was worn out, and Joe just naturally assumed the task of mobilizing forces when there was an emergency. The lucky ones whose lives she saved became her devout debtors, and during that winter she wove the web of connections that would sustain her after the fire.

The blacksmith's name was James Morton, and he was one of the few good men in the town. He felt an unassailable love for all humanity, including his ideological enemies, whom he considered errant out of ignorance, not intrinsic sinfulness. Incapable of a mean act, he could not imagine one in his neighbor; he preferred to believe that perverseness was a twist of character that could be remedied once exposed to the light of piety and affection. He came from a long line of Ohio Quakers, where he had worked with his brothers and sisters in an underground railroad for runaway slaves, first hiding them then leading them to free states and to Canada. His activities had drawn the ire of slaveholders, and one night a mob attacked their farm and set fire to the buildings; his family had watched without lifting a hand, because, faithful to their beliefs, they could not take up arms against a fellow man. The Mortons had to disperse and leave their land behind but they kept in close contact through the humanitarian network of abolitionists. James did not consider prospecting for gold to be an honorable way to earn a living because it did not create anything or perform a service. Riches debase the soul, complicate life, and engender unhappiness, he maintained. Besides, gold was a soft metal, useless for making tools; he could not understand the fascination it held for others. Tall, robust, with a luxuriant chestnut-colored beard, bright blue eyes, and muscular arms scarred from countless burns, lighted by the glow of his forge he was the reincarnation of the god Vulcan. In the town there were only three Quakers, men who cherished hard work and family, content with their lot, the only men who did not swear, drink, or frequent the whorehouses. They met regularly to practice their faith, modestly, preaching by example while patiently awaiting the arrival of a group of friends from the East who were coming to swell their community. Morton was often at Joe Bonecrusher's shack to help with victims of the epidemic, and there he met Esther. He would visit her, and pay her the regular fee, but all he did was sit with her and talk. He could not understand how she had chosen the life she had.

"Between my father's beatings and this, I prefer the life I have a thousand times over."

"Why did he beat you?"

"He accused me of provoking lust and inciting sin. He believed that Adam would still be in Paradise if Eve hadn't tempted him. Maybe he was right. . . . You see how I'm earning my living."

"There is other work, Esther."

"This isn't so bad, James. I close my eyes and think of nothing. It's just a few minutes and then it's over."

Despite the vicissitudes of her profession, the girl had kept the freshness of her twenty years, and there was a certain charm in her discreet and silent bearing, so different from that of her companions. There was nothing of the flirt about her; she was plump, with a placid, bovine face and a strong country girl's hands. Compared to the other doves, she was the least pretty, but her skin was glowing and her gaze gentle. The blacksmith didn't know when he had begun to dream about her, to see her in the sparks of his forge, in the flare of the hot metal and in the cloudless sky, until he was no longer able to ignore that cotton wool feeling wrapped around his heart, threatening to choke him. Nothing worse could happen than to fall in love with a loose woman; it would be impossible to justify in the eyes of God and his community. He decided to conquer temptation with sweat; he closed himself in his shop and worked like a madman. Some nights you could hear the loud ringing of his hammer until near dawn.

As soon as she had a fixed address, Eliza wrote Tao Chi'en at the Chinese restaurant in Sacramento, telling him her new name and asking his advice about combating dysentery because the only remedy she knew to prevent contagion was a piece of raw meat bound to the navel with a strip of red wool, the way Mama Fresia did in Chile, but that was not producing the hoped-for results. She missed Tao painfully; sometimes she awoke with Tom No-Tribe in her arms, imagining in the wooziness of half sleep that it was Tao Chi'en, but the boy's smoky odor quickly brought her back to reality. No one had the fresh salt-air scent of her friend. The distance that separated them was short in miles but storms made the route arduous and dangerous. She thought of riding with the mailman to continue her search for Joaquín Andieta, as she had in better weather, but weeks went by as she waited for an opportunity. It wasn't just the winter that got in the way of her plans. During that period the tension between American miners and the Chileans in the south of the mother lode had exploded. The Yanquis, fed up with the foreigners, joined together to run them out, but the Chileans fought back, first with weapons and then before a judge, who recognized their rights. Far from intimidating the aggressors, the judge's order merely fired them up; several Chileans ended up on the gallows or thrown off cliffs, and the survivors had to flee. In answer, they formed gangs of marauders, as many

Mexicans had done. Eliza realized that given her disguise as a Latin youth she could not risk being accused of some invented crime.

The last days of January 1850 witnessed one of the worst ice storms ever seen in those parts. No one dared leave shelter; the town seemed dead, and for more than ten days not a single customer came to the barn. It was so cold that at dawn water in the washbasins was frozen solid even though the stoves were kept burning, and some nights they had to bring Eliza's horse indoors to save it from the fate of other animals that woke up in blocks of ice. The girls slept two to a bed, and Eliza paired up with the Indian boy, for whom she felt a ferocious and jealous affection, which he returned with stubborn constancy. The only person among them who could compete with Eliza for the boy's affection was Joe Bonecrusher. "Some day I'm going to have a strong, courageous son like Tom No-Tribe, but much happier," Eliza wrote Tao Chi'en. "This little one never laughs." Babalú the Bad did not know how to sleep at night, and spent the long hours of darkness pacing from one end of the barn to the other in his Russian boots and seedy furs, with a blanket over his shoulders. He had stopped shaving his head and was sprouting a fuzz that matched his wolfskin jacket. Esther had knitted him a gosling-yellow wool cap that covered his head to the ears and gave him the look of a monstrous baby. He was the one who heard a few faint knocks that morning and had the good sense to distinguish it from the noise of the storm. He opened the door a crack, with pistol in hand, and found a bundle heaped in the snow. Alarmed, he called Joe, and between them, fighting to keep the wind from tearing the door off its hinges, they dragged it inside. It was a half-frozen man.

It was not easy to resuscitate their visitor. While Babalú rubbed him and tried to get some brandy down his throat, Joe waked the women, put more wood in the stove, and set water to heat for the bathtub, where they soaked him until gradually he began to revive, lose his blue color, and mumble a few words. His nose, feet, and hands were frostbitten. He was a campesino from the Mexican state of Sonora, he said, who had come to the California placers like thousands of his compatriots. His name was Jack, a name that doubtlessly wasn't his, but after all, no one else in that household used the one he was born with. For a few hours, Jack was several times on the threshold of death, but just when it seemed that nothing more could be done for him, he fought back from the other world and gagged down a few swallows of liquor. At about eight o'clock, when the storm had let up, Joe sent Babalú for the doctor. Overhearing her, the Mexican, who had been lying motionless, gulping for air like a fish, opened his eyes, and shouted an ear-splitting "No!" that startled everyone. No one was to know he was there, he commanded, with such ferocity that none of them dared cross him. Explanations were not necessary: it was obvious the man was in trouble with the law, and that town, with a gallows in the middle of the square, was the last place in the world a fugitive would want to look for asylum. Only the cruelty of the storm had forced him there. Eliza said nothing, but the man's reaction was no surprise to her: he smelled of evil.

After three days, Jack had regained some of his strength, but he lost the tip of his nose and two fingers on his left hand were showing signs of gangrene. Not even that convinced him of the need to see the doctor; he would rather rot by inches than hang, he said. Joe Bonecrusher gathered her people at the other end of the barn and held a whispered conference: his fingers had to be amputated. All eyes turned to Babalú the Bad.

"Me? Not fuckin' likely."

"Babalú, you sonofabitch. Don't be such a pantywaist!" shouted Joe, furious.

"You do it, Joe. I'm not good for things like that."

"If you can cut up a deer you can do this. What's a couple of lousy fingers?"

"An animal is one thing, a human being is something else."

"No! I can't believe it! This no-good sonofabitch, begging your pardon, girls, can't do me this one little favor. After everything I've done for you, you bastard!"

"Sorry, Joe. I've never harmed a hair on anyone's head."

"What are you telling me! You never killed anyone? You never did time in prison?"

"That was for stealing cattle," the giant confessed, near tears with humiliation.

"I will do it," Eliza interrupted, pale but decided.

Everyone stared at her, incredulous. Even Tom No-Tribe seemed a more likely candidate than the delicate Chile Boy.

"I'll need a really sharp knife, a hammer, a needle, thread, and clean rags."

Babalú sank to the floor with his huge head in his hands, horrified, while the girls got everything ready in respectful silence. Eliza reviewed what she had learned at Tao Chi'en's side when he extracted bullets and stitched up wounds in Sacramento. If she had watched that without blinking, she should be able to do this now, she thought. The most important thing, according to her friend, was to prevent hemorrhaging and infection. She had not watched him do amputations, but when he was treating unlucky patients whose ears had been cut off, he had commented that in other lands they cut off hands and feet for the same crime. "The executioner's ax is quick but it doesn't leave any tissue to cover the stump of the bone," Tao Chi'en had told her. He described what he had been taught by Ebanizer Hobbs, who had experience with war wounds and had shown him what to do. At least in this case it was only fingers, Eliza concluded.

Joe Bonecrusher poured enough liquor down the patient to render him unconscious, while Eliza disinfected the knife by heating it red hot. She had them sit Jack in a chair; she wet the hand in a basin of whiskey and then placed it on the edge of the table with the bad fingers separated from the others. She murmured one of Mama Fresia's magical prayers and when she was ready gave a wordless signal to the girls to hold down the patient. She positioned the knife on the fingers and hit it smartly with the hammer, driving the blade cleanly through the bones and into the wood of the table. Jack let out a yell from the depths of his guts but he was so drunk he didn't feel a thing as Eliza stitched the fingers and Esther bandaged them. The torture was over in a few minutes. Eliza stood staring at the amputated fingers, trying to keep from vomiting, while the women laid Jack on one of the mats. Babalú the Bad, who had kept his distance from the spectacle, walked up timidly, baby's cap in hand, and admiringly murmured:

"You're a real man, Chile Boy."

In March, Eliza quietly turned eighteen, still waiting for Joaquín to show up at their house one day, just as Babalú had said any man within a hundred miles would do. "Jack," the Mexican, had recovered after a few days and before his fingers healed had sneaked off at night without telling anyone good-bye. He was a sinister brute, and everyone was happy he was gone. He didn't talk much and was forever edgy, defiant, ready to spring at the hint of an imagined provocation. He showed no sign of gratitude for the help he had received, just the opposite; when the whiskey wore off and he learned that his trigger finger had been amputated, he let loose a string of curses and threats, swearing that the dog who had mutilated his hand would pay with his life. That was when Babalú's patience wore thin. He picked Jack up like a doll, lifted him up to his eye level, and said in the soft voice he used when he was about to explode:

"That was me. Babalú the Bad. Any problem with that?"

As soon as his fever was gone, Jack wanted to cash in on the opportunity to use the doves for his pleasure but, as one, they rejected him: they were not about to give anything away, and he had empty pockets, which they had observed when they undressed him to put him in the bathtub the night he had come to their door half frozen. Joe Bonecrusher took the trouble to explain to Jack that if they hadn't amputated his fingers he would have lost an arm, probably his life, and that he should be thanking his lucky stars that he had stumbled on to them. Eliza would not allow Tom No-Tribe to go anywhere near the man, and she approached him only to hand him food or change his bandages, because his odor of evil was as disturbing to her as a tangible presence. Babalú couldn't stand him either, and refused to speak to him all the time he was under their roof. He thought of the girls as his sisters and was wild whenever Jack obscenely tried to wheedle sex. Not even when he was most desperate would it have occurred to Babalú to use his companion's professional services; in his mind that would have been the same as incest. If his urges got too strong, he went to the local competition, and he instructed Chile Boy to do the same in the improbable case that he got over his missy-sissy habits.

Once when she was handing Jack a bowl of soup, Eliza worked up the courage to ask him about Joaquín Andieta.

"Murieta?" he asked, suspicious.

"Andieta."

"Don't know him."

"Maybe it's the same person," Eliza suggested.

"What do you want with him?"

"He's my brother. I came from Chile to find him."

"What's your brother look like?"

"He's not very tall, and he has black hair and eyes and white skin, like me, but we don't look alike. He's thin, muscular, brave, and passionate. When he talks, everyone listens."

"That's Joaquín Murieta all right, but he's not Chilean, he's Mexican."

"Are you sure?"

"Sure? I'm not sure of anything, but if I see Murieta I'll tell him you're looking for him."

It was the next night that he left, and they heard nothing more from him, but two weeks afterward they found a two-pound sack of coffee at the door. A little later when Eliza opened it to fix breakfast she found that it wasn't coffee but gold dust. According to Joe Bonecrusher, it could have come from any of the sick miners they had looked after, but Eliza had a strong intuition that Jack had left it as his payment. He was a man who didn't want to owe anyone a favor. On Sunday they learned that the sheriff was organizing a party of vigilantes to look for the murderer of a miner who had been found in the cabin where he had spent the winter alone, with nine knife wounds in his chest and slashed eyes. There was no trace of his gold, but because of the brutality of the crime they had placed the blame on Indians. Joe Bonecrusher, who did not want to get mixed up in any trouble, buried the two pounds of gold beneath an oak and ordered all her people to keep their mouths shut and not under any condition mention the Mexican with the amputated fingers *or* the sack of "coffee." In the course of the next two months, the vigilantes murdered a half dozen Indians and then forgot the matter because they had more pressing problems, and when the chief of the tribe came with great dignity to ask for an explanation, they killed him, too. Indians, blacks, and mulattos could not testify against a white man. James Morton and the other three Quakers in the town were the only ones who dared confront the mob at the lynching. Unarmed, they formed a circle around the chief, reciting from memory passages of the Bible that prohibited killing one's fellow man, but the crowd pushed them aside.

No one knew it was Eliza's birthday and there was no celebration, but even so, that night of March fifteenth was memorable for her, and for everyone else. Business was again booming at the barn. The doves were steadily occupied, Chile Boy was banging away at the piano with real gusto, and Joe was spinning optimistic tales. Winter hadn't been so bad, after all; the worst of the epidemic was past and they had no patients stretched out on the floor. That night a half dozen miners were drinking with true dedication while outside the wind was ripping branches from the pines. At about eleven, all hell broke loose. No one could explain how the fire began, but Joe always suspected the other madam. The wood caught fire like Roman candles and the curtains, silk shawls, and bed canopies flared up within seconds. Everyone got out safely, even managing to throw on a few blankets, and Eliza snatched up the tin box that contained her precious letters. Flames and smoke rapidly engulfed the building, and in less than ten minutes it was blazing like a torch as half-naked women and tipsy clients watched the spectacle in total helplessness. Eliza thought to count heads and realized with horror that Tom No-Tribe was missing. The boy had been fast asleep in the bed they shared. Without thinking, she grabbed a quilt from Esther's shoulders, covered her head, and ran inside, with one push flattening the thin partition of blazing wood, followed by Babalú, who yelled at her to stop, not realizing why she was dashing into the fire. Eliza found the boy standing stock-still in the swirling smoke, his eyes wide with fright, but perfectly serene. She threw the quilt over him and tried to pick him up, but he was very heavy and she was bent double by a fit of coughing. She dropped to her knees, pushing Tom to make him run outside, but he did not move and both of them would have been reduced to ashes had Babalú not appeared at that instant, picked up one under each arm, as if they were parcels, and bolted back outside to be greeted with loud cheers.

"Damned kid! What were you doing in there!" Joe scolded as she hugged the small Indian, covering his face with kisses and slapping his cheeks to make him breathe.

It was only because the shack was isolated that half the town didn't go up in flames, the sheriff commented later; he had plenty of experience with fires, they happened too frequently around there. A dozen volunteers had responded to the glow in the sky to fight the flames, headed by the blacksmith, but it was too late and all they could do was rescue Eliza's horse, which everyone had forgot in the confusion of the first minutes and was still tied in its lean-to, crazed with terror. Joe Bonecrusher lost everything she owned in the world that night, and for the first time was seen to lose heart. With the boy in her arms, she watched the destruction, unable to hold back the tears, and when all that remained was smoking embers she buried her face in the enormous chest of Babalú, whose eyelashes and eyebrows were singed. Seeing the surrogate mother whom they had thought invincible so vulnerable, the four girls burst out bawling, forming a cluster of petticoats, windblown hair, and trembling flesh. The support network, however, had begun to function even before the flames died out, and in less than an hour lodging had been found for everyone in various homes in town and one of the miners whom Joe had nursed through dysentery took up a collection. Chile Boy, Babalú, and the young Indian—the three males of the group—spent the night in the blacksmith's shop. James Morton laid two straw ticks with warm bedcovers beside the still warm forge and served his guests a splendid breakfast carefully prepared by the wife of the preacher who on Sundays shouted his loud denunciation of "such brazen exhibition of sin," as he referred to the activities of the two brothels.

"This is no time for prudery, these poor Christians are shivering," the reverend's wife had said when she showed up at the smithy with rabbit stew, a pitcher of hot chocolate, and cinnamon cookies.

That same lady went door-to-door collecting clothing for the doves, who were still in their petticoats, and the women of the town responded with generosity. They did not like to pass in front of the other madam's establishment, but they had of necessity dealt with Joe Bonecrusher during the epidemic and they respected her. So that was how the four ladies of the night went around for a while dressed as modest housewives, covered from neck to toe, until they could replace their splendiferous professional outfits. The night of the fire, the preacher's wife wanted to take Tom No-Tribe home, but the boy clung to Babalú's neck and no human power could pry him loose. The giant spent sleepless hours with Chile Boy curled up in one arm and the Indian in the other, piqued no little by the blacksmith's lifted eyebrows.

"You can get that idea out of your head, man. I'm no pansy," he sputtered indignantly, but he did not disturb either of the two sleepers.

The miners' collection and the pouch of gold dust buried beneath the oak were enough to install the victims in a house so comfortable that Joe Bonecrusher had about decided to give up her traveling company and settle down there. While other towns disappeared as the miners moved to new sites, this one grew, maintained its growth, and even thought of changing its name to one more dignified. At the end of winter, new waves of adventurers were climbing into the foothills, and the other madam was getting ready for them. Joe Bonecrusher now had only three girls, because it was obvious that the blacksmith was planning to steal Esther from them, but she wanted to see if she could work things out. Joe had won considerable respect with her compassionate works and she did not want to give that up: for the first time in her chaotic life she felt accepted in a community. That was far more than she had had in her Pennsylvania Dutch homeland, and at her age putting down roots did not seem like a bad idea. When Eliza heard those plans she decided that if Joaquín Andieta—or Murieta—had not appeared by spring she would have to tell her friends good-bye and keep looking for him.

Disillusion

At the end of autumn, Tao Chi'en received Eliza's latest letter, which had passed from hand to hand for several months, following him to San Francisco. He had left Sacramento in April. Winter in that city seemed to go on and on; the only thing that sustained him were Eliza's letters, which came sporadically, the hope that Lin's spirit would locate him, and his friendship with his fellow *zhong yi*. Tao had acquired books on Western medicine and with great pleasure had taken on the patient task of translating them line by line for his friend; in that way both absorbed at the same time a knowledge very different from their own. They found that in the West little was known about essential herbs, about preventing illness, or about *qi*, the bodily energy never mentioned in those texts, but also that Western medicine was more advanced in other aspects. With his friend, Tao spent days comparing and discussing, but study alone could not console him: isolation and solitude weighed on him so heavily that he abandoned the wooden hut and his garden of medicinal plants and moved to a hotel run by Chinese, where at least he heard his language and ate food to his taste. Even though his patients were very poor and he often treated them for nothing, he had saved money. If Eliza came back they would move into a house, he thought, but as long as he was alone the hotel was good enough. The other *zhong yi* planned to send for a young wife from China and settle in the United States where, despite the fact that he was a foreigner, he would have a better life than in his country. Tao Chi'en warned him against the vanity of the golden lilies, especially in America, where everyone walked so much and the *fan wey* made fun of a woman with a doll's feet. "Ask the broker to bring you a smiling and healthy wife; nothing else matters," he counseled, thinking of the brief passage through this world of his unforgettable Lin and how much happier she would have been with Eliza's feet and strong lungs. His wife was wandering somewhere, lost; she didn't know how to find her way in that foreign land. He invoked her in his meditation and in his poems but she did not come to him again, not even in his dreams. The last time he had been with her was that day in the hold of the ship, when she visited him wearing her green silk dress and peonies in her hair to ask him to save Eliza, but that had been somewhere near Peru, and since then he had traveled across so much water, land, and time that Lin was surely confused. He imagined her gentle spirit searching for him in this vast, unfamiliar continent, unable to find him. At the *zhong yi*'s suggestion, he commissioned an artist, a new émigré from Shanghai, to paint her portrait; he was a true tattoo genius, and although the painting followed Tao's precise instructions it did not do justice to Lin's diaphanous beauty. Tao Chi'en made a small altar for the portrait, where he would sit to summon her. He did not understand why solitude, which he had previously considered a blessing and a luxury, now seemed unbearable. The worst of his years as a sailor had been not having a private space for quiet and silence, but now all he wanted was companionship. The idea of ordering a bride, however, seemed ill-conceived. Once before, the spirits of his ancestors had found him a perfect wife, but behind that apparent good fortune was a hidden curse. He knew what it was to be loved in return, and now could never go back to the times of innocence when every woman with small feet and a sweet nature seemed enough. He felt condemned to live with the memory of Lin because no other woman could take her place with dignity. He did not want a servant or a concubine. Not even the need to have sons to honor his name and tend his tomb would induce him. He tried to explain all this to his friend but he got tangled up in words; there weren't enough in his vocabulary to express his torment. A woman is a creature useful for work, motherhood, and pleasure, but no cultivated and intelligent man would try to make her his companion his friend had said the only time Tao tried to confide his feelings. In China, one glance around made that reasoning understandable, but in America the relationship between husband and wife seemed different. To begin with, no one had concubines—at least not openly. To Tao Chi'en's mind, the few *fan wey* families he had met in this land of solitary men were beyond comprehension. He could not imagine how they behaved in private, given that apparently the husbands treated their wives as equals. It was a mystery that he was interested in exploring, like so many others in this extraordinary country.

Eliza's first letters were delivered to the restaurant, and as the Chinese community knew Tao Chi'en, they were not long in reaching him. Those lengthy missives, rich with details, were his best company. Remembering Eliza, he was surprised at how much he missed her, because he had never thought that friendship with a woman was possible, to say nothing of one from a different culture. He had almost always seen her in masculine clothing but he thought of her as totally feminine and was surprised that others accepted her disguise without asking questions. "Men never really look at other men, and the women think I'm an effeminate boy," she had written in one letter. To him, on the other hand, she was the girl dressed in white whose corset he had removed in a fishing hut in Valparaíso, the sick girl who had delivered herself without reservation to his care in the hold of the ship, the warm body snuggled against his on icy nights beneath the canvas roof; he heard her happy voice humming as she cooked, and remembered her serious expression when she helped him treat wounded patients. He no longer saw her as a young girl, but as a woman despite her airy bones and youthful face. He thought about how different she looked after she cut her hair and regretted not having kept the braid, a thought that had occurred to him at the time but had been discarded as a shameful bit of sentimentality. At least now he could have held it in his hands to summon the presence of that singular friend. When he meditated he never failed to send protective energy to help her survive the thousand deaths and possible disasters he tried not to think about, because he knew that one who thinks of bad things ends up convoking them. Sometimes Tao dreamed about Eliza and woke in a sweat; then he would throw his I Ching sticks to reveal the unseen. In those ambiguous messages, Eliza always appeared moving toward the mountain; that calmed him somewhat.

In September of 1850, Tao was present at the noisy patriotic celebration when California became the newest state in the union. The American nation took in the whole continent, from the Atlantic to the Pacific. By then, the fever for gold was beginning to take the shape of enormous collective disillusion, and Tao saw masses of debilitated and impoverished miners waiting their turns to sail back where they had come from. The newspapers estimated that more than ninety thousand were going home. Sailors were no longer deserting; on the contrary, there weren't enough ships to carry everyone who wanted to leave. One out of every five miners had died, of disease, cold, or drowning in the rivers; many were murdered or had shot themselves in the head. Foreigners were still coming, having embarked months earlier, but the gold was no longer within easy reach of any bold adventurer with a pan, a shovel, and a pair of boots. The time of solitary heroes was over and in their place were powerful companies equipped with machines able to open mountains with forceful bursts of water. Miners were working on salary and the ones getting rich were the impresarios, as avid for sudden wealth as the adventurers of '49, but much cleverer, like that tailor named Levi who was making pants with double seams and metal studs, the obligatory miner's uniform. At the same time that many were leaving the Chinese kept streaming in like mute ants. Tao Chi'en often translated the English-language newspapers for his friend, the *zhong yi*, who particularly liked the articles of a certain Jacob Freemont because they coincided with his own opinions.

"Thousands of argonauts are returning home defeated without having found the golden fleece, their odyssey turned into tragedy, but many others, though poor, are staying because now they cannot live anywhere else. Two years in this wild and beautiful country transforms men. The danger, the adventure, and the good health and vigor they have known in California are not found anywhere else. Gold fulfilled its function: it attracted the men who are conquering this region and making of it the promised land. That is irreversible . . ." wrote Freemont.

Tao Chi'en, however, felt that he was living in a paradise of greedy, materialistic, and impatient people whose obsession was to get rich quick. There was no food for the spirit; instead, violence and ignorance prospered. All other evils derived from those, he was convinced. He had seen a lot in his twenty-seven years, and did not consider himself a prude, but he was shocked by the standards of behavior and the impunity of crime. Such a place was destined to choke in the muck of its own vices, he maintained. He had lost hope of finding in America the peace he so desired; definitely, this was not the place for one who aspired to wisdom. So why was he so strongly attracted to it? He must avoid being bewitched by this land, as had happened to so many who had come here. He intended either to go back to Hong Kong or to visit his friend Ebanizer Hobbs in England where they could study and practice together. In the years that had gone by since he was shanghaied onto the *Liberty* he had written several letters to the English physician but during the days at sea it had taken a long time to get an answer, until finally in Valparaíso, in February of 1849, Captain John Sommers had received a letter for him and delivered it to him. In it, his friend told him that he was practicing surgery in London, although his true calling was to mental illnesses, a new field just being explored by science.

Tao Chi'en planned to work for a while in Dai Fao, the "great city" as the Chinese called San Francisco, and then sail to China in case Ebanizer Hobbs did not answer his most recent letter within a reasonable time. He was amazed to see how San Francisco had changed in little more than a year. Instead of the noisy camp of huts and tents he remembered, he saw a city with well-planned streets and buildings of several floors, organized and prosperous, with new dwellings going up everywhere. A catastrophic fire had destroyed several blocks three months earlier; one could still see the ruins of burned-out buildings, but the coals were not yet cool before everyone had taken hammer in hand to rebuild. There were luxury hotels with verandahs and balconies, casinos, bars, and restaurants, elegant carriages, along with an unattractive, badly dressed multicultural throng, among whom stood out the top hats of a few dandies. The rest were mud-covered, bearded types with the look of villains, although no one was who he seemed: the stevedore on the dock might be a Latin American aristocrat, and the coach driver a New York lawyer. After a minute's conversation with any of those intimidating-looking types, one might uncover an educated man who at the least pretext, with tears in his eyes, would pull out a wrinkled letter from his wife. And the opposite also happened: the foppish, well-cut suit might well conceal an unmitigated scoundrel. Tao did not see any schools in his walk through the center; instead he saw children working like adults, digging holes, carrying bricks, driving mules, and shining boots, but as soon as the breeze blew in the from the ocean they would run to fly kites. Later he learned that many of them were orphans, and that they roamed the streets in gangs, stealing food to survive. There were few women, and when one strolled elegantly down the street, traffic stopped to let her pass. At the foot of Telegraph Hill, where there was a semaphore flying flags to signal the registry of ships entering the bay, lay a few blocks in which there was no shortage of women: that was the red-light district, controlled by ruffians from Australia, Tasmania, and New Zealand. Tao Chi'en had heard of them, and knew it was no place for a Chinese man to venture by himself after sunset. Peering into shops, he saw they were offering the same goods he had seen in London when he stopped there. Everything came by sea, even a cargo of cats, sold individually like luxury items, to wage war against the rats. The forest of masts of ships abandoned in the bay was reduced to a tenth; many had been scuttled to make landfill for construction or had been converted into hotels, storehouses, jails, and even an insane asylum where poor wretches lost in the unreachable delirium of alcohol were sent to die. Such a haven was badly needed, since previously they had tied lunatics to trees.

Tao Chi'en headed for Chinatown and found that the rumors were true: his countrymen had built a complete city in the heart of San Francisco, where Mandarin and Cantonese were spoken, signs were all in Chinese, and the only faces were Chinese: the illusion of being transported to the celestial empire was perfect. Tao took a room in a decent hotel and prepared to practice medicine as long as necessary to earn a little more money because he had a long journey ahead of him. Something happened, however, that would overturn his plans and hold him in the city. "My karma was not to find peace in a monastery in the mountains, as I sometimes dreamed, but to fight a merciless, no-holds-barred war," he concluded many years later, when he could look back at his past and see clearly the roads he had traveled and those not taken. Months later, he received Eliza's last letter in a dirty, wrinkled envelope.

Paulina Rodríguez de Santa Cruz descended from the *Fortuna* like an empress, surrounded by her entourage and ninety-three trunks. Captain John Sommers' third trip with the ice had been true torment for him, the other passengers, and the crew. Paulina let everyone know that the ship was hers, and to prove it she contradicted the captain and gave arbitrary orders to the sailors. She had a stomach like an elephant and was not even slowed by seasickness; she was such a good sailor that her appetite merely increased. Her children continually got lost in the crannies of the ship even though their nannies never took their eyes off them, and when that happened the alarms sounded and they had to shut down the boilers because the hysterical mother screamed that her children had fallen overboard. The captain tried to explain as delicately as possible that were that the case she would have to resign herself to it, because the Pacific would already have swallowed them up, but she ordered him to lower the lifeboats. Sooner or later the children would surface, and after several hours of high drama they would resume their voyage. Paulina's objectionable little lap dog, however, did lose its footing one day and slip into the ocean in front of several witnesses, who watched without a word. Paulina's husband and brother-in-law were waiting on the dock in San Francisco with a row of carriages and wagons to transport the family and the trunks. The residence constructed for her, an elegant Victorian house, had been shipped in crates from England with numbered pieces and blueprints for putting it together; the wallpaper, furniture, harp, piano, lamps—even porcelain figurines and bucolic paintings to adorn it—were also imported. Paulina did not like it. Compared to her marble mansion in Chile, this new one looked like a dollhouse that threatened to collapse every time she leaned against a wall, but for the moment there was no alternative. And she needed only one look at the effervescent city to realize its possibilities.

"Here is where we are going to live, Feliciano. The first to arrive become aristocracy in a couple of years."

"You already have that in Chile, woman."

"I do, but you don't. Believe me, this will be the most important city of the Pacific."

"Founded by swine and whores!"

"Precisely. They are the ones most eager for respectability. No one will be more respectable than the Cross family. What a shame these people cannot pronounce our real name. Cross is a name for cheese makers. But after all, I suppose one cannot have everything."

That night Captain John Sommers went to the best restaurant in the city, eager to eat and drink well and forget his five weeks in the company of that woman. He had brought several boxes of the newest illustrated editions of erotic books. The success of the first had been stupendous, and he hoped his sister Rose would work up the spirit to write again. Ever since Eliza's disappearance she had been in a slough of sadness and had not once taken up her pen. His mood had been affected, too. "Shit, I am getting old," he said when he realized he was foundering in futile nostalgia. He had never had time to enjoy his daughter, to take her to England as he had planned; nor had he told her he was her father. He was fed up with deceit and mystery. The business of the books was another family secret. Fifteen years ago, when his sister had confessed that behind Jeremy's back she was writing lewd stories to keep from dying of boredom, he had come up with the idea of publishing them in London, where the market for erotica had prospered, along with prostitution and clubs for flagellants, the longer the rigid Victorian moral code was imposed. In a remote province in Chile, seated before a small dressing table of blond wood, with no source of inspiration but memories of her one love affair inflated and polished a thousand times over, his sister produced novel after novel signed by "An Anonymous Lady." No one believed that those steamy stories, some with a tone suggestive of the Marquis de Sade and already classics of their genre, were written by a woman. It was the captain's job to take the manuscripts to the editor, monitor expenses, collect the earnings, and deposit them in a London bank for his sister. It was his way of paying her for the huge favor she had done him by taking in his daughter and saying nothing. He could not remember Eliza's mother, but if the girl had inherited her mother's physical characteristics, she had undoubtedly gotten from him her urge for adventure. Where could she be? And with whom? Rose insisted she had gone to California after her lover, but the more time that passed, the more he doubted that. His friend Jacob Todd—now Freemont—who had made the search for Eliza a personal mission, assured him that she had never set foot in San Francisco.

Freemont met the captain for dinner, and then invited him to a frivolous show in one of the dance halls in the red-light district. He told Sommers that Ah Toy, the Chinese woman they had peered at through the holes in the wall, now had a chain of brothels and an elegant "salon" staffed by the finest Oriental girls, some barely eleven years old and trained to satisfy every whim. He said they weren't going there, however, but to see the Turkish harem dancers. Soon afterward they were smoking and drinking in a two-story building decorated with large marble tables, polished bronzes, and paintings of mythological nymphs pursued by fauns. Women of several races attended the clientele, served drinks, and presided over the gaming tables under the vigilant gaze of armed pimps, all dressed with eye-popping affectation. On both sides of the main salon, in private rooms, was high-stakes betting. That was where the real tigers gambled, risking thousands in one night: politicians, judges, merchants, lawyers, and criminals, all equals in the same mania. The performance was a fiasco in the eyes of the captain, who had seen authentic belly dancing in Istanbul and had no trouble recognizing that those clumsy girls were undoubtedly from the last group of whores to arrive from Chicago. The audience, most of whom were uneducated miners who couldn't have found Turkey on a map, whooped their approval of those odalisques barely covered by bead skirts. Bored, the captain drifted to one of the betting tables where with incredible dexterity a female dealer was shuffling the cards for monte. A different woman came up to him, grasped his arm, and breathed an invitation into his ear. He turned to look at her. She was a plump, common, South American, but she wore an expression of genuine happiness. He was about to send her on her way because he was planning to spend the rest of the night with one of the expensive whores he had visited on earlier trips to San Francisco when his eyes focused on her décolletage. Between her breasts was a gold brooch set with turquoise stones.

"Where did you get that?" he cried, gripping her shoulders with two hands.

"It's mine! I bought it!" she blurted out, terrified.

"Where!" and he shook her so roughly that one of the thugs sauntered toward them.

"Any trouble, mister?" he asked threateningly.

The captain made a sign that he wanted some time with this woman, and hustled her off to one of the cubicles on the second floor. He closed the curtain and with a single slap tumbled her back on the bed.

"You are going to tell me where you got that brooch or I'm going to knock all your teeth out, is that clear?"

"I didn't steal it, I swear. Someone gave it to me!"

"Who?"

"You won't believe me when I tell you."

"Try me!"

"A girl, a long time ago, on a boat . . ."

And Azucena Placeres had no choice but to tell that man possessed that a Chinese cook had given her the brooch in payment for looking after a poor little girl who was dying from a miscarriage in the hold of a ship in the middle of the Pacific Ocean. As she talked, the captain's anger turned to horror.

"What happened to her?" asked John Sommers, his head in his hands, stunned.

"I don't know, señor."

"I'll give you anything you want, woman, just tell me what happened to her," he begged, dropping a sheaf of bills in her skirt.

"Who are you?"

"I'm her father."

"She bled to death and we threw her body into the ocean. I swear, that's the truth," Azucena Placeres replied without a second's pause, because she thought that if that poor girl had traveled half the world hidden like a rat in a hole, it would be an unforgivable betrayal on her part to set the father on her trail.

Eliza spent the summer in the town because with one thing and another the days got away from her. First Babalú the Bad had a near fatal attack of dysentery, which set off a panic since the epidemic was supposed to be under control. For months there had been no cases to mourn except the death of a two-year-old boy, the first child to be born and die in that stopping-off place for newcomers and adventurers. That baby had put a seal of authenticity on the town, for now it was no longer an illusory camp with a gallows as its only reason to figure on the maps; it had a Christian cemetery and the tiny grave of someone whose entire life had been spent there. During the time Joe Bonecrusher's barn had been turned into a hospital, all of them had miraculously been spared from the epidemic—miraculously, because Joe didn't believe in contagion. She said everything was a matter of luck: the world is filled with plagues; some get them and some don't. That was why she didn't take precautions; she allowed herself the luxury of ignoring the commonsense warnings of the doctor and only under pressure boiled the drinking water. Once they had moved into a real house, they all felt safe; if they hadn't been infected before, they wouldn't now. But within a few days, Babalú was down; then it became the turn of Joe Bonecrusher, the girls from Missouri, and the beautiful Mexican. They succumbed with vile diarrhea, fevers you could fry an egg on, and uncontrollable chills, which in Babalú's case shook the house. Then came James Morton in his Sunday clothes to ask formally for Esther's hand.

"Oh, son, you couldn't have chosen a worse time," sighed Joe Bonecrusher, but she was too sick to object and between moans gave her consent.

Esther divided her belongings among her companions because she did not want to take anything to her new life, and they were married that same day, without much fuss, attended by Tom No-Tribe and Eliza, the only two of their company who weren't sick. A double row of Esther's former customers lined both sides of the street as the couple went by, shooting into the air and yelling congratulations. The couple moved into the blacksmith shop, determined to make it their home and forget the past, but still they went every day to Joe's house, taking hot meals and clean clothing to the ill. The unpleasant task of nursing everyone fell to Eliza and Tom No-Tribe. The town doctor—a young man from Philadelphia who for months had been warning that the water was polluted with waste from the miners upriver, without anyone's giving him the time of day—quarantined Joe's house. Their finances went from bad to worse but they did not go hungry, thanks to Esther and the anonymous gifts that mysteriously appeared at the door: a sack of beans, a few pounds of sugar, tobacco, small pouches of gold dust, silver dollars. To tend her friends, Eliza called on what she had learned in her girlhood from Mama Fresia and from Tao Chi'en in Sacramento, until finally one by one her friends began to recuperate, although for a long time they were unsteady and befuddled. Babalú the Bad had suffered the most. His Cyclops girth was unaccustomed to bad health; he lost weight and his flesh hung so loose his tattoos were unrecognizable.

During that time, a brief news items was published in the local newspaper about a Chilean or Mexican—no one was sure which—bandit named Joaquín Murieta, who was becoming famous up and down the mother lode. By then, violence was the rule in gold country. Disillusioned when they learned that sudden fortune, a mockery of a miracle, had come to only a few, the Americans accused foreigners of being greedy and of getting rich without contributing to the nation's prosperity. Liquor fired them up, and impunity in doling out punishment gave them an irrational sense of power. An American was never sentenced for crimes against another race; still worse, a white criminal often could choose his own jury. Racial hostility turned into blind hatred. Mexicans refused to accept the loss of their territory in the war, or to be run off their ranches and the mines. The Chinese bore abuse silently; they did not leave, but kept prospecting, not earning enough for a flea, but with such infinite tenacity that grain by grain they amassed wealth. Thousands of Chileans and Peruvians, who had been the first to arrive when gold fever blossomed, decided to return to their countries because it wasn't worth pursuing their dreams under such conditions. That year, 1850, the legislature of California approved a tax on mining operations designed to protect whites. Blacks and Indians were left out, unless they worked like slaves, and foreigners had to pay twenty dollars and renew rights to their claim monthly, which in practice was impossible. They couldn't leave the placers to travel several weeks to the city to obey the law, but if they didn't, the sheriff took over their mine and gave it to an American. The people in charge of enforcing those measures were chosen by the governor and earned their salaries from taxes and fines, a perfect setup for encouraging corruption. The law applied only to dark-skinned foreigners, even though according to the treaty that ended the war in 1848 the Mexicans had rights to American citizenship. Another decree was the last nail in the coffin: claims on their ranches, where they had lived for generations, had to be ratified by a court in San Francisco. This procedure took years and cost a fortune; in addition, the judges and constables were often the same ones who had appropriated the claims. In view of the fact that the law did not protect them, some Mexicans decided to act outside it, spiritedly throwing themselves into the role of outlaws. Men who formerly had been content to steal cattle now attacked solitary miners and travelers. Some gangs were famous for their cruelty; they not only robbed the victims, they took pleasure in torturing them before they killed them. There was talk of one particular *bandido* to whom they attributed, among other offenses, the terrible death of two young Americans. Their bodies were found tied to a tree, with signs of having been used as a target for knife throwers: their tormentors had also cut out their tongues, pierced their eyes, and cut off live flesh before leaving them to slowly die. This criminal was called Three-Finger Jack, and it was said that he was right-hand man to Joaquín Murieta.

Not everything was savagery, nevertheless; the cities were developing, and new towns were springing up and families moving in; newspapers, theater companies, and orchestras were organized, schools, churches, and banks were constructed, roads were built, and communications improved. There was stagecoach service and regular mail delivery. Women were less a novelty now, and a society was flourishing that aspired to order and morality, replacing the disaster of solitary men and prostitutes. There was an attempt to establish the rule of law and to return to the civilization forgotten in the delirium of easy gold. The town was given a respectable name in a solemn ceremony featuring a marching band and a parade, which Joe Bonecrusher attended dressed as a woman for the first time and backed by her entire company. Wives who had only recently arrived blanched when they saw the "painted women," but as Joe and her girls had saved so many lives during the epidemic they overlooked their activities. On the other hand, they declared war on the other brothel—a losing battle, nonetheless, since there was still only one woman for every nine men. At the end of that year, James Morton welcomed five families of Quakers who had crossed the continent in oxcarts, not for gold but drawn by the vastness of that virgin land.

By now, Eliza had no idea what trail to follow. Joaquín Andieta had evaporated in the confusion of the times and in his place had begun to materialize an outlaw with the same physical description and similar name, a figure she found impossible to identify with the noble young man she loved. The author of the letters she kept as her only treasure could not be the same person as the one to whom such horrendous crimes were attributed. The man she loved would never have associated with a cold-blooded killer like Three-Finger Jack, she was sure, but her conviction melted away at night when Joaquín appeared to her wearing a thousand different masks and bringing a thousand contradictory messages. She would wake up trembling, besieged by the raving specters of her nightmares. She had lost the ability to come and go from her dreams at will, as Mama Fresia had taught her as a child, nor could she decipher the visions and symbols that kept rattling in her head like pebbles rolling in the river. She wrote tirelessly in her diary, hoping as she did so that the images would acquire some meaning. She reread the love letters syllable by syllable, seeking clarifying signs but finding only deeper perplexity. Those letters were the one proof of her lover's existence and she clung to them so as not to lose her bearings completely. The temptation to fall into apathy as a way to escape the torment of continuing her search for Joaquín was becoming irresistible. She doubted everything: the embraces in the room of the armoires, the months buried in the hold of the ship, the baby that had bled out of her.

The financial problems that arose from Esther's marriage to the blacksmith, which deprived Joe's company of a quarter of their income overnight, and from the weeks the other girls had been laid low by dysentery, were so major that Joe nearly lost the house, but the thought of seeing her doves working for the competition spurred her to keep fighting adversity. They had gone through hell, and she could not let her girls slide back into that life, because much against her will she had become fond of them. She had always thought of herself as one of God's serious mistakes, a man condemned to the body of a woman, which is why she could not understand the maternal instinct that had budded when it was least convenient. She looked after Tom No-Tribe religiously, but she liked to point out that she did it "like a sergeant." None of that mollycoddling, it wasn't in her nature, and besides, the boy had to be strong like his ancestors; babying only screwed up a kid's manliness, she warned Eliza when she found her with Tom No-Tribe in her lap, telling him folktales from Chile. This new tenderness for her doves was a serious stone around her neck, and, to top everything off, they knew how she felt and had begun to call her Mother. Her gorge rose at that; she had forbidden them to do it, but they ignored her. "We have a business relationship here, goddamn it. I can't put it any straighter. As long as you work, you have a salary, a roof, food, and protection, but the day you get sick, get lazy on me, or get all wrinkled and gray . . . so long!" she groused. "Nothing easier than replacing you, the world is full of easy women." And then, all of a sudden, here came this syrupy sentimentality to foul up her life, something no madam in her right mind would ever permit. "All this crap happens to you because you're a nice person," Babalú the Bad teased her. And it was probably true, because while she was wasting precious time nursing sick people whose names she didn't even know, the other madam in town had refused to let anyone who was sick come near her place. Joe was getting poorer while her rival put on weight, had her hair bleached, and took a Russian lover ten years her junior with muscles like an athlete and a diamond set in one tooth. This competitor had expanded her business and on weekends the miners lined up at her door with money in one hand and hat in the other, for no woman, no matter how low she had sunk, would put up with an undoffed hat. Very clearly, Joe maintained, there was no future for her in the profession: the law didn't protect them, God had forgotten them, and all she could see ahead was old age, poverty, and loneliness. She considered taking in washing and baking pies to sell, meanwhile holding on to the trade in gambling and dirty books, but her girls were not interested in earning a living with such hard, and badly paid, work.

"This is a shitty profession, girls. Get yourselves married, go study to be teachers. Do something with your fucking lives and stop hanging around me," she sighed sadly.

Babalú the Bad, what's more, was tired of acting as a pimp and bodyguard. Their sedentary life bored him, and Joe Bonecrusher had changed so much that he didn't really feel like working with her any longer. If she had lost her enthusiasm for the profession, where did that leave him? In desperation he confided in Chile Boy, and the two of them entertained each other making fanciful plans to break free. They contemplated organizing a traveling spectacle. They talked about buying a bear and training it to box, so they could go from town to town challenging anyone brave enough to duke it out with the animal. Babalú was looking for adventure, and Eliza thought it would be a good opportunity to have company while she looked for Joaquín Andieta. Besides cooking and playing the piano she didn't have much to do at Joe's place, and the inactivity was making her out of sorts. She wanted to feel the freedom of the open road again, but she'd grown fond of these people and it broke her heart to think of leaving Tom No-Tribe. The boy was reading well now and was diligent in learning to write; Eliza had convinced him that when he grew up he should study to be a lawyer and defend the rights of the Indians instead of avenging the dead with bullets, as Joe wanted him to do. "You will be a much more powerful warrior that way, and all the gringos will be afraid of you." He still didn't laugh, but once or twice when he sat beside her to have her scratch his head, the shadow of a smile played over his angry Indian face.

Tao Chi'en walked into Joe Bonecrusher's house at three in the afternoon one Wednesday in December. Tom No-Tribe opened the door, invited him into the parlor—empty at that hour—and called the doves. Shortly thereafter the beautiful Mexican came into the kitchen where Chile Boy was kneading dough to announce that some Chinaman was asking about Elías Andieta, but Eliza was so preoccupied with her work, and with remembering her dreams of the night before in which there had been a blur of gambling tables and pierced eyes, that she didn't pay any attention.

"I'm telling you that some Chinese man is waiting for you," the Mexican repeated, and then Eliza's heart kicked like a mule in her chest.

"Tao!" she screamed, and shot out of the room.

When she got to the parlor, however, she found a man so changed that it took several seconds to recognize her friend. His queue was gone; he was wearing his hair short and combed back with brilliantine, round eyeglasses with wire frames, a dark suit with a frock coat, a three-button vest, and flared trousers. Over one arm was an overcoat and an umbrella, and in the other hand he held a top hat.

"God in heaven, Tao! What happened to *you*!"

"In America, you have to dress like the Americans." He smiled.

In San Francisco he had been attacked by three bullies, and before he could pull his knife from his sash they had knocked him out for the pure fun of mopping up a "celestial." When he came to, he found himself in an alley, covered with filth and with his queue cut off and wrapped around his neck. At that very moment, he decided to wear his hair short and dress like the *fan wey*. His new aspect made him stand out in Chinatown but he discovered that he was much better received outside it, and that doors opened that had been closed to him before. He was possibly the only Chinese man in the city who looked the way he did. A queue was considered sacred and the decision to cut it proved that he did not intend to go back to China but, rather, to stay in America, an unpardonable betrayal of the emperor, his country, and his ancestors. His clothing and his haircut, nevertheless, were also the source of a certain awe, for they indicated that he had access to the world of the Americans. Eliza could not take her eyes off him; he was a stranger she would have to get to know all over again. Tao Chi'en bowed several times, in his usual greeting, and she did not dare indulge the impulse to hug him that was burning inside her. She had often slept cuddled against him but they had never touched without the excuse of sleep.

"I think I liked you better, Tao, when you were out-and-out Chinese. I don't know you now. May I smell you?" she asked.

He stood very still, uneasy, while she sniffed him like a dog its quarry, at last recognizing the faint sea scent, the old, comforting odor. The haircut and severe tailoring made Tao look older; he had lost his lackadaisical air. He was thinner, and seemed taller, and his cheekbones stood out in his smooth face. Eliza observed his mouth with pleasure; she remembered perfectly his infectious smile and perfect teeth, but not how voluptuous his lips were. She caught a somber expression in his gaze but thought it must be the effect of his glasses.

"How good it is to see you, Tao!" she said as her eyes filled with tears.

"I couldn't come any sooner, I didn't have your address."

"But I like you now, too. You remind me of a grave digger, but a handsome one."

"That's what I'm doing now," he said, smiling, "digging graves. When I heard you were living in this place I thought you were fulfilling Azucena Placeres's prophecy. She said that one day you would end up like her."

"I told you in my letter that I earn my living playing the piano."

"Incredible."

"Why? You've never heard me, I'm not so bad. And if I could pass for a deaf-mute Chinese boy, I don't know why I couldn't be a Chilean piano player."

To his surprise, Tao Chi'en burst out laughing. It was the first time in months he had been happy.

"Did you find your lover?"

"No. I don't know where to look anymore."

"Maybe he doesn't deserve for you to find him. Come back with me to San Francisco."

"I don't have anything to do in San Francisco."

"And here? Winter is coming. In a week or two the roads will be impassable and this town will be cut off."

"It's very boring to be your stupid little brother, Tao."

"There is a lot to do in San Francisco, you'll see, and you won't have to dress as a man; there are women everywhere now."

"What about your plans to go back to China?"

"They're on hold. I can't leave yet."

Singsong Girls

In the summer of 1851 Jacob Freemont decided to interview Joaquín Murieta. Outlaws and fires were the chief subjects of conversation in California; they kept citizens terrorized and the press occupied. Crime was rampant and police corruption common knowledge; most of the force was composed of crooks more interested in protecting their partners in crime than the local populace. After one more raging fire, which destroyed a large area of San Francisco, a vigilante committee had been formed by outraged citizens, headed by the ineffable Sam Brannan, the Mormon who had spread the news of the gold. Companies of firemen pulling water carts by hand ran uphill and down, but before they reached a burning building flames would be leaping from the one beside it. The fire had begun when Australian "hounds" had splashed kerosene all through the store of a merchant who had refused to pay them protection money, and then torched it. In view of the indifference of the authorities, the committee had decided to act on its own. The newspapers clamored, "How many crimes have been committed in this city this year? And who has been hanged or jailed for them? No one! How many men have been shot or stabbed, hit over the head and beat up? And who has been convicted for that? We do not condone lynching, but who can tell what an indignant public will do to protect itself?" Lynchings were precisely the public's solution. Vigilantes immediately threw themselves into the task and hanged the first suspect. The numbers of these self-appointed enforcers grew day by day, and they acted with such excessive enthusiasm that for the first time outlaws took care to move about only in the full light of day. In that climate of violence and revenge, the figure of Joaquín Murieta was on the way to becoming a symbol. Jacob Freemont took it upon himself to fan the flames of Murieta's celebrity: his sensationalist articles had created a hero for Hispanics and a devil for Americans. Murieta was believed to have a large gang and the talent of a military genius; it was said that he was fighting a war of skirmishes that authorities were powerless to combat. He attacked with cunning and speed, descending upon his victims like a curse and then disappearing without a trace, only to show up a hundred miles away with another attack of unbelievable boldness that could be explained only by magic powers. Freemont suspected that there were several "Murietas," not one, but he was careful not to write that because it would have diminished the legend. On the other hand, he had the inspired idea of labeling Murieta "the Robin Hood of California," which immediately sparked a wildfire of racial controversy. To the Yanquis, Murieta represented what was most despicable about the greasers; and it was believed that the Mexicans hid him and provided him with weapons and supplies because he stole from the whites to help the people of his race. In the war they had lost the territories of Texas, Arizona, New Mexico, Nevada, Utah, and half of Colorado and California, and so for them any attack against the victors was an act of patriotism. The governor warned the newspaper against the rashness of making a hero of a criminal, but the name had already inflamed the public's imagination. Freemont received dozens of letters, including one from a young girl in Washington who was ready to sail halfway around the world in order to marry that "Robin Hood" and people stopped Freemont in the street to ask him details about the famous Joaquín Murieta. Without ever having seen him, the newspaperman described Murieta as a young man of virile mien, with the features of a noble Spaniard and the courage of a bullfighter. Quite by accident, Freemont had stumbled across a gold mine more productive than many in the mother lode. He decided he must interview this Joaquín, if the fellow really existed, and write his biography, and if it were all a fable he would turn it into a novel. His work as author would consist simply of writing in a heroic tone to satisfy the common man's tastes. California needed its myths and legends, Freemont maintained. To Americans, it had come into the union with a clean slate; they thought that the stroke of a pen could erase a long history of Indians, Mexicans, and Californians. For this land of empty spaces and solitary men, a land open to conquest and rape, what better hero than a bandit? Freemont packed his indispensables in a suitcase, stocked himself with a supply of notebooks and pencils, and set off in search of his character. The risks never entered his mind; having the dual arrogance of an Englishman and a journalist, he felt he was protected from any harm. In addition, traveling was by now effected with a certain ease; there were highways, and a regular stagecoach service connected the towns where he planned to make his investigations. It was not the way it had been when he had begun his work as a reporter, riding on mule back, forging a path through the uncertainty of hills and forests with no guide but insane maps that could lead one to wander in circles for all time. Along the way, he could see the changes in the region. Few men had made their fortune with gold but, thanks to adventurers who had come by the thousands, California was becoming civilized. Without gold fever, the conquest of the West would have been delayed by a couple of centuries, the journalist wrote in his notebook.

There was no dearth of subjects, such as the story of the young miner, a boy of eighteen, who after a year's backbreaking effort had gotten together the ten thousand dollars he needed to go home to Oklahoma and buy a farm for his parents. He was walking back to

Sacramento through the foothills of the Sierra Nevada one radiant day, with his treasure in a sack over his shoulder, when he was surprised by a band of ruthless Mexicans or Chileans, he wasn't sure which. All he knew for sure was that they spoke Spanish, because they had the impudence to leave a sign in that language, scrawled by knifepoint on a piece of wood: "Death to Yanquis." They were not content with beating and robbing him, they tied him naked to a tree and smeared him with honey. Two days later, when he was found by a patrol, he was raving. Mosquitoes had eaten away his skin.

Freemont put his talent for morbid journalism to the test with the tragic death of Josefa, a beautiful Mexican girl who worked in a dance hall. She arrived in the town of Downieville on the Fourth of July and found herself in the midst of a celebration promoted by a candidate for senator and irrigated with a river of alcohol. A drunken miner had forced his way into Josefa's room and she had fought him off, plunging her dagger deep into his heart. By the time Jacob Freemont arrived, the body was lying on a table, covered with an American flag, and a crowd of two thousand fanatics ignited by racial hatred was demanding the gallows for Josefa. Impassive, her white blouse stained with blood, smoking a cigarette as if the yelling had nothing to do with her, the woman was scanning the faces of the men with abysmal scorn, aware of the incendiary mixture of aggression and sexual desire she aroused in them. A doctor tried to take her part, explaining that she had acted in self-defense and that if they executed her they would also kill the baby in her womb, but the mob silenced him by threatening to hang him, too. Three terrified doctors were marched over to examine Josefa and all three declared that she was not pregnant, in view of which the impromptu tribunal condemned her in a matter of minutes. "Shooting these greasers is not the way to go," said one member of the jury. "We have to give them a fair trial and hang them in the full majesty of the law." Freemont had never had occasion to witness a lynching before, but this one he described in emotional sentences: how, about four in the afternoon, they had started to lead Josefa to the bridge where the ritual of execution had been prepared but she had haughtily shaken them off and walked to the gallows on her own. The beautiful woman climbed the steps without any help, bound her skirts around her ankles, placed the rope around her neck, arranged her black tresses, and bid them farewell with a courageous "*Adios, señores*" that left the journalist uncertain and the others ashamed. "Josefa did not die because she was guilty, but because she was Mexican. This is the first time a woman has been lynched in California. What a waste, when there are so few!" Freemont wrote in his article.

Following Joaquín Murieta's trail, he passed through established towns, with school, library, church, and cemetery, and others whose only signs of culture were a brothel and a jail. Saloons thrived in all of them, they were the centers of social life. Jacob Freemont would install himself there, asking questions, and so began constructing—with some truths and a mountain of lies, the life—or the legend—of Joaquín Murieta. The saloonkeepers painted him as a damned spic dressed in leather and black velvet, wearing outsize silver spurs and a dagger at his waist and riding the most spirited sorrel ever seen. They said he would ride into town, unchallenged, amid a jangle of spurs and his gang of cutthroats, slap his silver dollars on the counter and order a round of drinks for everyone in the house. No one dared refuse; even the bravest of men would down their drinks in silence under the villain's flashing gaze. For the constables, on the other hand, there was nothing splendid about him, he was nothing less than a vulgar murderer capable of the worst atrocities, who had managed to escape justice because all the greasers protected him. The Chileans thought he was one of them, born in a place called Quillota; they said he was loyal to his friends and never forgot to repay a favor, which was why it was good policy to help him, but the Mexicans swore he came from the state of Sonora and was an educated, handsome young man from an old and noble family and had turned to crime out of revenge. Gamblers considered him an expert monte player but avoided him because he had crazy luck in cards and a ready dagger that flashed into his hand at the least provocation. White prostitutes were dying with curiosity because it was rumored that this handsome and generous youth had the tireless cock of a stallion, but the Hispanic girls never expected to find out: Joaquín Murieta never used their services but often gave them tips they hadn't earned; they claimed that he was faithful to his sweetheart. They described him as a man of medium height, with black hair and eyes like coals, adored by his men, stalwart in the face of trouble, ferocious with his enemies, and gentle with women. Other people said he had the gross features of a born criminal, with a terrible scar right across his face, and that there was nothing of kindness, breeding, or elegance about him. Jacob Freemont selected the opinions that best suited his image of the bandit, and that was how he portrayed him in his articles, always with enough ambiguity that he could print a retraction in case he should someday meet his protagonist face to face. He looked high and low during the four summer months, without finding Murieta anywhere, but from the many different versions he contrived a fanciful and heroic biography. As he did not want to admit defeat, he invented in his articles brief meetings between cock's crow and midnight in mountain caves and forest clearings. After all, who was going to contradict him? Masked men, he wrote, led him on horseback with his eyes blindfolded; he couldn't identify them, but they spoke Spanish. The same fervent eloquence he had used years before in Chile to describe the Patagonian Indians in Tierra del Fuego, where he had never set foot, now served to pull an imaginary outlaw from his sleeve. He was becoming enamored of the character, and in the end was convinced that he knew him, that the secret meetings in caves were real, and that the fugitive himself had commissioned him to write about his feats because he thought of himself as the avenger of oppressed Spanish peoples and someone had to assume the responsibility of according him and his cause a proper place in the developing history of California. There was little journalism involved, but more than enough fiction for the novel Jacob Freemont was planning to write that winter.

When Tao Chi'en had reached San Francisco the year before, he had devoted himself to establishing the contacts he needed to exercise his profession of *zhong yi* for a few months. He had some money, but he wanted to triple it in a hurry. In Sacramento the Chinese community consisted of some seven hundred men and nine or ten prostitutes, but in San Francisco there were thousands of potential clients. Also, many ships were constantly crossing the ocean, and because there was no running water in the city, some gentlemen sent their shirts to be laundered in Hawaii or China, which allowed Tao to order his herbs and remedies from Canton without any difficulty. In San Francisco he would not be as isolated as in Sacramento. Here, too, there were several Chinese practitioners with whom he could exchange patients and information. He did not plan to open his own consulting office because he was trying to save money, but he could associate with another, already established, *zhong yi*. Once installed in a hotel, he had taken a walk around the quarter, which had spread in all directions like an octopus. Now it was a small city with sturdy buildings, hotels, restaurants, laundries, opium parlors, brothels, markets, and factories. Where before only cheap trinkets were for sale, now stood shops of Oriental antiques, porcelains, enamels, jewels, silks, and ivories. Rich merchants came there—not just Chinese but Americans as well—to buy goods to sell in other cities. The merchandise was displayed in a motley clutter, and the best pieces, those worthy of connoisseurs and collectors, were not set out in plain sight but were shown in the back of the shop to informed clients only. Down dark streets, some buildings housed rooms where serious players met to gamble. At those exclusive tables, out of view of public curiosity and the watchfulness of authorities, extravagant sums were bet, murky deals negotiated, and power exercised. American law had no bearing among the Chinese, who lived in their own world, with their own language, customs, and ancient laws. The "celestials" were not welcome anywhere; the whites considered them the lowest among the undesirable foreigners invading California, and could not forgive them for prospering. Americans exploited them however they could, attacked them in the street, robbed them, burned their shops and homes, murdered them with impunity, but nothing quelled them. The population was divided among five tongs; on arrival, every Chinese immigrant joined one of these brotherhoods, the one guarantee of protection, of finding work, and of assuring that at death one's body would be sent back to China. Tao Chi'en, who had avoided associating with a tong, now had to do so, and he chose the largest, the one most Cantonese affiliated with. Soon he was put in contact with other *zhong yi* and they explained the rules of the game to him. First of all, silence and loyalty: everything that happened in the quarter stayed inside its boundaries. No going to the police, not even in the case of life or death; conflicts were resolved within their kind, that was what the tongs were for. The common enemy was always the *fan wey*. Tao Chi'en once again found himself a prisoner of the customs, hierarchies, and restrictions of his days in Canton. Within a couple of days everyone had heard his name and he began to receive more patients that he could attend. He did not have to look for a partner, he decided, he could open his own office and make money in less time than he had thought. He rented two rooms above a restaurant, one to live in and the other for his work; he hung a sign in the window and hired a young assistant to spread word of his services and receive his patients. For the first time, he used Dr. Ebanizer Hobbs's system for following the history of the sick. Until then he had trusted his memory and intuition, but because of the growing number of patients, he began keeping records to note the treatment at each visit.

One afternoon in early autumn, Tao Chi'en's assistant came to him with an address on a piece of paper and a message to come as soon as possible. He attended his last patient of the day, and left. The wooden, two-story building decorated with dragons and paper lanterns was in the heart of Chinatown. One look was enough to tell him that this was a brothel. On either side of the door were small barred windows where he could see the faces of young girls calling to him in Cantonese: "Come in and do what you will with pretty Chinese girl." And for the benefit of white visitors and sailors of all races they repeated in indecipherable English, "Two bittie lookie, four bittee feelee, six bittee doee," as they exposed pitiful little breasts and tempted passersby with obscene gestures which, coming from those children, were a tragic pantomime. Tao Chi'en had seen them many times; he walked down that street every day and the mewing of the "singsong" girls pursued him, reminding him of his sister. What had happened to her? She would be twenty-three now, in the unlikely case that she was still alive, he thought. The poorest among the poor prostitutes began very early and rarely lived to be eighteen; by twenty, if they'd had the bad fortune to survive, they were ancient. The memory of that missing sister kept him from going to Chinese whorehouses; if he was maddened with desire, he sought out women of other races. The door was opened by a sinister-looking old woman with dyed black hair and eyebrows drawn with charcoal pencil, who greeted him in Cantonese. Once it was established that they belonged to the same tong, he was led inside. All the length of an evil-smelling corridor he saw the girls' cubicles; some were chained by an ankle to the bed. In the darkness of the hall he met two men adjusting their trousers as they left. The woman led him through a labyrinth of passages and stairways that covered an entire block before they descended rickety stairs into darkness. She indicated that Tao Chi'en should wait, and for a time that seemed interminable he waited in the blackness of that hole, listening to the muted noises of the nearby street. He heard a faint screech and something brushed his ankle; he kicked out and thought he had hit the creature, maybe a rat. The old woman returned with a candle and guided him through more twisting passageways until they came to a padlocked door. She took a key from a pocket and struggled with the lock until it opened. She held the candle high, lighting a windowless room in which the only piece of furniture was a board pallet a few inches above the ground. A wave of fetid odors struck them in the face and they had to cover nose and mouth in order to go in. On that platform were a small, cramped body, an empty bowl, and a burned-out oil lamp.

"Check her," the crone ordered.

Tao Chi'en turned the body over to find that it was already stiff. It was a child of about thirteen, with two circles of rouge on her checks and scars on her arms and legs. Her only clothing was a thin blouse. It was obvious she was nothing but bones, but she had not died of hunger or illness.

"Poison," he determined without hesitation.

"You don't say." The woman laughed as if she had heard something very funny.

Tao Chi'en had to sign a paper stating that the death was due to natural causes. The old woman stepped out into the corridor, banged a small gong twice, and a man promptly appeared, stuffed the body in a bag, slung it over his shoulder, and bore it off without a word as the procuress placed twenty dollars in the hands of the *zhong yi*. Then she led him through new labyrinths and left him finally before a door. It was to a different street, and it took Tao Chi'en a long time to find his way back to where he lived.

The next day he returned to the same address. Again there were the girls with rouged faces and crazed eyes, calling out in two languages. Ten years ago, in Canton, he had begun his practice of medicine with prostitutes; he had used them as rented flesh and to practice with his master's gold acupuncture needles, but he had never paused to think about their souls. He thought of them as one of the universe's misfortunes, yet another of the errors of creation, beings who suffered ignominy to pay for offenses in former lives and improve their karma. He felt sorry for them, but it never occurred to him that their fate might be modified. They awaited disaster in their cribs, exactly as a chicken in its coop in the market: that was their destiny. That was the anarchy of the world. He had walked down that street a hundred times without focusing on those small windows, on those faces behind the bars or the beckoning hands. He had some vague notion that they were slaves, but in China more or less all women were slaves; the most fortunate served fathers, husbands, or lovers, others, employers for whom they labored from dawn to dusk, and many were like these girls. That morning, however, he did not see them with the same indifference because something in him had changed.

He had not tried to sleep the night before. After he left the brothel he had gone to a public bath where he soaked for a long time to rid himself of the dark energy of his sick patients and the deep repulsion oppressing him. When he got to his office he sent his assistant home and brewed jasmine tea to purify himself. He had not eaten in many hours, but it was not the moment for food. He took off his clothes, lighted incense and a candle, knelt with his forehead to the ground, and said a prayer for the soul of the dead girl. Then he sat in meditation for hours, in total immobility, until he was able to isolate himself from the noise of the street and the odors of the restaurant and sink into the void and silence of his own spirit. He did not know how long he sat, absorbed, calling, calling Lin, until finally the delicate ghost heard him in the mysterious reaches she inhabited and slowly found her way, moving toward him with the lightness of a sigh, first nearly imperceptible but gradually more substantial, until he clearly felt her presence. He did not see Lin inside the room but, rather, in his bosom, in the very core of his tranquil heart. Tao Chi'en did not open his eyes, or move. For hours he sat in the same posture, separated from his body, floating in a luminous space in perfect communication with Lin. At dawn, once both were sure they would not lose one another again, Lin softly said good-bye. Then the acupuncture master had come, smiling and ironic as he had been in his best days, before he was beat down by the delirium of senility, and stayed with Tao, keeping him company and answering his questions until the sun rose, the neighborhood awoke, and he heard the discreet taps of his assistant at the door. Tao Chi'en got up, refreshed and renewed, as if after a peaceful sleep, dressed, and went to open the door.

"Close the office. I will not attend patients today, I have other things to do," he announced to his assistant.

The investigations of that day changed the course of Tao Chi'en's destiny. The girls behind the bars had come from China, picked up in the street or sold by their own fathers with the promise that they were going to the Golden Mountain to be married. Brokers selected the strongest and cheapest among them, not the most beautiful, unless it was a matter of a special order by wealthy clients who acquired them as concubines. Ah Toy, the clever woman who had invented the spectacle of the voyeuristic holes in the wall, had become the city's major importer of young flesh. For her chain of establishments she bought girls at the age of puberty because they were easy to tame and, after all, none lasted very long anyway. She was becoming famous and very rich; her coffers were overflowing and she had bought a palace in China where she planned to retire in her old age. She prided herself on being the Oriental madam with the best connections not only among Chinese but also influential Americans. She trained her girls to gather information, and so learned the personal secrets, political deals, and weaknesses of men who had power. If bribery failed, she had recourse to blackmail. No one dared defy her because everyone from the governor down lived in a glass house. Shipments of slaves came through the docks of San Francisco with no legal tie-ups and in full light of day. Ah Toy, however, was not the only trafficker; that vice was one of the most profitable and secure business dealings in California, as golden as the mines. Expenses were minimal, the girls were cheap, and they were transported in the holds of ships in large padded crates. They lived for weeks without knowing where they were going, or why; they saw daylight only when they were given lessons in their calling. During the crossing the sailors made it their business to train them, and by the time they got off the ship in San Francisco they had lost the last trace of innocence. Some died of dysentery, cholera, or dehydration; others managed to jump overboard during the minutes they were taken up to the deck to be washed down with saltwater. The rest were trapped; they spoke no English, they did not know that new country, they had no one to turn to. The immigration agents took bribes, turned a blind eye to the girls' obvious distress, and signed the false adoption or marriage papers without reading them. Newcomers were met at the dock by an old prostitute whose heart had turned to black stone. She herded them with a cane, like cattle, right through the center of the city, in plain view of anyone who wanted to look. The minute they crossed into Chinatown they disappeared forever in the subterranean labyrinth of dark rooms, false corridors, twisting stairs, hidden doors, and double walls where police never ventured because everything that happened there, they said, was the business of the Chinks, a yellow race of perverts with whom it was best not to meddle.

In an enormous below-street-level area ironically called "The Queen's Room," the girls confronted their fate. They were allowed one night's rest; they were bathed, fed, and sometimes forced to drink a cup of liquor to quiet them a little. At the hour of the auction, they were taken naked into a room crowded with buyers of every conceivable ilk who felt them, checked their teeth, put their fingers anywhere they pleased, and finally made their offers. Some girls were sold to high-class bordellos or the harems of the rich; the strongest often ended up with factory owners, miners, or Chinese farmers, where they worked for the remainder of their brief existences. Most stayed in the cribs of Chinatown. Old whores taught them their duties; they learned to tell brass from gold, so they would not be cheated, to attract clients and please them without complaint, however humiliating or painful their demands. To give the transaction an air of legality, the girls signed a contract, which they couldn't read, selling themselves for five years, but it was craftily calculated to ensure that they would never be free. For every day they were sick, two weeks were added to their time of service, and if they attempted to escape they were enslaved for life. They lived crammed into unventilated rooms divided by heavy curtains, laboring like galley slaves until they died. It was there Tao Chi'en went that morning, accompanied by the spirits of Lin and his acupuncture master. An adolescent scantily clad in a smock led him to a filthy straw mattress behind a curtain, held out her hand, and asked him to pay first. She took his six dollars, lay down on her back and spread her legs, her eyes fixed on the ceiling. Her pupils were dull and she was breathing with difficulty; he realized she was drugged. He sat beside her, pulled down her smock, and tried to stroke her head, but she screamed and bared her teeth, ready to bite him. Tao Chi'en moved away; he spoke to her a long time in Cantonese, without touching her, observing recent bruises, until the litany of his voice calmed her. Finally she began to answer his questions, more with gestures than words, as if she had lost the use of language, and he learned some details of her captivity. She could not tell him how long she had been there because counting days was a futile exercise, although it could not have been long since she still remembered her family in China with heartrending precision.

When Tao Chi'en estimated that his time behind the curtain was used up, he left. The same old woman who had received him the night before was waiting at the door but she gave no sign of recognizing him. From there Tao went to ask questions in saloons, gambling halls, opium parlors, and then visited other physicians in the quarter, until little by little he fit together the pieces of that puzzle. When the little singsong girls were too sick to keep working, they were taken to the "hospital," as they called the secret rooms he had seen the previous night, and left there with a cup of water, a little rice, and a lamp with oil enough for a few hours. The door was opened again a few days later when someone went in to be sure the girl was dead. If she was alive, she was killed; none ever saw sunlight again. Tao Chi'en had been called only because the usual *zhong yi* hadn't been available.

The idea of helping the girls wasn't his, he would tell Eliza nine months later, but Lin's and the acupuncture master's.

"California is a free state, Tao. Slavery is outlawed. Go to the American authorities."

"Not everyone enjoys freedom. White people are blind and deaf, Eliza. Those girls are invisible, like the insane and beggars and dogs."

"And the Chinese don't care about them?"

"Some do, like me, but no one is willing to risk his life defying the criminal tongs. Most people believe that if things have been run that way for centuries in China, there is no reason to criticize what goes on here."

"But that's very cruel!"

"It isn't cruelty. It's just that human life is not valued in my country. There are many, many people, and there are always more children than the family can feed."

"But in your mind those girls aren't garbage, Tao . . ."

"No. Lin and you have taught me a lot about women."

"What are you going to do?"

"I should have listened when you told me to come look for gold, you remember? If I were wealthy, I would buy them."

"But you aren't. Besides, all the gold in California wouldn't be enough to buy every one of them. You have to stop the traffic."

"That's impossible, but I can save a few if you help me."

Tao told Eliza that in recent months he had rescued eleven girls, but only two had survived. His formula was risky, and not very effective, but he couldn't think of another way. He had offered to treat the girls without charge when they were sick or got pregnant if in exchange they would hand over the dying girls to him. He bribed the old whores to call him when it was time to send a singsong girl to the "hospital"; he and his assistant would go to the brothel, load the dying girl onto a stretcher, and take her away. "For experiments," Tao Chi'en explained, although he was rarely questioned. The girl wasn't worth anything anymore, and this doctor's extravagant perversion saved the management the problem of getting rid of her. The transaction benefited both parties. Before taking the sick girl Tao Chi'en would hand them a death certificate and ask for the contract she had signed so there would be no claims. In nine instances, the girls were beyond help, and Tao's role was simply to be with them in their last hours, but two had lived.

"What did you do with them?" asked Eliza.

"I have them in my room. They are still weak, and one seems half crazy, but they will get well. My assistant stayed to look after them while I came to find you."

"I see."

"I can't keep them cooped up any longer."

"Maybe we can send them back to their families in China."

"No! They'll go right back to being slaves. They can be saved in this country, I just don't know how."

"If the authorities won't help you, good people will. We'll go to the churches and the missionaries."

"I don't think Christians are going to care about these Chinese girls."

"How little you trust the human heart, Tao!"

Eliza left her friend drinking tea with Joe Bonecrusher, wrapped up a loaf of freshly baked bread, and went to visit the blacksmith. She found James Morton at the anvil, sweating, naked from the waist up, wearing a leather apron and a kerchief tied around his forehead. The heat was unbearable and the place smelled of smoke and candescent metal. The forge was a large wood building with a dirt floor and a double door that was left open winter and summer during work hours. At the front was a large table for conducting business with customers, and behind it, the anvil. The instruments of Morton's trade hung from walls and roof beams, tools and wrought iron fashioned by Morton. At the rear, a ladder gave access to a loft that served as a bedroom, protected from the customer's eyes by an oilcloth curtain. The space below the loft was furnished with a tub for bathing and a table and two chairs; the only decorations were an American flag on the wall and three wildflowers in a vase on the table. Esther was ironing a mountain of clothes, her enormous belly bobbing and sweat pouring, but she was singing as she wielded the heavy irons. Love and pregnancy had made her beautiful, and peace lighted her like a halo. She took in washing, work as arduous as her husband's with his anvil and hammer. Three times a week she loaded a cart with dirty clothes, went to the river, and spent a good part of the day on her knees, soaping and scrubbing. If the sun was shining she dried the clothes on the rocks, but often she had to bring everything back wet. Then came the chore of starching and ironing. James Morton had not been able to persuade her to stop that brutal work; she did not want the baby to be born where they were and was saving every cent to move their family to a house in town.

"Chile Boy!" she cried, and welcomed Eliza with a hug. "It's been a long time since you came to visit."

"How pretty you're looking, Esther! I've really come to see James," she said, handing her friend the bread.

The man put down his tools, mopped sweat with his kerchief, and led Eliza to the backyard, where Esther joined them with three glasses of lemonade. The afternoon was cool and the sky cloudy but there were no signs of winter. The breeze bore the scent of newly mown hay and damp earth.

Joaquín

In the winter of 1852, the residents of northern California ate peaches, apricots, grapes, sweet corn, watermelon, and cantaloupe while in New York, Washington, Boston, and other important American cities people resigned themselves to seasonal scarcities. Paulina's ships brought from Chile the delights of the Southern Hemisphere's summer, which arrived unblemished in their beds of blue ice. Her business was doing much better than her husband's and brother-in-law's gold, even though they no longer got three dollars for a peach or ten for a dozen eggs. The Chilean peasants the Rodríguez de Santa Cruz brothers had working at their placers had been nearly wiped out by Yanquis who had appropriated the fruit of months of work, hanged the overseers, horsewhipped and cut off the ears of several men, and run off the rest. That episode had been published in the newspapers, but the Santa Cruz family learned the hair-raising details from an eight-year-old boy, the son of one of the overseers, who had seen the white men torture and kill his father. Paulina's ships also carried theater companies from London, opera from Milan, and musical theater from Madrid, companies that played for a short while in Valparaíso and then continued north. Tickets were sold months in advance, and on performance days San Francisco's best society, in gala finery, attended theaters where they sat beside rustic miners in work clothes. Ships did not return empty: they carried American flour, and passengers cured of the fantasy of gold returning to Chile as poor as they had left.

In San Francisco one saw everything but old people; the population was young, strong, noisy, and brimming with health. Gold had attracted a legion of twenty-year-old adventurers but the fever had passed. However, as Paulina had predicted, the city did not turn back into a wide spot in the road; on the contrary, it kept growing, with aspirations to refinement and culture. Paulina was in her element in that ambience; she liked the openness, the freedom, and the ostentation of that young society, exactly the opposite of the hypocrisy of Chile. She gloried in the thought of how her father would rage if he had to sit down at the table with a corrupt upstart become a judge, or a Frenchwoman of dubious past decked out like an empress. She had grown up within the thick stucco walls and grillwork windows of her paternal home, looking toward the past, dependent on divine punishment and the opinion of others. In California neither past nor scruples counted; eccentricity was welcomed and guilt did not exist as long as the offense remained hidden. Paulina wrote her sisters, with little hope that her letters would get past her father's censorship, to tell them about this extraordinary country where it was possible to invent a new life and become a millionaire or a beggar in the wink of an eye. It was the land of opportunity, open and generous. Through the Golden Gate came masses of beings escaping poverty or violence, hoping to find work and erase the past. It wasn't easy, but their descendants would be Americans. The marvel of this country was that everyone believed their children would have a better life than theirs. "Agriculture is the true gold of California. Farther than you can see are vast, sown fields; everything grows luxuriantly in this blessed soil. San Francisco has become a great city but it has not lost the character of a frontier outpost, and that enchants me. It is still the cradle of freethinkers, visionaries, heroes, and ruffians. People come from the most remote shores; you hear a hundred languages in the street, smell the food of five continents, see every race," she wrote. No longer a camp of solitary men, women had arrived, and with them society changed. They were as indomitable as the adventurers who came looking for gold; crossing the continent in oxcarts required a robust spirit, and these pioneer women had it. No namby-pambies like her mother and sisters; here Amazons like herself reigned. Day by day they proved their mettle, competing tirelessly and tenaciously with the hardiest men; no one called them the weaker sex, men respected them as equals. They worked in jobs forbidden to them elsewhere: they prospected for gold, worked as cowgirls, drove mules, tracked outlaws for bounty, managed gambling halls, restaurants, laundries, and hotels. "Here women can own land, buy and sell property, get divorced if they feel like it. Feliciano has to walk a fine line because the first thing he tries to get away with, I will leave him, all alone and poor," Paulina joked in her letters. And she added that California had the best of the worst: rats, fleas, weapons, and vices.

"People come west to escape the past and begin anew, but our obsessions pursue us, like the wind," Jacob Freemont wrote in a newspaper article. He himself was a good example, because changing his name, becoming a reporter, and dressing like an American had had little effect; he was the same man. The fraud of the missions in Valparaíso was behind him but now he was devising another, and he felt, as before, that his creation was taking over and he was irrevocably sinking into his own weaknesses. His articles on Joaquín Murieta had become the hottest item in the press. Every day came new testimonials confirming what he had written; dozens of individuals swore they had seen Murieta and described him exactly as the character Freemont had invented. He wasn't sure of anything anymore. He wished he had never written those stories, and at moments was tempted to retract them publicly, confess his lies, and disappear before the whole affair exploded and blew him to hell, as had happened in Chile, but he didn't have the courage to follow through. His prestige had gone to his head and he was dizzied by fame.

The story Jacob Freemont had been spinning had the earmarks of a dime novel. He wrote that Joaquín Murieta had been an upright, noble young man working honorably in the placers in Stanislaus, accompanied by the girl he was going to marry. When they learned of his prosperity, some Americans had attacked him, stolen his gold, beat him, and then raped his sweetheart before his eyes. There was nothing left for the unfortunate pair but to flee, and they set out for the north, far from the gold fields. They settled down as farmers, and cultivated an idyllic bit of land surrounded by forests and fed by a limpid stream, Freemont wrote, but they were not to find peace there, either, because once again Yanquis came and took what was his; the couple would have to find another way to survive. Shortly afterward Murieta showed up in Calaveras, dealing at monte while his bride prepared their wedding party in the home of her parents in Sonora. It was in the stars, however, that this man would never find tranquility anywhere. He was accused of stealing a horse, and without further ado a group of Yanquis tied him to a tree and savagely lashed him in the town square. That public humiliation was more than a proud young Latino could bear, and his heart turned cold. It wasn't long before the body of a white man was found cut up in pieces like a hen for a stew, and once his parts were put back together they recognized one of the men who had shamed Murieta with the horsewhipping. In the following weeks all the other participants fell one by one, each tortured and killed in some novel way. Just as Jacob Freemont wrote in his articles: never had such cruelty been seen in a land of cruel men. In the next two years the name of the outlaw cropped up everywhere. His gang stole cattle and horses, ambushed stagecoaches, attacked miners in the placers and travelers on the road, defied the constables, killed any careless American they came upon, and openly mocked the law. Every unpunished crime and excess in California was attributed to Murieta. The terrain lent itself to disappearing; there were plenty of fish and game to be had in its hills and valleys and rivers and woods; a horseman could ride for hours through the high grass without leaving a trail, and it had deep caves to take shelter in, secret mountain passes where a man could throw off pursuers. The posses that rode out to capture the wrongdoers returned empty-handed, or died in their attempt. All this Jacob Freemont described with florid rhetoric, and no one thought to ask for names, dates, or places.

Eliza Sommers worked for two years in San Francisco at Tao Chi'en's side. During that time, she left twice, during the summers, to search for Joaquín Andieta, following the same procedure she had used before: joining other travelers. The first time she went with the idea of looking until she found Andieta or until winter began, but after four months she returned, exhausted and ill. In the summer of 1852 she started out again, but after retracing the route she had followed previously, and later visiting Joe Bonecrusher, now thoroughly immersed in her role as Tom No-Tribe's grandmother, and James and Esther, who were expecting their second child, she had returned home after five weeks because she couldn't stand the anguish of being away from Tao Chi'en. They were so comfortable in their routines, paired in their work and as close in spirit as an old married couple. She collected everything published about Joaquín Murieta and memorized it, as she had Miss Rose's poems when a little girl, although she tried to ignore the references to the outlaw's sweetheart. "They invented that girl to sell newspapers; you know how the public is fascinated by romance," she argued to Tao Chi'en. On a brittle map she tracked Murieta's steps with the determination of a navigator, but the available information was vague and contradictory: routes crisscrossed like the web of a demented spider, leading nowhere. Although at first she had rejected the possibility that her Joaquín was the one responsible for the bloodcurdling attacks, she soon was convinced that that person jibed perfectly with the young man she remembered. He, too, had rebelled against abuses and was obsessed with helping the downtrodden. Maybe it wasn't Joaquín Murieta who tortured his victims but his gang, someone like that Three-Finger Jack, whom she believed capable of any atrocity.

She kept wearing men's clothing because it contributed to the invisibility so necessary in the quixotic mission Tao Chi'en had enrolled her in. It had been three and a half years since she had worn a dress, and she'd had no news of Miss Rose, Mama Fresia, or her uncle John; it seemed a thousand years that she had been chasing an increasingly improbable chimera. The days of the furtive embraces with her lover were long behind her; she wasn't sure of her feelings and she didn't know whether it was love or pride that was driving her to wait for him. She was so caught up in her work that sometimes whole weeks went by without her remembering him, but suddenly a memory would lunge out at her and leave her trembling. Then she would look around her, confused, unable to identify the world in which she found herself. What was she doing wearing trousers and surrounded by Chinese? She had to make an effort to shake off the confusion and remember that she was there because of the intransigence of love. Her mission was not to be helping Tao Chi'en, she would think, but to search for Joaquín; that was why she had come so far, and look for him she would, even if it was just to tell him face-to-face that he was a damned deserter and he had ruined her youth. That was her reason for having set out three times before; she lacked the will, however, to start again. She had gone to Tao Chi'en to announce her determination to take up her pilgrimage but the words stuck like sand in her throat. She could not abandon this strange companion fate had sent her way.

"What will you do if you find him?" Tao Chi'en had asked her once.

"When I see him I will know whether I still love him."

"And if you never find him?"

"I will live with that doubt, I suppose."

Eliza had noticed a few premature gray hairs at her friend's temples. At times the temptation to bury her fingers in that thick black hair, or her nose in his neck to get the full effect of his ocean scent, was unbearable, but now she did not have the excuse of sleeping on the ground rolled up in a blanket, and opportunities to touch one another were nonexistent. Tao was working and studying too hard; she could tell how tired he must be although he was always impeccably groomed, and kept his calm in even the most trying moments. He faltered only when he came back from a sale leading a terrified girl by the arm. He would examine her to see what condition she was in and hand her over to Eliza with necessary instructions, then lock himself in his room for hours. "He is with Lin," Eliza would conclude, and an inexplicable pain would imbed itself deep in a hidden corner of her heart. In truth, he was. In the silence of his meditation, Tao Chi'en would try to recover his lost aplomb and rid himself of the temptation of hatred and anger. Gradually, memories, desires, and thoughts would slip away, until he felt his body dissolving into nothingness. For a time, he ceased to exist, until he reemerged transformed into an eagle, soaring effortlessly, borne by cold, limpid air that lifted him above the highest mountains. From there he could look down on vast prairies, endless forests, and rivers of pure silver. Then he knew perfect harmony, like a fine instrument resonating with the heavens and the earth. Floating among milky clouds, superb wings outstretched, he suddenly would feel Lin with him. She materialized at his side, another splendid eagle suspended in the infinite heavens.

"Where is your joy, Tao?" she asked.

"The world is filled with suffering, Lin."

"Suffering fulfills a spiritual purpose."

"This is merely useless sorrow."

"Remember that the sage is always joyful because he accepts reality."

"And evil, must he accept that, too?"

"The only antidote is love. And, incidentally . . . when will you marry again?"

"I am married to you."

"I am a ghost. I cannot visit you your whole lifetime, Tao. It is very difficult to come when you call me; I do not belong in your world any longer. Marry, or you will be an old man before your time. Besides, if you do not practice the two hundred twenty-two positions of love, you will forget them," she teased with her unforgettable crystalline laugh.

The auctions were much worse that his visits to the "hospital." There was very little hope of helping the dying girls, and if that happened it was a miraculous gift; on the other hand, he knew that for every girl he bought, dozens were condemned to infamy. He would torture himself imagining how many he could rescue if he were wealthy, until Eliza reminded him of the ones he had saved. The two of them were joined by a delicate web of affinities and shared secrets, but also separated by mutual obsessions. The ghost of Joaquín Andieta was fading; in contrast, Lin's spirit was as detectable as the breeze or the sound of waves on the shore. All Tao Chi'en had to do was summon her and she came, always smiling, as she had been in her lifetime. Far from being Eliza's rival, however, she had become her ally, although Eliza never knew that. Lin was the first to realize that Eliza and Tao's friendship was closer to love, and when her husband rebutted that there was no place in China or in Chile for a couple like them, she always laughed.

"Do not say foolish things; the world is large and life is long. It is all a question of taking a chance."

"You cannot imagine what racism is like, Lin; you always lived among your own kind. Here no one cares what I do or what I know; to white people I am just a revolting Chinese pagan, and Eliza is a greaser. In Chinatown I am a renegade without a queue who dresses like an American. I don't belong anywhere."

"Racism is nothing new. In China you and I believed that the *fan wey* were all savages."

"Here the only thing they respect is money, and apparently I will never have enough."

"You are mistaken. They also respect the person who commands respect. Look in their eyes."

"If I follow your advice, I'll be shot at the first street corner."

"It's worth the chance to try. You complain too much, Tao, I cannot recognize you. Where is the courageous man I love?"

Tao Chi'en had to admit that he felt bound to Eliza by countless fine threads, each easily cut but when twisted together forming strands like steel. They had known each other only a few years but they could look to the past and see the obstacle-filled road they had traveled together. Their similarities had erased differences of race. "You look like a pretty Chinese girl," Tao had said in an unguarded moment. "You have the face of a handsome Chilean," she had immediately answered. They were a strange pair in the quarter: a tall, elegant Chinese man with an insignificant Spanish boy. Outside Chinatown, however, they were nearly invisible in the multifaceted throngs of San Francisco.

"You cannot wait for that man forever, Eliza. It is a form of madness, like gold fever. You must set a deadline," Tao said one day.

"And what do I do with my life when the time is up?"

"You can go back to your country."

"In Chile a woman like me is worse off than one of your singsong girls. Would you go back to China?"

"That was my intention, but I am beginning to like America. There I would be Fourth Son again. I'm better off here."

"So am I. If I don't find Joaquín, I'll stay here and open a restaurant. I have everything I need: a good memory for recipes, love of the ingredients, a good sense of taste and touch, an instinct for seasonings . . ."

"And modesty, too." Tao Chi'en laughed.

"Why should I be modest about my talent? Besides, I have a nose like a hound. A good nose should be worth something; all I have to do is smell a dish to know what's in it, and how to make it better."

"You can't do that with Chinese cooking."

"You eat such strange things, Tao! Mine would be a French restaurant, the best in the city."

"I will make you a deal, Eliza. If within one year you do not find this Joaquín, marry me," said Tao Chi'en, and both burst out laughing.

After that conversation, something changed between them. They felt uncomfortable when they were alone, and although alone was what they wanted to be, they began to avoid it. The longing to follow Eliza when she went to her room often tortured Tao Chi'en, but he was stopped short by a blend of shyness and respect. He felt that as long as Eliza was clinging to the memory of her former lover he should not go near her, but neither could he continue to walk a tightrope indefinitely. He imagined her in her bed, counting the hours in the expectant silence of the night, she, too, sleepless with love, but for another, not him. He knew her body so well that he could sketch it in detail, down to the most secret mole, even though he had not seen her naked since the days he had looked after her on the ship. He daydreamed that if she fell ill he would have an excuse to touch her, but then he was ashamed at the thought. The spontaneous laughter and quiet tenderness that had used to bubble up between them was now replaced with oppressive tension. If they brushed against each other by accident they pulled back, embarrassed; each was aware of the other's presence or absence, the air seemed laden with presages and anticipation. Instead of sitting down to read or write in quiet companionship, they parted ways as soon as work in the consulting room was finished. Tao Chi'en would visit bedfast patients, meet other *zhong yi* to discuss diagnoses and treatments, or go to his room to study Western medical texts. He hoped to earn a permit to practice medicine legally in California, a project he had confided to no one but Eliza and the spirits of Lin and his acupuncture master. In China a *zhong yi* began as an apprentice and then worked on his own, which was why medicine hadn't changed for centuries but had preserved the same methods and remedies. The difference between a good practitioner and one who was mediocre was that the former had a talent for diagnosing and the gift of using his hands to heal. Western doctors, however, followed a demanding program of study, kept in contact with one another, and were up-to-date on new discoveries; they had laboratories and morgues for experimentation and exposed themselves to the challenge of competition. Science fascinated Tao, but his enthusiasm was not seconded in a community faithful to tradition. He followed all the latest advances and bought every book and magazine he could find on those subjects. His curiosity for modern ways was so great that he had to write his venerable master's adage on the wall: "Knowledge is of little use without wisdom, and there is no wisdom without spirituality." Science isn't everything, Tao repeated to himself, in order not to forget. In any case, he needed American citizenship—very difficult to obtain because of his race, but that was the only way he could remain in that country without being a permanent outsider. And he needed a title; with a title he could earn a lot more. The *fan wey* knew nothing about acupuncture or the herbs used in Asia for centuries; they considered him a kind of witch doctor, and their scorn for other races was so profound that slave owners on southern plantations sent for a veterinarian when a Negro fell ill. They held the same opinion of the Chinese, but there were a few visionary doctors who had traveled, or had read about other cultures, and were interested in Eastern techniques and the thousand drugs in the Oriental pharmacopoeia. Tao kept in touch with Ebanizer Hobbs in England, and both lamented in their letters the great distance that separated them. "Come to London, Dr. Chi'en, and give an acupuncture demonstration to the Royal Medical Society. You will leave them openmouthed, I promise you," Hobbs wrote. He had always said that if they combined their knowledge they would be able to raise the dead.

An Unusual Pair

Several singsong girls died of pneumonia from the winter cold, and Tao Chi'en couldn't save them. Twice he was called while the girls were still alive; he managed to get them home but they died in his arms a few hours later, delirious with fever. By then, the quiet tentacles of his compassion had spread across North America, from San Francisco to New York, from the Río Grande to Canada, but that extraordinary effort was only a grain of salt in an ocean of misery. Things were going well in his practice, and everything he was able to save, or obtained through the charity of a few wealthy patients, went toward buying the youngest girls in the auctions. He was recognized now in that subculture, and had the reputation of being a degenerate. No one had ever seen alive any of the adolescents Tao acquired "for his experiments," as he called them, but no one really cared what happened behind his closed doors. As a *zhong yi* he was the best; as long as he did not create a scandal, and limited himself to the little whores, who were no more than animals, anyway, they left him in peace. In answer to curious questions, Tao Chi'en's loyal assistant, the only person qualified to give information, said only that his employer's mysterious experiments resulted in the exceptional knowledge that was so beneficial for his patients. By that time Tao Chi'en had moved to a fine house on the edge of Chinatown a few blocks from Union Square, where he held his clinic, sold his remedies, and hid the girls until they were able to travel.

Eliza had learned the rudiments of Chinese necessary for communicating on an elementary level; the rest she improvised with pantomime, drawings, and a few words of English. The effort was rewarding; it was much better than posing as the doctor's deaf-mute brother. She could not write or read Chinese but she recognized the medicines by their smell, and as a safeguard she marked the bottles with a code of her own invention. There were always patients waiting for the gold needles, the miraculous herbs, and the comfort of Tao Chi'en's voice. More than one asked himself how that man who was so wise and affable could be the person who collected corpses and child concubines, but as they were not absolutely sure what his vices consisted of, the community respected him. He had no friends, it was true, but neither did he have enemies. His good name spread beyond the confines of Chinatown and some American doctors consulted him when their knowledge was insufficient—always very quietly, for it would have been embarrassing to admit that a "celestial" had anything to teach them. That was how Tao had occasion to treat certain important figures in the city, and to meet the celebrated Ah Toy.

The madam had summoned Tao Chi'en when she heard that he had helped the wife of a judge. She was suffering a rattle like castanets in her lungs, so bad that at times it threatened to choke her. Tao Chi'en's first impulse was to refuse, but principle was overshadowed by his curiosity to see at close hand the legend and her surroundings. In his eyes, she was a viper, his personal enemy. Knowing what Ah Toy represented for Tao, Eliza put enough arsenic in his bag to dispatch a team of oxen.

"Just in case," she explained.

"Just in case *what*?"

"She may be very sick. You wouldn't want her to suffer, would you? Sometimes you have to help someone die."

Tao Chi'en laughed heartily but did not remove the bottle from his satchel. Ah Toy received him in one of the deluxe "retreats" where the client paid a thousand dollars a session but always left satisfied. Besides, she maintained, "If you need to ask the price, this is not the place for you." A Negress in a starched uniform opened the door to Tao and took him through several drawing rooms where beautiful girls in silk robes were lounging. Compared with their less fortunate sisters they lived like princesses; they ate three times a day and had daily baths. The house, a true museum of Oriental antiques and American conveniences, reeked of tobacco, stale perfumes, and dust. It was three in the afternoon but the heavy drapes were drawn; no breeze ever freshened those rooms. Ah Toy was sitting in a small study crammed with furniture and birdcages. She was much smaller, younger, and more beautiful than Tao had imagined. She was carefully made-up but she wore no jewels, was simply dressed, and eschewed the long fingernails that indicated wealth and leisure. His eyes were drawn to her miniscule, sandal-shod feet. Her gaze was penetrating and hard, but she spoke in a caressing tone that reminded Tao of Lin. Damn her, Tao Chi'en sighed, defeated with her first word. He was impassive as he examined her, cloaking his repugnance and agitation, not knowing what to say to her because to lecture her for trafficking was not only futile, it was dangerous and would call attention to his own activities. He prescribed *mahuang* for her asthma and other remedies for cooling her liver, curtly warning her that as long as she lived closed up behind those drapes, smoking tobacco and opium, her lungs would continue to wheeze. The temptation to leave the poison with instructions to take one pinch daily flitted past like a nocturnal butterfly and he shivered, shocked by that instant of doubt, because until then he had believed he would never be angry enough to kill anyone. He left hurriedly, certain that in view of his rudeness, the woman would never call him again.

"Well?" asked Eliza on his return.

"Nothing."

"What do you mean, *nothing*! Not even a little tuberculosis? She won't die?"

"We are all going to die. That snake will die an old woman. She is as strong as a buffalo."

"Most evil people are."

As for Eliza, she knew that she was at a definitive fork in her road and that the direction she chose would determine the rest of her life. Tao Chi'en was right: she had to set a deadline. She couldn't ignore any longer the suspicion that she had fallen in love with love and was trapped in the morass of a legendary passion with no link to reality. She tried to remember the feelings that had driven her to embark on this consuming adventure but she couldn't. The woman she had become had little in common with the moonstruck girl of the past. Valparaíso and the room of the armoires belonged to a different time, to a world that was disappearing in the mist. She asked herself a thousand times why she had hungered so desperately to belong body and soul to Joaquín Andieta when in truth she had never been totally happy in his arms, and could explain it only in terms of first love. She had been ready to fall in love when he came to the house to unload some cargo; the rest was instinct. She had merely obeyed the most powerful and ancient of calls, but it had happened an eternity ago and seven thousand miles away. Who she was then and what she had seen in him she could not say, only that now her heart was far away from there. Not only was she tired of looking for him, but deep down she did not want to find him; at the same time, though, she could not go on riddled with doubts. She needed an ending for that phase in order to begin a new love with a clean slate.

By the end of November her anxiety was too great, and without a word to Tao Chi'en she visited the newspaper office to speak with the famous Jacob Freemont. She was taken to the editorial room where several journalists were working at their desks, surrounded by appalling disorder. They pointed to a small office behind a glass-paned door and she went in. She stood before the desk, waiting for the Yanqui with red sideburns to look up from his papers. He seemed to be about medium height, with freckled skin, and had a faint aroma of candles. He was writing with his left hand and his head was propped on his right; she could not see his face, but then, beneath the scent of beeswax, she perceived a familiar odor that carried a vague, distant, childhood memory. She bent slightly toward him, discreetly sniffing, at the very instant the newspaperman looked up. Surprised, they stared at each other from uncomfortably close quarters, then simultaneously drew back. Eliza recognized him from his scent, despite the years, the eyeglasses, the sideburns, and the American garb. Miss Rose's perennial suitor! The same Englishman who had faithfully attended the Wednesday musicals in Valparaíso. Paralyzed, she could not escape.

"What can I do for you, young fellow?" asked Jacob Todd, removing his eyeglasses to clean them with his handkerchief.

The speech Eliza had prepared was wiped from her brain. She stood with her mouth open, hat in hand, sure that since she had recognized him he would know her; but he carefully fitted his glasses back on and repeated the question without looking at her.

"It's about Joaquín Murieta," she stammered, her voice squeaking higher than usual.

"You have information about that outlaw?" The newspaperman was immediately interested.

"No, no. . . . Just the opposite, I came to ask you about him. I need to see him."

"You remind me of someone, kid. Haven't we met somewhere?"

"I don't think so, señor."

"Are you Chilean?"

"Yes."

"I lived in Chile some years ago. Beautiful country. Why do you want to see Murieta?"

"It's very important."

"I'm afraid I can't help you. No one knows his whereabouts."

"But you have talked with him!"

"Only when Murieta summons me. He gets in touch with me when he wants some episode of his published. Nothing modest about the man, he likes his fame."

"What language do you use when you talk?"

"My Spanish is better than his English."

"Tell me, señor. Is his accent Chilean or Mexican?"

"I couldn't say. I repeat, kid, I can't help you," the journalist replied, standing to indicate the end of the conversation, which was beginning to annoy him.

Eliza quickly said good-bye, and Freemont stood with a quizzical look, watching as she picked her way through the uproar of the editorial room. That boy looked familiar, but he couldn't place him. Several minutes later, after his visitor had vanished, Freemont remembered Captain John Sommers' request and the image of young Eliza flashed through his memory. Then he connected the name of the outlaw with that of Joaquín Andieta and understood why she was asking. He choked back a groan and ran outside, but Eliza had disappeared.

Tao Chi'en and Eliza Sommers did their most important work at night. In the darkness they disposed of the corpses of the poor creatures they couldn't save and took the survivors across the city to their Quaker friends. One by one, girls emerged from hell to leap blindly into an adventure with no return. They lost all hope of returning to China or of seeing their families again; some would never again speak their language or see anyone of their race. They would have to learn a skill and work hard the rest of their lives, but anything was paradise compared to the life they had been living. The girls Tao was able to buy adapted better. They had been caged in large crates and subjected to the lust and brutality of the sailors but they were not completely broken in spirit and had kept some potential for recovery. The less fortunate, who were freed at almost their last breaths from the "hospital," never lost the fear that like a disease in the blood would consume them for the rest of their days. Tao Chi'en hoped that with time they would at least learn to smile occasionally. As soon as they regained strength, and understood that they would never again be forced to submit to a man but would always be refugees, their rescuers took them to the home of abolitionist friends, a station in the underground railroad, the group the blacksmith James Morton and his brothers belonged to. Ordinarily these Quakers took in fugitives from slave states and helped them get established in California, but in this instance they had to operate in the opposite direction, sending Chinese girls from California far away from traffickers and criminal gangs, finding homes for them, and some way to earn a living. The Quakers assumed the risks with religious fervor; for them their charges were innocents soiled by the human baseness placed in their path as a test. They welcomed those waifs so wholeheartedly that they often reacted with violence or terror; they did not know how to accept affection, but the patience of those good people slowly won them over. The girls were taught a few indispensable phrases in English, given an idea of American customs, shown a map to at least give them an idea of where they were, and an effort was made to introduce them to some form of work while they waited for Babalú the Bad to come for them.

That behemoth had at last found a good way to use his talents: he was an indefatigable traveler who loved to stay up all night, and he craved adventure. When they first saw him, the singsong girls would run and hide in terror, and it would take a great deal of persuasion on the part of their protectors to calm them. Babalú had learned a song in Chinese and three magic tricks that he used to bedazzle and to blunt the fright of that first encounter but he had refused to give up his wolf skins, his shaved head, his pirate earrings, or his formidable array of weapons. This kind giant always stayed a couple of days, until he convinced his lambs that he was not a devil and had no intent of eating them, then set off with them by night. Distances were carefully calculated in order to reach the next refuge by dawn, where they would rest during the day. They traveled by horseback; a carriage was useless because a major part of the journey was through open country, avoiding the main roads. They had discovered that it was much safer to travel in darkness, as long as they knew where they were, because bears, snakes, highwaymen, and Indians slept like everyone else. Babalú would leave the girls safe in the hands of other members of the vast network of freedom. They ended up on farms in Oregon, laundries in Canada, and craft studios in Mexico; some were hired as family servants and some were even wed. Tao Chi'en and Eliza often received news through James Morton, who kept track of every fugitive rescued by his organization. From time to time they would receive an envelope from some distant spot and when they opened it find a paper with a poorly written name, a few dried flowers or a drawing, and then congratulate themselves on having saved another of the singsong girls.

Occasionally Eliza shared her room for a few days with a newly rescued girl but she never revealed that she was a woman, something only Tao knew. She had a spacious room behind her friend's consulting office, the best in the house. Its two windows looked out on a small inner patio where medicinal plants for Tao's practice and aromatic herbs for the kitchen were grown. They often fantasized about moving to a larger house where they would have a proper garden, not merely for practical purposes but also for pleasuring their eyes and memories, a place where they would cultivate the most beautiful plants from China and Chile and construct a pergola where they would sit and drink tea in the evening and in the early morning admire the sunrise over the bay. Tao Chi'en had noticed Eliza's diligence in beautifying the house, the care with which she cleaned and organized, how she always kept small bouquets of fresh flowers in every room. He had never enjoyed such refinements; he had grown up in total poverty, and the acupuncture master's mansion had lacked a woman's hand to make it homelike. Lin had been too fragile to have strength for domestic tasks. Eliza, on the other hand, like a bird, had the instinct to nest. She invested in the house part of what she earned by playing the piano a couple of nights a week in a saloon, and by selling meat pies and tarts in the Chilean barrio. She had contributed curtains, a damask tablecloth, kitchen utensils, and a set of fine china. For Eliza, the good manners she had learned as a child were essential; she made a ceremony of the one meal she and Tao shared each day; she set a beautiful table and blushed with satisfaction when Tao applauded her efforts. The everyday chores seemed to do themselves, as if by night generous spirits cleaned the doctor's office, brought the records up to date, tiptoed into Tao Chi'en's room to gather his dirty clothes, sew on his buttons, brush his suits, and change the water in the roses on his desk.

"Don't drown me with attentions, Eliza."

"You said that Chinese men expect women to serve them."

"That is in China, but I never had that good fortune. You're spoiling me."

"I was trying to. Miss Rose said that to be a man's master you have to let him get used to living well, and then when he misbehaves you withdraw your favors."

"But wasn't Miss Rose a spinster?"

"By choice, not lack of opportunities."

"I am not planning to misbehave, but how will I manage on my own after you leave?"

"You won't have to. You're not at all bad-looking, and there will always be some bad-natured woman with big feet ready to marry you," she replied, and he laughed with delight.

Tao had bought beautiful furniture for Eliza's room, the only one in the house decorated with some luxury. Walking together through Chinatown, Eliza often admired traditional Chinese furniture. "It's very handsome, but heavy. The mistake is to use too much of it," she said. He gave her a bed and armoire of dark, carved wood, and then she chose a table, chairs, and bamboo screen. She did not want a silk spread, like the ones used in China, but something more European: white embroidered linen with large pillowcases of the same fabric.

"Are you sure you want to spend that much, Tao?"

"You are thinking of the singsong girls . . . ?"

"Yes."

"You yourself told me that there wasn't enough gold in California to buy them all. Don't worry, we have enough."

Eliza repaid him in a thousand subtle ways: by respecting his silence and hours of study, by helping him in the consulting office, with her bravery in the work of rescuing the girls. To Tao Chi'en, nevertheless, her best gift was her irrepressible optimism, which forced him to fight back when shadows threatened to envelop him completely. "If you go around so sad, you won't have the strength to help anyone. Let's go take a walk, you need to smell the forest. Chinatown smells of soy sauce," and she would take him by carriage to the outskirts of the city. They would spend the day in the open air, romping like children, and that night he would sleep like an angel and awake vigorous and happy.

Captain John Sommers anchored in the port of Valparaíso on March 15, 1853, exhausted by his voyage and the demands of his employer, whose most recent whim was to tow a whaling-ship-size slab of glacier from southern Chile. Her current idea was to make sorbets and ices to sell, since the price of fresh vegetables and fruit had declined sharply once agriculture had begun to prosper in California. Gold had attracted a quarter of a million immigrants in four years' time but the bonanza had passed. Even so, Paulina Rodríguez de Santa Cruz did not plan ever to leave San Francisco. In her fiery heart she had adopted that city of heroic immigrants where still there were no social classes. She had personally supervised the construction of their future home, a mansion at the top of Nob Hill with the best view of the bay, but she was expecting their fourth child and wanted it to be born in Valparaíso, where her mother and sisters could coddle her sinfully. Her father had suffered an opportune stroke, which left half his body paralyzed and his brain softened. Infirmity had not changed the character of Agustín del Valle but he feared death and, naturally, hell. Setting off for the other world with a string of mortal sins behind him was not a good idea, his relative, the bishop, had repeated ad nauseum. Of the womanizer and hellraiser he had been, nothing remained—not out of repentance but because his battered body was no longer capable of such deviltry. He heard mass every day in the chapel of his home and stoically bore the reading of the Gospel and the countless rosaries his wife recited. None of those things, however, made him any more benign toward his tenants and employees. He was still a despot to his family and the rest of the world, but part of his conversion was a sudden and inexplicable love for Paulina, the daughter who had left home. He forgot that he had repudiated her when she had run away from the convent to marry "that Jew boy" whose name he could never remember because the family wasn't of his class. He wrote Paulina calling her his favorite, the only child who had inherited his temperament and his vision for business, begging her to come home because her poor papa wanted to hug her before he died. Is that old tyrant really sick? a hopeful Paulina asked her sisters in a letter. He was not, actually, and no doubt would live on for years driving everyone crazy from his wheelchair. In any event, it was Captain Sommers' lot to be saddled on his most recent voyage with his employer, her screaming brats, her hopelessly seasick servants, a boatload of trunks, two cows for the children's milk, and the three lapdogs with a French courtesan's ribbons on their ears that had replaced the precious pooch drowned on Paulina's first voyage. To the captain, the trip seemed eternal, and he was terrified at the thought that soon he would have to take Paulina and her circus back to San Francisco. For the first time in his long life as a sailor he considered retiring, to spend the time he had left in this world on dry land. His brother, Jeremy, was waiting on the dock and drove him home, making excuses for Rose, who was suffering from a migraine.

"You know that she is always ill on Eliza's birthday. She has never been the same since the child's death," he explained.

"I wanted to talk to you about that," the captain replied.

Miss Rose had never known how much she loved Eliza until she was gone; the realization of her maternal love had come too late. She blamed herself for the years she had treated Eliza so casually, with an arbitrary and chaotic affection, the times she had completely forgotten her, too caught up in her own frivolities, and when she did remember would find that the child had been in the patio with the hens for a week. Eliza had been the nearest thing to a daughter she would ever have; for nearly sixteen years she had been her best friend, her companion in games, the only person in the world who touched her. Miss Rose ached with pure loneliness. She missed her baths with the child, when they splashed happily in water scented with mint and rosemary. She remembered Eliza's small, skillful hands washing her hair, rubbing her neck, polishing her fingernails with a piece of chamois, helping her dress her hair. At night she would lie awake, her ear cocked for the girl's footsteps as she brought her small glass of anisette. She would have given anything to feel Eliza's good-night kiss on her forehead. Miss Rose had stopped writing, and she had canceled the musical gatherings that had once been the hub of her social life. She had lost her flirtatious spirit and was resigned to growing old ungracefully: "At my age nothing is expected of a woman but to be dignified and smell good," she would say. She had not created a new dress in years; she continued to wear her old ones and had failed to notice that they were out of style. The little sewing room stood abandoned, and even the collection of bonnets and hats languished in their hatboxes because Rose had opted to wear the black mantle of Chilean women when she went out. She spent her time rereading the classics and playing melancholy airs on the piano. As punishment, she deliberately and methodically sank into boredom. Eliza's absence became a good pretext for wearing mourning for the pain and privations of her forty years, especially her lost love. That was like a thorn under her fingernail, a constant, mute sorrow. She regretted having raised Eliza with a lie; she could not imagine why she had invented the story of the basket with the batiste sheets, the improbable mink coverlet and gold coins, when the truth would have been far more comforting. Eliza had a right to know that her adored uncle John was, in fact, her father, and that she and Jeremy were her aunt and uncle, that she belonged to the Sommers family and was not an orphan adopted out of charity. Miss Rose recalled with horror the time she had dragged Eliza down to the orphanage to frighten her. How old would she have been then? Eight or ten, a mere child. If only she could start over; she would be a very different mother. To begin with, she would have sympathized with Eliza when she fell in love instead of opposing her; if she had, her adoptive daughter would be alive, she sighed; it was her fault that Eliza had run away and died. Why hadn't she remembered her own experience, realized that the women of their family were always deranged by their first love? And saddest of all was not having anyone she could talk to about Eliza, because Mama Fresia was gone as well, and her brother Jeremy clenched his lips and stalked off to his room whenever she mentioned the girl. Miss Rose's grief infected everything around her; in the last four years the house had had the heavy air of a mausoleum, and the quality of their meals had deteriorated so badly that she was eating nothing but tea and English biscuits. She had not engaged a decent cook and, in fact, was not seriously looking. She was indifferent to how the house appeared; there were no flowers in the vases and half the plants in the garden were dying for lack of care. For four winters, the flowered summer cretonnes had hung in the parlor because no one had made the effort to change them at the end of the season.

Jeremy never reproached his sister; he ate whatever was put before him and said nothing when his shirts were badly ironed and his suits not brushed. He had read that single women are given to perilous indispositions. In England, a miraculous cure had been developed for hysteria, which was to cauterize certain points with a red-hot iron, but such advances had not yet reached Chile, where holy water was employed for those ills. It was, in any case, a delicate matter, one difficult to mention to Rose. It never occurred to him to comfort her, the habit of discretion and silence between them was very old. He tried to please her with gifts he bought from the contraband off the ships, but he knew nothing about women and came home with monstrosities that soon disappeared into the back of the armoires. He never suspected how many times his sister had crept near when he was smoking in his easy chair, on the verge of collapsing at his feet, resting her head on his knees, and weeping till she could weep no more, but at the last instant she would retrace her steps, fearful, because any word of affection between them would have come out as irony or unpardonable sentimentality. Stiff-backed, morose, Rose kept up appearances out of discipline, with the sensation that nothing but her corset held her together and if she removed it she would break apart. There was no hint of her former merriment and mischievousness, nor of her bold opinions, her rebellious behavior, her impertinent curiosity. She had become what she had most feared: a Victorian spinster. "It's The Change; women of her age become unstable," the German pharmacist diagnosed, and prescribed valerian for her nerves and cod-liver oil for her pallor.

Captain John Sommers joined his brother and sister in the library to tell them the news.

"Do you remember Jacob Todd?"

"The cad who defrauded us with that yarn about missions in Tierra del Fuego?" asked Jeremy Sommers.

"The same."

"He was enamored of Rose, if I recall correctly." Jeremy smiled, gratified that at least they had been spared that prevaricator as a brother-in-law.

"He changed his name. Now he calls himself Jacob Freemont, and he's a newspaperman in San Francisco."

"Egad! So it is true that in the United States any scoundrel may begin a new life?"

"Jacob Todd paid for his offense several times over. I think it is splendid that there is a country where a man can have a second chance."

"And honor means nothing?"

"There are other things besides honor, Jeremy."

"Is there anything else?"

"What do we care about Jacob Todd? I imagine you haven't b-b-brought us here to talk about him, John," Rose stammered from behind her vanilla-perfumed handkerchief.

"I was with Jacob Todd, that is, Freemont, before I sailed. He told me that he saw Eliza in San Francisco."

For the first time in her life, Miss Rose thought she was going to faint. She felt her heart pounding, her temples about to explode, as a wave of blood rushed to her face. She gasped, unable to articulate a word.

"You cannot believe a word the man says! Did you not tell us that a woman swore she had seen Eliza on a ship in 1849, and that she had not the slightest doubt she had died?" rebutted Jeremy Sommers, striding back and forth across the library.

"That's true, but she was a harlot, and she had the turquoise brooch I gave to Eliza. She may have stolen it and lied to protect herself. What reason would Jacob Freemont have to deceive me?"

"None, other than he is a four-flusher by nature."

"That's enough, please," Rose begged, making a colossal effort to get the words out. "The only thing that matters is that someone saw Eliza, that she isn't dead, that we can find her."

"Do not raise your hopes, dear sister. You do not see that this is a pure fantasy? It would be a terrible blow for you if it is proven that this news is in error," Jeremy warned.

John Sommers related the details of the meeting between Jacob Freemont and Eliza, including the information that the girl was dressed as a man and was so at ease in those clothes that the newspaperman had never doubted he was talking with a boy. He added that he and Freemont had gone together to the Chilean barrio to ask about her but they didn't know what name she was using, and no one could, or would, tell them where she was. He explained that Eliza had doubtlessly gone to California to join her lover, but something had gone wrong and they hadn't met, since the purpose of her visit to Jacob Freemont had been to inquire about an outlaw with a similar name.

"It must be Joaquín Andieta. The man is a thief. He decamped to escape the law," Jeremy Sommers sputtered.

It had been impossible to hide the identity of Eliza's lover from him. Miss Rose had had to confess that she often went to see Joaquín Andieta's mother to ask for news, and that the unfortunate woman, poorer and sicker at each visit, was convinced her son was dead. There was no other explanation for his long silence, she maintained. She had received one letter from California dated February 1849, a week after he had arrived there, in which he told her of his plans to leave for the placers and repeated his promise to write her every two weeks. Then nothing more: he had disappeared without further word.

"Does it not seem strange that Jacob Todd would recognize Eliza out of context and dressed as a man?" asked Jeremy Sommers. "When he knew her, she was a child. How long ago was that? At least six or seven years. How could he imagine that Eliza was in California? This is absurd!"

"Three years ago I told him what had happened, and he promised to look for her. I described her in detail, Jeremy. Besides, Eliza's face never changed much. When she left here she still looked like a little girl. Jacob Freemont kept an eye out for a long time, until I told him that she might be dead. Now he has promised to renew his search; he was even thinking of hiring a detective. I expect to have more concrete news on my next voyage."

"Why can we not forget this matter once and for all?" sighed Jeremy.

"Because, brother, she is my daughter, for God's sake!" the captain exclaimed.

"I am going to California to look for Eliza," Miss Rose interrupted, jumping to her feet.

"You are not going anywhere!" her older brother exploded.

But she had already left the room. John's news had been an injection of new blood for Miss Rose. She was absolutely certain she would find her adopted daughter, and for the first time in four years she had a reason to go on living. To her amazement, she found that her old strength was intact, lurking in some secret part of her heart, ready to serve her as it had before. Her headache vanished as if by a charm; she was perspiring, and her cheeks were pink with euphoria when she called the servants to go with her to the room of the armoires to look for suitcases.

In May of 1853 Eliza read in the newspaper that Joaquín Murieta and his follower, Three-Finger Jack, had attacked a camp of six peaceful Chinese, held them by their queues, and slit their throats. Then they had strung the heads from a tree, like a cluster of melons. The roads were ruled by the bandits, no one was safe in the region, everyone had to move about in large, heavily armed groups. The outlaws murdered American miners, French adventurers, Jewish peddlers, and travelers of any race, although usually they did not attack Indians or Mexicans, the Yanquis saw to them. Terrorized settlers bolted doors and windows, men with loaded rifles stood guard, and women hid, because no one wanted to fall into the grasp of Three-Finger Jack. It was said of Murieta, however, that he never abused a woman and that on more than one occasion he had saved a young girl from being brutally ravished by his gang. Inns refused to put up travelers because they feared that one of them might be Murieta. No one had seen him in person, and descriptions varied, although Freemont's articles had created a romantic image of the bandit that most readers accepted as authentic. In Jackson they formed the first group of volunteers charged with hunting down the outlaws; soon there were vigilantes in every town and an unprecedented manhunt was set in motion. No one who spoke Spanish was free of suspicion, and within a few weeks there were more summary lynchings than there had been in the previous four years. Speaking Spanish was enough to make a man a public enemy and to attract the wrath of sheriffs and constables. The final outrage came when Murieta's gang was fleeing a party of American soldiers that was close on their heels and in midflight detoured and attacked a camp of Chinese. Soldiers arrived seconds later to find several men dead and others dying. It was said that Joaquín Murieta was enraged by Asians because they rarely defended themselves, even when they had weapons; the celestials feared him so much that the mere sound of his name threw them into a panic. The most persistent rumor, however, was that Murieta was recruiting an army, and that in partnership with wealthy Mexican ranchers in the area was planning to foment an uprising, stir up the Hispanic population, massacre Americans, and either return California to Mexico or form an independent republic.

In answer to popular demand, the governor signed a decree authorizing Captain Harry Love and a group of twenty volunteers to hunt Joaquín Murieta for a period of three months. They assigned a salary of one hundred and fifty dollars a month to each man—not much considering that they had to provide their own horses, weapons, and provisions, but even so the company was ready for action in less than a week. There was a reward of a thousand dollars on Joaquín Murieta's head. As Jacob Freemont had pointed out in his newspaper, they were condemning a man to death without knowing his identity, without having proved his crimes, and without a trial:

Captain Love's mission was tantamount to a lynching. Eliza felt a mixture of horror and relief that she could not explain. She did not want those men to kill Joaquín, but they might be the only ones capable of finding him: all she wanted was to be sure, she was tired of shadowboxing. At any rate, it was not very likely that Captain Love would be successful where so many others had failed. Joaquín Murieta seemed invincible. The myth was that nothing but a silver bullet could kill him, because two pistols had been emptied point-blank into his chest and he was still galloping up and down Calaveras County.

"If that beast is your lover, you'd be better off never to find him," was Tao Chi'en's comment when Eliza showed him the newspaper cuttings she had collected for more than a year.

"I don't think it's him."

"How do you know?"

In her dreams she saw her former lover in the same worn suit and same threadbare but crisply ironed shirts of the days when they had made love in Valparaíso. He came with his tragic air, his intense eyes, his smell of soap and sweat, took her by the hands as he had then, and spoke feverishly of democracy. Sometimes they lay together on the pile of drapes in the room of the armoires, side by side, without touching, completely dressed, listening to creaking boards lashed by winds from the sea. And always, in every dream, Joaquín had a star of light on his forehead.

"And what does that signify?" Tao Chi'en wanted to know.

"No evil man has light on his forehead."

"It's only a dream, Eliza."

"Not one, Tao, many dreams."

"Then you are looking for the wrong man."

"Maybe, but I haven't wasted my time," she replied without further explanation.

For the first time in four years she was again aware of her body, which had been relegated to an insignificant plane from the moment Joaquín Andieta told her good-bye in Chile on that doleful December 22 in 1848. In her obsession to find the man she had renounced everything, including her femininity. Somewhere along the way she had lost what made her a woman and turned into a strange, asexual creature. Sometimes, riding through woods and hills, exposed to the assault of the winds, she remembered the advice of Miss Rose, who bathed in milk and never allowed a ray of sun to touch her porcelain skin, but Eliza could not brood about such matters. She endured difficulties and punishment because she had no alternative. She considered her body, like her thoughts, her memory, or her sense of smell, an inseparable part of her being. She had never understood what Miss Rose was referring to when she spoke of the soul because she could not differentiate it from the whole of her person, but now she was beginning to get a glimpse of what it was. The soul was the immutable part of her being. The body, in contrast, was the fearsome beast that after years of hibernation was roaring back, filled with demands. It came to remind her of the ardor of the desire she had savored briefly in the room of the armoires. Since that time she had never felt any true urgency for love or physical pleasure, as if that part of herself was in profound, permanent slumber. She attributed that to the pain of having been abandoned by her lover, to the fear of finding herself pregnant, to her journey through the labyrinths of death on the ship, to the trauma of the miscarriage. Her body had been so mistreated that dread of finding herself in that condition again was stronger than the impulses of youth. She felt that she had paid too high a price for love, and that it would be better to avoid it altogether; but something had changed in the last two years she had been with Tao Chi'en, and suddenly love, like desire, seemed inevitable. The obligation to dress like a man was beginning to be a heavy burden. She remembered the little sewing room, where at that very moment Miss Rose must be stitching another of her exquisite dresses, and she was deluged by a wave of nostalgia for those fragile afternoons of her childhood, for five o'clock tea in cups Miss Rose had inherited from her mother, for the outings when they went to buy smuggled fripperies from the ships. And what had become of Mama Fresia? Eliza could see her, grumbling in the kitchen, fat and warm, smelling of sweet basil, always with a wooden spoon in her hand and a pot boiling on the stove, like an affable witch. She yearned for that long-lost female companionship, the sense that she was a woman again. She did not have a large mirror in her room in which to study that feminine being struggling to emerge. She wanted to see herself naked. Some days she awakened at dawn, feverish from impetuous dreams in which the image of Joaquín Andieta with a star on his forehead imposed itself upon visions from the erotic books she used to read aloud to Joe Bonecrusher's doves. In those days she had read with remarkable indifference because the descriptions evoked nothing in her, but now they came like lewd phantoms to haunt her in dreams. Alone in her beautiful room of Chinese furniture, she used the dawn light filtering weakly through the windows to make a rapturous exploration of her body. She took off her pajamas, studied with curiosity the parts of her body she could see, and ran her hands over the rest, as she had in the days she was discovering love. She found that little had changed. She was slimmer, but she also seemed much stronger. Her hands were roughened by sun and work, but the rest of her body was as pale and smooth as she remembered. It amazed her that after being crushed so long beneath a sash that she still had small, firm breasts, with nipples like garbanzos. She let down her hair, which she hadn't cut in four months, and fastened it at the back of her neck, then closed her eyes and shook her head, enjoying the weight and texture of the live animal of its length. She wondered at that nearly unknown woman with curved thighs and hips, small waist, and the curly, springy thatch on her pubis so different from the smooth, silky hair on her head. She lifted an arm to measure its length, appreciate its form, look at her fingernails from a distance; with the other hand she felt along her side, the ripples of her ribs, the hollow of her underarm, the contour of her arm. She paused at the most sensitive points of wrist and inner elbow, wondering whether Tao felt the same tickle at those spots. She caressed her neck, traced the outlines of her ears, the arch of her eyebrows, the line of her lips; she wet a finger in her mouth and then touched it to her nipples, which hardened with the contact of the warm saliva. She ran her hands down her hips to learn their shape, and then sensually, to feel the smoothness of her skin. She sat on her bed and stroked her legs from feet to groin, noticing for the first time the nearly imperceptible golden fuzz on her legs. She parted her thighs and found the mysterious cleft of her sex, soft and moist; she sought the bud of her clitoris, the very center of her desires and confusions, and, as she touched it, immediately came the unexpected vision of Tao Chi'en. It was not Joaquín Andieta, whose face she could barely remember, but her loyal friend who came to fuel her febrile fantasies with an irresistible blend of ardent embraces, gentle tenderness, and shared laughter. Afterward she smelled her hands, awed by the powerful aroma of salt and ripe fruit her body emitted.

Three days after the governor had put a price on the head of Joaquín Murieta, the steamship *Northerner* had anchored in the port of San Francisco carrying two hundred seventy-five sacks of mail and Lola Montez. She was the most famous courtesan in Europe but neither Tao Chi'en nor Eliza had ever heard her name. They were on the dock by accident, there to pick up a box of Chinese medicines brought by a sailor from Shanghai. They thought the reason for the carnival atmosphere was the mail—there had never been such a large number of sacks—but the festive fireworks made them reconsider. In that city accustomed to all manner of wonders a mob of curious men had congregated to see the incomparable Lola Montez, who had traveled across the isthmus of Panama preceded by the throbbing drums of her fame. She was carried from the dinghy in the arms of a pair of lucky sailors who set her on the ground with the reverence due a queen. And that was precisely the attitude of that celebrated Amazon as she accepted the cheers of her admirers. The hubbub caught Eliza and Tao Chi'en unaware; they had no inkling of the beauty's history, but other spectators quickly brought them up to date. Montez was an Irishwoman, a bastard of common stock who passed herself off as a noble Spanish ballerina and actress. She danced like a goose, and had nothing of an actress except excessive vanity, but her name invoked licentious images of great seductresses, from Delilah to Cleopatra, which was why so many delirious crowds went to applaud her. They did not go because of her talent but to witness firsthand her perturbing wickedness, her legendary beauty and fiery temperament. With little craft other than impudence and audacity, she filled theaters, ran through fortunes, collected jewels and lovers, threw epic rages, declared war on Jesuits, and had been thrown out of several cities, but her crowning feat was to have broken a king's heart. Ludwig I of Bavaria had been a good man, parsimonious and prudent, for sixty years, until Lola popped up in his life, worked him over, and left him limp as a straw doll. The monarch had lost his judgment, his health, and his honor, while she emptied the royal coffers of his small kingdom. The besotted Ludwig gave Lola everything she wanted, including the title of countess, but could not get his subjects to accept her. The woman's low habits and outrageous whims provoked the hatred of the citizens of Munich, who finally poured out into the streets to demand that the king's lover be exiled.

Instead of quietly disappearing, Lola met the armed mob with a horsewhip and they would have chopped her to bits had her faithful servants not forcibly stuffed her into a carriage and taken her to the border. Desperate, Ludwig abdicated his throne and prepared to follow her into exile, but stripped of his crown, his power, and his bank account, the beauty found little of interest in him and left the old man flat.

"So her only virtue is her bad reputation," said Tao Chi'en dismissively.

A group of Irishmen unhitched the horses from Lola's carriage, harnessed themselves in place, and pulled her to the hotel through streets carpeted with flower petals. Eliza and Tao Chi'en watched her pass by in a glorious procession.

"That's all this country of madmen needed," sighed the Chinese without a second look at the beautiful Lola.

Eliza followed the carnival for a few blocks, half amused and half admiring, while Roman candles and pistols flashed all around. Lola Montez was carrying her hat in her hand; her black hair was parted in the middle with curls over her ears, and her eyes were a hallucinatory midnight blue; she was wearing a skirt of crimson velvet, a blouse with lace at the neck and wrists, and a bolero embroidered with bugle beads. Her attitude was mocking and defiant; she was fully aware that she embodied the men's most primitive and secret desires and symbolized all that was most feared by defenders of morality; she was an idol of perversity and she loved the role. In the excitement of the moment, someone tossed a handful of gold dust over her and it clung to her hair and clothing like an aura. The vision of that young woman, triumphant and fearless, shook Eliza. She thought of Miss Rose, as she did more and more often, and felt a surge of compassion and tenderness for her. She remembered her armored in her corset, back straight, waist constricted, sweating under her five petticoats. "Sit with your knees together, stand up straight, never be in haste, speak in a low voice, smile, do not make faces because that causes wrinkles, be silent and feign interest, men are flattered by women who listen to them." Miss Rose, with her scent of vanilla, always obliging. But she also remembered her in her bath, nearly naked in her wet nightdress, eyes shining with laughter, hair wild, cheeks pink, chattering happily: "A woman can do anything she wants, Eliza, as long as she does it discreetly." Lola Montez, however, did what she wanted openly; she had lived more lives than the boldest adventurer, and had done it proudly, as a beautiful woman. That night a pensive Eliza went to her room and stealthily, like someone committing a crime, opened the suitcase with her dresses. She had left the case in Sacramento when she left to look for her lover the first time, but Tao Chi'en had kept it for her, thinking that someday she might want it. When she opened it, something fell out; surprised, she saw her pearl necklace, her payment to Tao Chi'en for smuggling her onto the ship. She stood for a long time with the pearls in her hand, deeply moved. She shook out the dresses and laid them on the bed; they were wrinkled and smelled musty. The next day she took them to the best laundry in Chinatown.

"I am going to write Miss Rose, Tao," she announced.

"Why?"

"She is like my mother. If I love her this much, I am sure she loves me back. Four years have gone by; she must think I'm dead."

"Would you like to see her?"

"Of course, but that isn't possible. I'm going to write just to ease her doubts, but it would be nice if she could answer me. Do you mind if I give her this address?"

"You want your family to find you," he said, and something cracked in his voice.

She looked at him and realized that she had never been so close to anyone in this world as she was at that moment to Tao Chi'en.

She felt the man in her own blood, with such ancient and fierce certainty that she marveled at the time she had spent by his side without realizing. She missed him even though she saw him every day. She longed for the carefree days when they were good friends; everything had seemed simpler then, but neither did she want to turn back. Now there was something unfinished between them, something much more complex and fascinating than their old friendship.

Eliza's dresses and petticoats had come back from the laundry and were laid out on her bed, wrapped in paper. She opened the suitcase and took out her white stockings and high-button shoes, but left the corset inside. She smiled at the thought that she had never dressed as a woman without help, then put on the petticoats and tried on the dresses one by one in order to choose the one most appropriate for the occasion. She felt alien in those clothes and got tangled in the ribbons, laces, and buttons; it took her several minutes to button the boots and get her balance under so many petticoats, but with each garment she put on she was overcoming her doubts and confirming her desire to be a woman again. Mama Fresia had warned her about the risks of womanhood: "Your body will change, your thoughts will be jumbled, and any man will be able to do what he wants with you," she had said, but now Eliza did not fear those risks.

Tao Chi'en had attended the last patient of the day. He was in his shirt sleeves and had taken off the jacket and tie he always wore out of respect for his patients, following the counsel of his acupuncture master. He was perspiring, because the sun hadn't set and it had been one of the few hot days of that July. He thought he never would get used to the caprices of the San Francisco climate, where summer wore the face of winter. It usually dawned with a radiant sun but within hours a thick fog rolled in through the Golden Gate or a chilling wind blew off the sea. He was sterilizing the needles in alcohol and arranging his medicine bottles when Eliza came in. The assistant had left and at the moment there was no singsong girl in their care; they were alone in the house.

"I have something for you, Tao," Eliza said.

Tao Chi'en looked up; he was so startled that a bottle dropped from his hands. Eliza was wearing an elegant dark dress trimmed with white lace. He had seen her only twice in women's clothing in Valparaíso, but he had not forgotten how she had looked.

"Do you like me this way?"

"I like you any way." He smiled as he removed his eyeglasses to admire her from a distance.

"This is my Sunday dress. I put it on because I want to have a portrait taken. Here, this is for you," and she handed him a pouch.

"What is this?"

"My savings . . . for you to buy another girl, Tao. I planned to look for Joaquín this summer, but I'm not going. I know now I will never find him."

"It seems that like everyone who came to California we found something different from what we were looking for."

"What were you looking for?"

"Knowledge, wisdom, I don't remember. Instead I found the singsong girls, and look at the mess I'm in."

"Why are you so unromantic, Tao? My God! Gallantry demands that you say you also found me."

"I would have found you anyway, it was predestined."

"Not the old story about reincarnation."

"Of course. In every incarnation we will keep meeting until we work out our karma."

"It sounds frightening. Whatever the case, I am not going back to Chile; but I'm not going to keep hiding, either, Tao. I want to be myself."

"You always have been."

"My life is here. That is, if you want me to stay and help you."

"And Joaquín Andieta?"

"Maybe the star on his forehead means he is dead. Imagine. All this long, dreadful journey in vain."

"Nothing is in vain. You don't *go* anywhere in life, Eliza, you just keep walking."

"The part we've walked together hasn't been bad. Come with me, I am going to have my portrait taken to send to Miss Rose."

"Can you have one made for me?"

They walked arm in arm to Union Square, where there were several photography shops, and chose the one that looked the best. In the window was a collection of images of forty-niners: a young man with a blond beard and determined expression, holding a pick and shovel; a group of miners in shirt sleeves, eyes fixed on the camera, very serious; some Chinese on the banks of a river; Indians panning for gold with finely woven baskets; pioneer families posing beside their wagons. Daguerreotypes were in vogue; they were the link to distant friends and family, proof that they were living the gold adventure. It was said that in Eastern cities many men who had never been to California had their portraits made in mining garb. Eliza was convinced that the extraordinary invention of the photograph had dealt the death blow to painters, who rarely caught a likeness.

"Miss Rose had her portrait painted with three hands, Tao. It was by a famous artist, but I don't remember his name."

"Three hands?"

"Well, the painter put two, but she added another. Her brother Jeremy nearly died when he saw it."

She wanted to put her daguerreotype in a fine gilt and red velvet frame for Miss Rose's desk. She had brought Joaquín Andieta's letters to immortalize them in the photograph before she destroyed them. Inside the shop were enough backdrops for a small theater: canvases of flowery pergolas and lakes with herons, cardboard Greek columns garlanded with roses, even a stuffed bear. The photographer was a small, hurried man whose words tumbled out and who leapt about like a toad among the implements in his studio. Once they had agreed on the details, he sat Eliza at a table with the love letters in her hand and fitted a metal bar behind her with a support for her neck, not unlike the rod Miss Rose had insisted on during Eliza's piano lessons.

"This is to keep you from moving. Look at the camera and don't breathe."

The gnome disappeared behind a black cloth; an instant later a white flash blinded Eliza and a scorched smell made her sneeze. For the second portrait she put the letters aside and asked Tao Chi'en to help her fasten the pearl necklace.

The next day Tao Chi'en went out early to buy a newspaper, as he always did before opening the office, and was met with a six-column headline: Joaquín Murieta had been killed. He returned home with the paper pressed to his chest, wondering how to tell Eliza, and how she would receive the news.

At dawn on July 24, after three months of riding through California in a game of blindman's bluff, Captain Harry Love and his twenty mercenaries had come to the Tulare valley. By then they were sick and tired of chasing ghosts and following false trails; the heat and mosquitoes had put them in a foul mood and they were beginning to despise one another. Three summer months of forced march through these dry hills with the sun beating down on their heads was a lot of sacrifice for what they were being paid. They had seen the posters in the towns offering a thousand dollars' reward for the capture of the bandit. On more than one they had seen a scrawled, "I will pay five thousand," and signed Joaquín Murieta. They were looking foolish, and there were only three days left before time ran out: if they returned empty-handed they wouldn't see a cent of the governor's thousand dollars. But this must have been their lucky day because just when they were losing hope they had come across a group of seven unguarded Mexicans camping under some trees.

Later the captain would say that they were wearing the finest clothes and had only purebred horses, reasons enough to awaken their suspicion, and that was why they rode over to ask for identification. Instead of complying, the suspicious characters made a run for their horses but before they could mount they were surrounded by Love's guard. The one person who olympically ignored the attackers and walked on toward his mount as if he had not heard any warning was the one who seemed to be the leader. He was unarmed except for a hunting knife at his belt; his guns were strapped to his saddle, but he never fired a shot because by then the captain had his pistol to the man's forehead. A few steps away the other Mexicans watched, transfixed, Love would write in his report, ready to come to their leader's aid at the first careless move by the guards. Suddenly they all made a desperate attempt to escape, perhaps with the purpose of distracting the guards, while their leader, with one formidable leap, was on his restless stallion and bursting through their lines. He did not get far, however, because a blast from a shotgun caught his horse, which rolled to the ground vomiting blood. Then the outlaw, who was none other than the famous Joaquín Murieta, Captain Love claimed, took off like an antelope, and they had no choice but to empty their pistols into his chest.

"Don't shoot anymore, you've done your job," the man said before he slowly sank to the ground, dead.

That was the story dramatized in the press, and no Mexican was left alive to tell his version of events. The heroic Captain Harry Love proceeded to cut off the head of the supposed Murieta with one slash of his sword. Someone noticed that one of the victims had a mutilated hand, and it was immediately assumed that this was Three-Finger Jack, so they cut off his head, too, and for good measure added the hand. The twenty guards went galloping toward the nearest town, some miles away, but the heat was hellish and Three-Finger Jack's head was so full of bullet holes it began to disintegrate, so they threw it by the side of the road. Pursued by flies and a terrible stench, Captain Harry Love realized that he would have to preserve the remains or he would never get them to San Francisco to collect the deserved reward, so he immersed them in great jars of gin. He was welcomed as a hero: he had liberated California from the worst outlaw in its history. But as Jacob Freemont reported, the matter was not entirely cleared up; the story smelled of fabrication. To begin with, no one could prove that events had happened as portrayed by Harry Love and his men, and it was somewhat suspicious that after three months of fruitless searching they would find seven Mexicans just when the captain most needed them. Nor had anyone been able to identify Joaquín Murieta: Freemont himself went to see the head and could not be sure it was the bandit he knew, although it certainly resembled him, he said.

For weeks the remains of the presumed Joaquín Murieta and the hand of his abominable sidekick Three-Finger Jack were exhibited in San Francisco before being taken on a triumphal tour through the remainder of California. The lines of the curious stretched around the block and there was no one who hadn't taken a close look at the sinister trophies. Eliza was one of the first to go, and Tao Chi'en accompanied her because he did not want her to undergo such a test alone, even though she had received the news with amazing calm. After an eternal wait in the sun, it was finally their turn and they went inside. Eliza clung to Tao Chi'en's fingers but moved forward with determination, indifferent to the river of sweat staining her dress and the trembling that shook her bones. They found themselves in a dark room badly lighted by yellow candles emitting a breath from the tomb. Black cloth covered the walls and in one corner a valiant pianist was thumping out funereal chords with more resignation than real feeling. On a table draped like a catafalque sat the two glass jars. Eliza closed her eyes and let Tao Chi'en guide her, sure that the beating of her heart was drowning out the chords from the piano. They stopped; she felt her friend's grip grow stronger on hers; she gulped a mouthful of air and opened her eyes. She stared at the head for a few seconds and then let herself be led outside.

"Was it him?" asked Tao Chi'en.

"I am free," she replied, holding tightly to Tao's hand.

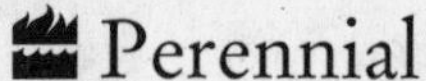

Books by Isabel Allende:

MY INVENTED COUNTRY: *A Nostalgic Journey Through Chile*
ISBN 0-06-054564-X (New in hardcover from HarperCollins*Publishers*)
ISBN 0-06-055926-8 (unabridged audio) • ISBN 0-06-055927-6 (unabridged CD)

Allende's highly personal memoir acknowledges the role of memory and nostalgia in shaping her life, her books, and her very connection to that most intimate place of origin—Chile.

PORTRAIT IN SEPIA: *A Novel*
ISBN 0-06-093636-3 (paperback) • ISBN 0-06-621401-7 (large print edition)
ISBN 0-694-52599-5 (unabridged audio) • ISBN 0-694-52654-1 (unabridged CD)

Allende brings back some of her characters from *Daughter of Fortune* to tell the story of Aurora del Valle who, raised in a privileged environment with no recollection of her first five years, decides to confront the mystery of her past.

DAUGHTER OF FORTUNE: *A Novel*
ISBN 0-06-093275-9 (paperback)
ISBN 0-380-82101-X (mass market paperback) • ISBN 0-694-52251-1 (audio)

A sweeping portrait of an unconventional woman carving her own destiny in California during the Gold Rush of 1849—an era marked by violence, passion, and adventure.

APHRODITE: *A Memoir of the Senses*
ISBN 0-06-093017-9 (paperback)

A rich celebration of the pleasures of the sensual life. Under the aegis of the Goddess of Love, Allende combines personal narrative and a treasury of erotic lore.

THE INFINITE PLAN: *A Novel*
ISBN 0-06-092498-5 (paperback)

One man's search for love and his struggle to come to terms with a childhood of poverty and neglect. *The Infinite Plan* is a powerful tale of loneliness and love, betrayals and hurdles, and defeats that finally lead to acceptance and reconciliation.

PAULA
ISBN 0-06-092721-6 (paperback)

A powerful, soul-baring memoir filled with bizarre ancestors, delightful and bitter childhood memories, amazing anecdotes, and intimate secrets meant to be told in whispers.

Want to receive notice of author events and new books by Isabel Allende?
Sign up for Isabel Allende's AuthorTracker at www.AuthorTracker.com

Available wherever books are sold, or call 1-800-331-3761 to order.

Don't miss Isabel Allende's debut Young Adult novel!

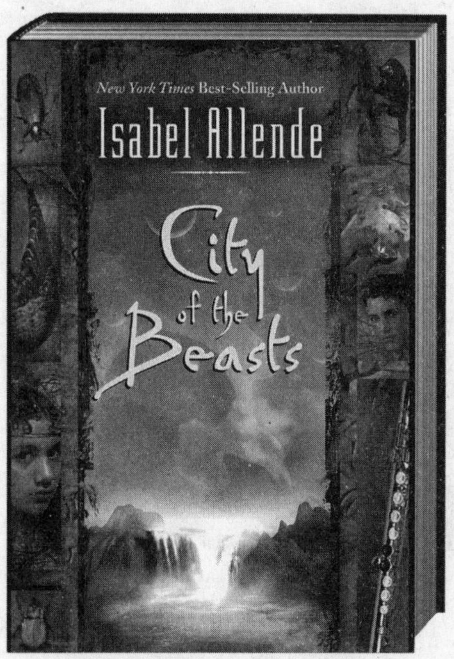

ISBN 0-06-050918-X (hardcover)
ISBN 0-06-051076-5 (audio)

"Acclaimed author Isabel Allende's first YA novel, part thrilling survival adventure, part coming-of-age journey, blends magical realism with grim history and contemporary politics in a way that shakes up all the usual definitions of savagery and civilization."
—ALA Booklist (starred review)